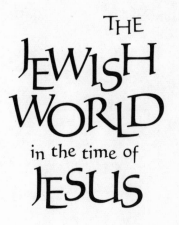

THE JEWISH WORLD
in the time of
JESUS

By CHARLES GUIGNEBERT

Late Professor of Christianity at the Sorbonne

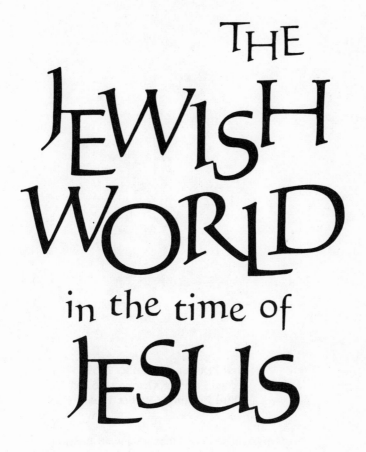

THE JEWISH WORLD

in the time of

JESUS

With An Introduction by Dr. Charles Francis Potter

UNIVERSITY BOOKS  *New Hyde Park, New York*

First Printing, December 1959
Second Printing, October 1961
Third Printing, October 1965

Library of Congress Catalog Card No. 59-14528

Manufactured in the United States of America

CONTENTS

BOOK III

THE REAL NATURE OF JEWISH RELIGIOUS LIFE IN PALESTINE

BOOK IV

HELLENISTIC JUDAISM

FOREWORD

By Charles Francis Potter

(M.A., S.T.M., Litt.D.)

(Author, THE STORY OF RELIGION, HUMANIZING RELIGION, THE FAITHS MEN LIVE BY, THE GREAT RELIGIOUS LEADERS)

It is a singular satisfaction for both scholar and layman to have THE JEWISH WORLD IN THE TIME OF JESUS reprinted in excellent format at this time, for there is so much in this particular book that needs to be repeated now.

Nothing is so powerful as an idea whose time has come; surely today, in the light of the coincident discoveries in the caves of Judean Qumran and Egyptian Chenoboskion, the truth of Guignebert's clear and scholarly message is apparent. If we dare to pull aside "the veil wherewith early Christian imagination has shrouded him," we shall see that Jesus "is plainly inexplicable except as the product of his environment."

When Guignebert's books were first translated into English they were regarded as shocking to Christian sensibilities. In 1933, only two years before the present book appeared in French, he had published his *Jésus*. When Knopf issued the English translation, JESUS,* it was given front-page treatment in the *New York Times Book Review* the Sunday before Christmas (December 22, 1935). P. W. Wilson, the reviewer, was shocked that any scholar should dare to say that "Paul has deliberately sacrificed Jesus to Christ," or that "Matthew and Luke, if they agree as to the birthplace of Jesus, give quite irreconcilable accounts of the birth." Wilson was particularly horrified at the last sentence of the book, in which Guignebert averred that Jesus' religion was not the Christian religion: "he neither foresaw it nor desired it." He also objected to Guignebert's agreement with the scholar Wellhausen in saying "that enthusiasm engendered Christianity, but it was the enthusiasm of the disciples, not that of Jesus." The reviewer lamely charged the great French scholar (who was then completing his third decade at

---

*JESUS was reprinted in 1955 by University Books

vii

the Sorbonne as Professor of History of Christianity) with teaching a "cubist scholarship," and condemned it as a "cart so clever it pulls the horses."

When that review appeared, Guignebert's next book, the one you are now reading, had already come out in France, and four years later was published in an English translation. But World War II was already starting in 1939, and by the time it was over no one but a few scholars had seen or even heard of the book, important to all though it was, and is!

THE JEWISH WORLD IN THE TIME OF JESUS is one of the very few books which has not been made obsolescent by the revolutionizing discoveries of ancient manuscripts in the Qumran Caves by the Dead Sea. By an extraordinary inferential anticipation, Guignebert reached the conclusion, to which honest Bible students are now being reluctantly driven, that the Judaism from whose bosom Christianity sprang was not the orthodox "Old Testament" Judaism of an earlier time but the sectarian syncretistic Judaism expressed variously by the Essenes, Nazarenes, Covenanters, Zealots, and the pre-Christian Jewish Gnostics.

Guignebert arrived at so accurate a preview of the Scrolls findings by his skill as an historian trained in the Sorbonne atmosphere of careful scholarship, which overlooks no clue and weighs all evidence with meticulous objectivity. Like his contemporary and colleague Adolphe Lods, who took the Chair of Hebrew Language and Literature at the Sorbonne in 1906, the year that Guignebert was made Professor of the History of Christianity there (both leaving in 1937), and like the distinguished scholar A. Dupont-Sommer, specialist in Hebrew at the Sorbonne for some years now, Guignebert made honest announcement of his findings and their theological significance, even when the truth proved embarrassing to Jew and Christian alike.

The work and frank statements of Dupont-Sommer about the importance of the Scrolls made possible Edmund Wilson's famous piece in *The New Yorker* which awakened the American public to the existence of the dynamite that had been discovered in the Qumran caves a decade before — knowledge which had been concealed by what Editor Theodore A. Gill of *The Christian Century* well termed "the unforgivable scholarly reticence which had kept us in the dark too long." Edmund Wilson captioned one of his chapters "What Would Renan Have Said," and spoke of Dupont-Sommer as "carrying on what may be called the Renanian tradition.

A hundred years ago the thirty-seven-year-old Renan,

already noted as a researcher in Semitic philology and for his brilliant essays in the history of religion, became a candidate for a professorship in Hebrew at the Collège de France. Opposition developed from the Church, which he had left in his early twenties. The emperor, perhaps to let the opposing prelates cool off, sent Renan to Phoenicia, where he studied the important inscriptions which became the foundation of his *Corpus Inscriptionum Semiticarum*.

Upon Renan's return, he was elected in 1862 to the Chair of Hebrew in spite of his opponents, but in his first lecture he referred to Jesus Christ as "an incomparable Man." To the powerful priests, who considered the Galilean to be God Himself Who had temporarily assumed human form, Renan's words were blasphemy and heresy, and they made such an outcry that the young professor was suspended as a disturber of the public peace.

He returned to writing, and quickly finished and published in 1863 his soon-famous *Vie de Jésus*, the first book of his great seven-volume *History of the Origins of Christianity*. In it Renan presented Jesus in direct, simple, scientific fashion, as a critical objective historian should, and of course the Galilean emerged from the beautiful prose of this master writer as indeed "an incomparable Man," a great Teacher, an inspired and inspiring human religious leader. The reaction in orthodox Christian Europe and America was so violent that within a year fifteen hundred controversial books and pamphlets were published, and the name of Ernest Renan became anathema throughout the Christian world.

Yet, quietly underneath the surface, his ideas percolated into the consciousness of laymen and even caused doubts and recasting of ideas and doctrines by the clergy. Among critical scientific Biblical scholars, many of his ideas and interpretations were in time adopted, often without giving him credit. The appellation of "higher criticee" was handicap enough without foolishly shouldering the opprobrium of Renan's alleged atheism.

A few scholars of the "Renanian tradition" did proudly acknowledge their debt to the Great Heretic, and continued and extended his truth-telling scholarship. And this is where Guignebert comes in, especially with his JEWISH WORLD IN THE TIME OF JESUS.

This book contains Guignebert's best thinking: it is his fine and characteristic contribution to the solution of the riddle of the personality of Jesus. And the book is directly in the Renanian tradition: it bridges the gap between Renan and Dupont-Sommer. Its importance will be gradually but increasingly recognized as we study the recently discovered evidence of the Essene provenance of Jesus' teachings.

In his introduction to this book, Guignebert points out that Renan wrote in 1887 that "the whole development of Christianity had its roots in the Judaism of the first and second centuries before Christ." But Guignebert goes even further and emphasizes that it was in and among the Jews of the Diaspora, the dispersed Jews among the Gentiles, the Jews who had left the strict orthodoxy of the temple worship, that the Christian religion got its start. He says (page 2):

> "Undoubtedly the seed sown by Jesus was Jewish seed, and its earliest growth was Jewish, but_ the. fostering earth ... was a Hellenistic soil in which Greece and the East mingled their fertilizing elements. That it was at Antioch ... the metropolis of the Hellenistic world that the Nazarenes were first called *Christians*, is a fact of profound symbolic significance."

The "soil in which Greece and the East mingled their fertilizing elements" is seen in the Qumran hymns and the fourth Christian gospel, and their eastern Persian dualistic angelology and demonology, astrology and eschatology. These theological and doctrinal vitamins nourished the Jewish seed and produced, under the hot desert sun of the Wady Qumran, strange religious variants and saltations, such as the ascetic monkish frères of the New Covenant, the wide-ranging devoted followers of the eremitic John Baptist, and the wider-ranging disciples of the other martyr, the evangelist Jesus, whose sect found its name in Antioch, its organizer in Tarsus, and its operational centers in Alexandria, Constantinople, and Rome.

It was Renan, as Edmund Wilson says, who "called attention to the first emergence in the 'interestamental' apocrypha of certain characteristic Christian themes," and Dupont-Sommer noted that fact. Dupont-Sommer has pointed in particular to the Enochan books, which were never really printed between the Testaments, and are more often called pseudepigrapha than apocrypha by Protestant scholars.

At any rate, Enoch is the Ethiopian in the woodpile in the scholars' backyard right now. The word is permissible and proper, for it was in Ethiopia that the canny Scot, James Bruce, found three copies of "The Lost Book of Enoch" and brought them back in 1773. They were in Geez, ancient Ethiopic, and it was a long time before they were translated, and still longer before the public was told what was in "The Book of Enoch," then thought to be one book, but now known to be a small library of celestial travel-stories, interspersed with parables and beatitudes, all attributed to the Patriarch Enoch, "the seventh from Adam."

These pre-Christian books had been banished from third and fourth century Christendom because they contained too much that was by then supposed to be a special, new, and unique revelation of truth given to the world first through Jesus and His disciples. The books just disappeared, to be hidden for long centuries in far-off Ethiopia and in the Qumran Caves, in one of which were lately found fragments of ten manuscripts of Enoch, a fact not widely publicized.

Renan told the world about the "Book of Enoch" as soon as he found out about the Ethiopic manuscripts. And Christians just wouldn't believe him! The Reverend William J. Deane, in a book published in Edinburgh in 1891, who wouldn't "dignify the author by name," protested that in Renan's book "we are asked to believe that our Lord and His apostles, consciously or unconsciously, introduced into their speech and writings ideas and expressions most decidedly derived from Enoch."

Dr. Deane was shocked that this impious author dared to call Enoch "the Semitic Milton" whose writings furnished the gospel writers and apostles with "their conceptions of the resurrection, judgment, immortality, perdition, and of the universal reign of righteousness under the eternal dominion of the Son of Man." The Reverend consoled his readers with the assurance that "Few unprejudiced persons will agree with the author of this opinion, whose aim seems to be to throw discredit upon the superhuman origin of Christianity and to trace it to merely human development."

It was true that the vast majority of Christians continued to believe as Dr. Deane did, rather than even read Ernest Renan's comments on Enoch, much less read The Book of Enoch itself. The very word "apocryphal" had already, in colloquial usage, lost its meaning of "secret" and had acquired the connotation of "spurious" or "false." Nevertheless the more progressive English and American Bible scholars were much intrigued by Renan's statement and wished the Book of Enoch were available in English that they might check Renan's startling assertions.

In 1892 there appeared a reissue of Archbishop Laurence's long out-of-print translation of Enoch, first issued in 1821, and again in 1833 and 1838, but unnoticed for over half a century. And Canon Charles' more critical translation and study of Enoch, based on twenty more manuscripts discovered during the nineteenth century, came out in 1893. Renan had died the previous year, just too early to read the Oxford Don's well-documented exposition of the tremendous influence which Enoch had had on the New Testament.

Charles' book, perhaps because it was technical and meticulously scholarly, full of quotations and references in a dozen languages, attracted little opposition, even among Biblical students. Charles assumed too much background knowledge on the part of his readers. The second edition, in 1912, was even more repelling, as was also the huge two-volume work which Charles edited, APOCRYPHA AND PSEUDEPIGRAPHA OF THE OLD TESTAMENT, including introductions, translations, and commentaries by eminent scholars on all the known interbiblical and non-canonical scriptures, published by Oxford in 1913. In it, both Ethiopic and Slavonic Enoch were buried among the other strange apocalyptic books.

But the Renan tradition was already being revived at the Sorbonne by Charles Guignebert, who had been in the Chair of the History of Christianity for seven years when Charles' monumental two-volume book appeared. And when this present volume, THE JEWISH WORLD IN THE TIME OF JESUS, first appeared in English in 1939, its legitimate place in that great tradition was apparent. Five of Renan's books are listed in the bibliography, and he is frequently quoted in text and footnotes. The Enochan literature is given proper recognition, with ample attention paid to the influence of the apocalyptic books on Jesus, Paul, and the writers of gospels and epistles.

Most significant of all, in this book published in 1935 (French) and 1939 (English), is the extended treatment given the Essenes, the Hellenists, the Gnostics, and other fringe Jewish sects, and the careful appraisal of the nature and extent of their influence on the group of Jesus-followers, who termed their faith "The Way."*

It was the "natural responsiveness to contact with foreign patterns of thought," a normal development among all neighboring peoples, which caused the blending of Persian, Hellenistic, and Essenic ideas with a basic Judaism, a blend which became in time the early Christian theology. It was not due to "deliberate, premeditated and conscious borrowing," Guignebert points out.

Jesus was the natural product of his environment. All religious leaders arrive that way. As our author says, so temperately and cogently.

"The phenomenon is not in the least unusual or surpris-

---

*The most surprising prediction, prophecy, or anticipation by Professor Guignebert is on page 173: "§It is unfortunate that the secret books of the Essenes, mentioned by Josephus, have perished, leaving no trace. The likeness of the eschatological views of the Essenes . . . to Enoch's version of Paradise, has led to the suggestion that their books were of an apocalyptic nature [and that] this sect is responsible for all the apocryphal writings which pass under the name of Enoch . . . Perhaps some chance discovery may add to the documentation of the subject."

Guignebert died in August 1939, just as the first English version of this book appeared. The revised date of the discovery of the Qumran Dead Sea Scrolls is the spring of 1945.

ing ... but just because it happens to apply to the *people of God*, religious prejudice — Christian more than Jewish — has long stood in the way of its recognition. It is impossible for anyone who still denies it to understand the historical process which led up to the birth of Christianity."

This is the main message of this book — that religions come by natural evolution and not by miraculous creation by divine fiat, and that Judaism and Christianity are not only no exceptions to that law, but rather excellent illustrations thereof. One detects a recurrent note of surprise on the author's part that good Christian and Jewish people either cannot see, or refuse to admit, so patent a fact. He hammers home the evidence that the whole Judeo-Christian theological complex is a "normal development," the "natural response to contact with foreign patterns of thought," and therefore a "phenomenon" neither "unusual nor surprising in the least."

The great majority of Christians retain the myth of "the faith once delivered to the saints." Thinkers who could not accept that official faith, after the councils had (with some difficulty) determined just what that faith was, were deemed heretics, and were persecuted, imprisoned, and burned by the thousands.

Patiently, like a good teacher, Guignebert brings to the attention of his readers, evidence after evidence, proof after proof, that every culture with which the Jews came into contact, early or late, contributed to the shaping and reshaping of Judaism.

The Messiah idea, considered by so many Jews and Christians to be peculiarly Jewish (or Christian), is shown to have been taken from the Iranian "saoshyant" or savior, the messiah of the Zoroastrian religion of "the Medes and Persians which changeth not" but which the Persians adopted very likely from the Assyrians and Babylonians.

Another foreign influence was early Gnosticism, to which the author devotes considerable interesting treatment, making observations which will be better appreciated now that the Gnostic library of forty-four books, discovered in a cave halfway up a cliff at Chenoboskion (Nag Hammagi) in Upper Egypt in 1946, is at last being translated from the Coptic.

So, not only the Qumran manuscripts discovery in the many caves above the Dead Sea, but the newest archaeological miracle find (which some scholars hold equally important for Christian origins) in the Egyptian cave, show almost startlingly the timeliness of this republication of Charles Guignebert's THE JEWISH WORLD IN THE TIME OF JESUS.

THE JEWISH WORLD IN THE TIME OF JESUS

FROM THE PROPHETS TO JESUS

INTRODUCTION

JUDAISM AND CHRISTIANITY

JUDAISM ABOUT THE TIME OF JESUS

JESUS was born among Jews on Jewish soil, and his message was for Jews alone. In its origin, therefore, and in so far as it is dependent on its traditional founder, Christianity must be considered a Jewish phenomenon. When Jesus ended his ministry, it was not yet a religion, but at least it was the embodiment of a great hope. Jews first carried it into Greek soil, where an extraordinary success awaited it, and there, too, it found its first home in the hearts of Jews, or of those who were already influenced and prepared for its reception by Jewish propaganda. Finally it was only under the protection of the privileges which the Jewish *nation* had acquired in the Empire that the first Christian communities were able to spring up and take root without exciting the suspicion of the Roman authorities.

Even after the "heresy of the Nazarenes," as the Jews came to call it, had become an independent religion, Judaism never ceased to influence it, either directly or by the hostile reaction which it created.[1]

Indeed, not only has the Jewish Bible been preserved as the Sacred Book, the Bible of the Christian Church, but the liturgical traditions, the forms of worship, and even the religious customs of the Jews have all left a deep imprint on Christian life.[2]

[1] **CCLXV**, 248 *ff.*, makes a special effort to define this influence of Judaism on Christianity after the two religions became separated.

[2] W. O. E. Oesterley, *The Jewish Background of the Christian Liturgy*, London, 1925. *Cf.* **IV**.

1

The very hostility of the early Church to the synagogue, and the tenacity with which the Christian clergy sought to guard against any possible invasion of the Jewish spirit or of Jewish propaganda, were often determining factors in the decisions and even in the development of the institutions of the Christian Church.[1]

These are the established facts, obvious to anyone who has made a careful study of Israel at the period just before the Christian era, which led to the conclusion, once generally accepted, that Christianity was nothing more than a Hellenized Judaism. In 1860 Michel Nicolas could write :—" *Christianity sprang from the bosom of Judaism ; if it has any direct and immediate antecedents, it is there that we must seek them* "—thus alleging his interest in Christianity as his motive for undertaking a study of the *Religious Doctrines of the Jews.*[2] Towards the end of his life Renan still maintained that " *the whole development of Christianity had its roots in the Judaism of the first and second centuries before Christ.*"[3] He also claimed that " *the countries which were the first to surrender to primitive Christianity were those which Judaism had already conquered during the two or three centuries before Jesus Christ.*"[4]

Today the position does not seem quite so simple. Undoubtedly the seed sown by Jesus was Jewish seed, and its earliest growth was Jewish, but the fostering earth, which nourished it with life-giving juices till it became first a vigorous sapling and then a mighty tree, was a Hellenistic soil in which Greece and the East mingled their fertilizing elements. That it was at Antioch that the new religion first received its name, and that it was in the metropolis of the Hellenistic world that the Nazarenes were first called *Christians*, is a fact of profound symbolic significance.[5]

It may well be that many Hellenistic influences did not reach Christianity directly but rather by way of the Judaism of which they had already made a partial conquest. This consideration is enough in itself to conjure up a picture of

---

[1] **XLVII**, i, 277 *ff.* ;   304 *ff.*   [2] **CCLXXX**, preface, p. 1.
[3] **LXXI**, v, 380.   [4] **LXXI**, v, 222.
[5] The first Christians called themselves by names in use among the sects of that time, such as the *elect* (ἐκλεκτοί: Rom. viii. 33 ; xvi. 13 ; Col. iii. 12 ; 2 Tim. ii. 10), the *saints* (ἅγιοι : Rom. viii. 27 ; xv. 25), the *faithful* (πιστοί : Col. i. 2 ; Ephes. i. 1), the *disciples* (μαθηταί : Acts ix. 26 ; xi. 26), the *brethren* (ἀδελφοί : Gal. i. 2 ; 1 Cor. v. 11 ; Phil. i. 14), or any other designation of the same sort (*cf.* **DACL**, i, under *Chrétien*). In a passage from Acts (xi. 26) we learn that *it was at Antioch that the disciples took the name of Christians* (*Loisy, Actes*, 470) or *were called Christians* (ἐγένετο . . . χρηματίσαι . . . τοὺς μαθητὰς χριστιανούς). There is no reason for questioning this evidence.

Judaism which would have astonished Nicolas and, no doubt, even Renan himself. As we observe the contamination of the Jewish world by the Hellenistic East, and perhaps even by the true East itself, we can no longer think of it as a domain straitly enclosed by the thick and thorny fence of legalism. It is not wholly confined within the wider boundaries of the post-exilic writings of the Old Testament, the Deuterocanonical books, as much Alexandrine as Jewish, and the Apocryphal books, but even extends beyond that larger field where Josephus and Philo are our guides.

We must, therefore, include under the name of Judaism the whole vast but confused and heterogeneous complex of ideas, beliefs, feelings, tendencies, customs and observances, differing according to age and source, which characterized the Jews—or at least some of the Jews—of the period just before the birth of Jesus. And we have to consider, not only the inhabitants of Palestine itself, but also those Israelite groups which were scattered over the Græco-Oriental world, for, if it be admitted that Hellenism exerted most of its influence on Christianity through the medium of Judaism, the Judaism in question is that which flourished outside Palestine, the Judaism growing on Greek soil. To all appearance the Jewish activities which had the widest, the deepest, and the most lasting effect on Christianity emanated from the environment of the *Dispersion*.[1] Was not Paul himself a Jew of Tarsus in Cilicia ?

In this volume we shall attempt to give an account of the Jewish world of Palestine into which Jesus was born and in which he lived. We shall then go on to discuss the meaning of the Judaism of the *Dispersion*—the *Diaspora*—the environment in which Christianity became aware of itself and began to achieve its destiny.

BIBLIOGRAPHICAL NOTE

A complete bibliography of the subject may be found in the works of Schürer and Juster, referred to below. I shall only mention here a few particularly useful books. In the notes I shall limit myself, as far as possible, to those books which are most easily accessible to the reader.

(A) SOURCES. I. *The Hebrew Bible* ; *Biblia hebraica* edit., Kittel, Leipzig, 1913. Greek.—H. B. Swete, *Old Testament in Greek according to the Septuagint*, Cambridge, 1887–94. Translations.—(*a*) French : A. Crampon, *La Sainte Bible* (2nd ed.), Paris, 1905 ; *La Bible du Centenaire* (**V**) (in course of publication) ; (*b*) German : Kautzsch (**XLVIII**) ; (*c*) English : *The Revised Version*.

All the information needed for a careful study of the text is to be found

---

[1] **CCXCIV**, i, 193 ; **CCLXXXIV**, 216 *ff.* ; **CCLVIII**, XVI (a letter from Pfleiderer to the author).

in L. Gautier, *Introduction à l'Ancien Testament*, Paris, 1914 ; C. Steuer-nagel, *Lehrbuch der Einleitung in den Alten Testament mit einem Anhang über die Apokryphen und Pseudepigraphen*, Tübingen, 1912 ; W. Nowack, *Hand Kommentar Zum Alten Testament*, Göttingen, 1894 *et seq.*, 13 volumes, each volume forming a separate work, by a well-known specialist.

II. The *Targumim* and the *Midrashim* : see Articles in **DB** and **JE**.

III. The *Talmud* : all the necessary information is in Strack, *Einleitung in den Talmud* (4th ed.), Leipzig, 1908 ; new edition, 1930 ; Oesterley and Box, **CCXCIX,** parts I and II ; J. Derenbourg, article *Talmud* in the *Enc. des Sciences religieuses*, Paris, 1882, vol. xii ; M. J. Schwab, *Le Talmud de Jérusalem*, vol. i (2nd ed.), Paris, 1890.

IV. The *Apocryphal Books* : everything essential is to be found in **EB, DB** and **CE** under *Apocrypha*, texts, translations and commentaries ; Fabricius, *Codex pseudepigraphicus Veteris Testamenti*, 2 vols., Hamburg, 1713 and 1723 ; **CCLXIX,** German translation with notes and com-ments ; **CCLIV,** the same in English. Martin is publishing a similar work in French under the title, *Les Apocryphes de l'Ancien Testament*. Finally there are : **LXXV,** iii, par. 32 ; V. L. Couard, *Die religiösen und sittlichen Anschauungen der Alttestamentlichen Apokryphen und Pseudepi-graphen*. Gütersloh, 1907.

V. *Contemporary Authors.* (*a*) Josephus : B. Niese, *Flavii Josephi Opera*, 6 vols., Berlin, 1888–95 ; French translation **XLVI** in course of publication ; English translation, *The Works of Flavius Josephus*, W. Whiston (re-edited by Margoliouth), New York, n.d. Other trans-lations are noted in **LXXV,** i, 101 *ff.* (*b*) Philo : L. Cohn and P. Wendland, *Philonis Alexandrini Opera*, Berlin, from 1895 ; German translation, Cohn, *Die Werke Philos von Alexandrien*, Breslau, from 1909 *et seq.* (unfinished).

(B) Special Works. I. French : **XIII** ; **LXXXIV** ; **LXXI** ; **XLVII** (essential) ; **CCLXXIV** (part 3) ; **III** ; C. F. Jean, *Le Milieu biblique avant J.-C.*, I, Paris, 1922 ; II, 1923 ; III, 1936.

II. German : **LXXV** (1st edit. translated into English, New York, 1891, 7 vols.) is still the essential work ; O. Holtzmann, *Neutesta-mentliche Zeitgeschichte* (2nd ed.), Tübingen, 1906 ; **LXXIV** ; **CCXCI** ; **CCLII** ; **CCLXXVIII** ; **CCLIII** (essential).

III. English : **LXIII** ; **CCLXVII** ; **CCLV** ; **CCLXXIX** ; **XXXIII.**

BOOK I

THE POLITICAL AND RELIGIOUS CONDITION OF PALESTINE

CHAPTER I

THE COUNTRIES OF PALESTINE

I

PALESTINE

WHEN Jesus appeared in Israel the great mass of Jews were still living in Palestine. Palestine was a part of Syria under Roman rule, and comprised three main political divisions.[1]

To the south lay Judæa, " gloomy Judæa," as Renan calls it, a series of rocky plateaux furrowed by deep gorges, the chief of which, the valley of the lower Jordan, ends in the enclosed basin of the Dead Sea. Judæa lay between the Dead Sea and the Mediterranean, stretching down through Idumæa towards Sinai, and up past Samaria towards Carmel. After A.D. 6., when Augustus deposed Herod the Great's son, Archelaus, on account of his shocking administration and intolerable tyranny, this region was under the direct rule of a Roman procurator.

To the north Palestine embraced *Galilee*, consecrated by Gospel tradition as the birthplace of Jesus. This stretched between the Jordan Valley, which opened out round the Lakes of Huleh [2] and Gennesaret, and Phœnicia, which abutted on Syria. It combined with *Peræa*, the district beyond the lower Jordan ($τὸ πέραν τοῦ ποταμοῦ$), to form the Tetrarchy of Herod Antipas, another son of Herod the Great, who had his headquarters there until Caligula exiled him to Lyons in A.D. 39., although Augustus had previously transferred the Greek cities of Peræa to the direct authority of the Governor of Syria.

[1] For a general description *cf.* **LVII,** 19–44. More technical details are given in Abel, *Géographie de la Palestine*, I, Paris, 1933, II, 1938, which also contains a fairly detailed analytical table.

[2] Nowadays most scholars have ceased to identify this lake with the *waters of Merom* (Joshua xi. 5 and 7). I therefore give the modern name.

5

Lastly, on the *north-east*, lay the districts of *Batanœa*, *Gaulanitis*, and *Trachonitis*, between the upper Jordan and the Syrian desert, which were all grouped under the rule of a third Herod, Philip. These areas contained Jewish colonies, but were not themselves really Jewish. Philip, a prince with definite Hellenistic leanings, was even able to have a coinage struck with his image, which he would not have dared to do if the Jewish element had been dominant in his states.

Moreover, the inhabitants of Palestine were far from being all Israelites. Apart from the various not inconsiderable Semitic elements, Arabs to the south, and Phœnicians towards the coast, numbers of Greeks had landed at seaboard towns, such as Berytus, Tyre, Sidon, Ptolemaïs, Cæsarea and Joppa, or had come south from the Hellenized parts of Syria in the days of the Seleucids, and had settled in different parts of the country. But although they were well received by the Herodian princes, they did not find Judæa or the neighbouring states very attractive, apart from the coast towns. They got no sympathy or encouragement from the genuinely Jewish population, which was too dense to allow them a really comfortable existence in its midst. Nor could this lean and barren land offer either resources for their enterprise, or an adequate means of livelihood. On the other hand they formed large settlements in Galilee, especially in the busy and flourishing towns of Bethsaida, Capernaum, and Magdala, on the shores of the Lake of Gennesaret ; and a little later they colonized Tiberias. Already they had peopled Peræa, especially its northern section known as the *Decapolis*, or the *Ten Cities*, south-east of the Lake, where they had enjoyed special privileges from Rome ever since 63 B.C. ; and finally, they had formed important settlements in Philip's Tetrarchy, through which ran the roads connecting Damascus with the coast.

It is necessary to get a clear idea of these countries of Palestine, since they not only constitute the setting of the Gospel story, but they give us its atmosphere, and throw its incidents into such clear relief that they have even been called the *Fifth Gospel*.[1]

[1] There is a bibliography of this subject in **LXXV**, i, section 2 B, and in F.-M. Abel, *Géographie de la Palestine*, i.—Smith, *Historical Geography of the Holy Land* (4th edit.), New York, 1907 *ff.* ; M. Brückner, *Das Fünfte Evangelium, das heilige Land*, Tübingen, 1910 ; C. Foster Kent, *Biblical Geography and History*, London, 1911, especially chaps. xxiii and xxiv ; Ph. J. Baldensperger, *The Immovable East*, London, 1913 ; V. Schvoebel, *Die Landesnatur Palästinas*, erster Teil, Leipzig, 1914 ; G. Dalman, *Les itinéraires de Jésus*, Paris, 1930. A good deal of interest will be found in Fr. Robert Koeppel, S.J., *Palästina. Die Landschaft in*

II

GALILEE

The familiar claim that Galilee has not changed since ancient times is ill founded. We have only to compare Galilee as it is today with the descriptions given by ancient writers to realize the extent of Turkish ravages. Nevertheless, what we may call the *character* of the country has not suffered any profound change, and the environment of the Gospels—that is, the environment which the three Synoptic Gospels reflect—still persists in the daily life and ordinary customs of the people, even to the present day. A traveller who reaches Palestine with his mind full of the scenes of the Gospel narrative will find those scenes re-enacted before his eyes so faithfully as to leave little to the imagination.[1]

It is perhaps unnecessary to describe the whole of Palestine, since it does not all concern Jesus directly, but we must at least glance at Galilee where he was born and grew up.[2]

At the time of the conquest and division of the Promised Land, the southern part of Galilee fell to the lot of the tribes of Naphtali and Asher, the northern part to those of Zebulon and Issachar, according to tradition.[3] Later on Solomon must have held the district as a private possession since he seems to have given twenty Galilean cities to Hiram, King of Tyre, as payment for the costly materials the latter supplied for the construction of the Temple and the royal Palace.[4] But in the eighth century B.C. the Assyrians of Tiglathpileser extended their conquests to the south of Syria, and seized the territory of Naphtali, dispossessing its rightful occupants, though whether by massacre, deportation, expulsion or voluntary exile, or by all four methods at once, is not clear.[5] In any case genuine Jews do not seem to have been very numerous in any part of

Karten und Bildern, Tübingen, 1928, and the collection of photographs called *Das heilige Land*, Munich, 1927. For maps consult Hermann Guthe, *Bibelatlas* (2nd edit.), Leipzig, 1927.

[1] *Cf.* in particular A. Mitrie Rihbany, *The Syrian Christ*, Melrose, 1921.

[2] In addition to the books mentioned in note 1, p. 6, see Merrill, *Galilee in the time of Christ*, London, 1891; the article on *Galilee* in **EB** (which gives a good map); **LXXVII**, particularly book I, chaps. vii and viii; Bertholet, **III**, chap. i, and **CCLXXII**, 381 *ff.*

[3] Joshua xii. 23; xx. 7; xxi. 32. According to Judges i. 30–3, the invaders did not drive out the original inhabitants, but agreed to accept tribute from them. The Israelites cannot have been so very numerous.

[4] 1 Kings ix. 10 *ff.*

[5] 2 Kings xv. 29, only speaks of deportation to Assyria.

this northern region of Palestine. Be that as it may, their place was soon filled by the neighbouring Phœnicians and Aramæans, until the Jews fell into the habit of calling this lost territory *Galil-ha-Goyim* or the *Circle of the Gentiles*.[1] They did not renounce their claim to it but they do not seem to have made any attempt to re-establish their rights until the end of the Persian period. [2]

They did not succeed until the time of the Maccabees in the course of the second century B.C.[3] The Jews had completely regained possession long before the birth of Jesus ; the former Gentile inhabitants had either accepted circumcision or moved elsewhere,[4] and the country was referred to simply as *Galil*, the *Circle*, or *Galilee*.

It was not of any great extent, measuring something like fifty miles from north to south and twenty-two from east to west. It fell naturally into two distinct divisions, called by Josephus [5] Lower Galilee (ἡ κάτω Γαλιλαία) to the south, and Upper Galilee (ἡ ἄνω Γαλιλαία) to the north. Lower Galilee is a land of plateaus and hills whose highest points scarcely reach 2,000 feet. Between them lie small fertile plains, like those of *Zebulon* and *Tor'an*, and they fall away to the west towards the plain of *Jezreel*, the *Esdraelon* of the Greeks, which means the *Sowing of God* (literally, *God sows*). Northward, about the latitude of the coastal town of Ptolemaïs, the country is traversed by a deep depression, through which rivers flow in opposite directions, some towards the bay of Acre, and some to the Lake of Tiberias. Beyond this depression lies Upper Galilee. Its mountains are not particularly high—the crowning peaks are under 4,000 feet—but they are huddled closely together and are fairly rugged. Rain is not scarce, owing to the neighbourhood of Lebanon which attracts the clouds, hence the soil is fertile and trees grow readily.[6] In ancient times, walnuts, figs, vines and palms, and all the Mediterranean fruit-trees, flourished there. Their quality and abundance were renowned throughout Palestine and made Galilee the centre of an active trade.[7]

---

[1] Isaiah viii. 23.   Joshua xx. 7 ; xxi. 32 ; 1 Kings ix. 11 ; 1 Chron. vi. 76, have simply *Gālil*.

[2] **CCLXXVIII**, ii, 420, note 3.

[3] 1 Macc. v. 21–3, on Simon's expedition to Galilee to bring back the Jewish settlers whose position there still seemed to him insecure.

[4] Jos., *B.J.*, iii, 2.

[5] Jos., *B.J.*, iii, 3, 1 ; ii, 20, 6 ; *Vita*, iii, 7.   For a general description of the mountains, see Abel, *Géographie*, 59 *ff.* ; 75 *ff.* ; 349 *ff.* ; for lakes and waterways, 137 *ff.* ; 447.

[6] Jos., *B.J.*, iii, 2, notes this.   [7] **LXXVI**, 151.

Josephus was astonished at the richness of Galilee.[1] It must be confessed that the present aspect of the country does not entirely justify his enthusiasm, but even allowing for a slight exaggeration into which the contrast with sun-baked Judæa may have led him, he may well have found Galilee a gracious and fertile country where life was pleasant and easy. On this point both ancient and modern witnesses are agreed.[2]

A pilgrim from the west, who visited Galilee in the sixth century, was scarcely less enthusiastic than Josephus had been. He wrote, " *It is a paradisal country, rivalling Egypt in its grain and cereals, and, although so small, surpassing her in wine and oil and fruit.*" Nowadays the aqueducts built by the Romans have long been in ruins, dead trees have not been replaced because the land-owners feared to add to their already crushing burden of taxation, fields lie fallow and empty ; yet still in April the land near the ruins of Capernaum and Chorazin is covered with a marvellous mantle of flowers, billowing out to the oleanders of the wretched wadis. Around its little mountain towns like Nazareth or Cana, olives, figs and vines grow sturdily enough wherever they can find a drop of moisture for their roots. Everywhere tranced nature waits for human industry to call it back to life, and gives the impression that if it had not been frustrated by centuries of almost incredible neglect it would never have fallen asleep. The success achieved by the recent efforts of a few Zionist colonies in the plain of Jezreel, and by various religious orders (notably German Lazarists) and Jewish settlers on the plain of Gennesaret, north-west of the Lake, is enough to prove how quickly this soil, abandoned for hundreds of years to grazing sheep, or feebly scratched here and there by the ploughshares of indolent Arabs or Bedouins, would respond to suitable agricultural methods.

Such a country, surrounded as it was by barren and intractable lands, naturally attracted a large population.[3] Josephus tells us it contained fifteen fortified towns and 204 villages, the least of which numbered 15,000 souls ! Of course this is an absurd exaggeration, but it is one which the author would not have ventured if his first impression of the actual density of the population had not given him grounds for it. And the ruins which still strew the countryside bear witness to a prosperity that must once have been considerable.

[1] Jos., *B.J.*, iii, 3, 2 ; iii, 10, 8 ; *Vita*, 45.

[2] **CCCI**, 64 ; von Soden, *Palästina* (3rd edit.), Leipzig, 1911, p. 12 ; J. Revel, *Chez nos ancêtres*, Paris, 1888, p. 119. *Cf.* Ch. Guignebert, *Vie cachée de Jésus*, p. 172, note 4.

[3] Jos., *B.J.*, iii, 2 ; *Vita*, 45.

The Galileans were an active, hard-working and energetic people who were not content to live merely on the fruits of the earth and of the Lake, which was rich in fish.[1]   They drew large profits from the great merchant caravans which passed through the country on their way from the coast to the Transjordan district.   The west bank of the Lake, where two trade routes met, was the economic centre of the whole district. Here lay several towns that are often mentioned in the Gospels, though not always with approval; Chorazin, Capernaum, Magdala, and further south, within reach of some famous hot springs and in what Josephus tells us is the very best part of Galilee ἐν κρατίστοις τῆς Γαλιλαίας [2]—Tiberias.[3]   But when Jesus was born Tiberias had not yet come into being.   It was not till A.D. 26 that Herod Antipas founded it, and its name was a compliment to the Emperor Tiberius.   It was built on the site of an ancient necropolis, which made it unclean for the Israelites, so it was populated by foreigners—not all of the best class—and seemed more like a Greek city.   Many Jews finally abandoned their scruples and settled there, attracted by the opulence of the place and delighted by its amenities, but it seems improbable that Jesus ever visited the city.

The population of Galilee was very mixed, although Jewish in external appearance owing to the fact that strangers residing there tended to adopt Jewish customs (with more or less sincerity and good will), in order to live more easily among the Jews, who were intolerant of foreign ways.   This is why the Judæans, proud of their own alleged racial purity, rather looked down on the Galileans as half-breeds, more or less under suspicion of defilement.[4]   From our point of view these people stand out as being strikingly unlike the rest of the Jews. The special nature of their country and the little labour needed to extract an abundant livelihood from it,[5] their motley racial character, their habitual contact with travellers from other lands, and their comparative remoteness from Jerusalem, all combined to set them apart from the remainder of the Israelites.

[1] The name Bethsaida means the *house of the fisheries* (*cf.* **LXXVI,** 154 *ff.*) ; it was a town on the north bank of the lake.   As for Magdala, its real name, *Magdal Nounaiya*, should be rendered *the Magdal of the fishes.*

[2] Jos., *Ant.*, xviii, 2, 3 ;   *B.J.*, ii, 9, 1.

[3] **LXXV,** i (4th edit.), 433 ; ii (3rd edit.), 169 *ff.* ; **LXXVI,** 131.

[4] **CCCI,** 22 ; **LXXV,** ii, 20 ; **XXV,** ii, 264 *ff.* ; **LXXVI,** 131.

[5] The country would never have produced much of its own accord, as a glance at its present condition proves.   There are no trees left in *the Garden of Gennesaret.*   Schwalm (**LXXVI,** 151) reckons one palm tree at El-Mejdel and three or four at Tiberias, but this is an understatement : I counted at least ten between Tiberias and Capernaum.

They had the reputation of being gay and optimistic, kindly, and even generous.[1] Peasants for the most part, they led simple, healthy lives, scarcely touched by the intellectual problems that perplexed the inhabitants of Judæa. Their religion was simpler and less troubled by speculation than that of their neighbours to the south, who were somewhat contemptuous of their simple faith.[2] They were firm in their allegiance to the nationalist ideals of Israel, and this stout patriotism might easily be regarded as disaffection.[3]

Nevertheless there was one blemish in this idyllic picture. The Galileans were not all above suspicion, and at the time of Jesus the mountain fastnesses of Upper Galilee still harboured brigands whom an inadequate police force was unable to suppress.[4] These outlaws found the spoil of passing caravans or of lonely farms at the edge of the plain exceedingly tempting. Moreover, all the people of Palestine had the reputation of taking readily to brigandage by land or sea.[5] So much so, that it seems to have been a condition of reception among the Essenes that the novice should swear that he would not turn bandit.[6]

It has been written,[7] " *If Umbria is the key to St. Francis, Galilee is in a sense the key to Jesus of Nazareth.*" It is certainly not a key that will open all the locked doors that confront our curiosity, but it is not to be despised. The atmosphere of Galilee offers valuable assistance to him who seeks to visualize the external features of Jesus' personality, and may even aid in the understanding of the spirit and character of his teaching. If the Prophet had been born in the harsh region of the south, in the midst of toil and hardship, anxiety and unrest, the fragments of his life and teaching that remain would create a very different impression of the man. It is not without significance perhaps that while the Judaism of Galilee brought forth Jesus and the Gospels, the Judaism of Judæa produced John the Baptist and the Talmud.[8]

[1] This doubtless accounts for the Rabbinical eulogy cited by Schwalm (158), *viz.* : *The Galileans care more for honour than for wealth.*

[2] **LXXVI**, 131 *ff.* Cf. *John*, vii, 52 : ἴδε ὅτι ἐκ τῆς Γαλιλαίας προφήτης οὐκ ἐγείρεται.

[3] **CCLXVII**, i, 290.

[4] **CCCI**, 171 ; Jos., *Ant.*, xvii, 10, 4 *ff.* ; *Vita*, 11.

[5] **XLVII**, ii, 202 *ff.*   [6] Jos., *B.J.*, ii, 8, 7.

[7] Cheyne, in **EB**, art. *Galilee*, col. 1631, § 6.

[8] **LXXV**, ii (3rd edit.), 20 ; **CCCI**, 67. Naturally this method of approach leads to misconceptions if carried too far. The character of John the Baptist does correspond to the tendencies of a certain section of the Judæans, but we do not know his exact background. On Judæa, see J. Jeremias, *Jerusalem zur Zeit Jesu. Eine Kulturgeschichte. Untersuchung zur neutestamentlichen Zeitgeschichte*, 2 vols., 1927.

CHAPTER II

THE SOURCES

I

LATE JUDAISM

ANY attempt to consider this problem statically would be doomed to failure, because the precise dating of social conditions, and especially of religious conditions, is scarcely ever possible ; and in any case we can only arrive at the true character of the facts in question, their meaning and scope, by an inquiry into their origins. The obvious difficulty of this method should not prevent us from making the attempt. Life is manifested in movement ; hence it is movement, transformation, in a word *evolution*, that we must try to capture in this survey of the Palestinian world, and we should have little hope of understanding the problem on the basis of a rigid chronology.

The Germans have a convenient term for the Judaism of the period which we are about to study. They call it *das Spätjudentum*. This may be rendered in English by the term *Late Judaism*, by analogy with the *Early* and *Late Roman Empire*. Late Judaism refers to the 250 years of existence of the Jewish State " *as opposed to the ancient history of the people of Israel.*" [1] And the Jewish world does indeed undergo such a profound transformation during this time that it is no longer comparable with its former state before the Babylonian Captivity.

Let us first of all take stock of the various available sources for the history of Late Judaism and see how much help we may expect from them. [2]

It is an artificial distinction which separates sources dealing with religious history from those concerned with politics, for

---

[1] **CCLXVI**, i, 27.

[2] For bibliography see **LXXV**, i (4th edit.), 10–31 (archæology, chronology, numismatics and epigraphy) ; iii (3rd edit.), 135–562 (literature) ; also **XLVII**, i, 1–179, and **CCLIII**, 47–52. *Cf.* Gunkel, *Israëlitische Literatur* in *Die Kultur der Gegenwart*, vii, Leipzig, 1906, 51–102, and **CCLIII**, 6–47.

in such an environment and in such an age there was nothing that was not in some way connected with religion. It is therefore merely for the sake of clearness that I propose to separate the documents mainly concerned with the political aspect of Jewish life from those which deal with its religious aspect. All I shall do in the way of amplification will be to note an occasional name or date and to fix accurately the few landmarks that are absolutely necessary for the understanding of our problem.

II

THE REMAINS OF THE HISTORICAL LITERATURE

Of all the wealth of literature, Jewish, Greek, and even Latin, produced during this period, only fragments remain. Many works are only known by their titles, or by a few meagre fragments; and no doubt an even greater proportion has disappeared completely, leaving no trace. At the present time our principal, indeed almost our sole sources of information are the two Books of the Maccabees and the works of Josephus. Such scanty additions as are possible come first from Greek and Latin historical writings which deal with this period and then from the Rabbinical literature whose chronology is so uncertain that it must be used with great caution.

In Aramaic *maqqaba* means " hammer," while *maqqabi* is the "hammerer." Hence, when Judas, the third son of Mattathias and the head of the Jewish State from 165–161 B.C., was surnamed *Maccabæus*, it was because he had caused the enemies of Israel to feel the crushing weight of his arm. In the same way Charlemagne's grandfather, Charles, who conquered the Arabs at Poitiers, received the name of *Martel*. The epithet remained in the family of Judas, and was used on several occasions to honour those who championed the Jewish faith against the Greeks. Jewish writers sometimes refer to the First Book of Maccabees [1] as the *Book of the Hasmonæans*, because the grandfather of Mattathias was called *Ehashmon* (Greek ʼΑσαμωναῖος = Asmonæus, or Hasmonæus.[2] All his successors are included under this designation).[3]

The First Book of Maccabees covers the period from 175–

---

[1] *Cf.* B. Niese, *Kritik der beiden Makkabäerbücher*, Berlin, 1899.

[2] Jos., *Ant.*, xii, 6, 1.

[3] *Cf.* **LXXV**, i, 32 *ff.* ; iii, 139 *ff.* ; 159 *ff.* ; **EB**, art. *Maccabees (First Book)* and *Maccabees (Second Book)* ; **CCLXIX**, i, 24 *ff. Les Livres apocryphes de l'Ancien Testament*, published by the *Société biblique de Paris* in 1909, anonymously, is the best French translation.

135 B.C., the second from 175–161. Hence 1 Maccabees starts with the accession of Antiochus Epiphanes in 175 and ends with the death of Simon, the third of the Maccabees, in 135. It is a record of military and political history, given in chronological order. The author is unknown. We can only infer that he was an ardent patriot and of Palestinian origin, since he gives many details which could only be of interest to someone who knew the country well. He may not have taken an active part himself in the events he chronicles, but he certainly knew those who did, and he delights in political discussion. In accordance with his strong *Hasmonœan* feeling he speaks well of the High Priest throughout the book.[1]

The redaction of the book must have taken place *after* the accession of John Hyrcanus, in 135 B.C., since this prince is mentioned in xvi, 23–4, and *before* 63 B.C., the date of Pompey's activities in Jerusalem, for the author would not have spoken so highly of the Romans if he had known of their outrage on the Holy City. All things considered, the work may be assigned to the period between 100 and 70 B.C.

It was written first in Aramaic and then translated into Greek, not without undergoing certain changes in the process, if we accept the view that the version used by Josephus differed somewhat from ours.[2] This, however, is not certain. The author made use chiefly of first-hand information and the traditions which he had collected himself. He added several official documents, and alludes on at least two occasions (ix, 22 and xvi, 24) to earlier writings known to him.[3] He was evidently not without literary experience, and even shows some skill in the presentation of his material.

The man himself gives the impression of being a good Jew, pious and honourable, somewhat credulous, but conscientious and moderate in his judgments. In speaking of the enemies of Israel he shows a restraint which is unusual in one of his race. He is deliberately silent on occasion ; for instance, he does not breathe a word about the frightful scandal caused by the impious behaviour of the two High Priests, Jason and Menelaus ; but at least he does not try to give false impressions, or to fill the gaps with inventions of his own. We may not feel

---

[1] 1 Macc. v. 62 ; xiii. 3 ; xiv. 25 ; xvi. 2 ; etc.

[2] Destinon, *Die Quellen des Josephus*, 1882, p. 8 *ff.* Only the Greek version has survived.

[3] We read in ix, 22, that "*the rest of the acts of Judas . . ., which made him famous, have not been written,*" from which we may assume the existence of written documents used by our author to substantiate his narrative. xvi, 24, indicates that other acts of John Hyrcanus are written in the *book of his priesthood.*

complete confidence in the documents he quotes or the figures he supplies or the speeches he reports, but the same reservation applies to all ancient historians, even the most famous. He resembles them and can bear comparison with them.

We cannot say as much for the author of the Second Book of Maccabees. It purports to be an abridged version of a work by Jason of Cyrene, of which we know nothing from any other source.[1] But, as 2 Maccabees has every appearance of being a rhetorical amplification rather than a summary, it would not be surprising if its alleged model existed only in the author's imagination. He was probably an Egyptian Jew whose motive for writing was rather the desire to edify his Greek-speaking co-religionists than to preserve a record of events. Greek was his mother tongue ; he wrote it with care and discrimination, and not without success. He leaves us completely in the dark as to his personal history, but his violent hatred of foreigners, his theocratic convictions, his strict legalism, and his belief in the resurrection of the dead, all suggest that he was an adherent of the *Pharisaic* movement.[2]

The date of the work is very uncertain. Josephus did not know it, but both Philo (*Quod omnis probus liber*) and the author of the Epistle to the Hebrews (xi, 35 *ff*.) had read it. We shall perhaps not be very far wrong in assigning it to the end of the first century B.C. Its sources (or those of Jason of Cyrene) are unknown. The author did not use 1 Maccabees, for he omits or transposes many of the events there chronicled and shows various other discrepancies, particularly in the chronology. We have reason to think that, even if the alleged book of Jason did exist, it was merely compiled from oral and untrustworthy traditions. Whenever 1 Maccabees and 2 Maccabees disagree the presumption is in favour of the former. 2 Maccabees must be read with caution.

Little will be said here of two other works concerned with the same family, 3 and 4 Maccabees, because neither of them deals with our particular period. 3 Maccabees is a kind of brief historical romance, compiled between A.D. 1 and 70, and apparently intended for the edification of the Jews of Egypt. 4 Maccabees is not really a narrative at all, but a philosophical dissertation which asserts the sovereignty of reason over the passions.

The same caution needed in the use of 2 Maccabees must also be used when we approach Josephus.[3]

---

[1] On this Jason, *cf.* **LXXV**, iii (3rd edit.), 359 *ff*.
[2] 2 Macc. vii. 9–11 ; xii. 43–5 ; xiv. 23, 29, 36, 46.
[3] **LXXV**, i, 74 *ff*. ; **XXV**, ii, 364 *ff*. ; more recently, Laqueur, *Der jüdischer Historiker Flavius Josephus*, Giessen, 1920 ; **CCLXVIII** (im-

He was a Jew of Jerusalem, of priestly family, born in A.D. 37 or 38, the first year of Caligula's reign. According to his own account he showed such startling precocity that he was visited, at the age of fourteen, by the priests and " elders " of the city, who came to ask him for explanations of certain points of the law. When he had made the round of all the Palestinian schools, learnt all that the Pharisees could teach him, imbibed the doctrines of the Sadducees, and exhausted the mysteries of the Essenes, he spent a further period of three years in the desert under the direction of a hermit named Banos. Before he was twenty he had accomplished this vast voyage of study and experience, and could henceforth establish himself securely in the safe harbour of Pharisaism. These unrestrained boastings are interesting because of the light they throw on what a Jew of that time, who wished to gain a reputation for piety and sacred learning, regarded as the best sources of information and religious experience.

In A.D. 64, when Josephus was twenty-six, he was sent to Rome to plead for the liberation of two Pharisees who were imprisoned there. A Jewish comedian named Alityros presented him to Poppæa, who was already well disposed towards the Synagogue. Thanks to her intervention he was successful in his mission, and received several handsome presents in addition. It is probable that on leaving Italy he took with him, if not any enduring devotion to Rome, at any rate a strong impression of the might of Rome, and the conviction that it would be madness for the Jews to challenge it. Hence, when, soon after he had returned to his own country, the great revolt of 66 broke out, he took part in it with no illusions as to its outcome. But he did not on that account hold aloof from it, and in this he showed himself a true Jew. His reason told him that the adventure was foolish and doomed to disaster, but his heart whispered : " Who knows ? It may be that Jahweh will intervene ! " He was allotted the important and honourable duty of defending Galilee, probably through the favour of the High Priest, Joshua ben Gamala. He does not seem to have thrown himself very ardently into his task ; at any rate he failed. Trapped in the fortress of Jotapata, he surrendered on conditions which add no lustre to his reputation, and his conqueror Vespasian gave him an immediate welcome

portant bibliography in appendix, p. 291) ; St. J. Thackeray, *Josephus, the Man and the Historian*, New York, 1929, mainly followed by Lagrange, **LI**, p. xi and Index. Eisler's study, **CCLXXXIX**, i, 3 *ff., Der Streit um das sogenannte Testamentum Flavianum*, must also be taken into account in spite of its peculiar angle of approach.

which bears witness both to his friendship with Rome and to
the zeal he had shown during the revolt. He was present in
the Roman camp during the siege of Jerusalem and did his
best to hasten the capitulation [1] of the city by haranguing its
defenders from the foot of the walls. He clearly considered it
a lost cause and feared that the Jews would suffer for their
obstinacy.

After the Holy City had been taken and sacked, he judged
it wiser not to expose himself to the vengeance of some over-
zealous patriot, and followed Titus back to Rome. The Emperor
gave him hospitality there and after his death, according to
Eusebius,[2] the Romans even put up a statue in honour of his
memory. This reveals his character, which was that of an
intelligent realist, quick to seize and act on anything that
would be to his own advantage. Whether the story of the
statue is true or not (and if it is it only proves that he knew
how to flatter his all-powerful protectors), it is a fact that he
was accorded the honour of Roman citizenship and took the
name of Flavius, as became an intimate of Vespasian and Titus.
On the other hand, his compatriots looked on him as a common
traitor, and felt only loathing for him. Even to the present
day Jewish writers are quite uncompromising in the attitude
they adopt towards him.[3] In reality his case is rather a
complex one. It is perfectly true that he became Romanized,
just as it is true that he was Hellenized, writing in Greek and
keeping abreast of Greek culture. But for all that he was not
really a Hellenist, that is, an Israelite transformed by his
Gentile environment. His religion was much more akin to
that of the Pharisees than of Philo.[4] Fundamentally he
remained a Jew—and, in certain respects, even a good Jew ; he
was, in the gospel sense, *a Herodian*.[5] No doubt he wrote in
his own defence, and tried to whitewash his conduct, since his
enemies were so unscrupulous in their attacks. But his primary
object in composing his works was to clear the Jews from the
contempt in which they were held in Rome ; and he believed
that his conduct was governed by patriotic motives.

In truth he was more a victim of circumstances than a

[1] He relates (in *B.J.*, v, 13, 3) that on one occasion he nearly met his
death from a stone which one of the defenders hurled at him in reply.

[2] Eus., *H.E.*, iii, 9. He probably died during the first few years of
the second century, for the *Vita* dates from after the disappearance of
Herod Agrippa II, the last of the Herodians, who died in A.D. 99 or 100.

[3] Thus Graetz (**XXV**, ii, 401) accuses him of spitefully applauding
when he witnessed the sufferings of the heroes.

[4] **CCLXV**, 66, n. 1.

[5] **CCLXVIII**, 33.

traitor, and it was his misfortune to be without illusions or self-sacrifice at a time which demanded the abandonment of both egoism and discretion.

Of the four works from his pen that have survived, three form part of his plan for raising the Jews in the estimation of the cultured Romans. These are : (1) *The Jewish War* (περὶ τοῦ ᾿Ιουδαϊκοῦ πολέμου), in seven books, authorized for publication by the Emperor ; (2) *Jewish Antiquities* (᾿Ιουδαϊκὴ ᾿Αρχαιολογία), a history of the Jewish people from their beginnings to the time of the Great Rebellion, in twenty books ; (3) *Contra Apion* (the Greek title is lost but must have been προς τοὺς ῞Ελληνας or περὶ τῆς τῶν ᾿Ιουδαίων ἀρχαιότητος),[1] an apologia for the Jewish race, inspired by the anti-Semitic insults of a Greek grammarian named Apion ; (4) *The Life* (Φλαουίου ᾿Ιωσήπου βίος), which appears as an appendix to the *Antiquities*, is a personal defence dealing especially with the accusations made against him by his fellow-countryman, Justus of Tiberias.

We have in Josephus an educated man who writes both Greek and Aramaic[2] with equal skill. It is unfortunate that in general we know nothing of his sources except from his own use of them, so that we are unable to form an estimate of their authority or of the way in which he has handled them. On the other hand we get a clear idea of his *attitude*, which is not that of the historian who chronicles and explains, but of the apologist who accommodates his facts and the conclusions he draws from them to his own preconceived ideas and theories. His authority, which was very great in ancient and mediæval times,[3] is now much diminished. He is accused of such daring *flights of fancy* as the transformation of the Pharisees and Sadducees into philosophical sects who discuss free-will and the immortality of the soul ; of *wilful omissions*, such as that of all reference to the Messianic expectations of the Jews—since he thought it wiser not to draw the attention of the Romans to one of the chief causes which Israel gave them for anxiety ; and of *inter-*

---

[1] Porphyry, *De abstinentia*, iv, 11 ; Orig., *C. Celsum*, i, 16 ; iv, 11 ; Eus., *H.E.*, iii, 9.

[2] Josephus wrote the *B.J.* in Aramaic, and then made a Greek version of it (*C. Apion*, i, 9). It is, however, unlikely that he had any remarkable knowledge of Greek ; he had his manuscript revised before publication (*cf.* **CCLXVIII**, chap. xiv). He was also the author of various works which have not survived.

[3] **LXXV**, i (4th edit.), 93, recalls St. Jerome's saying, *Ad Eustochium*, 35 : *Josephus Græcus Livius* ; F. Jackson (**CCLXVIII**, p. xi) still considers him *an historian of exceptional value*. This is an exaggerated estimate.

pretations which are obviously and consciously false, such as that which throws the whole responsibility for the revolt on to a few fanatics, so that the Jewish people as a whole may appear blameless in the matter. The figures which he gives are always doubtful, and the dialogues scattered through his pages do not give any greater impression of authenticity than those with which Livy afflicts us. Even with regard to the official documents which he claims to have copied, we have often good grounds for suspecting him of having altered, misinterpreted or actually forged them. Wherever we are in a position to check him we find him allowing himself the most deplorable liberties with his sources. He inspires little confidence even as an eye-witness, being much addicted to exaggeration, a failing in which he indulges with a sort of cynicism, heedless even of absurdity. And lastly, he assumed a burden which was beyond his powers, and the last books of the *Antiquities* show signs of weariness and a certain slackening in care.

Taken all in all, neither the man nor his work is of the first quality ; yet if some misfortune had robbed us of the *Antiquities* and the *Jewish War* we should not even be able to attempt a reconstruction of the Græco-Roman period of Jewish history, for what other documents we possess are of value solely in relation to these works. Also it is only fair to add that Christian scribes have not shown a proper respect for the text, which they have often shamelessly interpolated and also have perhaps deliberately mutilated.[1]

It is a pity that we do not possess, side by side with the works of Josephus, those of his enemy Justus ben Pistos, known as Justus of Tiberias.[2] He too wrote a history of the Jewish war, and composed a *Chronicle* extending from the time of Moses to that of Agrippa II. These books were still known to Photius in the ninth century, but they have not come down to us. Even more valuable perhaps would be the works of Nicholas of Damascus, tutor to the children of Antony and Cleopatra, and a friend of Herod the Great, which were Josephus's main source outside the Bible.[3] But these have perished, together

---

[1] A. Berendts, *Die Zeugnisse vom Christentum im Slavischen de bello judaico des Josephus*, Leipzig, 1906, and Schürer's critique of it in **TLZ**, 1906, col. 262 *ff*. Quite recently R. Eisler has attempted to reinstate the Slavonic Josephus, and has convinced Salomon Reinach, but I cannot believe he has won his case, for reasons which I have given in the volume of this series which relates to Jesus (*Jesus*, Eng. trans., 19, 149, 281 *ff*.). On the other hand the same scholar has given striking examples of the way in which Christians of the Middle Ages maltreated Jewish texts. *Cf.* **CCLXXXIX**, i, the plates at the end of the volume.

[2] **LXXV**, i, 58 ; **XXV**, ii, 433.   [3] **LXXV**, i, 50 *ff*.

with the writings of Timogenes of Alexandria, Posidonius of Apamæa and others whose loss we equally deplore.

Now and again we get a little help from some other Greek or Latin author, whom I shall mention as occasion arises.[1] Epigraphy and papyrology relate only to Egyptian Judaism, but they sometimes provide instructive comparisons and should not be ignored in studying the Palestinian world.[2] And finally the Rabbinical literature furnishes us with occasional information about the political history of the time, information which we must always make use of with caution.

III

THE STRICTLY RELIGIOUS DOCUMENTS

All the sources already mentioned, and the writings of Josephus in particular, provide us with a good deal of information, but the definitely religious documents fall into *four groups*. These are : (1) a certain number of Jewish writings which have been received into the canon of the Jewish Bible in spite of their late date ; (2) various works more or less similar to the above and known as the *Deuterocanonical* books ; they have been the subject of much discussion from early times and only a few have been admitted into the Alexandrian canon ; (3) apocryphal writings universally regarded as such, the most interesting being apocalyptic in character ; and (4) the genuine Rabbinical literature.[3]

A. At the head of the first group comes the book of Job, which raises the difficult problem of God's relation to the misfortunes of the righteous. Critics are divided as to its date, but there are several cogent arguments in favour of the post-exilic period. For instance, there is a certain flavour of scepticism with regard to divine justice, which can hardly be dated earlier than the Return, or at most before the Exile ; again, the universalistic conception of God is only characteristic of this period ; and, lastly, the book is pervaded by a sort of humanitarianism which is not in keeping with what is known

---

[1] List of references in **LXXV**, i, 107 *ff*. The texts are collected and translated into French in Th. Reinach, *Textes d'auteurs grecs et romains relatifs au judaïsme*, Paris, 1895.

[2] C. K. H. Wright, *Light from Egyptian papyri on Jewish history before Christ*, **LXXV**, i, 65 *ff*.

[3] All the necessary information is to be found in the various Dictionaries of the Bible, in particular **EB** and **DB**, and in **HRE**, **JE** and **EJ**. *Cf.* **XXXIX** (*Job*, 75 *ff*. ; *Ecclesiastes*, 107 *ff*. ; *Ben-Sira*, 125 *ff*.).

of ancient Israel.[1]   The angelology of the book leads to the
same conclusion.   Hence the beginning of the third century B.C.
seems a probable date.

The Psalms present the same problem of date,[2] which is no
easier to solve than in the case of Job.   The titles, whose textual
tradition is uncertain, such as *To David, To Asaph*, seem to
refer, not to the probable author, but only to the collection
from which the particular psalm is taken—for the five books
into which the Psalms in their present form are divided are
made up of borrowings from earlier collections.   It is possible
that a few of these poems, definitely intended for liturgical
purposes, date from before the Exile, but the tone and feeling
of the majority point to that later period which now concerns
us.[3]

The book known as Ecclesiastes is really called " *The words
of the Preacher, the son of David, King of Israel in Jerusalem*." [4]
It opens with the famous words : " *Vanity of vanities . . .*",
which give the keynote of all the rest.   It is the work of a
sceptic, or at least of a disillusioned pessimist.   It seems most
extraordinary that a writing of this nature, so frankly setting
forth its negative quietistic philosophy of indifference, should
ever have been received into the canon.   It is earlier than
Ecclesiasticus (*The Wisdom of Jesus, the son of Sirach*),[5] which
was composed about the year 200 or a little later ; but we do
not know whether to place it towards the end of the Persian
domination or just before the time of the Maccabees.

The Book of Daniel [6] is an apocalypse belonging to the
period of Antiochus Epiphanes (175–164 B.C.).   Inspired by
the oppression of the Seleucid king, the author chooses the
reign of the Chaldæan king, Nebuchadnezzar, for the setting
of his story.   The work first appeared in Aramaic, but was

---

[1] **LXX,** 669 and Steuernagel in **XLVIII,** ii, 296.   On the matter and
spirit of the book see Lods, *The Prophets of Israel and the Rise of Judaism,*
book iii, chap. ii, § ii, 335 *ff.*

[2] See Lods, *op. cit.,* pp. 347 *ff.*

[3] *Psalms,* in **V,** 1920, pp. 186 *ff.*; **XLVIII,** ii, 106; **EB,** under *Psalms*
(*Book*), § 7–14 ; A. Causse, *L'Ancienne poésie cultuelle d'Israël et les
origines du Psautier,* after **RHPR,** i–ii, 1926 ; **LIX** (3rd edit.), 36.

[4] See Lods, *op. cit.,* pp. 341 *ff.*   **EB,** art. *Ecclesiastes* ; Budde in **XLVIII,**
ii, 384.   St. Jerome renders the Hebrew *Koheleth,* meaning " preacher,"
as *concionator* ; this is the meaning of the Greek *Ecclesiastes,* one who
addresses the *ecclesia* or assembly.

[5] Ben-Sira xviii. 6 is taken to be an echo of Eccles. iii. 14 and Ben-
Sira xlii. 24 is reminiscent of Eccles. vii. 14.

[6] **EB,** art. *Daniel* (*Book of*) ; Marti, in **XLVIII,** ii, 416 ; **LXXV,** iii
(3rd edit.), 186 ; Charles, *A critical and exegetical commentary on the book
of Daniel,* Oxford, 1929.

subsequently translated into Greek with various additions,
notably the famous story of the chaste Susanna (xiii, 1–64),
the tale of Bel and the Dragon (xiii, 65 to xiv, 42), and perhaps
the Three Hebrew Children in the Fiery Furnace (iii, 8–97).
This is the first apocalypse to take the form of a prophecy ;
but the events which it is supposed to foretell are darkly wrapped
in figures and symbols. Daniel holds an important part in the
history and formation of Messianic belief in Israel and largely
contributed to the Palestinian unrest which found expression
in the Great Rebellion.

B. The above-mentioned *Wisdom of Jesus, Son of Sirach,*
the Ecclesiasticus of the Vulgate,[1] belongs to the second group.
It was originally written in Hebrew, but was translated into
Greek fifty years later in Egypt by the author's grandson, as
the preface tells us. The author himself was probably a Scribe,
well balanced, not dominated by legalism, and chiefly interested in morality. It is probably this last characteristic which
has earned him the title of Ecclesiasticus, since his work must
have seemed particularly suitable for educational purposes.
The wisdom of Ben-Sira often seems banal, little concerned
with religion.[2]

Ben-Sira may be compared with another book of Wisdom,
that attributed to Solomon,[3] which has done so much to redeem
his tarnished reputation. It need hardly be said that the son
of David is not the author. After interminable discussions,
ranging over a period of about 250 years, the critics can tell us
no more of the date of the work than that it was written some-
time between 250 B.C. and A.D. 40, though they seem to show
a slight preference for the first century A.D. It is certain that
the author was an Alexandrian Jew. There are few works of
greater interest from the point of view of the Hellenization of
Israel. It is the forerunner of Philo, and although neither
Plato, Pythagoras, nor the Stoics are mentioned, their influence
is everywhere manifest.

Baruch [4] seems to be a patchwork of fragments of various

---

[1] **EB**, art. *Ecclesiasticus* ; Ryssel in **CCLXIX**, i, 230 *ff.* ; **LXXV**,
iii, 157 *ff.* ; **LXX**, 651 *ff.* ; *Les Apocryphes de l'Ancien Testament,*
385 *ff.*

[2] If an example is needed, here is one which is typical, though very
indelicate : xxxi. 20, . . . *The pangs of sleeplessness, vomitings and colic
are the lot of the intemperate ;* 21, *If thou hast allowed thyself to eat im-
moderately, arise and evacuate and thou shalt have rest.*

[3] **EB**, art. *Wisdom (Book of)* ; Siegfried in **CCLXIX**, i, 476 *ff.* ; **LXXV**,
iii, 377 *ff.* ; *Les Apocryphes de l'A.T.,* 582 *ff.*

[4] **LXXV**, iii (3rd edit.), 223 *ff.* ; **CCLXIX**, i, 402 ; *Apocr. de l'A.T.,*
358 *ff.*

dates and origins. The discussions it has provoked have not yet led to even an approximate agreement, and we shall be well advised to make as little use of it as possible.

The second book of Esdras, Tobit, Judith and Esther, all belong to the period of late Judaism. They are *paranetic* in character, intended for the encouragement and exhortation (παραίνεσις) of their readers.

C. A special place among apocryphal works must be assigned to the Apocalypses, since they are a special feature of Judaism.[1] These *Revelations* constitute a literature of edification and encouragement, intended to comfort Israel in the midst of its trials and misfortunes. Down to the time of the total ruin and dispersion of the Jewish people, every national disaster was followed by an outbreak of these apocalypses. If, as some have said, the Persian mind was metaphysical, certainly the Jewish was apocalyptic.[2] The basic conviction that underlies all these writings, though it is expressed and given concrete form in different ways, is that the present humiliation of Israel is in itself the sign of its triumphant exaltation in the near future. The wheel has almost come full circle and Jahweh is about to stretch out his hand on behalf of his people. Jesus was born into an apocalyptic atmosphere.[3]

It will be necessary to return to and enlarge on this all-important element in the religious life of the Jews; hence it will suffice for the present to mention the chief apocalyptic books which will be referred to later. These are: (1) The Book of Enoch,[4] a composite work which is difficult to disentangle. As far as we can tell, most of it was written in Palestine between 200 and 150 B.C. (2) The Book of Jubilees[5]; (3) The Sybilline Oracles,[6] which are probably of Alexandrian origin. The first edition apparently belonged to the second century B.C., but they were worked over again and again, and were later largely remodelled by the Christians. Their special point of interest is the testimony they bear to the Jewish belief that all Gentiles would be converted to the true faith before the last

---

[1] EB, art. *Apocalpytic Literature*; LXXV, iii (3rd edit.), 190 *ff.*; CCLXVI, i, 44–7; CCLXXX, 266 *ff.*; CCLXXVI, i, 163 *ff.*; CCLIII, 242 *ff.*; LI, 70 *ff.* on the apocalyptic literature in general, its character, themes, etc.

[2] CCLXV, 69 *ff.*

[3] CCLV, 93 *ff.*; 108; CCCIII, 49.

[4] LIX (3rd edit.), 44 *ff.*; CCLIX, ii, 217; LXXV, iii, 190; Fr. Martin, *Le livre d'Hénoch traduit sur le texte éthiopien*, Paris, 1906; Short bibliography in LI, 109, n. 3.

[5] CCLXIX, ii, 177 *ff.*; LXXV, iii, 421.

[6] Bibliography in LI, 116, n. 1, 503; CCLXIX, ii, 31 *ff.*

days.[1] (4) The Testament of the Twelve Patriarchs.[2] (5) The Assumption of Moses.[3] (6) The Psalms of Solomon,[4] etc.

We possess only a small fraction of this apocalyptic literature,[5] which, fostered by the national obsession, was produced in great quantities. It naturally included many ephemeral works which perished with the hopes they had momentarily succeeded in arousing. It is surprising that we should be so relatively well supplied with these works, which are full of interest though often difficult to interpret.

D. The term *Rabbinical literature* comprises the writings of the Jewish scholars (doctors of the Law) whose teaching and schools grew up from the Return, and more particularly from the time of the earlier Hasmonæans.[6] This literature was exclusively occupied with the Law, with the purpose of clearing up obscurities in the text and giving an exposition of its precepts. It made a study of the *cases* which arose out of the sacred text, and gradually evolved a comprehensive religious and moral jurisprudence as well as a code of daily behaviour.

This immense work had two main objects. (1) It sought to make the letter of the Law comprehensible to the people of Palestine, who had as a whole forgotten Hebrew by the time they returned from the Exile ; and to this end it produced the *Targums*. (2) It commented on and supplemented the Law on all points where unforeseen questions had arisen, the results of this labour being the *Midrash* and the *Talmud*.

Originally the word *Targum* [7] meant a translation of any kind, but in this connexion it refers to an Aramaic version of a Biblical text first written in Hebrew. Aramaic was spoken among the Mesopotamian conquerors of Israel and had begun to make its way into Palestine, along with the products of Oriental trade, even before the Captivity. It became the language of the exiles and also of those humble folk who had remained in Palestine under the Babylonian yoke. After 536,

---

[1] **CCLV**, 103.

[2] **CCLIX**, ii, 458 *ff.* ; **LXXV**, iii, 252 *ff.* ; **LI**, 122 *ff.* A good recent book is R. Eppel, *Le piétisme juif dans le Testament des Douze Patriarches*, Strasbourg, 1930.

[3] **LI**, 237 *ff.*

[4] Bibliography in **LI**, 150 *ff.* ; Viteau, *Les Psaumes de Salomon*, Paris, 1911.

[5] *Cf.* M. R. James, *The lost Apocrypha of the Old Testament*, London, 1920.

[6] **EB**, art. *Scribes*.

[7] **EB**, art. *Text and Versions*, § 65, and *Aramaic language*, § 6 ; **CCXLIX**, 39 *ff.* ; **LXXV**, i, 147 *ff.* Jastrow, *A Dictionary of the Targumim, the Talmud Babli and Yerushalmi and the Midrashic Literature*, London, 2 vols., 1903.

when Cyrus, King of Persia, allowed the Jews to return to Palestine and set about reorganizing their religious life, they had to appoint in each synagogue an official called a *targoman* (*cf.* the *dragoman* of our embassies and legations in the Near East), whose duty it was to give a rendering, in the vulgar tongue, of the Scriptures which were read aloud in Hebrew. For a long while these translations remained oral and individual, the *targoman* improvising, or appearing to do so, as he read ; but gradually they became crystallized into a fixed version. The practice was then extended from the *Torah* (the Law) to the *Nebiim* (the Prophets), and at last even to the *Kethubim* (the Sacred Writings), though this final development took place too late to concern us here.

The earliest references to written *Targums* take us back to the third century B.C. ; but nothing is left of these ancient documents. We have a *Targum* on the Pentateuch, known as the *Targum of Onkelos*, from the name of a Scribe who was supposed to have been a pupil of the Rabbi Gamaliel the Elder (about A.D. 70). Actually Onkelos was not the author but merely the compiler of the work, which probably dates from about the middle of the first century A.D., though some critics put him as late as the first half of the second century, making him contemporary with Rabbi Eliezer and Rabbi Joshua. He made use of earlier *Targums*. The theory is that the book, originally compiled in Palestine, was re-edited later in Babylon, which accounts for its being sometimes referred to as the *Targum Babli*. The *Babylonian Talmud* makes use of it. For us its special value is in reference to post-exilic exegesis and theology. Specially noteworthy is its evident desire to get rid of the anthropomorphism of the Bible narrative and to emphasize the transcendence of God.[1]

The *Jerusalem Targum* (*Yerushalmi*) is also on the *Pentateuch* and has come down to us in two editions, one complete, the other abridged. The former is known as the *Targum of Pseudo-Jonathan*[2] and may perhaps be assigned, though not with certainty, to the first decades of the first century. The other is not earlier than the seventh century, since it gives the names of a wife and a daughter of Mahomet.

For the *Prophets* we have a *Targum of Jonathan*, the date of which seems rather less uncertain ; but it is rather a paraphrase of the original than a genuine translation. *Ezra,*

---

[1] Characteristic examples illustrating these tendencies in **CCXCIX, 46**.

[2] The reference is to Jonathan ben Uzziel, said to have been a pupil of Hillel's, but the work has long ceased to be attributed to him. *Cf.* **LXXV, i, 151**.

Nehemiah, and *Daniel* being comparatively late have no early *Targums.*[1] As for the *Targums* on the *Kethubim,* they belong to the early Middle Ages,[2] and do not concern us here.

Our main interest in this collection of *Targums* is in the light they throw on the way in which the authors understood the Hebrew text and more especially the *Torah,* whose interpretation was fundamental for those whose whole religion was based, ultimately, on the Law of Jahweh and its meaning. Thus the *Targums* try to extricate God from the awkward situations caused by the anthropomorphisms of the Old Testament writers. They emphasize the activity of his *Word (Memra)* and his *Visible Glory (Shechinah),* and they are aware of the rôle of the Messiah.[3] Further discussion will make clear the importance of all these ideas.

The word *Talmud* [4] means " study," " doctrine " or " discipline." What corresponds to the word is, theoretically, the collection of the teachings of the great Rabbis traditionally preserved in two volumes of vast, though unequal extent, namely the *Jerusalem Talmud (Yerushalmi)* and the more voluminous *Babylonian Talmud (Babli).*

A Jew may read his Bible without attempting to penetrate beyond its literal meaning (*peshat*) ; but, if he wishes to probe the deeper meaning of the text, he applies to the *letter* a method of interpretation known as *midrash* (plural *midrashim*), a word whose root (*darash*) is used in the *Targums* and in the *Talmud* with the meaning to " examine," " weigh," " interpret," and ultimately, " to teach." [5] From the moment the *Scribes* (*sopherim*) take up the study of the Law, they produce *midrash.*[6] But the Scribes lead on to the Rabbis, indeed they are *rabbis* themselves, for the word is no more than a title meaning " master "—in this case a mastery of the text and meaning of the Law. The *midrashim* form the substance of the Rabbinical teaching.[7]

This teaching consisted of : (1) expositions in narrative form, elaborating and elucidating a chosen biblical passage.

[1] Also Dan. ii. 4 to vii. 28 and Ezra iv. 8–vi. 18 ; vii. 12–26 are in Aramaic.

[2] **CCXCIX,** 56 *ff.*   [3] **CCXCIX,** 48 *ff.*

[4] See Bibliographical Note on pp. 3–4. In addition, **JE,** xii, art. *Talmud* ; *Encycl. Britannica,* xxvi, art. *Talmud* ; **DB,** v, art. *Talmud* ; **CCXCIX,** 57 *ff.* ; J. Fromer, *Der Talmud. Geschichte, Wesen und Zukunft,* Berlin, 1920. Lagrange's article in **LI,** xv, is based on Strack.

[5] **LXXV,** ii, 330 *ff.* ; **CCXCIX,** 58 : " *to lecture* " on the Law and on the Old Testament generally.

[6] The first rather vague allusion to this practice is in Neh. viii. 2–8.

[7] **JE,** art. *Midrashim,* and **CCXCIX,** 64 *ff.,* enumerate and examine the most important tractates which constitute the *midrash.*

These are the *haggadoth* (plural of *haggadah*, meaning " story " or " narration ") ; (2) explanatory notes and commentaries on legal prescriptions, customs, and rituals. These are the *halachoth* (plural of *halachah*, which means a " rule " or " binding obligation "). Thus there was a *midrash haggadah* and a *midrash halachah*, often without any very definite line of demarcation, especially in the earlier written *midrashim*. Later on the distinction became sharper ; and the learned doctors would deliberately specialize in one branch or the other.

The *midrashim* thus approach the exegesis of the Scriptures from the two points of view defined above. Those which survive are grouped into thirty-one major collections and a few of lesser importance. Most of them took shape between the first and fifth centuries A.D., but some of them may reflect earlier teachings. They are generally distinguished from the *Talmud* proper, although they are the products of the same tendencies and the same method.

As the doctors of the Law were frequently faced with special combinations of circumstances or particular cases of conscience for which the sacred text made no provision, to meet these difficulties they gradually created a body of supplementary prescriptions which they called the *Oral Law* (*the Torah by word of mouth*), and which went back, so they said, to Moses himself. Side by side with the *Scriptures* (= *writings*) there is the *Tradition*, which is a necessary adjunct to every sacred book.[1] By the beginning of the Christian era there was already a considerable accumulation of these pseudo-traditional teachings, but they were too confused to be of much use. The Rabbinical schools of Hillel and Shammai are said to have conceived the idea of gathering all this scattered learning into some more or less organized collection. This is the origin of the *Mishnah*, meaning " Second "[2]—that is, the Second Law.[3] Each school probably had its own *Mishnah*, based on the tradition of its own teachers, but it was quickly realized how valuable a complete collection would be for the whole community. This great work was accomplished by a certain Jehudah-ha-Nasi, towards the end of the second century A.D. His collection has come down to us unimpaired except for such alterations, of varying importance, as it has undergone in the course of its long history.

The *Mishnah* is the basis of the *Talmud*, acknowledged as

---

[1] *Cf.* Guignebert, *L'Évolution des Dogmes* (2nd edit.), chap. iv.
[2] Bibliography in **CCXCIX**, 97.
[3] In Greek, δευτερώσις. *Cf.* Jerome, *Ep.*, 121, *Ep.*, 18, ad *Damasum* ; **LXXV**, i, 113, n. 1. The word could also mean " repetition," for the verb *shanah* means " to repeat," " to teach by means of repetition," **CCXCIX**, 98.

such by both the *Yerushalmi* and the *Babli*. It comprises a vast collection of commentaries, glosses, explanations, amplifications and various applications of the biblical text.[1] But in addition, each *Talmud* also contains an immense amount of haggadic material (much more in the *Babli* than in the *Yerushalmi*). The *Mishnah* is the work of the *Tannaïm* (" teachers " or " reciters "), who were divided into four generations, covering the period from A.D. 70 to 200, whilst five generations of *Amoraïm* (" interpreters " ?), from A.D. 220 to 500, were responsible for the *Talmud*. The first compiler of the *Babli* was Rabbi Ashi, of Sura in Babylonia, about 430. No doubt many other writers have since had a hand in developing this tremendous collection, which the Jews, overwhelmed by its bulk, have called the " Ocean of the *Talmud*."

The contents of the *Talmud* are extraordinarily varied and unequal in value. It contains history, legends, theological, moral and even astrological speculations, in fact everything ; but it is the *halachic* material, that is to say the whole body of teachings relating to religious jurisprudence, which forms the main content of the work, and this must be the guide of anyone who wishes to study the religious ideas and beliefs of Late Judaism. The historical use of anything derived from the *Talmud* is a delicate matter requiring great caution. Its compilers had neither the means nor the will to be troubled by critical scruples, and sometimes even disdained considerations of common sense. Neither the *Midrashim*, nor the *Mishnah*, nor the *Talmud* itself are very reliable from this point of view. Their chronology, where they have any, is vague and confused ; the attribution of teachings to a particular doctor often seems doubtful ; and there are irritating anachronisms by which characters are introduced into scenes far removed in time from the period in which they lived. One Jewish scholar has even said that anachronism was the *vital principle of the Haggadah* [2]

---

[1] The *Mishnah* consists of 63 tractates divided into 6 sections or *sedarim* (analysed in CCXCIX, 99 *ff.*). References are made by giving the name of the particular tractate in question, *e.g. Mishnah, Berakoth*, 20[a]. (*Berakoth*, or the *Benedictions*, is the first tractate of the collection. The figure 20[a] corresponds to the paging of the standard edition of Daniel Bomberg : *Babli*, 12 vols., Venice, 1520–3, and *Yerushalmi*, 1 vol., Venice, 1524.) Sometimes the *Tosephta* (" addition " or " supplement ") is also included. This again is divided into 6 *sedarim*, which more or less correspond to those of the *Mishnah*. *Cf.* CCXCIX, 180.

[2] Cited by Kalthoff, *Was wissen wir von Jesus?*, Berlin, 1904, p. 39. For instance, these writings will often give the *day* on which an event occurred, but not the *year* ! *Cf.* S. Zeitlin, *Megillat Taanit as a source for Jewish chronology and history in the Hellenistic and Roman period*, in *Jewish Quart. Review*, New Series, vol. ix, 1918, and vol. x, 1919.

—that is to say, of history as set forth by the whole Rabbinical literature.

The tractates of the *Mishnah* from which we shall be drawing most of our material are those which actually deal with the religious life, namely *Berakoth* (" the Blessings "), *Shabbath*, *Pesachim* (" the Passover "), *Yoma* (" the Day of Atonement "), *Sanhedrin*, and above all *Pirke Aboth* (" the Sayings of the Fathers "). The Fathers in question were the ancient Rabbis who were supposed to have been the founders of the tradition, and the surest means of understanding early Rabbinical thought is by an examination of their moral precepts. Unfortunately, however, that work of critical exegesis which is indispensable to a study of this composite literature has as yet only dealt with a few sections.[1] It is to be hoped that some day the valuable historical information which may lie buried there will be sifted and evaluated as it is not at present. But even now these confused documents often serve as a means of comparison for the interpretation and estimation of our other sources. In no case should a Rabbinical text be relied on without mature consideration.

Finally, if our information about Late Judaism is not always sound, at least there is enough of it to allow of that collation of evidence which marks the first stage of criticism, and this is no small gain. Even if we limit ourselves to a very cautious use of sources that are not yet well sifted, there is still enough evidence to enable us to reconstruct the conditions which dominated the religious life of the Jews just before the Christian era, and the tendencies which determined its course; and that is the essential thing. If we are careful not to demand too much of the sources and to consult them with discretion, we shall find that they will on the whole give satisfactory answers to our questions.

[1] Most of the work already accomplished is to be found in the more recent critical translations, viz. : Paul Fiebig, *Ausgewählte Mischnatractate in deutscher Uebersetzung*, Tübingen, 1905 *ff.* ; Latzarus Goldschmidt, *Der Talmud*, Berlin, in course of publication, to be completed in 12 vols. G. Beer, O. Holtzmann and E. Krauss, *Die Mischna*, text, translation and commentary, in course of publication, Giessen, 1913 *ff.* The S.P.C.K. has issued a series of translations (London, 1919 *ff.*) : Oesterley, *Pirké Aboth* and *Shabbath*; Lukyn Williams, *Berakoth* ; Box, *Yoma*, etc. The best publication of this type which, however, only deals with one tractate as yet, is A. Cohen, *The Babylonian Talmud : Tractate Berakot*, Cambridge, 1921. The two great works undertaken by L. Goldschmidt in Leipzig and N. Schlögl in Vienna are still far from completion, but will eventually provide between them a complete German translation, with commentary, of the *Babli* (*Der babylonische Talmud*).

CHAPTER III

THE POLITICAL SYSTEM

THE HISTORY OF PALESTINE DURING THE PERIOD PRECEDING THE BIRTH OF JESUS

AT the time of the birth of Jesus Palestine had already long lost her political independence. Indeed, her geographical position gave her little hope of preserving it. In her corner of Asia she was the highway linking north and south, east and west. She had always been a small state, even in the days of her legendary splendour under David, and when, immediately after Solomon's death, she was split up into two kingdoms which were soon in a state of chronic hostility, it was inevitable that she should become the battlefield and the prey of her mighty neighbours. First Egypt and Assyria despoiled her, then Persia, then the Hellenized Lagids and Seleucids, and finally Rome. Not one of the upheavals which shook this part of the Orient passed her by, and none left her unscathed. Her history was a very tissue of calamities. I shall only recall here a few dates and facts to which reference will be made later.[1]

I

THE EXILE AND THE RETURN

About the beginning of the sixth century, when the conflict between Necho, King of Egypt, and Nabopolassar, King of Babylon, came to an end, Palestine fell into the hands of the Mesopotamians. She chafed under their rule and was soon in a state of revolt. Thereupon the Chaldæans returned in full force, took and sacked Jerusalem (585 B.C.), and led away to their own country, in successive deportations, the greater part of the population. This is what is known as the Exile, the deportation *super flumina Babylonis*—the Babylonian Captivity. Of the numbers thus exiled we have no knowledge, but they

[1] See Lods, *op. cit.*, part ii, book i, chaps. i–iii. Full bibliography in **LXXV**, i, 169 *ff*.

probably did not include the humbler folk, workmen and peasantry, whom the conquerors left in peace in their own country.

In 538, when Cyrus, King of Persia, had broken the might of the Chaldæans and taken Babylon, he gave permission for the exiles to return. Not all of them did so, for many had prospered in Mesopotamia and preferred to remain there, but a considerable number came back, and this is called the *Return from Exile* or the *Restoration*. It was, of course, a restoration of the Jewish nation, and not of the Jewish State, for Palestine was placed under the authority of a Persian satrap. But the new rulers of Israel, who were perhaps not altogether lacking in sympathy for Jahwism, tolerated and even encouraged the rebuilding of the religious life of its adherents. From this point of view at least, the repatriated Jews did regain a certain measure of autonomy.

No doubt it fell short of their desires, for there were constant skirmishes between themselves and their governors, and they gladly welcomed Alexander when he arrived in Palestine after the battle of Issus in 332 B.C.[1] Their new ruler restored all the hopes that his predecessor had failed to fulfil; but little came of them, for in the course of his short career his attention was absorbed by countries other than Palestine. At his death in 323, Antigonus, Seleucus and Ptolemy, three of his generals, all laid claim to the part of his Empire that included Palestine. It fell finally to Ptolemy, Antigonus having perished in the Battle of Ipsus in 301.

The domination of the Egyptian Kings lasted about a hundred years. It was constantly threatened by the Syrian Seleucids, and never won the hearts of the Jewish people—though no doubt to have done this would have been beyond the power of any conqueror whatever. During the reign of Ptolemy Philopator, the malcontents of Palestine helped Antiochus III to drive out the Egyptians. Antiochus governed in their stead, and there was a state of friendly alliance during a peaceful interlude which lasted several years. Unfortunately, however, Antiochus IV, called *Epiphanes* (175–164 B.C.), determined to Hellenize all his provinces and, not realizing what a delicate operation this would be in the case of a Jewish country, went about it with such haste, want of tact, and arbitrary violence that the inhabitants of Palestine were soon provoked to dan-

---

[1] **XXV**, ii, 51. Due allowance being made for exaggeration in Josephus's remarkable story in *Ant.*, xi, 8, 5, which depicts Alexander as making a triumphal entry into Jerusalem, going into the Temple and there reading the prophecy of his own victory from the Book of Daniel.

gerous rebellion.[1] The Jews most bitterly resented his violation of the Temple, which he plundered twice and rededicated to Zeus.[2] Possibly the priestly aristocracy of Jerusalem would have bowed its head to the yoke and attempted to make terms with the victor, but the common people were less accommodating and hated with equal violence both the foreign prince who insulted their God and those renegades who could tolerate such sacrilege.

From this time two parties make their appearance, the Hellenists, who yielded to the pressure put upon them by Antiochus, and the Ḥasidim (ʼΑσιδαίοι),[3] who held fast to the ideals of the scribes. But for the tactless impetuosity of the Seleucid, the former, who were rich and influential, might have gained the day, but his lack of diplomacy was a great advantage to the second party, which succeeded in gaining the leadership of the people.[4]

II

The Revolt of the Maccabees and the Hasmonæan Dynasty

The High Priest Onias had been driven out by his rival Menelaus, with the help of Antiochus,[5] and had taken refuge in Egypt, where in 170 B.C., by the permission of King Ptolemy VI, he founded the temple of Leontopolis, on the ruins of an ancient heathen shrine near Heliopolis, that it might take the place of the desecrated Temple of Zion. But in the meantime there was growing unrest and dissatisfaction in Palestine, which came to a head in 167 in open rebellion, under the leadership of a certain Mattathias, a priest who had left Jerusalem and taken refuge at Modin.[6] He managed to hold the plain,

[1] **LXXV,** i, 169 *ff.* ; 179 *ff.* ; 210 *ff.* ; **LXXXVIII,** 247 ; **LXIII,** 8 *ff.* Epiphanes was an ill-balanced man. According to Athenæus, Polybius called him ἐπιμανής or the " madman," and not ἐπιφανής, " the illustrious one, on account of his behaviour " (διὰ τὰς πράξεις). Actually the facts Polybius cites in support of this theory (xxvi, 10) are not convincing. The epithet ἐπιφανής stands for the formula ὁ θεός ἐπιφανής, meaning " the god made manifest," a title already assumed by Ptolemy V. It was in common use among the Seleucids after Antiochus IV.

[2] *The Abomination of Desolation* (βδέλνγμα τῆς ἐρημώσ εως), spoken of in Dan. xi. 31 and xii. 11, meant the erection of an altar to Zeus on the site of the great altar of the Temple.

[3] 1 Macc. ii. 42 ; vii. 13.   [4] **LXXV,** i, 189.

[5] Jos., *Ant.,* xii, 5 ; 2 Macc. iv.

[6] 1 Macc. ii. 1 ; i. 15–28. Modin lay to the west, between Jerusalem and Lydda. *Cf.* **LI,** chap. iii. For the consequences of the Maccabæan movement, see chap. vi, and for the fall of the Hasmonæans, chap. viii, which gives a short account of each of the princes.

and even more successfully the mountains, until his death in 166. One of his sons, Judas, called *Maccabæus*, carried on the work, and after a series of brilliant victories interspersed with some crushing defeats, lost his life in a battle against the Syrian General Bacchides in 161. His brother Jonathan managed to gain a measure of independence, chiefly owing to internal dissensions of the Seleucid Kingdom, but in the end he also fell in battle like Judas (143 B.C.). The last brother, Simon, also was able to establish himself, owing to the weakness of the Syrian princes caused by their continual rivalry. He came to an end by a conspiracy in 135, leaving a son, John Hyrcanus. The latter was at first severely defeated by Antiochus Sidetes, but when Antiochus was killed by the Parthians in 128 he was able to consolidate his position and began to assume regal state. It was his son Aristobulus who first took the *title* of King (in 104 or thereabouts). Hitherto the power of the Maccabees had remained very precarious ; they had been more like guerilla leaders than established rulers. Even the successors of John Hyrcanus—Aristobulus, Alexander Jannæus, his wife Alexandra, Hyrcanus II and Aristobulus II—would never have maintained their position but for the anarchy that still paralysed the neighbouring powers. Meanwhile, more and more they gradually assumed the customs and manners of petty oriental princes.

Meanwhile the Romans had long been watching with interest every move in this political game.[1] In 63 B.C., when there was civil war between the Jewish princes Hyrcanus II and Aristobulus II, Pompey, whom the affair of Mithridates had brought into the vicinity of Palestine, was called in to arbitrate. He seized Jerusalem, made Hyrcanus High Priest, and sent Aristobulus to Rome.

That was the end of the Hasmonæan dynasty.[2] In reality the Jews exaggerated the prosperity and independence which they imagined themselves to have enjoyed under the rule of the descendants of Mattathias. Later on they created a legendary picture of the power of these petty princes,[3] and in the end it brought disaster upon them because they thought that they only needed another Judas Maccabæus to free themselves from the Roman yoke, and more than once they were too easily induced to believe that they had found him. They

---

[1] **LXXV,** i, 302 *ff.*

[2] The name comes from Mattathias' grandfather, *Hashmon*, and was applied to all his descendants.

[3] 1 Macc. iii. 4 says of Judas : " *In his acts he was like a lion, like a lion's whelp roaring did he hurl himself upon his prey.*"

failed to realize that the external situation had been completely transformed. Rome had them in her grasp and would not let them go. When they struggled she merely tightened her hold.

In 47 B.C. Cæsar appointed an active and ambitious Arab named Herod,[1] son of a certain Antipater, to be governor of Judæa, and it was by Roman consent that this man took the title of King of the Jews (40 B.C.) and became *rex socius*, the friend and ally of the Roman people. He needed extraordinary gifts of discretion and adaptability and a rare opportunism to keep on good terms with the varied succession of governors sent by Rome to the East, and to hold his position until his death in 4 B.C. He found special favour with Augustus owing to his unfailing deference to the Imperial will, and his loyalty to his *societas*. He followed a policy of Hellenization, restoring ruined cities and founding new ones, building theatres and arenas, and even flaunting the Roman emblems in Jerusalem itself, to the horror of strict Jews. In his palace were to be found a *Hall of the Cæsars* and a *Hall of Agrippa*.[2] In short, he was a remarkably shrewd man. His crimes have often been emphasized. There is no need either to deny or to exaggerate them. They should be viewed in the perspective of his time, since his acts seemed more natural and therefore less disturbing to his contemporaries than they do to us today. He compares not unfavourably with several of his predecessors who, with an equal capacity for evil, did far less good. " *In the days of King Herod* " [3] Palestine prospered, and was at least at peace, at whatever cost in heavy taxation and despotic control. This brilliant monarch sacrificed the future to the present, and solid reality to dazzling display. Later on he was charged with " *having reduced to penury a people whom he had found in great prosperity* " (Jos., *B.J.*, v, 6, 2). His extortionate fiscal policy was probably the cause of most of the disturbances which broke out at his death.[4]

His kingdom was then divided among his three sons, according to the provisions made in his will.[5] Of the three, Antipas

[1] **LXXV**, i, 360 ; W. Otto, *Herodes. Beiträge zur Gesch. des letzten jüdischen Königshauses*, Stuttgart, 1913, col. 3–164 ; **XXV**, ii, 214 *ff.* ; Hugo Willrich, *Das Haus des Herodes*, Heidelberg, 1929, chaps. i–iv ; **LI**, 164 *ff.* : bibliography and study of sources followed by a fairly detailed analysis.

[2] Jos., *Ant.*, xv, 9, 3. Herod even built pagan temples, but only outside Judæa (Jos., *Ant.*, xv, 9, 5). On the building activities of the Herods *cf.* **XLVII**, i, 341.

[3] **CCLXVIII**, 133 *ff*.

[4] **CCLXXII**, 277 *ff.* ; 281, which emphasizes the errors and indiscretions of Herod's economic policy.

[5] **LI**, chap. xi ; **LXXV**, i, 425 *ff.*

and Philip kept their territories, but in A.D. 6, after ten years of cruelty and tyranny, Archelaus was deprived of his by Augustus and banished to Vienne in Gaul.[1] No sooner was he on the throne than the Pharisees persuaded a considerable section of his subjects to revolt against him, while at the same time a deputation of the malcontents was sent to Rome to beg that Judæa might be placed under the authority of the governor of Syria.[2]

But this was not the solution adopted by Augustus in A.D. 6. He placed Judæa under a procurator. The other two Herods, who were officially known as *tetrarchs*, considered themselves and were no doubt considered by their subjects as *kings*.[3] It is clear that both Herod Antipas in Galilee and Philip in Batanæa, Gaulanitis and Trachonitis did their utmost to make a good impression in Rome.

Of Herod Antipas we know little, except that he was a great builder like his father,[4] that in Luke (xiii. 32) he is called " *that fox* " (which suggests that he gave the impression of being tricky and cunning), and that he caused a great scandal by marrying Herodias, the wife of one of his half-brothers— a story which the Gospel tradition connects with the death of John the Baptist. Jesus would certainly clash with such a man, or at least with his police officials. This petty king enjoyed enough independence to make a war on his own account, in a small way ; namely, his unsuccessful campaign against his father-in-law, the Arabian King Aretas. Josephus tells us however that generally " *he liked peace and quiet.* " [5]

In spite of his Hellenizing activities he was careful of Jewish susceptibilities, he sent gifts to the Temple, he refrained from having his image on the coinage, and even associated himself with a protest against the procurator Pilate's sacrilegious introduction of votive shields into the Sanctuary.[6] Moreover we have reason to be somewhat suspicious of the sincerity of his Hellenizing zeal, which may easily have cloaked much cunning and some nefarious designs. He may even, at one moment, have cherished the dream of freeing himself from the

---

[1] Jos., *Ant.*, xvii, 13, 2 ; **LXXV**, i, 449 ; Otto, *op. cit.*, 165 *ff.* He had the title of *ethnarch*.

[2] **LXV**, 89 ; **XXV**, ii, 247.

[3] Mark vi. 14 : ὁ βασιλεύς Ἡρώδης.

[4] As shown particularly by the founding of Tiberias and the restoration of Beth-Ramtha, which he named *Livia*. *Cf.* **LXXV**, i, 432 *ff.*

[5] Jos., *Ant.*, xviii, 7, 2 : ἀγαπῶν τὴν ἡσυχίαν. On his character see **LXXV**, i, 431 *ff.* ; Otto, *op. cit.*, col. 175 *ff.* ; **EB**, art. *Herod (Family of)*, § 7.

[6] **LXXV**, i, 434 *ff.*

overlordship of Rome. Such at least was the accusation made
by his neighbour Herod Agrippa (A.D. 37) whom Caligula had
appointed to succeed Philip when the latter died in 34. Antipas
could not deny the existence of his arsenals, but explained
that he feared an attack from the Arabs. The Emperor was
unconvinced, and after deposing him, banished him to Lyons
where he may have had him put to death, on which point we
have no certain information.[1] The informer, Herod Agrippa,
took over his territories. Whatever the real intentions of
Antipas may have been, this episode, with its disastrous sequel,
proves how slight was his imagined independence.

His brother Philip [2] was no better off from this point of
view, and in other ways much worse, since he had received the
least attractive portion under his father's will. His state was
so fragmentary that we can only gain a rough idea of it by
comparing various passages in Josephus.[3] Philip himself had
a fair reputation, both as an administrator and a judge ; he
was a prudent man who showed no inclination to enlarge his
domains or to meddle in the affairs of others. He shared the
family passion for building. It was he who founded Cæsarea,
near the source of the Jordan, and rebuilt Bethsaida, on the
north-east shore of the Lake of Gennesaret, renaming it *Julias*
in honour of Augustus' daughter Julia. As most of his subjects
were *goyim* (Greeks and Syrians), he could Hellenize as much
as he liked, and put his image on the money, side by side with
those of Augustus and Tiberius. It was the first time that
coins struck by a Jewish prince had borne the representation
of a human figure ; but in truth Philip would scarcely have
been considered a genuine Jew.[4] He seems to have spent his
leisure in study. He was interested in scientific research and
was popularly supposed to have solved the problem of the
source of the Jordan by proving that the river flowed out of
the Lake of Phiale [5] by means of a subterranean channel.
According to the itinerary given by Mark, Jesus must have
made at least one excursion into Philip's territories. In fact
Marcan tradition stages one of its most celebrated scenes, the
Confession of Peter,[6] in the neighbourhood of Cæsarea.

---

[1] Dio Cassius, xlix, 8, rather suggests an execution.
[2] **LXXV**, i, 425 *ff.* ; **LXXIII**, 146 ; **EB**, art. *Herod (Family of)*, § 11.
[3] Jos., *Ant.*, xvii, 8, 1 ; xiv, 4 ; xviii, 46 ; *B.J.*, ii, 6, 3.
[4] **LXXV**, i, 430 and n. 10.
[5] Jos., *B.J.*, iii, 10, 7.
[6] Mark viii. 27–33 ; Matt. xvi. 13–28. *Cf. Jésus*, 236 (English translation, 283).

III

THE RULE OF THE ROMAN PROCURATORS

After the removal of Archelaus, his ethnarchy was turned into a *procuratorial province* of the second class and was governed by an official with the rank of *procurator* (Gk. ἐπίτροπος).[1] Josephus claims [2] that the province came under the administration of Syria, but he probably mistook the special missions which the Syrian governor undertook from time to time in Palestine for a regular and permanent control. The mere fact that the procurator possessed the *jus gladii*, that is to say, full powers of criminal jurisdiction, is enough to prove his official independence.[3]

His usual place of residence was Cæsarea, the coastal city which Herod the Great had founded about 19 B.C. on the site of the ancient Tower of Strato, and which now lies in ruins. But whenever he anticipated possible disturbances, as for instance during the great religious festivals that attracted thousands of pilgrims to Jerusalem every year, he would move up into the Holy City and instal himself there till the danger was past. He controlled all the local authorities, civil and religious. He could both nominate and depose the High Priest, according to what he regarded as his own interests or those of Rome. He kept the priestly equipment for the great rituals shut up in the Antonia [4] and only allowed the priests to have it when it was required for some particular festival. In this sense therefore he played the part of guardian and supervisor to the Jewish cult ; but his chief concern was really to see that the taxes were duly collected and to keep the peace. This was no easy task with a people like the Judæans, touchy, irascible, and ready to flare up at the least provocation, frequently taking offence at what must have seemed to a Roman, unversed in the intricacies of the Law, the most frivolous trifles. Even a watchful and well-informed procurator must still have been uneasy in the midst of this utterly alien population. And the prospect of a revolt was all the more alarming in that he

---

[1] Jos., *Ant.*, xx, 6, 2 ; *B.J.*, ii, 8, 1. They are also called ἡγεμών, a general term equivalent to the Latin *praeses*. This is the word used in the New Testament (Matt. xxvii. 2 ; Luke xx. 20, etc.). *Cf.* also Jos., *Ant.*, xviii, 3, 1, where ἔπαρχος, meaning *praefectus* (*Ant.*, xix, 9, 2), and ἐπιμελητής, meaning *curator* (*Ant.*, xviii, 4, 2), also occur.

[2] Jos., *Ant.*, xvii, 13, 5 ; xviii, 1, 1.

[3] **LXV**, xi, 91, n. 1.

[4] This was a Hasmonæan building, which Herod had turned into a fortress. It overlooked the Temple Courts.

had only a mere handful of Roman troops with which to parry it.[1] These fears were fully justified by the event.

Roman prudence inclined the procurator to be cautious and diplomatic in his dealings with these suspicious and susceptible Jews. Hence the small change which the people used almost exclusively was minted locally, and, although it bore the Emperor's name, it did not display his image. Hence also all Gentiles without exception were debarred, on pain of death, from entering the sacred courts of the Temple. Even the cohorts assigned to Jerusalem would leave their standards at Cæsarea, so that the pious population might be spared the sight of these idolatrous emblems. We can picture the small Roman force, returning from some raid against the Arabs, carefully skirting the city to avoid wounding the tender susceptibilities of the inhabitants by an appearance in the streets. It was inevitable that as governors of different dispositions succeeded one another, each enjoying a wide discretion, the character of the administration must also have varied from time to time. But there was no procurator fortunate enough to discover the secret of winning the hearts of the people or exorcizing their resentment and distrust. Under every ruler they grumbled and complained, sometimes more, sometimes less, but always bitterly.

The actual administration was in the hands of local authorities, to whom Rome allowed, as always, a considerable discretion. We are not very well informed on this subject.[2] It seems likely that the Romans had subdivided the three main regions of Judæa, Samaria and Idumæa into smaller administrative units, but of these we know scarcely anything. One gathers the existence of *toparchies*, each consisting of a town and its environs, sometimes forming a district of considerable size. We know of eleven of these toparchies in Judæa,[3] including that of Jerusalem, which was also the Jewish capital, important not only as the focus of the religious life of the race, but also as the seat of the *council* or *Sanhedrin*, which had authority over the whole country. We shall deal with the Sanhedrin later on.

---

[1] He was allowed a division of cavalry and 5 cohorts of infantry, perhaps some 3,000 men, mainly recruited in Samaria and Syria, at Cæsarea and Sebaste (Jos., *Ant.*, xx, 8, 7). Sebaste is the Greek name of the city of Samaria. Normally one cohort formed the garrison of the tower Antonia.

[2] **LXXV**, ii, 175 *ff.* ; **LXIII**, 137 and n. 4.

[3] Pliny, *Hist. Nat.*, v, 70 ; Jos., *B.J.*, iii, 3, 5. Probably small towns were attached to more important ones and the whole of Idumæa formed a single toparchy ; but the details of the whole arrangement are very obscure.

Here as elsewhere in the Empire the basis of local organization was the *city council*, a Sanhedrin (συνέδριον) employing
a staff of clerks (κωμογραμματεῖς) [1] and scribes. Since the
Jerusalem Sanhedrin was responsible for the returns of the
Roman taxes, it seems to have been the duty of the Sanhedrins
of the toparchies to raise them. All that Rome required of
her subjects was to pay up and keep quiet, and whoever fulfilled
these conditions was reasonably sure of being left in peace.
But the fiscal burden was heavy, and it must have been
extremely hard for the Jews to bear it patiently, especially
as it was supervised and enforced by *goyim*.

Coponius, the first procurator, arrived in Judæa in A.D. 6
or 7. With him came Quirinius, governor of Syria, charged
with the duty of collecting the personal possessions of Archelaus,
which the Emperor had confiscated, and of taking a census
of persons and property with a view to assessing the taxes.
The Jews objected to this inquiry, which augured them no
good, and some serious rioting ensued.[2] In the province of
Gaulanitis, east of the Jordan opposite Galilee, a certain Judas
of Gamala, called Judas *the Galilean*, formed an alliance with
a Pharisee named Sadduk, and attempted to repeat the successful rising of the Maccabees. Needless to say, he failed ;
but his venture seems to have been the starting-point of the
extremist party of patriots and religious fanatics—indeed it
was difficult to be one without the other—known as the *Kannaïm*
or " Zealots." [3] They were not strong enough to prevent the
inauguration of the Roman system of taxation. In general the
fiscal obligations of the Jews consisted of a *land tax* (*tributum
agri*) payable in kind, and a *poll tax* (*tributum capitis*) which
was levied on every male child over fourteen and every female
over twelve ; only the aged were exempt.[4] But there was also
additional burdensome taxation. There were taxes on revenue
and on cattle, and, in addition, indirect charges on imports and
exports—town and harbour dues, bridge tolls, market fees and
the like. Money raised by means of direct taxation was collected by Roman officials, but the rest of the work was farmed
out, and Judæa suffered in consequence from the abuses which
this particular form of exploitation always brings in its train.
This explains why the *publicani* (τελῶναι) were held in such
ill repute throughout the country. Their name came to be

[1] **LXV**, xi, 94 ; *cf.* Jos., *Ant.*, xvi, 7, 3.
[2] **LXXV**, i, 486 *ff.* ; **XXV**, ii, 252 ; **LI**, 212.
[3] Jos., *B.J.*, iv, 3, 9 ; iv, 5, 1 ; iv, 6, 3 ; vii, 8, 1.   *Cf.* Hamburger,
Real Enc. für Bibel und Talmud, Leipzig, 1870–94, part ii, 1286 *ff.*
[4] **XXV**, ii, 249.

synonymous with that of *sinner* or *transgressor of the divine Law*.[1]

Such a form of government should not in itself have been intolerable to a nation long accustomed to an alien yoke, and one moreover whose native princes, particularly Herod and Archelaus, had not been sparing in their demands. In fact, as has already been said, the Pharisees of the opposition had actually begged Rome to take over the reins of government from the tyrant Archelaus not so long before. But if certain groups could regard Roman rule as an heroic remedy for unbearable ills, and if the few rich and powerful families who constituted the Jewish aristocracy of Judæa even found it agreeable on account of their natural sympathy with these aristocratic conquerors, the people were much less inclined to accept the yoke. They combined a deep and fervent religious feeling with a scrupulous exactness of observance; and their hatred of the rule, even the very presence of these *goyim*, sprang more from fanaticism than from nationalism. It was their misfortune that in their impatience they failed to realize their utter helplessness against the power of Rome. Any trifle became a cause for discontent,[2] which soon grew into a state of chronic exasperation, rendering them open to any rash suggestion. When the Zealots maintained that to obey the Romans was a violation of the divine Law, since Jahweh was the only Lord who could claim their obedience, they were only voicing the opinion of the majority of the Jews.[3] And as time passed and the Roman bondage seemed heavier or hopes grew brighter, the revolutionaries gained more and more adherents and the moderate party, composed of the nobles of Jerusalem and Temple dignitaries, and of those who possessed property, or were in favour with the Romans, could no longer hold them in check.

To give the procurators their due, their task was by no means an easy one.[4] Those whom they governed accused them all more or less of injustice, high-handedness and outrageous cupidity. We have not enough information at our disposal to measure the truth underlying these vociferous charges, nor can we form any clear idea of such disputes as are described in Jewish sources. The Romans probably sometimes abused their power and acted without tact, and tended to be over-hasty and to display uncontrolled severity. When we

---

[1] **XXV**, ii, 253; **LXIII**, 140.   [2] **XXV**, ii, 253.
[3] The ideal of the Kannaïm was *a Jewish republic with God as its president and the Law for its constitution.* **XXV**, ii, 250.
[4] **LI**, 215 *ff.*

hear that Valerius Gratus, who was procurator from A.D. 15–20, deposed five High Priests in succession, we are tempted to wonder if he was actuated less by his devotion to the interests of Rome than by some shady scheme for private gain. However, not one of the first five procurators, Coponius, Ambivius, Rufus, Gratus and Pilate, seems to have forgotten that the headstrong Jews needed tactful handling, and even those with a natural preference for violent methods did not resort to force without careful consideration.

In A.D. 41, by the decree of Claudius, Judæa and Samaria were once more ruled over by a Jewish King, Herod Agrippa [1] (grandson of Herod the Great), who was a personal friend of the prince, and had already enjoyed the favour of Caligula. But even this was not enough to allay the bitterness of the Zealots, and the hatred of the Jews for Rome. This hatred burned most fiercely in Judæa, but it was shared by the fellow-countrymen of Jesus, and the city of Tiberias was a permanent reminder that the *goyim* were still in control of their tetrarchy.

Two points in this account need special emphasis. *Firstly*, when Jesus came into the world the Jews had been for several centuries in constant contact with men of other races : these foreigners had even subdued their country and settled in it. Palestine had been conquered successively by Persia, Greece and Rome, all countries characterized by strongly individual civilizations ; and each in succession had made systematic attempts to impose its own culture on Israel. *Secondly*, the Jews had never grown used to servitude. They were for ever kicking against the pricks and had even made efforts to free themselves. This was not so much because the material conditions of their present status compared very badly with those of their former liberty, for they had been little better off under Herod or the Hasmonæans than they were under the Cæsars. It was rather that they felt that the rule of the Gentile was a menace and an outrage to their religion. This was the real root of the matter, the motive of their rebellions and the source of all their hopes, for they could not believe that Jahweh would permanently refuse his aid to those who were fighting his own battles. From the moment when the Jews first lost their independence, the salient feature of their history is the way their nationalism was moulded and dominated by their religion. When the Chaldæans carried away the flower of the Judæans to Babylon, Israel was just beginning to undergo the levelling

[1] Jos., *Ant.*, xix, 5. After the death of Herod Agrippa in A.D. 44, Palestine was once more governed by procurators.

effect of the characteristic cultural patterns of the Semitic world ; it was losing its originality and its religious exclusiveness was weakening. It was the exile which renewed and strengthened these elements.

CHAPTER IV

RELIGIOUS CONDITIONS

I

THE EXILIC PROPHETS

THE Exile had severely tried the faith of Israel.[1] The sight of those long trains of exiles journeying towards the Euphrates might well raise a doubt whether God was mindful of his covenant with Abraham and with Moses. Indeed, could a God be truly omnipotent who had failed to save his people from such a fate ? Was it not rather a proof of the greater might of the gods of Babylon, a proof that they and not Jahweh merited the allegiance of the discerning ? On the other hand, if God were really all-powerful, could he also be just ? There were Jews who did in fact lose heart and apostatized from Jahweh. But during the Exile itself great prophets arose [2] who set themselves to strengthen the backsliders, to dispel the clouds of doubt and discontent, and to proclaim to the exiles the unfailing justice and power of Jahweh. For the sole source of their humiliation lay in themselves, in their unfaithfulness to the Covenant and their tolerance of strange gods ; and it was expedient as well as right that they should humble themselves and bow down in contrition before Jahweh who, having pardoned them, would in his own good time shower upon them once more the benefits of his grace and favour.

The most typical of these inspired writers, whose heroic faith lifted the hearts of the exiles and no doubt saved Jahwism from extinction, was Ezekiel.[3] His harsh and bitter book exercised a decisive influence over the Jews, since it caused

---

[1] I have limited myself here to the mention of such facts as are essential to the development of my theme. For their further elucidation the whole of the second part of Lods, *The Prophets of Israel and the Rise of Judaism*, should be read.

[2] For an account of the prophets of the Captivity and of the Return see Lods, *op. cit.*, part ii, book i, chaps. ii and iv.

[3] On the man and his work see Lods, *op. cit.*, 211 *ff.* ; 214 *ff.* ; 227 *ff.*

them to realize the necessity for a thorough purification of their religion, and gave them the idea of the *Torah*, or Law, a rigorous code based on an exact ritual.

Second Isaiah [1] was written late in the Exile, by an unknown author. He was not one of those who languished *super flumina Babylonis*, but his origin remains obscure. His work begins at chapter 40 of the canonical book of Isaiah. He is not so much a prophet as a compiler of prophecies, but above all he is a powerful preacher whom we shall find, later on, to have been the source of many religious ideas.[2] He was no visionary as Ezekiel claimed to be,[3] and he is far more confident than his predecessor, probably because by the time he wrote the Triumph of Cyrus was becoming evident, and this prospect gave some hope to the captives. Ezekiel belonged to a priestly family, and Loisy has justly pointed out that " the priest may be seen in the ritualism of the prophet." This combination is unusual ; as a rule priest and prophet represent different trends. Ezekiel was not a rabid nationalist. He devoted himself wholly to the service of Jahweh, and to the re-establishment of the cult, no doubt feeling that once that was secured the rest would follow of its own accord. He therefore counselled submission to the Chaldees and all his fervour found expression in his religious claims. The most interesting thing about him from our point of view is that he did not draw his message from his own consciousness. What he did was to co-ordinate the ideas that were current at the time, ideas that were logically inevitable for those whose object it was to reconcile the misfortunes of Israel with the character of Jahweh.

It could not be denied, however, that God had for the time forsaken Jerusalem. He had turned his face from the ruins of Zion, and Sinai, his ancient habitation, knew him no more. He had withdrawn himself to *the holy mountain* [4] somewhere in the dim north. But the day would come when he would leave this distant retreat, and return to his purified and repentant people ; a return which the prophet heralds and describes (Ezek. xl. *ff.*). The Temple was destroyed, and until it was rebuilt there was no possibility of instituting a cult which could find favour in the sight of Jahweh ; therefore his wrath must be appeased by other means. To this end Ezekiel insists on the practices which separated the Jews from the *goyim*, practices such as the observance of the Sabbath and

[1] **CCXXIII** ; **LXVII**, 259 *ff.* ; **VIII**, 34. See also Lods, *op. cit.*, 238 *ff.*
[2] **LXVII**, 259 *ff.*   [3] *Cf.* Ezek. i. 1 *ff.*
[4] Ezek. i. 4 ; xxviii. 14. Perhaps this is to be connected with the traditional Eden.

the strict rite of circumcision, although the latter was not even mentioned in the Deuteronomic code and had originally no connexion with Jahwism.[1] It comes to be the special sign of the Covenant and of faith in God's promises. Under Ezekiel's influence greater stress was laid on the power of prayer and on the efficacy of fasting ; in fact the chief concern of the exiles was to devise and practise a course of pious conduct which would serve to avert the just anger of their God.

Hitherto fasting had probably not played a very important part in the religious life of the Jews. It was simply a part of their funeral rites. But during the Exile the exiles seem to have instituted a practice of commemorating all the calamities of their history by days of mourning and atonement, which were kept with every possible manifestation of grief and penitence. Thus fasting gradually came to be considered a necessary preliminary to any important undertaking, and for a strict Jew every undertaking of importance had its religious aspect.

This was the first sign that marked the transformation of Jahwism into a pre-eminently stern and gloomy religion. From this time onward the Jews began to see everything as an occasion for expiation, and even introduced expiatory sacrifices into what had once been joyful festivals. Ezekiel called upon his readers to give themselves up to perpetual self-examination, and meditation on their sins. Henceforward the chosen people lived in a perpetual consciousness of guilt, and this brooding on their degradation was not calculated to cheer or reassure its members or to make them very good company for their neighbours. It resulted in the development of scruples and of formalism, and an extreme regard for details of observance, very different from the essentially moral religion of the pre-exilic prophets.

Certainly the tendencies which Ezekiel represented were not entirely new in Israel. What the prophet did was to shift the emphasis so that what was inconspicuous and of minor importance in the older Jahwism now stood clearly and permanently in the foreground. According to Loisy,[2] "*Ezekiel did more than any other writer to prevent Judaism from understanding its own history.*" One might almost accuse him of doing the same thing with regard to "*its religion.*" Moreover, not all his hatred of alien gods could free the mind of this formidable seer from the images of pagan mythology.[3] He, and he alone,

[1] Tradition placed the adoption of circumcision during the sojourn in Egypt : Joshua v. 2 *ff.* *Cf.* **CCLXXIV**, 270 *ff.* ; **VIII**, 45.
[2] **LIX**, 215.
[3] *Cf.* the remarkable visions of chap. xi ; **LIX**, 216.

is responsible for that exploitation of Gentile myths which is such a feature of Jewish apocalyptic literature. At first sight this more or less unconscious syncretism seems strange in any-one so narrow and bigoted in his religious views. But I take it to be a proof of the compelling influence of the Babylonian environment; Babylon, mother of so many myths and mysteries, has set her seal on the very fanatic who denounces her. This is an extraordinarily instructive point.

But it is not only a more complex and crystallized ritual that develops in Ezekiel's imagination—if indeed it did not already exist in the attitude of the exiled Jews. The idea of Jahweh is also modified, and becomes more spiritual. This is perhaps a result of the dispersion of the Jews which followed the Assyrian conquests.[1] God expanded, so to speak, with the expansion of the area over which his worship spread. Doubtless Ezekiel's conception is still fairly anthropomorphic. Jahweh speaks to him directly [2]; the prophet apparently sees his hand and it grasps him [3]; and finally he is allowed to look upon God's *glory*, the dazzling radiance of his person.[4] Nor is he at all sure that the abominable gods of the nations are non-existent or powerless. On the other hand, Second Isaiah, who dwells chiefly on hopes for the future, is apparently a pure monotheist. According to him there is no god but God, " *it is he that sitteth enthroned upon the circle of the earth . . . that stretcheth out the heavens as a curtain, and spreadeth them as a tent to dwell in* " [5]; he is the creator and ruler of the universe. And the supreme manifestation of his glory will be the conversion of the nations.[6]

II

THE RETURN

The prophets of the Exile evidently anticipated a mass return of the descendants of those who were exiled in 586; but when Cyrus actually sanctioned their departure it was not a very large band that set out for Judæa, under the leadership of Sheshbazzar.[7] The number has been given as 50,000, but this is only a very doubtful approximation. Certainly those whose

[1] **CCLXXIV**, 252 *ff*.   [2] Ezek. i. 28; ii. 2; iii. 16, etc.
[3] Ezek. ii, 9 and iii. 14; viii. 3, etc.
[4] Ezek. i, 28; iii. 23; viii. 4, etc.
[5] Isa. xl. 22. It is only necessary to read chaps. xl. and xli. to appreciate the attitude of the author.
[6] Isa. xlix. 6.
[7] **LIX**, 3rd edit., 191. On the Return and the beginnings of the Restoration, *cf*. Lods, *op. cit.*, 265 *ff*.

devotion to the Promised Land caused them to forsake Babylon, where they were well established by this time, were outnumbered by the Jews who had never left Palestine and had therefore not shared the religious upheaval experienced by the exiles. These " people of the land " (am-haareṣ) still preserved the Jahwism of the time before that crisis, the religion characterized by heathen tendencies, which Ezekiel had denounced as the cause of all the sufferings of Israel. It had even deteriorated, for during this time when there was no Temple and no priests, its essential exclusivism had loosened, and in particular the practice of mixed marriages, which Jahwism, essentially a male religion,[1] had never condemned, had become firmly established by common usage. The returned exiles soon realized how ill their own religion would harmonize with the prevailing laxity, but, instead of making them adopt a policy of caution and conciliation, the increasingly hostile atmosphere only served to aggravate their irritation and uneasiness. In spite of their small number they enjoyed a certain moral and material ascendency, and their work in reorganizing the Temple cult (the Temple was rebuilt, 420–415 B.C.), and in gradually restoring religious life to its ordered routine, gave them an unassailable prestige in the eyes of the whole Jewish world. And above all they could rely on the financial and moral support of the large and wealthy colony which they had left behind in Mesopotamia. This was unquestionably the deciding factor in the ultimate triumph of the spirit of the Return ; in fact, the men who did most of all to bring about that triumph, namely Nehemiah and Ezra,[2] were actually sent to Judæa as delegates from the voluntary exiles in Babylonia. But for this energetic co-operation on the part of the expatriated Jews, the inertia of the uneducated mass who clung to the old tradition would probably have succeeded in swamping the pietistic impulse of the Return, and the subsequent history of Israel would have taken a very different course.

It was natural that the Jews who returned from the Exile should bring with them a strong enthusiasm and some illusions. At first they even succeeded in infecting the Judæan villagers with their excitement until they too believed they were living on the eve of a miracle. It was whispered that Zerubbabel, one of the leaders of the Return, might well prove to be the Messiah. But it was soon evident that this was not the case,

[1] LIX, 2nd edit., 225. Jahwism also included females, but their obligations were both less numerous and less important than those of males. Cf. CCLXXIX, ii, 129 ff.
[2] Cf. Lods, op. cit., 296 ff.

and at once a reaction of despair set in, a reaction known to us chiefly through the book of Malachi,[1] who set himself to combat it. The puritans cast about for some fresh failure on the part of Israel, which might account for God's further delay in manifesting his complete reconciliation with his people, and they found it in the mixed marriages. Serious complications at once arose.

It was in order to extricate themselves from these difficulties and strengthen their authority that the Jews of the Return made their appeal to the Babylonian colony, which responded by sending Nehemiah and Ezra to their aid. The envoys had the approval, and perhaps even the support, of the King of Persia.[2] They carried out the necessary reforms and achieved a measure of success in the fight against mixed marriages.[3]

The most obvious consequences of the ensuing state of affairs were as follows: (1) The establishment of a priesthood in Jerusalem which made the Temple the absolutely exclusive centre of the cult, and which became a sort of living symbol of Jewish individualism. The Persians left the Jews free only in their religious beliefs: it was therefore natural that they should look upon the priests as the rightful representatives and champions of their liberty. (2) The disappearance of the official prophetic movement, which had represented religion in its spontaneous, emotional form, the religion which finds its sustenance in the hearts of the devout rather than in priestly rites, and which therefore has no place in a well-regulated theocracy. (3) The ascendancy of the Scribes, who were found to be essential if the salvation of Israel lay in the strict observance of the law, since the need of interpretation was immediately felt, and cases of conscience began to arise out of their environment. The business of the Scribe is religious jurisprudence, which does not blend easily with religious emotion.

There is one fact of which we must never lose sight. *From the Return onwards the history of the Jews is essentially that of their religion.* The returned exiles of Jerusalem found their sole motive of existence under the Persian rule in its preservation and in the reorganization of the cult. The Temple became the focus of their whole life. Even so it is possible that they were occasionally subject to stirrings of that spirit of rebellion which was later to ruin their descendants, and we find hints of at least one attempted revolt under Artaxerxes Ochus (359–338). But since the Persians never interfered in any way with their beliefs and observances, they did not as yet feel any very

---

[1] *Cf.* Lods, *op. cit.,* 275 *ff.*   [2] Ezra vii. 1–10.
[3] *Cf.* Lods, *op. cit., loc. cit.,* especially 303 *ff.*

desperate longing for political independence. The animosity which they gradually developed towards their conquerors proves nothing beyond their native intolerance, and the long duration of Persian rule. No doubt a satrap did not have to treat them very badly for them to find his rule insufferable.

Under the Seleucids, on the other hand, Israel had to put forth all its strength to resist the Hellenistic influences which were primarily threatening its religious customs. Hence the resistance assumed a religious character, under the leadership of the priestly class. At last, when the danger became too urgent, under Antiochus Epiphanes (d. 164),[1] a rising broke out, the revolt of the Maccabees.

This was the beginning of a Holy War, in which Israel managed to regain a measure of political independence, and accepted the domination of the family through which Jahweh had manifested his power. Under the Hasmonæan Maccabees, who were both kings and priests,[2] from 167 to 40 B.C., Jewish life remained, as was inevitable, essentially religious. But under the Roman rule during the reign of the Herods, who curried favour with the victor by accepting his customs, there was a recrudescence of the old latent hostility, that attitude of smouldering hatred against the Gentile and the foreigner, whom the Jews always suspected, though without cause, at least at the time of the birth of Jesus, of harbouring designs against their ritual customs and their beliefs.

Thus during the five centuries preceding the birth of Christ Jewish energies seem to have been wholly focussed on one object, that of retaining their religious individuality at all costs. This all-absorbing interest led to the production of two significant phenomena, brought about, however, more by the force of circumstances than by any preconceived plan. These were (1) the organization, partly political, of the priestly caste, and (2) the increased attention paid to legalism and to the strict observance of the law, which had now come to be regarded both as the irrefragable barrier which separated the Jews from the *goyim*, and as the guardian of the faith and hope of Israel.

[1] For the whole period, *cf.* **LXXV**, i, 165 *ff.*
[2] Jonathan was the first to assume both titles at once.

CHAPTER V

THE POWER OF THE PRIESTHOOD

I

THE SANHEDRIN

ABOUT the time of Jesus the priestly authority expressed itself through the *Great Council*, or *Sanhedrin*, which sat in Jerusalem.[1] We have little knowledge concerning its origin and development, its method of election, or even its functions. The Rabbis of the *Talmud* liked to stress its great antiquity; their story was that it had grown out of the council of the seventy elders of Israel whom Jahweh had commanded Moses to assemble in the "*tent of meeting*" (Num. xi. 16). They imagined for this assembly an unbroken continuity from that distant date to Talmudic times. In this they were completely mistaken, for there is no connexion between the possibly fictitious Sanhedrin of Numbers and that of the Gospels, nor between the latter and the " Sanhedrin " known to the redactors of the *Talmud*, which was a kind of learned Academy with certain judicial powers, and existed from the time of the Great Rebellion until the tenth century or later.

The Sanhedrin with which we are concerned dates in all probability from the time of Antiochus the Great, or at the very earliest from the Persian domination. At this period Jewish life had suffered very much the same restrictions as those imposed later by the Greeks and Romans, and it was natural that Israel should have felt the need of some organization to regulate its internal affairs. Ezra speaks of *Elders*,[2] and Nehemiah of *nobles* and *rulers*.[3] Exactly who these people were and how they were organized we cannot tell, but it is not unlikely that they represented a council of the nobles of Israel, both priests and laity.[4] Be that as it may, it is under

---

[1] Bibliography in **LXXV**, ii, 188 *ff*; **XLVII**, i, 400, n. 4.—Strack, *Synedrium* in **HRE**; Hamburger, *R. Enc.*, art. *Synedrion*, and again in the Supplement, art. *Obergericht*.

[2] Ezra v. 5 and 9; vi. 7 and 14; x. 8.

[3] Neh. ii. 16; v. 7; vii. 5.   [4] **LXXV**, ii, 191.

Antiochus the Great (223–187 B.C.) that we find the first clear evidence of a *gerousia*.[1] This is the term Josephus uses and it is enough in itself to brand the council as an aristocratic institution. The High Priest presided over it and the priestly aristocracy dominated its proceedings, except perhaps when the High Priest happened also to be the secular ruler or *ethnarch*, as was the case with several of the Hasmonæans. These princes were suspicious of the Temple personnel.

There is every reason to believe that this *gerousia* was essentially the same institution as the *synedrion* of the Roman period.[2] The term came into use in the reign of Hyrcanus II (*i.e.* after 69 B.C.). It was applied to an organized body which appears to have combined the functions of High Court of Justice and administrative council.[3] We can deduce the latter function from the alarming repercussions which a change of governors would sometimes produce in the Sanhedrin. Thus Josephus informs us that Herod celebrated his accession by having every member of the council executed (Jos., *Ant.*, xiv, 9, 4).

At this time the Sanhedrin was the special province of the priestly aristocracy, who were undoubtedly the prevailing, though not the exclusive element in the council. Josephus makes the definite assertion that after the death of Herod and the deposition of Archelaus " *the administration of the state was in the hands of an aristocracy* " and " *the government of the nation was entrusted to the High Priests.*" [4] But the priesthood was not in complete control, for the Sanhedrin must have included a certain number of lay members, and we must also allow for the growing power of the *Doctors of the Law*, or *Scribes*, who had had a place in it ever since the time of Queen Alexandra (69 B.C.) and had gained considerable influence during the reign of King Herod. This is why Schürer is justified in his con-

---

[1] Jos., *Ant.*, xii, 3, 3.

[2] The texts on which this assumption is based are collected in **LXXV,** ii, 192.

[3] According to Jos., *Ant.*, xix, 9, 3 *ff.*, it was before this συνέδριον that the young King Herod was summoned to answer for his behaviour and actions in Galilee. — Bücheler (*Das Synedrium in Jerusalem*, 1902) maintains that there were two *councils*, having respectively religious and civil jurisdiction. Such a division of authority would have been quite foreign to the customs and feelings of the Jews, and there is no proof that it existed. *Cf.* **CCL,** i, 9.

[4] Jos., *Ant.*, xx, 10, *in fine* : ἀριστοκρατία μὲν ἦν ἡ πολιτεία . . . τὴν δὲ προστασίαν τοῦ ἔθνους οἱ ἀρχιερεῖς ἐπεπίστευοντο. Note that Josephus does not always call the Council συνέδριον. He also uses the term βουλή (*B.J.*, ii, 15, 6 ; ii, 16, 2, etc. *Cf.* **LXXV,** ii, n. 18). The New Testament has the expression πρεσβυτέριον (Luke xxii. 66 ; Acts xxii. 5) and γερουσία (Acts v. 21).

clusion that in the Roman period the Sanhedrin was composed of two elements : " *the priestly nobility of the Sadducean group and the Pharisaic doctors.*" [1]

We do not know the exact numbers of the Sanhedrin, nor how its membership was maintained. There is a tractate on the Sanhedrin in the *Mishnah*,[2] but it supplies no satisfactory answer to these questions. We read in i, 6, that " *the Great Sanhedrin is composed of 71 members and the little Sanhedrin of 33.—How can you tell that the Great Sanhedrin should have 71 members ?—It is written : Gather unto me seventy men of the elders of Israel ; and these, with Moses, make 71. Rabbi Jehuda is of opinion that there should be only 70 (including Moses).*" The scriptural reference is to Numbers xi. 16. It is not impossible that the Sanhedrin really did conform to this text by fixing its numbers at 70 or 71, though it is equally likely that the Talmudic Rabbis suppressed the real membership in favour of the sacred number. On the whole the statement of the *Mishnah* seems plausible.

The aristocratic character of the Sanhedrin makes it probable that its members did not change from year to year, and were not elected, but that they were co-opted for life [3]; it is also possible that some or all of the members were appointed directly or indirectly by the Romans during the period of their domination. It is a problem which we cannot solve.

On the other hand, we do know that the members were not all of equal rank or privilege. The tractate called *Sanhedrin* makes the following statement (iv, 2) : " *In cases where there is no question of a death sentence, anyone (i.e.* any member) *may give judgment, but in the trial of capital offences only priests, Levites and those Israelites who are qualified to ally themselves with a priestly family by marriage shall do so.*" Israelites thus qualified were those who were free from all taint of mixed marriage and could supply proof of a Jewish lineage that was both ancient and undefiled. As to the component elements of the council both Josephus and the New Testament refer to *High Priests* (ἀρχιερεῖς), *Scribes* (γραμματεῖς) and *elders* (πρεσβύτεροι) as belonging to it. The primacy clearly belonged to the *High Priests*, who were sometimes given the significant

---

[1] **LXXV**, ii, 197.

[2] There are several critical translations in English and German. *Cf.* Herbert Danby, *Tractate Sanhedrin. Mishnah and Tosefta*, London, 1919, pp. xvi–xviii.

[3] **LXXV**, ii, 199. A passage that supports this hypothesis will be found in *Sanhed.*, iv. 4.

title of οἱ ἄρχοντες,[1] or *chiefs*. It is obvious that these men neither were, nor had been, all High Priests. The term ἀρχιερεῖς must have been used to designate any of the higher offices of the priesthood, and even members of those families qualified to fill them.

Josephus has a sentence in his *Antiquities* that seems to hint at a sort of executive committee within the Sanhedrin. He is telling the story of a dispute between Herod Agrippa II and the Temple personnel.[2] Claudius had made this son of Herod Agrippa I King of Chalcis, and had added the courtesy title of "*King of the Temple*." Agrippa then proceeded to build out a balcony from the palace, giving him an excellent view of all that went on in the sanctuary ! The priests retorted by building a wall to block his view, but having made sure that the procurator, Festus, was sympathetic,[3] Agrippa gave orders to have it pulled down again. Thereupon the Jews appealed to the Emperor, Nero, for they declared that they could not outlive the destruction of any part of the Temple. With the permission of Festus they sent to Rome "*the ten foremost men with the High Priest Ishmael and Elkias the treasurer.*" [4] The question is whether this was an *ad hoc* delegation consisting merely of ten distinguished persons, or an organized group with recognized functions. If we accept the second explanation, as I am inclined to think we should, the group must almost certainly have consisted of members of the Sanhedrin.[5]

Further, when we are told at the beginning of the description of the Atonement ritual in the *Mishnah* (*Yoma*, i, 1), that the High Priest leaves his apartment and goes into the "*Hall of the Assessors*," this surely gives us the clue as to where the committee usually sat.

We are better informed as to the question of who presided over the Sanhedrin. The *Mishnah* [6] would have us believe the Council was under the guidance of a president (*nasi*) and a vice-president (*ab-beth-din*), heads of the schools of Scribes, like Gamaliel I, and his son Simon ; but these are Rabbinical fantasies induced by memories of that other Sanhedrin which flourished after A.D. 70, and which we have been at pains to distinguish from the one we are now discussing. Both Josephus

---

[1] Acts iv. 5 : τοὺς ἄρχοντας καὶ τοὺς πρεσβυτέρους καὶ τοὺς γραμματεῖς ἐν Ἱερουσαλήμ. Texts in **LXXV**, ii, 200, n. 34 and 35.

[2] **LXXV**, ii, 222. *Cf.* Acts iv. 6 : Ἄννας ὁ ἀρχιερεὺς καὶ Καιάφας καὶ Ἰωάννης καὶ Ἀλέξανδρος καὶ ὅσοι ἦσαν ἐκ γένους ἀρχιερατικοῦ.

[3] Festus held office from A.D. 60 to 62. *Cf.* **LXXV**, i, 779.

[4] *Ant.*, xx, 8, 11 : τοὺς πρώτους δεκὰ, καὶ Ἰσμάελον τὸν ἀρχιερεα καὶ Ἑλκίαν τὸν γαζοφύλακα.

[5] **LXXV**, ii, 201 *ff.*   [6] **LXXV**, ii, 202 ; **CCLXXXI**, 3, n. 7.

and the New Testament witness to the leadership of the High Priest. Josephus represents this dignitary as the guardian of the laws, and tells us that he acted as judge in litigation and cases of crime, and even as an arbiter for other courts in difficult cases.[1] This is in harmony with the evidence of the New Testament,[2] and there is certainly no reason to waive this evidence in favour of Rabbinical tradition.[3] In point of fact the first president of the Sanhedrin to take the title of *nasi* was Rabbi Judah, who is supposed to have compiled the *Mishnah* at the end of the second century A.D. The belief that it was the High Priest who presided over the Sanhedrin gives a characteristic touch to the picture of a governing body which corresponds to what might have been expected of a people whose whole life was centred in its religion.

The question of the scope of its power has given rise to a good deal of discussion.[4] There is no doubt that it was held in great respect by all the Jews ; the point is whether its decisions were legally binding outside Palestine. Quite possibly during the rule of the procurators its legal validity was confined to Palestine or even to the province over which the procurator had power, but its *moral* authority was none the less recognized outside—in Galilee for instance, or wherever there were organized Jewish communities.[5] It represented a great spiritual force which to some extent counterbalanced the material power of the alien rulers.

The Sanhedrin dealt with every problem that had any connexion with religion, however remote. There were the offences dealt with by the Law, questions of marriage and divorce, heretical opinions, genealogies, the calendar, and all those cases on which it was often difficult to get a clear ruling, but which were of great importance for the Jews.[6] It also acted as the civil court for Jerusalem and as a court of appeal or arbitration for the other toparchies.[7] The general opinion is that it could try criminal cases as well but could not pronounce the death sentence without the sanction of the Roman governor.[8] The chief evidence for this is the Gospel accounts of the trial of Jesus, particularly the perfectly definite statement which John puts into the mouths of the Jews (xviii. 31), namely, " *It is not lawful for us to put any man to death.*" But the opinion also receives support from various other facts. For instance, we

---

[1] *C. Ap.*, ii, 23 ; *Ant.*, iv, 8, 14.

[2] Acts v. 17 *ff.* ; vii. 1 ; ix. 1–2 ; xxii. 5 ; xxiii. 2, etc. ; Matt. xxvi. 3 and 57.

[3] **LXXV**, ii, 205. [4] **XLVII**, ii, 142. [5] **LXXV**, ii, 206.

[6] **LXIII**, 143. [7] **XLVII**, 2, 148 *ff.* ; **LXV**, xi, 94 ; **LXXV**, 208 *ff.*

[8] **LXV**, *loc. cit.* ; **LXXV**, ii, 209.

note that under Herod the right of criminal jurisdiction appears
to belong not to the Sanhedrin but to the King himself ; but
since we know that he and all the Herodians had small respect
either for tradition or for what we may call *legality*, their policy
with its obvious intention of reducing the Sanhedrin to a purely
religious court, is no proof whatever that they were legally
entitled to make these restrictions, but rather suggests the
opposite.[1]   Further, it seems quite certain that when Rome
took over the direct rule and restored to the Sanhedrin its
former powers, the scope of the council was rather enlarged
than restricted ; though this did not prevent the procurator
from making use of his *jus gladii*, without reference to any
Jewish court, in the case of brigands or seditious subjects, or
from using any coercive measures which he thought necessary
in the interests of Rome or of public tranquillity.[2]

Are we then to believe that the powers of the Sanhedrin
did not include that of pronouncing the death penalty ?   Jewish
Law specified a number of capital offences, especially in religious matters.   Could its exponents legally pronounce and
enforce the sentence ?   Juster [3] has made a detailed study of
the Talmudic texts which, together with the New Testament,
have formed the chief basis for the negative reply generally
given to this question.   He makes it clear that, contrary to
the usual assumption, the Sanhedrin had full liberty to inflict
the death penalty on Jews for religious offences.   It is true
that after A.D. 70 it only kept these rights on sufferance.   It
would have been strange if the government of the second and
third centuries had allowed it a privilege which had been with-
held before the Great Rebellion, but it is understandable that
a practice which had been generally recognized in the first
century should not have been formally prohibited later.

II

THE TEMPLE

The Sanhedrin then was the most powerful weapon of the
priestly class,[4] who made use of its authority to enforce the
material submission of the rank and file of Jews to the dictates

[1] **XLVII**, ii, 128–30, where the main facts are mentioned in the notes.
[2] " *In fact all the cases dealt with by the procurators are cases of sedition
or of banditry* " (**XLVII**, ii, 147).   A list of these cases is given in a note.
[3] **XLVII**, ii, 133 *ff*.
[4] It sat in some special place which Josephus refers to as βουλή or
βουλευτήριον (*B.J.*, v, 4, 2 ; vi, 6, 3), and which must have been on the
eastern side of the Temple mountain.   *Cf.* **LXXV**, ii, 210 *ff*.

of the Law. By means of it they could command or forbid ; and by its means also they had the opportunity of turning every case into a religious problem and setting up a religious —or perhaps we should say a *clerical* standard by which every-thing in Israel should be judged.

But the priests had a further hold over the people, for they were the natural and acknowledged guardians of the Temple, whose duty and privilege it was both to preserve the cult and to administer it. Thus the High Priest, who was the head of the priesthood, enjoyed very considerable power, not only in strictly religious matters, but also through his leadership of an organization in which the boundaries separating politics from religion and theocracy were so ill-defined.

The most important effect of the Restoration had been to establish the supremacy of the clerical element in the Jewish state over the lay population. As a natural result of the vicissitudes of the political life of the chosen people, the High Priest (*kohen haggadol*) had become their real head, just as the restored Temple had become the real centre of their life.[1] It was about the middle of the Persian period that the High Priest attained this position, which he kept until the reign of Herod.

I have already mentioned that when the Hasmonæans, who came of priestly stock, became kings, they also assumed the title and office of High Priest,[2] which was the easier for them in that their predecessors in the second capacity had already taken the rank of princes. They held fast to the dual principle which ensured their possession of the office and its transmission, namely, that it was *for life* and was *hereditary*. It was further reinforced by all the material and moral authority of the *gerousia*, since it was the High Priest who presided over the Council.

It goes without saying that the power of the priesthood had diminished after the intervention of Rome, and under the tyranny of the Herods. In the first place, the precious dual principle mentioned above no longer functioned ; the High Priesthood had ceased to be hereditary and tenable for life. Herod and the Romans set up High Priests and pulled them down again as their interest or their fancy might dictate. And,

[1] **LXXV**, ii, 215 ; **CCLXVIII**, 275 *ff.*

[2] Schürer rightly observes (**LXXV**, ii, 315, n. 2) that the princely rank of the Jewish High Priests was no exception in this part of the Orient. The inscription of Tabnith, King of Sidon, which was discovered in 1887, reads : " Tabnith, priest of Astarte, King of Sidon, son of Eshmunazar, the priest of Astarte, King of Sidon." *Cf. Rev. Archéologique*, 1887, 2. The dynasts of Chalcis were described on their coins as both ἀρχιερεῖς and τετράρχαι.

secondly, another influence—that of the *Doctors of the Law*, which we shall discuss later—had grown up alongside that of the priesthood, and the frequent clashes of opinion between the Temple and the Schools helped to weaken the prestige of the High Priest.[1] But for all that he was still the *Primate* of the Jewish nation, for the Jews still held that the priesthood played an essential part as mediator between God and his people.[2] His moral authority remained very great even though it was now shared with the Rabbis, and he still preserved his all-important privilege of presiding over the Sanhedrin. If the High Priests could no longer be regarded as a dynasty they did constitute a very special and exclusive aristocracy, for they were invariably chosen from the same small group of families.

It must not be forgotten that in the post-exilic period the whole Jewish nation only possessed *one altar*, and that this altar was inaccessible to the lay population and the lower orders of Temple priests, the High Priest alone having the full sacerdotal powers required for the acceptance of Jahweh. In the old days Israel had certainly not practised such a rigid exclusivism, but these theocratic innovations and the priestly encroachments which were responsible for them had gained such a firm hold that they were attributed to Moses, that is to say, to Jahweh himself. Already the ritual customs of pre-exilic days had passed out of the memory of Israel.[3]

The practice of selecting the High Priest from a small group of families had two results. On the one hand, the families in question gained in prestige by his reflected glory, and, on the other, they did what they could to strengthen his position, since his downfall would immediately and vitally affect their own security. Even to belong to one of these privileged families was a considerable distinction. Thus we find Josephus placing the *sons of the High Priests* (υἱοὶ τῶν ἀρχιερέων) side by side with the High Priests themselves (ἀρχιερεῖς) in his list of the most important Jews who took sides with Rome in the Great Rebellion.[4] These sons of the High Priests are also referred to in the *Mishnah* [5] as the rightful authorities on matrimonial law, as though a well-recognized tradition had already established them firmly in that capacity. Another passage [6] tells us that letters addressed to the sons of the High Priests sometimes reached the Temple from foreign lands, a fact which at any

---

[1] **EB**, art. *Priest*. [2] **LXXV**, ii, 225.
[3] **EB**, art. *Priest*. On the origins of these institutions, which had been suspended long before Jesus was born, *cf.* **XVIII**.
[4] Jos., *B.J.*, vi, 2, 2. [5] *Kethaboth*, xii, 1.
[6] *Mishnah. Ohaloth*, xvii, 5.

rate serves to prove that these aristocratic families enjoyed a very wide reputation.[1] We shall be considering later the part the High Priest played in the Judaism of the Dispersion. But in Palestine, however much his position might be questioned or challenged, he remained supreme, and when he officiated in state in the Temple, surrounded by all the pomp and ceremony of one of the great festivals, the people who thronged behind him forgot for a moment the humiliation of their earthly lot, forgot the Greek or the Roman yoke, and were lifted up with him to Jahweh, their God.[2]

The High Priest himself received the support not only of the caste of High Priests and sons of the High Priests, but also of the entire priestly class.[3] This was an exclusive caste which only recognized legitimate children of the stock of the " Sons of Aaron." [4] Every aspirant to the priesthood had first to validate his genealogy. This was no empty formality. At the time of the Return there was a general investigation, and all families failing to pass the test were rigorously excluded from the priesthood. Josephus boasts that he discovered his own family tree (or enough information to enable him to reconstruct it) " in the public registers " (ἐν ταῖς δημοσίαις δέλτοις), that is, among the archives. Precautions were also taken to keep the blood of the priestly families from defilement. A priest might only wed a virgin or a widow of Israel.[5] And even a descendant of Aaron who fulfilled all the required conditions was not certain of admission. He had first to be nominated by the Sanhedrin and undergo a rather elaborate ritual of consecration, lasting seven days.[6]

Once consecrated, a priest was considered holy and the Law hedged him round with special prohibitions, so that he might be sure of preserving the ritual purity necessary to his office.[7]

He was, in fact, set apart from the rest of the Jews. He was maintained by the offerings of all kinds which poured into the Temple, only a small part of which were consumed on the altar to the glory of Jahweh.

---

[1] LXXV, ii, 223.

[2] See the eulogy of the High Priest, Simon, son of Onias, in Ecclus. l., especially verse 11 ff.

[3] EB, art. Priest ; LXXV, ii, 226 ff.

[4] Exod. xxviii. and xxix. ; Lev. viii. and ix. ; Num. xvii. and xviii.

[5] The High Priest himself could only marry a virgin, who had to be chosen, at any rate in the first century A.D., from a priestly family. Cf. Philo, De monarchia, ii, 11 : μόνον γυναῖκα παρθένον, ἀλλὰ καὶ ἱέρειαν ἐξ ἱερέων.

[6] LXXV, ii, 231.

[7] Num. xix. ; Lev. xxi. 1–4 ; 11–12 ; Ezek. xliv. 25–7.

The Levites were not of the same rank as the priests.   Before the Exile the distinction was not very clear ; but later it was well marked.   They were not allowed to take any part in the cult, or even to enter the inner sanctuary.   Their business was to see that the Temple was adequately protected, to mount guard at the gateways, and to sing in the choirs.   The cult itself was in the sole charge of the priests.[1]   It was inevitable that these men, whose function was the conservation of the cult, should represent the tendency of religion to become static.[2] A great part of the esteem in which they were held was due to their position as functionaries of the Temple.

III

THE TEMPLE WORSHIP

The Temple was the centre of Jewish national life.[3]   In its service Israel found the communal satisfaction of its deepest and most vital impulse, and at least an illusion of national unity. We can see by the wealth of detail given in the *Mishnah* and the *Gemara*, which were compiled many years after its destruction, the place which it held in the minds and affections of the Jews.

This is not the place for a description of the Temple ceremonies or the daily life of the priests and Levites who took part in them.   Suffice it to say that the cult required the services of priests of all ranks, and the Temple staff must have been very large, since Josephus reckons it at twenty thousand souls.   It was divided into twenty-four " courses," each course being responsible for the service during one week.[4]   Every course therefore included priests, Levites and a company of laymen, called a *maamad,* or " station."   Thus the whole population was divided up among the twenty-four groups, and any layman living in or near Jerusalem had to make his appearance at the Temple and be present at all the ceremonies of the cult whenever the turn of his station came round.   Those who lived further from Jerusalem were supposed to assemble in their own

---

[1] **EB,** art. *Temple Service,* § 35.

[2] **EB,** art. *Priest,* characterizes these as part of the " *unprogressive traditional side of religion.*"

[3] *Cf.* **CCLIII,** 97–118, which deals particularly with the overshadowing of the Temple cult by the Law.   It was really the *Torah* that united the Jews, not the Temple.

[4] Jos., *Vita,* i, 1, claimed to belong to the first of these courses (*mismar* = ἐφημερία), which had also included the Hasmonæans.   It was Joarib's course (1 Macc. ii. 1).

synagogues instead, to pray and to read from the Scriptures, so that the whole course might unite at least in spirit with what was taking place at the Temple itself. Hence it was only a small fraction of each *maamad* that actually took part in the Temple rites.

The personnel of the Temple [1] was composed of (1) *dignitaries*, that is to say the High Priest (*kohen haggadol*), the Captain of the Temple (*segan*) who commanded the armed guard which performed police duties and if necessary defended the Temple against attack; his inferior officers, called *seganim* (probably corresponding to the στρατηγοί of Luke xxii. 4); and the heads of the twenty-four courses; (2) *priests* and *Levites*; (3) *treasurers* (*gizbarim*, Greek γαζοφύλακες), all those officials concerned with general administration, with the commissariat, and with various kinds of equipment, offerings and treasures; (4) *porters* to open and shut the gates at the proper times and prevent Gentiles (*goyim*) from entering, and police agents; (5) special functionaries who prepared for the daily public services, and (6) *musicians* (*mesorerim* = ψαλμῳδοί, ἱεροψάλται, ὑμνῳδοί), who were mainly drawn from three Levitical families. They were very numerous, and were also divided into twenty-four courses.[2]

The organization of the Temple was thus a complicated business and even its ordinary routine involved the co-operation of a host of men specially dedicated to the service of Jahweh. The duties of a Temple servant may have lacked variety [3] by reason of constant repetition, but they were both absorbing and important—and were so considered by the whole Jewish community. No provision was made for the teaching of the Law in all these ritual activities, but although the Temple did not teach, it set an example of rigorous exactness in all that concerned the cult, and its leaders, with the support of the Sanhedrin, did everything in their power to ensure the obedience of Israel to the prescriptions of Jahweh.

The central event in the life of the Temple was the daily sacrifice on behalf of the people, which was publicly offered to Jahweh morning and evening. It was accompanied by a lengthy and imposing ceremonial, following a detailed ritual, and was accompanied by many private sacrifices. Our infor-

---

[1] **LXXV**, ii, 262 *ff.*

[2] **EB**, art. *Temple Service*, §§ 35 and 36.

[3] I am speaking only of their duties in the Temple. Apart from their weeks of service, they could choose whatever employment they liked, provided it was honourable. Many of them were merchants. *Cf.* **CCL**, i, 82.

mation on this subject is derived from the *Mishnah* and is not always very clear. On feast-days and on the Sabbath there were additional sacrifices and an even more elaborate ceremonial. The point which calls for special notice in all this is the way in which the whole population was associated in the most important act of the cult, the act which really linked the celebrant with his God ; namely, the sacrifice. This act was both symbolic of the nature of the relation between Jahweh and Israel, and a manifestation of God's actual presence (which no Jew could doubt) in the midst of his people on the Temple hill.

No matter where he had built his house or pitched his tent, every Jew lifted his eyes and his heart to this chosen spot, the holiest of all the holy places sanctified by God's majesty. And the Temple was almost as much the centre of the public life of Jerusalem as it was the shrine of the national religion. The inner courts were sacrosanct and closed to all profane activities, but in the outer enclosures gatherings of all kinds took place, and the treasure chambers where Jahweh's gifts were stored served also as strong-rooms in which costly private possessions might be deposited for safe keeping. The stricter Jews even came to feel that this mingling of the sacred and the profane, and this thoroughly practical use of the holy place, was not entirely satisfactory. They complained, for instance, that the Temple was used as a thoroughfare, and that trivial transactions took place on the threshold of the House of God. For instance, money-changers had their booths in the outer courts, where they provided pilgrims with supposedly *pure* money in which to pay their Temple dues.

This brief outline will be enough to show the nature and importance of the authority exercised by the priesthood in the Jewish world of Palestine, and at the same time to set the Gospels in the historical perspective necessary for their right understanding.

CHAPTER VI

THE LAW. THE SCRIBES. THE SYNAGOGUES

I

THE TORAH

THE keystone of this whole edifice of priestly authority was the *Torah*. In its name the High Priest, the priesthood, and the Temple itself as an institution, claimed and exacted the obedience of Israel. The word *Torah* means " doctrine " or " teaching," in particular, " religious teaching." It is generally rendered by *the Law*, following the Septuagint, and also Josephus and Paul, who use ὁ νόμος ; but this is not an exact equivalent. The term *Law*, with its suggestion of formalism, rigidity and dryness, fails to represent the infinite variety of meaning in the word *Torah*.[1] The sovereignty of the *Torah* is one of the essential factors of Late Judaism and demands special attention. The Law had always been the central interest of the Jews, but it had never attained, before the exile, the absolute and despotic sway which it exercised over post-exilic Judaism.[2] This was due in part to the determination of the priesthood of the Return, but above all to the disappearance of that natural check to formalism, the phenomenon of *Prophecy*.

At the beginning of the *Restoration* prophecy as an institution was already at the point of death,[3] though it produced Haggai and Zechariah. It seems strange to find Nehemiah, who played an important part in the reorganization of Israel after the Return, placing the prophets in the enemy camp. " *Remember*," he says, " *O my God, Tobiah and Sanballat according to their misdeeds, and also the prophetess Noadiah, and the rest of the*

[1] Bibliography : **LXXV**, ii, 305 *ff.* ; 464 *ff.* ; **CCLIII**, 119 *ff.* ; **CCLXIII**, 60 *ff.* ; **XXXIII**, 30 *ff.*

[2] **LXXV**, ii, 305.

[3] **LIX**, 238. It is quite possible that the disappearance of prophetic activity has been exaggerated, and that although the institution had decayed the tendency persisted. The careers of John the Baptist and of Jesus himself constitute arguments of some weight in favour of such a view.

prophets, that would have put me in fear." [1] This hostility is
natural, for the Law (of which Nehemiah is the exponent) must,
in its strict and narrow form, always hate and fear the prophet,
the mystic, that independent and often unorthodox element
in religion. For the inspiration of the prophet is emotional
in character, and emotion has small patience with the shackles
of immutable law. After the Return prophecy merges into
apocalyptic, and with the book of Daniel the former begins
to be superseded by the latter.

This form of prophetism may strengthen and uplift religious
emotion, but it does not encourage the spontaneous outpourings
of natural piety. On the other hand there is no difficulty
whatever in reconciling it with legalism. The future belonged
to the *Doctor of the Law*, the man whose function it was,
to expand and adapt, to add interpretations, explanations,
commentaries and glosses to the traditional ordinances of
Jahweh.

Till then the *Torah* had been alive. That is to say, it had
undergone whatever alteration, revision and expansion was
necessary to keep it more or less in harmony with the various
requirements of successive generations. But the Law codified
and published by Ezra and Nehemiah was the work of the
Scribes and priests of the Captivity. It had no relation to life,
no possibility of immediate application, and reflects an ideal
of static perfection, the familiar clerical desire for some settled
and final scheme of organization. Its motive was to establish
a theocracy, and at the same time to authenticate and justify
it. Priestly authority is by nature conservative ; one could
scarcely imagine it otherwise. And, although the exegesis of
the Scribe might mould or stretch the meaning of the text to
cover cases that the lawgivers had not foreseen, it had to start
with the assumption that the text itself was fixed and inviolable.
The law was believed to contain the absolute and unquestionable
will of God, and its prohibitions were in a sense a test of the
unquestioning obedience due to the Lord of all, a test making
the same demands on the pious Jew as the *tabu* upon the Tree
of Knowledge made on Adam in Eden. Hence the *Torah* itself
became the object of an actual cult. It was personified as the
well-beloved daughter of God, begotten before the world began [2] ;
Jahweh was said to devote his leisure hours to its study, to
observe it himself and to read aloud from it on the Sabbath.[3]

---

[1] Neh. vi. 14.

[2] Ecclus. xxiv. 8 *ff.* ; Baruch iii. 27–iv. 2. *Cf.* **CCLXVI**, i, 74.

[3] **LXXXVIII**, 296 ; L. de Grandmaison, *Jésus-Christ*, Paris, 1928, ii,
8–9 and note. This notion may seem less incongruous if the reader bears

Needless to say, there was no mention of the alterations and embellishments which it had often received from the hands of man. Moreover, the paradox was ignored by which the God of justice and of mercy, whom the prophets had proclaimed as universal and absolute, was invested with the moods and caprices of some local deity, granting Israel a unique and certain means of gaining his favour through the study and practice of a complex code of rites and observances better suited to the worship of the Baals of Canaan, and in fact mainly derived from this source.[1] The universal opinion in Palestine was that of Ben-Sira : "*All these things are the book of the covenant of the most high God, even the law which Moses commanded for an heritage unto the congregations of Jacob.*"[2]

Henceforth the *Torah* could only be regarded as the unalterable Rule and absolute standard of all religious life ; the sole and immediate source of God's truth. And it followed that the constant reading and pondering of the Scriptures came to be looked upon as the religious exercise *par excellence*, far more necessary even to the layman than participation in the cult, which, owing to his lack of special knowledge, could only be a passive one. The piety of Israel was measured in terms of its extreme veneration for the Law even more than by the exactness of its observance, for in practice certain concessions had to be made, otherwise the life of the community would not have been tolerable, but these concessions rather added to than detracted from the respect in which the letter of the law was held. And any member of a Jewish community who failed in the necessary reverence might be dealt with very severely.[3]

As a matter of fact, the *Torah* does not promulgate dogmas or metaphysical ideas, or even, properly speaking, any system of ethics. It makes definite and final statements about the will of God and his omnipotence, and lays down certain *practical* rules, either *negative* (prohibition) or *positive* (commands). The strict observance of these rules is an absolute necessity for the good Jew, because only by this means can he retain that legal purity upon which a right relationship with Jahweh depends. The effort to preserve this purity easily becomes an

in mind the story from Raymond of Capua (*Légende majeure de Sainte Catherine de Sienne*, i, chap. xi, 112), in which Jesus comes daily in person to read the Psalms with the saint in her cell.

[1] Ecclus. xxiv. 22.

[2] LVIII, 513. On the content and various aspects of the *Torah*, *cf.* CCLIII, 119.

[3] Philo himself emphasizes this danger. *Cf.* C. Conybeare, *Myth, Magic and Morals*, London, 1910, 158.

obsession. It gives birth to innumerable minor rules of ever-increasing particularity, which seek to anticipate and provide for every conceivable shortcoming.[1]

Disagreement might arise over the interpretation and consequent application of one of these rules. This produced disputes of surprising bitterness among the Jews, showing at least the importance attached to the solution of the problem. I will cite only one random instance [2] out of many. At the time of the celebration of the Feast of the Tabernacles, the Priest-King, Alexander Jannæus (104–78 B.C.), was officiating before a congregation of the people. Instead of pouring the lustral water on the altar he made as though to sprinkle it on the ground, thus affirming his choice between two forms of ritual, each of which claimed its adherents. Unfortunately most of those present belonged to the opposing faction, whose ceremonial had been slighted. They had come to the feast, as custom required, bearing a palm in one hand and a lemon or citron in the other, and Jannæus had hardly made his ill-timed gesture when the crowd, seized with violent indignation, began to pelt him with the fruit. The prince was furious and ordered his guard of mercenaries to attack the mob, which they did, leaving the ground strewn with dead and wounded.[3]

The casuistry which grew up around the *Torah* will be considered later in connexion with the doctors and Scribes who were responsible for it. It is enough to say here that it formed a dense and almost impenetrable jungle whose tortuous paths only the initiate might tread. He, and he alone, would have the inestimable advantage of knowing whether or not it was lawful to eat an egg laid on the Sabbath ; whether he might, on that day of rest, set up a ladder against his dovecote to examine the cause of some disturbance there, or whether water poured from a clean vessel into an unclean one contaminated the source as well. The observance of the Sabbath raised especially thorny points and the scrupulous Jew had to make use of all his alertness and discernment to avoid the many pitfalls it presented.

[1] CCCII, i, 100, n. 1.
[2] Jos., *Ant.*, xiii, 13, 5 ; xiii, 98 *ff.*
[3] I. Lévy (CCLXXVII, 243 and n. 3) doubts the authenticity of this incident because it reappears in the *Babylonian Talmud* (*Sukkah*, 48, *b*) in a different setting, the hero on this occasion being not Jannæus but an anonymous Sadducean priest. If the incident itself is genuine, as M. Lévy believes, I do not see why the *Talmud* should be preferred to Josephus. In any case, whether it was a question of a priest or a king, the main point of the story, the fury of the people, remains unchanged.

The natural deduction would be that all this dry legalism, this hypertrophied scrupulosity, which Renan rightly calls the " *rust of religion*," ended by utterly extinguishing the flame of true religion in Israel, but this was not the case.   The spirit of legalism was counterbalanced by a new and very different impulse which was manifested in the Psalms.   They are imbued with a spirit of warm and spontaneous personal piety, that seems like a direct heritage from the religion of the Prophets. Probably the explanation is that the immediate result of the Return was a strong wave of spiritual life out of which the Psalter sprang.

It is clear that the written Law, ascribed to Moses, was accorded supreme and absolute authority ; but this was only theoretical.   In practice this authority appertained to the interpretation " *according to the tradition*." [1]   In itself the *Torah* was simply the dead letter.   What gave it vitality was the work of the Scribes who adapted it to the needs of the moment and brought it into contact with the daily life of men. I have already pointed out that the redactors of the *Targums* had no hesitation in altering any passages which might offend the susceptibilities of their contemporaries, and this tendency was general in Israel about the time of the birth of Jesus. Passages of the Scriptures which seemed out of date were either ignored or else so transformed that they acquired a new meaning.[2]   Even the *Midrash* completely misrepresents a number of the old ideas which it undertakes to clarify and explain.   But after all the tractate *Sopherim* tells us that God taught Moses forty-nine different ways of interpreting the Law,[3] which leaves the commentators quite a comfortable margin.[4]

The *Torah* alone could not have nourished and sustained the vitality of the religious life of Israel ; what provided the necessary flexibility and variety was the *tradition*.   Custom

[1] This is the παράδοσις τῶν πρεσβυτέρων ; Mark vii. 3–5 ; Matt. xv. 2 ; Jos., *Ant.*, xiii, 16, 2.   *Cf.* Gal. i. 14 ; **CCLXVI**, i, 38 ; **CCLIII**, 153–161.

[2] **CCLXXX**, 155.

[3] **CCLXXX**, 33–37.

[4] It is, moreover, a relevant fact that in the time of Jesus the *Nebiim*, or Prophets, were considered canonical together with the *Torah* ; which accounts for the phrase, " *the Law and the Prophets* " which occurs in the Gospels and in the writings of the Rabbis (**EB**, art. *Canon*, § 42, and **CCLIII**, 142 *ff*.).   Moreover, some of the *Kethubim* were already generally accepted as part of the Scriptures (*cf.* Ben-Sira's Prologue.   1 Macc. vii. 16 cites Psalm lxxix. 2, as Scripture : κατὰ τὸν λόγον ὃ ἔγραψε).   These writings yield even more readily than the *Torah* to the ingenuity of the commentators.

(*minhag*) had always played a large part in the everyday life
of the Jews, and Ezra reckoned with this when he drew into
the orbit of the *Torah* a number of ancient practices which were
quickly added to the code sponsored by Jahweh.   The first
function of the commentators was to elicit from the Scriptures
such religious precepts as seemed suitable to the age in which
they lived, and to study God and man and their mutual relations
so that the best possible balance might be struck between the
will of the Creator and the interests of his creatures.   It was
the fulfilment of this task, at once doctrinal and ethical, which
gave rise to the *Haggadah*.[1]   In the second place, the commentators strove to subject the precepts of the *Torah* to a searching
legal analysis, with a view to defining them more rigidly, and
also to enlarging the scope of their application.   They sought
to follow them out to their logical conclusions and to seize
and express the true meaning of the *unwritten Law*, which was
soon held to be just as much the acknowledged word of Jahweh
as the Scriptures themselves.   This accretion, mainly legisla-
tive, constitutes the *Halachah*.[2]   It was this twofold stream of
exegesis which nourished the religious life of Pharisaism, without
which Judaism would certainly have foundered.

II

THE SCRIBES, DOCTORS OF THE LAW

The heading of this section refers to the men who carried
out this vast work of adaptation, namely, the *sopherim*, or
Scribes, whose appearance I have mentioned earlier as one of
the outstanding phenomena of the Restoration period and as
an essential factor in the building up of legalism.[3]   Among the
other names by which the Scribes were sometimes known are
hakhamim (" wise men ") and *Rabbis* (" masters ").[4]   They
had also the courtesy titles of *abba*, meaning " father," and
more (" guide," Greek καθηγητής).

Most scholars consider the Scribes (with the Synagogue
which really developed from them) as the most distinctive
creation of the post-exilic period.   Their influence dates from

---

[1] **XXXIII**, 83 *ff.* ; **CCLXXIX**, i, 161 *ff.*
[2] **XXXIII**, 86 *ff.* ; **CCLXXIX**, i, 161, 319 and Index.
[3] Bibliography in **LXXV**, ii, 312 *ff.* ; O. Holtzmann, *Die jüdische Schriftgelehrtsamkeit*, 1901 ; **EB**, art. *Scribes*. Cf. **CCLIII**, 162 *ff.*
[4] This name, which became the usual one, only dates from the time of Christ. *Cf.* **LXXV**, ii, 316.   In Greek the commonest term is γραμματεύς, but we also find νομικός, νομοδιδάσκαλος, διδάσκαλος (Luke ii. 46). Josephus uses ἱερογραμματεύς, σοφιστής, ἐξηγητής τῶν πατρίων νόμων.

the time when Jahwism began to be identified with the application of the Law, and to become more and more the religion of the Book,[1] since *nomocracy* seems to be the natural and inevitable complement of *hierocracy*. But we have reason to believe that the earliest Scribes arose during the Exile, when the Jews turned their attention to the relation between the observance of the *Torah* and the state of Israel at that time. It was not in Palestine that Ezra matured, yet in the book that bears his name (Ezra vii. 11) we find him characterized as " *the priest, the scribe, even the scribe of the words of the Lord, and of his statutes.*" Nehemiah (viii. 1) refers to him in similar terms and depicts him expounding the law to the people.

As Jewish life was reorganized along the lines laid down in the Law of Ezra, the Scribes gradually gained in importance and their special type of learning took definite shape. Probably the pioneers of the movement, the men who first undertook to study the *Torah* from a purely human and practical point of view and to make it legally applicable to doubtful cases, belonged to the priestly class. But as the priests yielded to political influences and allied themselves ever more closely with the aristocratic followers of the long line of foreign rulers (Persians, Greeks and finally Romans), the Scribes became more definitely experts and specialists and became distinct from the priestly class.[2]

The next step was for each Scribe to found a school (*Beth-ha-Midrash*) of which he was the *Rabbi*, and in which his teaching was followed more or less closely according to the amount of prestige he enjoyed. His disciples surrounded him with an atmosphere of reverent devotion.[3] In theory he was unpaid and had to practise some other profession for a livelihood.[4]

The passion with which these doctors guarded and protected the *Torah* united them into a political party when its authority was threatened. Thus, when Antiochus Epiphanes made his attempt to Hellenize Israel, it was the Scribes who incited the *ḥasidim* to their stubborn opposition. The stand made by these *ḥasidim* should not be confused with the Maccabean revolt, which was a much more *popular* movement. It seems that the Scribes and *ḥasidim* only rallied somewhat grudgingly to the

[1] **CCLXVI**, i, 35.   **LXXV**, ii, 313.   [2] **EB**, art. *Scribes*, § 14.
[3] *Pirké Aboth*, iv, 12.   **LXXV**, ii, 317 quotes various passages from the *Talmud* that take this completely filial relationship of pupils to master for granted.
[4] Texts in **LXXV**, ii, 318.

standard of Judas Maccabæus, and that as soon as the principle
of national independence was established, they reassumed their
old complete autonomy in their schools.[1]

Their strength lay in the fact that they did not devote
themselves solely to a theoretical study of the *Torah*, but were
also occupied in elucidating and defining its practical application. They were not only jurists and canonists, but also
moralists and casuists.[2] The tractate of the *Mishnah* called
Pirké Aboth ("the Sayings of the Fathers") quotes the threefold
injunction which is supposed to have emanated from the celebrated *Great Synagogue* of 444 : "*Be prudent in judgment;
make many disciples; put a fence about the Torah,*" and in the
midst of the disasters of Israel the Scribes set themselves to
follow this advice. Even the capture and destruction of
Jerusalem in A.D. 70 did not hinder them, for the tradition of
the Exile yielded explanations for all the trials of their people,
explanations which made their sufferings easier to bear and
even held out hopes of reward. They regarded these misfortunes as the chastisement which they had deserved at the
hand of Jahweh, and believed that Israel would soon receive
the due recompense of his justice and his fidelity to his Promise.
After the destruction of the Holy City by Titus, the Scribes
dispersed to various centres in Jamnia, Tiberias, Lydda and
Babylon, and it was in the schools which they founded in these
places that the compilation of the *Talmud* began.

About the time of Jesus the *sopherim* were distracted by
various different scholastic tendencies. There is no reason to
believe that there was any actual clash of doctrines, but the
schools varied somewhat in their spirit, and the divergence is
noticeable in the details of their interpretations of the Law.
They were well aware of these differences, and although we
cannot clearly envisage or even understand the disputes to which
these differences gave rise, there is no doubt as to their intensity.
This characteristic of the intellectual life of these academic
centres is important if we are to understand the religious ideas
they promulgated. The reader should bear in mind that they
really were *schools*, and not *sects*.

Their differences centred round two famous leaders, Hillel
and Shammai.[3] The first represented a more liberal tendency,
a somewhat less stringent observance ; the second was in favour
of a rigorous orthodoxy. But the evidence we have hardly

---

[1] EB, art. *Scribes*, § 15 ; **LXXV**, ii, 319.
[2] **CCLXVI**, i, 37.
[3] **LXXV**, ii, 359 ; **CCLXVI**, i, 42 ; **CCLXXX**, 97 *ff.* ; **CCLXXIX**, Index
(*Hillel, Shammai*, and *Schools of S. and H.*); **CCLXXII**, 329 *ff.*

seems to justify an opposition which appears to have been both strenuous and prolonged.   Any general statement of the position must necessarily be inadequate and over-simplified, but we might perhaps say that Hillel, in his exposition of the obligations imposed by the *Torah*, emphasized neighbourly love and a spirit of conciliation, while Shammai, in similar cases, insisted on strict observance and of the absolute authority not only of the commands of the Torah but of the jurisprudence of the Scribes.[1]   The story runs that a Gentile with inclinations to become a proselyte came to Hillel one day and asked him what was the essential commandment of the *Torah*, and Hillel replied : " *Do not unto others as you would not that they should do unto you.*"   This saying, so thoroughly in the spirit of the Gospel, which occurs in Matthew vii. 12 and Luke vi. 31, in the form of the *Golden Rule*, has given rise to the theory that Hillel was the real teacher of Jesus.   Hillel allowed divorce (that is the putting away of the woman) only when she was guilty of adultery, whereas according to Shammai she might be divorced for spoiling her husband's dinner.

It is difficult for us to realize the immense reputation and undisputed authority attained by some of the Scribes.[2]   The common people looked up to them with reverence, and women of all ranks showed them special favour, which Josephus attributes to their supposed intimacy with Jahweh.[3]   In spite of this respect, however, the people were not always docile.   For example, although the general feeling among the Scribes was against the impulsive acts of violence that accompanied a revolt, it was by no means always possible to prevent them.[4]

The New Testament always classes the Scribes with the *Pharisees*, who also represented in Israel the legalistic and exclusivist party, but who constituted neither a sect nor a school.   They are named together as though complementary to one another : *e.g.* " *Scribes and Pharisees, hypocrites,*" in Matthew xxiii. 13.   The redactor has not confused them, but connects them, as is frequently the case in the literature of Late Judaism.   Moreover, it is perfectly natural that the Pharisees, whose aim was to live according to the Law, should have been regarded as the allies—or even the followers and disciples—of the Scribes, who were the interpreters of that

---

[1] *Pirké Aboth*, i, 12–15.   **CCLXV** cites many examples, drawn from the *Talmud*, of divergences between the two schools.

[2] **LXXV**, ii, 351 *ff*.   The reader who wishes to learn something of the early Rabbis whose illustrious names were handed down in the tradition should read the whole of the first chapter of the *Pirké Aboth*.

[3] Jos., *Ant.*, xvii, 2, 4.   [4] **XLVII**, i, 221, n. 1.

Law. Certain passages of the New Testament clearly express this close agreement. For instance, Mark (ii. 16) has " *The Scribes of the Pharisees* " (οἱ γραμματεῖς τῶν φαρισαίων), and in Luke v. 30 we find " *The Pharisees and their Scribes* " (οἱ φαρισαῖοι καὶ οἱ γραμματεῖς αὐτῶν).

Nevertheless the Scribes must not be identified with the Pharisees,[1] nor must the Pharisees be regarded as a party led by the Scribes ; for there were Scribes who were not Pharisees at all.[2] It is none the less true that the Pharisees found in the Scribes—those leaders and inspirers of Judaism on its legalistic side which they also represented—a solid support and justification. As for the Scribes, they may appear to be mere casuists and hair-splitters, but this is really a superficial view, which only considers the letter of their religion and not the feeling underneath. These subtle dialecticians, obstinate and vain, full of absurd pedantry about trivial details of ritual and observance, were nevertheless at heart deeply pious, exponents of a religion characterized by a broad humanity.[3] It is difficult to form a convincing picture of their attitude with its contrasting elements, for the modern world has nothing like it. But we should do well to bear in mind that far from being crushed or oppressed by the minuteness and complexity of their practical exegesis of the *Torah*, they were exalted and delighted by it. The *Torah*, which they made so burdensome, was no burden for them. On the contrary they rejoiced in it, finding in its every word the visible sign of Jahweh's love for his people. To the pious Jew, living in constant contact with the Law, which was in a sense his very life, the fulfilment of any one of these prescriptions, which seem to us so wearisome, was an act of infinite gratitude to God, who had deigned to vouchsafe this Law to Israel.

Delight in the Law is then the keynote of the lives of the Rabbis,[4] and we must add to this, *pride in the Law*, pride in being singled out by Jahweh's special grace for the unique privilege of actually knowing the divine will and therefore being able to live according to it. They possessed in the *Torah* the

---

[1] **CCLXV**, 39.

[2] **CCLXXXVI**, 11 ; **CCLXV**, *loc. cit.* : *Die Schriftgelehrten bildeten ein Stand, die Pharisäer eine politisch-religiöse Richtung.*

[3] **CCLXII** ; **CCL**, i ; **CCXCVII**, 7 *ff.* Lagrange, **LI**, 7 *ff.*, disputes this conclusion. He still maintains that *the whole of Judaism is confined within the limits of its jurisprudence* and that the Rabbis *cared little for the cultivation of piety* since for them *obedience to the Law was all that mattered.* These opinions, intended to glorify the mystical side of the Christian religion at the expense of the Scribes, seem somewhat out of date.

[4] Montefiore, in **CCLXVII**, 59 *ff.*

very embodiment of that will ; there they could examine his
every act of justice and love, and contemplate the visible proof
of his favour, and their hearts glowed with a perpetual gratitude.[1]
We must insist [2] that the real concern of the Scribes was not
juridical, but religious. It was not a matter of simply interpreting and administering a code but of setting forth the divine
revelation and correlating the will of Jahweh with the realities
of daily life. This explains the many Rabbinical precepts
which are not the outcome of legalistic scruples but of pious
meditations and moral considerations. Pirké Aboth (i, 1)
attributes the following saying to Simon the Just, who is
supposed to have been contemporary with the *Great Synagogue* :
" *The world is founded on three things : on the Torah, on the
worship of God, and on almsgiving.*" These ideas are expressed
in *maxims* and in *parables* which are extraordinarily similar to
the parables and maxims of the Gospels. I merely note this
correspondence in passing, as we shall return to it later.
Scholars like Nicolas, Wellhausen and Schürer have been somewhat misled by the dry and pedantic appearance of the old
Rabbinical literature. A close and sympathetic study of the
tradition as it is preserved to us in the older parts of the
Mishnah [3] gives evidence of a religion that was far more ardent,
more vital and sincere than is generally suspected. In its
essential simplicity it resembled the religion of Jesus ; indeed
the two teachings have more than a little in common, though
until recently no one perceived it. There are historians who
still share the opinion of Nicolas,[4] that " *there is undoubtedly
a great gulf between the religion of the Synagogue and the religion
of Jesus.*" Nicolas based his arguments on the contrast between
the *formal* obedience demanded by the doctors without reference
to *motives* or *feelings*, and the emphasis Jesus laid on the *sub-
jective springs of action ;* it was a choice between *moral autom-
atism* and *moral initiative*. But, as he admitted himself, this
opposition was not new. It had divided the schools long before
the coming of Christianity, and could be traced back to the
old antagonism between formal legalism and the more spiritual
religion of the Prophets.

I am emphasizing these biased opinions because I believe
them to be of great importance. The writers of the Gospels

---

[1] **CCXCVII**, 29 *ff.*   [2] **XXXIII**, 158.

[3] *Pirké Aboth*, i, 1 and 5, treats of the charitable works which are one
of the three corner-stones of the world, and of Josiah ben Jochanan's
injunction to leave the house unbarred and welcome needy wayfarers as
though they were honoured relatives. Nothing could be more in harmony with the spirit of the Gospels.

[4] **CCLXXX**, p. vi.

were hostile to the Jews, above all to the Jewish doctors; and they naturally gave the impression of an impassable gulf separating Jesus from the Pharisaic Scribes. But this is a distortion of the facts. The chasm was not really of very alarming proportions and there were bridges which crossed it. When all is said, early Christianity arose on a foundation not widely different from that of the *sopherim*, and historically speaking the career of Jesus would be practically inconceivable without the preliminary work accomplished by these men. It is the Christian spirit which shines out from the canonical Psalms and the Psalms of " Solomon," although both are from Pharisaic sources.[1] They are a witness to the intensity of Jewish spiritual life.

III

THE SYNAGOGUE

The link between the Scribes and the people was the *synagogue*.[2] It is an expression of religious life whose origins go back to a practical need and not to a question of principle. Neither its beginnings nor its workings in this early period of its history are very easy to trace. The *word* is Greek ($\sigma\nu\nu\alpha\gamma\omega\gamma\eta$) and means " assembly." It has several equivalents in the language of Hellenized Judaism, which mean the " assembly," or the community, as well as the synagogue.[3] Josephus, for instance, sometimes uses *sabbateion* ($\sigma\alpha\beta\beta\alpha\tau\varepsilon\tilde{\iota}o\nu$), which describes the synagogue by its chief function, that is to say, as a place where men congregated on the Sabbath.[4] The Palestinian word is *keneseth*, including both the place and the gathering held there.

The uncertainty as to the origin of the synagogue has given rise to several rather divergent theories. According to the Jews of Jesus' day the founder was of course Moses himself.[5] Friedländer, on the other hand, goes so far as to maintain [6] that it was the creation of Hellenized Judaism, and was introduced into Palestine by the Essenes, who were themselves under Greek influences. But this thesis has not found much favour,[7] especially in view of the passage from Psalm lxxiv., (v. 8), which runs, " *They have burned up all the synagogues of*

---

[1] **CCLVII,** 29. *Cf.* Psalm lxxiii. 25 ; xlii. 2.

[2] Bibliography in **LXXV,** ii, 427. *Cf.* **EB,** art. *Synagogue* ; **DB,** art. *Synagogue* ; *cf.* **CCLIII,** 171 *ff.*, which deals chiefly with synagogue worship ; **CCLXXIII,** chap. 1, and **CCLXXIX,** 281–307.

[3] **XLVII,** i, 416, note.   [4] Jos., *Ant.*, xvi, 6, 2.

[5] Jos., *C. Ap.*, ii, 17 ; Philo, *Vita Mos.*, iii, 27.

[6] **CCLVIII,** 53 *ff.*   [7] **CCLXVI,** i, 37 and note ; **CCL,** i, 1.

God in the land," [1] which can hardly mean anything but the synagogues. Friedländer's contention that the earliest non-Essene Judæan synagogues (those of the Libertines, the Cyrenæans and the Alexandrians) belonged to the Jews of the Dispersion really proves very little, since the authors of the Acts, which is the source of our information, would not have been concerned with any others. It would be difficult to prove the absence of *others*, that is to say, synagogues of purely Palestinian origin, in Jerusalem about the time of Jesus' death. Wellhausen [2] supports the more logical hypothesis that the synagogue dates from the Exile and arose in Babylon out of the necessity of providing some local centre as a substitute for the Temple in maintaining the continuity of worship among the exiles. A similar necessity gave the synagogues of the *Diaspora* their extreme importance.

For my own part, I am prepared to believe that the first steps were taken during the Exile, by pious men (*hasidim*) who wished to find a common expression for their unswerving devotion to Jahweh,[3] but I am inclined to think that it was in Palestine during the Persian period that the institution really took definite form. In that case its rise would have been a result of the stress laid by Ezra and Nehemiah on the knowledge of the *Torah*. The dissemination of this knowledge demanded a new centre of religious instruction for the people, since the Temple, which was, moreover, unavailable to more than a small section of the community, was not concerned with teaching.

In principle, there was certainly nothing in this innovation hostile to the Temple ; the synagogue was rather its complement,[4] and wherever priests were found, they played an important part in its organization. Later, when the synagogues had become the special domain of the Scribes, they were perhaps not always well disposed to the priestly dignitaries of the Temple; but this attitude should not be regarded as more than a question of tendencies and personal feeling.

The synagogue was not a temple, for Gentiles were not excluded from its meetings, though it was true that they might advance no further than the threshold.[5] It was a *meeting-*

---

[1] This is the only text that makes any allusion to the synagogue in the Old Testament and its Apocrypha.

[2] **LXXXVIII**, 193. [3] **CCLXXIII**, chap. v. [4] **CCL**, i, 2.

[5] **CCC**, i, 85. This was certainly true of synagogues on Hellenic territory, but may possibly not apply to those of Palestine. Ps. Justin, *Cohortatio ad Graecos*, 13, advises Gentiles who wish to learn something of the origins of the Christian faith (in this case the Messianic passages in the Law and the Prophets) to attend the Jewish synagogues.

place for the pious. But it differed from one of our own churches, which, although a consecrated place, is open to unrestricted public use. A synagogue presupposed the existence of an organized community ; it was the place where men and women became aware of themselves as a community and sought edification. From another angle we may look upon it as the organ of legalistic supervision and control,[1] a centre of religious instruction ; for it was in theory the seat of a spiritual government which ordered and disciplined the lives of the people.

As it was not a temple, the synagogue had no *minister*. A priest might occupy an important position in it, but it would be as a *teacher*, not in his official capacity. The recognized leader was the *Rabbi*, or doctor of the Law. But the privilege of teaching in the synagogue was not confined to him. On the contrary, any Jew who felt ready and able to do so, whether he were a member of the community or simply a passing stranger, might ask and obtain permission to expound the Scriptures. The synagogue was thus a thoroughly democratic institution. It might almost be described as a sort of *popular religious university*.

Here the worship was confined solely to the reading of the *Torah* and the *Nebiim*.[2] The scriptural passage read formed the basis of a commentary and the text of an address in which ingenuity and learning of the speaker had free scope. Naturally any professional *master*, or Rabbi, who happened to be present would make the most of such an opportunity. The singing of Psalms and congregational prayers completed the religious activities of the meeting, but, strictly speaking, there were no sacrifices and no liturgy, and this is what gives the synagogue its unique place among the religious institutions of antiquity. Here was seen, for the first time, a cult whose members worshipped wholly *in spirit and in truth* and whose rites were no more than organized individual impulses, only restricted by the need to ensure the order and edification of the meeting.

Unfortunately little is known of the organization or development of synagogues in Palestine.[3] There is more evidence

---

[1] EB, art. *Synagogue*, § 4.

[2] At first no doubt the readings consisted only of a short lesson from each of these sections. Later on it was the rule that 21 verses from each should be read. According to the *Massoretic* divisions, the Sabbath lessons, or *sedarim*, consist of 8 or 9 verses each (*cf.* CCL, i, 7). The whole *Torah* was read through every three years. But the evidence for this whole subject is very scanty, and it is surely unwise of the Jewish scholar Abrahams to base the description of the lessons and commentaries in the synagogue on such a doubtful passage as Luke iv. 17. *Cf.* LXXV, ii, 533, n. 123.

[3] Vitringa, *De Synagoga vetere*, 821 *ff.*, 915, 929, 941 ; LXXXIV, 326 *ff.* ; CCCII, i, 102 *ff.*

concerning the synagogues of the Dispersion but it would be unwise to apply this to Palestine, for it is quite possible that the practice of these two great sections of the Jewish world did not exactly correspond. There may well have been variations from district to district, even from town to town, and indeed it is difficult to see what central authority could possibly have laid down or enforced strict rules for the direction and organization of a synagogue. Quite a small number of Jews—probably a minimum of ten [1]—could constitute the initial group. This little community, of which its synagogue was both the centre and the symbol,[2] was usually led by a *council of elders*, either co-opted or elected. This was an administrative council under the direction of either *one*, or *three* officials (in Greek, *archisyn-agogoi*), who maintained order and regulated the finances of the synagogue, collecting subscriptions, authorizing expenditure, and agreeing on the best use to be made of such offerings as were received. An official called a *ḥazzan* (ὑπηρέτης), who was a kind of beadle and schoolmaster, kept order at the meetings (sometimes a very necessary duty), and was responsible for the correct reading of the Scriptures. It was also his duty to teach the children to read and write so that they might be able to gain a proper knowledge of the *Torah*.

There was a meeting in the synagogue every evening,[3] but the whole community was under no obligation to assemble there except on the Sabbath or for the special religious festivals. In this way the religious rhythm of the synagogue coincided more or less with that of the Temple. As a centre and focus of community life it was full of vitality and vigour. The members all knew one another and were quick to notice lapses and equally ready to encourage and applaud manifestations of piety, that being the sole standard by which anyone in the group was ever judged. The synagogue was used not only for reading, listening, singing and praying, but also for discussion, an exercise for which the Jews soon showed a peculiar talent. They took to this intellectual warfare so readily and derived such pleasure from it that arguments would be started on every possible occasion, and they became more and more passionately addicted to subtle and ingenious interpretations. The Scribes who had done so much to develop this very spirit naturally welcomed its appearance in the synagogue, and if their teaching, which was the fruit of their own schools, remained rigid, they themselves revelled in this propitious atmosphere.

As a rule the founding of a synagogue cannot have been a

---

[1] This was the *minian*, or *number*. *Cf.* **CCC**, i, 84 *ff*.
[2] **EB**, art. *Synagogue*, § 9.   [3] **EB**, art. *Synagogue*, § 10.

matter of great expense,[1] hence they probably sprang up throughout the country. Doubtless every village had one and a town more than one, in some cases a considerable number. The total for Jerusalem at the time of its destruction (A.D. 70) has been put as high as 480, which must have meant that the community served by each was very small. There is nothing strange about this co-existence of the synagogue and the Temple if we remember the special function of the former, that of disseminating among the people the particular kind of religious instruction necessary for their understanding and proper observance of the requirements of the Law. It formed the popular platform of the *sopherim*.

No doubt the synagogues vied with each other, just as the schools did, in the subtlety of their interpretation of the *Torah*, and like those academic institutions, any synagogue possessing the services of a Rabbi specially skilled in this work would carry the subtlety of its exegesis of the Scriptures to the point of absurdity.[2] In fact—and this is the heart of the matter— the synagogue came to be more and more the focus of Jewish religious life. It provided the men of that day with all they found most congenial, so that even with the destruction of the Temple, in A.D. 70, the religion of Israel sustained no essential or devastating loss. For if it was returned exiles who had set up the *Torah* as at once the centre, the motive and the object of religious life, it was the synagogue, aided by the School, which had been the real Temple of this new cult.[3] This practical replacing of the house of Jahweh on the mountain of Zion by the synagogue had happened gradually, and as it were unconsciously, but it effected serious changes in the organization of the Jewish religion none the less. The reader should not forget the extremely important part played by the synagogue in fixing the canon of the Bible, accepting or rejecting various works, and making the final decision by which certain books were stamped and consecrated as *Scriptures*.

Further, neither the synagogue nor the School could confine itself entirely to the niceties of the theoretical interpretation of the *Torah*. The Jews are an intensely practical race and

---

[1] Recent excavations have unearthed the ruins of what must have been very costly and imposing synagogues, but the finest of them (*e.g.* those of Capernaum and Chorazin) seem to belong to the Christian era. *Cf.* R. D. G. Orfali, *Capharnahum et ses ruines*, Paris, 1912.

[2] There is a general account of the *theological system* of the synagogue in **CCLXVI**, i, 43 *ff.*, but the reader should beware of *deducing* too much from this or creating some artificial synthesis which had no counterpart in real life.

[3] **CCLXXIX**, ii, 12.

they demanded an equally detailed study of its *application,* an exhaustive system of legalistic prescriptions based on a minute survey and analysis of every problem and action of the ordinary Israelite in the course of his daily life.   Thus it was through the medium of the synagogue that the whole existence of the Jews became enmeshed in the web of pious obligations that is generally regarded as the distinguishing mark of Late Judaism.[1]   This often exaggerated and even childish insistence on formalism is no really inherent part of authentic Jahwism. On the contrary, it is quite alien to the spirit of the ancient religion of Israel.

IV

ISRAEL, THE PEOPLE OF THE *TORAH*

Henceforward, therefore, the Jews must be looked on as the *people of the " Torah."* [2]   Anyone who failed in his study or practice of it paid the penalty of his neglect in the contempt of the rest of the community, but the man who showed himself well versed in its precepts and scrupulous in his observance was rewarded with universal honour and respect.   Here was the pearl without price, the ultimate, inalienable wealth of Israel. Denuded of riches and property, all his resources gone, the Jew still had the *Torah,* his indestructible and supreme possession.[3] His fear of his pagan overlords could never prevail against the sacred fear of the law, no matter how harsh their rule.   In such a cause no suffering could be too severe,[4] and no risk could be too great, since God must certainly assist a righteous cause. This conviction that Jahweh could not fail to help the devout was the cause of that indomitable and unfailing fanaticism which inspired one section of the Jews and which would now and then suddenly infect the whole population.   Even if the enterprises undertaken in the cause of the *Torah* seemed to fail, the participants were at least sure of a recompense in heaven ; but in spite of this there was no calculation or bargaining about the sacrifices of the faithful.   The *Pirké Aboth* (i, 5) ascribes the following pronouncement to Antigonus, a pupil of Simon the Just : " *Be not as slaves who serve their masters for a recompense, but be rather as slaves who serve their masters without hope of reward, and may the fear of Heaven be upon you.*"   This is

---

[1] **LXXV**, ii, 464, the section entitled *Das Leben unter das Gesetz.*
[2] For explanations and essential additions to all that follows, see Lods, *op. cit.,* book iii, chap. iii : *Religion.*
[3] Jos., *C. Ap.,* ii, 38 : ὁ γοῦν νόμος ἡμῖν διαμένει.
[4] Jos., *op. cit.,* i, 8.

the true expression of what the pious Israelite felt in his heart
to be the claims of the *Torah*.

There is no denying that this constant effort to live according
to the spirit and the letter of the *Torah*, and not to transgress
the narrow boundaries it imposed, did tend to imprison the
pietists in a somewhat rigid formalism. Their material and
moral expansion was hampered by a network of narrow and
exacting prescriptions which might well have a hardening effect
on their hearts. It was all too easy for the strict Jew to mistake
his superficial exactness of observance for a genuine religious
feeling which he was far from experiencing. A glance at the
Mishnah tractate called *Shabbath* leaves the reader overwhelmed
by the number and the triviality of the prescriptions which
burdened the pious Israelite.[1] The rest on the Sabbath had
been definitely enjoined by Exodus xx. 8, which runs :
" *Remember the Sabbath day, to keep it holy. Six days shalt thou
labour, and do all thy work : but the seventh day is a sabbath
unto Jahweh, thy God. In it thou shalt not do any work, thou,
nor thy son, nor thy daughter, thy manservant, nor thy maid-
servant, nor thy cattle, nor the stranger that is within thy gates.*"
The obvious meaning of the passage is perfectly clear, but it
becomes complicated when the doctors attempt an exact
definition of the words *labour* and *work*, for such a definition
can only be given by making a complete list of *every possible
case* in which a careless man might conceivably be *working* or
labouring without realizing it.

In *Shabbath* (vii, 2) the list includes thirty-eight prohibitions,
which seems fairly comprehensive. But this does not settle
the question, for the careful student of the twenty-first prohibition (against *making a knot*) or the twenty-second (against
undoing a knot) may well feel doubts as to exactly what constitutes a *knot*, and a whole chapter (xv) is devoted to giving
the decisions and opinions of the Rabbis on this vital problem.
Again, a Jew is strictly forbidden to trace *two letters* on the
Sabbath day. But this raises all kinds of difficulties—What
letters can it refer to ? From what alphabet ? Formed by
what hand or implement ? *Shabbath* (xii, 3–6) does not rest
till it has examined every conceivable hypothesis. And so it
is throughout the work. Every word of every precept becomes
the text of an interminable harangue, a pretext for quibblings
and hair-splittings, pedantries and sophistries until the smooth
course of ordinary life is seriously menaced. How, for instance,
could all domestic affairs be completely interrupted for twenty-
four hours ? Who was to light the fires, or look after the

[1] **LXXV**, ii, 170 *ff.*

animals, which could scarcely be expected to conform to an ultra-strict observance of the day of rest ? One could go on piling up instances of such ridiculous and extravagant *cases* indefinitely.[1]   And yet, as I have said, it would be a serious mistake to regard the religion of the *Torah* as mere academic casuistry in which the deadweight of legalism had extinguished every gleam of genuine feeling. The profound and ardent gratitude which every good Jew felt for the *Torah* itself, as the special gift vouchsafed by Jahweh to his people, is sufficient proof to the contrary.

The real drawback of this passion for strict observance was the utter lack of proportion it engendered. In practice the neglect of some trivial ruling of the doctors aroused as much horror and indignation as a serious breach of the Law itself. A strict Jew would consider it nearly as reprehensible not to wear those woollen tassels or fringes called *zizith* (the κράσπεδα of the Gospels) on the border of his garment, or to put the little box (*mesusah*) containing certain parts of the book of Deuteronomy (vi. 4–9, and xi. 13–21) on the right-hand door-post of his house, or to bind the *tephillim* (the φυλακτήρια of Matt. xxiii. 5) about his head and forearm before praying,[2] as not to pray at all. Yet the pious man was supposed to spend much time in prayer,[3] since he not only had to recite the *Shema*[4] morning and evening and at midday, the *Shemoneh-Esreh*,[5] or benedictions, at meal-times, and the special prayers linking him with the celebration of the two daily sacrifices of

---

[1] Schürer has made a special study of the points raised with reference to the observance of the Sabbath (**LXXV**, ii, 470 *ff.*) and to legal purity (tractate *Kelim*, 478 *ff.*).

[2] These were strips of leather, one of which was bound about the fore-head, and the other wound seven times round the left forearm. The one worn round the head held in place a little box containing pieces of parchment inscribed with three texts (Exod. xiii. 1–10 ; Deut. vi. 4–9 ; and Deut. xi. 13–21[a]). The other was fastened to a piece of parchment bearing the same texts.

[3] **LXXV**, ii, 186 *ff.*

[4] *Shema = Hear* : it is the first word of a prayer made up of a combination of Deut. vi. 4–9 ; xi. 13–31, and Num. xv. 37–41. *Cf.* **CCXCIX**, 162 *ff.*, and **CCLXXIX**, i, 291 *ff.*

[5] The *Shemoneh-Esreh = the Eighteen Benedictions. Cf.* **CCXCIX**, 164 *ff.* ; **LI** translates the text established by G. Dalman ; **CCLXXIX**, i, 292 ; ii, 212. In the introduction to his translation of the *Mishnah*, O. Holtzmann disputes the theory that the *Shema* was in use in the time of Jesus. He considers that it was introduced about A.D. 40–50 ; and that the *Shemoneh-Esreh* was after 70 and probably as late as A.D. 100. But no doubt the prayers existed before they became obligatory, or at least the *prayer-book* of the pious Jew included something very similar to them.

the Temple, but was also under obligation to take part in the communal prayers at the synagogue.

There is a danger of not making sufficient distinction between the ramifications of Rabbinical theory and the common practice of the people. If critics would bear the origin of the *Mishnah* in mind, they would be less likely to exaggerate its effects and to picture Judaism as bound and fettered by a kind of strait-jacket of legalism. A careful examination soon makes it clear that the academic discussions of the Schools and the somewhat pedantic formalism of the synagogue represent only one aspect of the Jewish religion.

Such an examination reveals a number of religious ideas which seem to have little connection with the *Torah* or with any other part of the Scriptures, but which nevertheless loom large in the daily life of the people. The so-called *Deutero-canonical* and *Apocryphal* books bear witness to their existence,[1] but the scientific study of this evidence has so far proved unfruitful, because those who have engaged in it have remained satisfied with purely theoretical ideas, and have ignored the complex and more elusive realities underlying them.[2] Such a study has also been prejudiced by the common custom of regarding Judaism as something absolutely unique and complete in itself. R. Dussaud has rightly pointed out that a closer acquaintance with the ancient East has made it clear that the stock of moral ideas, which had so long been considered the exclusive prerogative of the Jews, were in reality the common property of all the ancient oriental civilizations.[3] And what is true of Early Judaism, which is his especial concern, applies no less to the Late Judaism which forms the subject of this book.

---

[1] R. H. Charles, *The Book of Enoch*, 2nd edit., Clarendon Press, 1912, has an introduction of 112 pages which abounds in facts and ideas on the question before us.

[2] **XLVII**, i, XVI.   [3] **CCLVI**, 283.

BOOK II

INNOVATIONS AND FOREIGN INFLUENCES

CHAPTER I

THE ORIGIN OF INNOVATIONS. GOD AND HIS HYPOSTASES

WHEN Michel Nicolas was writing seventy-five years ago, scholars had already begun to realize that traditional Judaism had undergone certain changes during the post-exilic period. It was said that these innovations were due to that slow process of natural evolution from within to which the *Targums* and the *Midrash* bear witness. The possibility of outside influences was only very grudgingly admitted, and where these could not be wholly denied they were reduced to the level of unconscious suggestions, as indefinable today as they would have been for the Jews whose religion they affected.[1] The most important innovations which were supposed to have penetrated current Judaism—or so-called *popular Judaism*—by way of the *Haggadah*, consisted of speculations on the *nature of God*, on the rôle of *good and bad angels*, on the *future life* and its rewards and punishments, and on the *messianic expectation*.

Modern opinion is not satisfied with this somewhat superficial view. It finds the position more complex, and the origin of these innovations seems less obvious.

I

THE ORIGIN OF INNOVATIONS

The strict traditionalist cannot, of course, admit even the possibility of alterations and developments in the religion revealed to the chosen people, but there is not a single liberal

[1] This attitude was taken up by Michel Nicolas himself, in his *Doctrines religieuses*, and also by Albert Réville (*cf.* **CCCII**, i, 152 *ff.*). Even Schürer, with all his vast and detailed erudition, shares their point of view on the whole.

critic today who denies that Judaism did evolve, and that this evolution was an inevitable result of the mere passage of time. Jahwism which was at once the creator and the product of Jewish life could not have failed to vary with the needs and aspirations of the society which gave it birth. For instance, the Jews of Jesus' day could not possibly picture their God in exactly the same terms as their forefathers in the reign of David. But this spontaneous, internal development—a process that might even be termed *autogenous*—will not account for all the *innovations* which the historian encounters in Israel just before the Christian era. To begin with, we must take into account the work of the Scribes. These men sincerely believed that all they did was to secure the tradition by explaining and elucidating it, but in reality they could not help modifying it, often profoundly. For instance, the attempt of the *Targums* to get rid of the crude anthropomorphism of the old Bible stories affords a good illustration of the *re-focusing* which modernized the ancient beliefs. We must also pay special attention to the trend of popular feeling, tending to emphasize the ideas which satisfy the desires of the people or *minister to their needs*, such as the Messianic hope, demonology, and all kinds of marvels and miracles. None of these elements would have come to fruition without the popular impulse. Finally, there is the problem of foreign influences.

This question is still a very controversial one, but it can no longer be ignored.[1]

For a long time critics refused to admit that foreign influences on Judaism were anything but *peripheral* or *tangential* (Wellhausen), or *only bearing on matters of detail*,[2] or else maintained that they were of late date, that is to say, not earlier than the second century A.D. There seems to be no longer any possibility of doubting the existence of older, deeper and more extensive influences than these. Moreover, as I have said, Palestine occupied a position of unusual importance and interest in the Mediterranean Orient as a thoroughfare and meeting-

[1] Bibliography in **CCLXVI**, i, 44 *ff.* ; **CCLIII**, 302 *ff.* ; **VIII**, 116–60 ; Gunkel, *Der Einfluss Babyloniens auf die israelitische Religion*, Göttingen, 1903 ; Wellhausen, *Skizzen und Vorarbeiten*, vi, 1889 ; Bertholet, *Das religiongeschichtliche Problem des Spätjudentums*, Tübingen, 1909 ; Erik Stave, *Ueber den Einfluss des Parsismus auf das Judentum*, Giessen, 1920. On this last influence, *cf.* particularly **CCLXXVIII**, ii, 59 *ff.* ; **CCLXXIV**, especially the 3rd section of chap. ii ; **CCLXXI** ; **LXVII**, 227 *ff.*, 273 *ff.*, 304 *ff.* ; **LI**, 388 *ff.* (maintaining the non-existence of influences).

[2] Such as the seven eyes that Jahweh was supposed to have graved on the stone mentioned in Zech. iii. 9, and the figure of *Satan* as he appears in Job, Chronicles, Zechariah, and Ecclesiasticus. Nicolas as early as 1860 (**CCLXXX**) recognized Persian influence here.

place for the many varied streams of cultural influences which
had made their impact upon her, sometimes in successive waves,
sometimes in a conjoined attack. Recently discovered documents clearly prove the influence of the Babylonians, the
Egyptians, the Hittites and the Ægeans on ancient Palestine,
an influence which the Israelite conquest did not efface or
interrupt.[1] Unless the Jewish religion is to be regarded as a
continual miracle, it is difficult to see *a priori* how Palestine
on the one hand, subjugated by the Egyptians, Chaldæans and
Persians, by the Lagids and Seleucids and by the Hellenized
Romans, that is to say, by peoples whose culture and religion
were well established,[2] and on the other surrounded by populations of the same race as her own or nearly akin, and, finally,
in constant communication with the Jews scattered throughout the Mediterranean Orient,[3] could possibly have held absolutely aloof from all infiltrations and contaminations and
preserved her native beliefs perfectly intact. A mere reading
of the Prophets is enough to dispose of this remarkable
hypothesis.

An illustration will make this clear. Israel dwelt for three
generations in Mesopotamia, under the shadow of Babylon, the
great city whose thought had influenced the whole Hellenic
and Asiatic world so lastingly and so profoundly, and had
already left its mark on the redaction of the opening chapters of
Genesis. Is it possible to imagine that Jahwism was absolutely
unaffected by this contact ?

It is equally unlikely that the inhabitants of Palestine
should have remained impervious to all influences emanating
from the girdle of Hellenized cities that encircled the Holy
Land after the Return.[4] This would have been as great a
miracle as the one already referred to. The fact that there
has been such an obstinate refusal to recognize these obvious
realities simply proves that the assumption of such miracles
dominated the study of the history of Judaism—and of Christianity.[5] Even when the belief in miracles began to wane

---

[1] *Cf.* **CCLXXIV**, 19–36.

[2] Persian religion made strenuous efforts to extend its influence in the
wake of the Achemenid conquests. *Cf.* **CCLXXVIII**, ii, 86.

[3] **CCLIII**, 432 *ff.*, emphasizes the *Diaspora* as a source of foreign
influences.

[4] The relevant material is to be found in **LXXV**, i, 188 *ff.* ; Nielsen
(**CCXCVIII**, 31 *ff.*, 389 *ff.*) rightly stresses this Hellenistic influence, which
dates back to the third century B.C. and shows itself chiefly *in einer
Vergeistigung der Göttergestalten.* The translation of Greek commercial
terms into Aramaic is further proof of this contact : **CCLXXII**, 270 *ff.*

[5] P. Lagrange still affirms that anything really new in these so-called
innovations was derived from supplementary Divine revelations.

it left behind it a kind of hypnosis, which regarded Judaism as something so completely apart from all other religions (Christianity excepted) that the others were only seen through a cloud of repulsion and contempt.   They forgot that when Israel borrowed from its neighbours it might have done so for the most part involuntarily and even unawares.   A religion, like an individual, can only put up an adequate defence when it is fully conscious of the danger threatening it.   And they forgot that a faith is only alive as long as it is evolving, and that the only way it can evolve is by selecting what it needs for its growth from its environment.   Flesh and blood cannot be created out of a void.

It is now fully proved that even before the Exile Jewish civilization—which means first and foremost the Jewish religion —could not be regarded as an indigenous growth,[1] but that it had drawn its constituent elements from the stock of ideas and beliefs common to the Semitic peoples of the Orient.[2]   There is no need to enlarge on the confusion into which the conservative ranks were thrown (with good reason) by the recent discovery of Babylonian tablets of a much earlier date than the book of Genesis, giving a story of the creation and the flood, so like the Biblical account that it has every appearance of being its source.   Orthodox tradition received a no less disturbing shock when the Morgan expedition discovered the Code of Hammurabi at Susa in 1901 or 1902, and revealed its relation with the so-called Law of Moses.   These ancient documents prove conclusively that the alleged isolation of early Judaism was purely legendary and that the tendencious inventions and fanciful interpretations of the priests who compiled the *Torah* of the Return should not be regarded as historical fact.

In the same way Late Judaism contains a number of elements foreign to early Jahwism.[3]   Its cosmology, its angelology, its demonology, its mythology, its eschatology present many analogies with those of Babylon, Iran and even Egypt.   Nicolas had already [4] recognized Mazdean influences in Jewish angelology and demonology, and to some extent in the apocalyptic books, but he believed that the germs of all this were already contained in the native religion of Israel, although without Iranian influence it might have developed somewhat differently.

---

[1] CCLVI, 283. *Cf.* CCCVIII, 190.

[2] On this important point *cf.* L. W. King, *Legends of Babylon and Egypt in relation to Hebrew Tradition*, London, 1918 ; G. A. Barton, in *Archœology and the Bible*, Philadelphia, 1916, attempts to minimize in his conclusions the results to which he is led by his study of the text ; **XLV.**

[3] CCLXXIV, 248 *ff*.   [4] CCLXXX.

This is really to say that Judaism was modified by its environment. There is also a whole group of ideas about God, the soul and its immortality which are reminiscent of Greek thought. These borrowings are disconnected and contradictory, hard to analyse or define, but they are obvious enough, and even a superficial examination will convince the reader of their extreme importance in the religious life of the Jews.[1] It matters little whether this power of assimilation constituted the strength or the weakness of Judaism; it suffices to establish the fact. This fact, however, is difficult to discern, because of the syncretistic complexity of those influences again at work in Israel after the Return. It is not superfluous to repeat that syncretism was the normal religious form throughout the East, whether Asiatic or Hellenized, and such a universal tendency cannot have failed to affect the Jewish faith.

During the Greek and Roman periods the people of Palestine were still influenced by Iran and Mesopotamia through the relations which they maintained with the Jewish colonies on the banks of the Euphrates. But it was the Hellenistic movement, both on its cultural and on its religious side, that most deeply affected the Judaism of this time. Any Jew who wished to extend his trade beyond the borders of Palestine was forced to learn Greek, for no matter which way he turned he would encounter towns that were Hellenic or at least Hellenized. And with the language as their natural vehicle came ideas, concepts, fashions and customs. Greek philosophy,[2] by reason of its obvious *intellectual* superiority to anything of native origin, that is to say, the greater resources which it offered to the Jew who was interested in the realm of the mind, soon made its attraction felt. And along with Greek thought, the whole Hellenistic culture, then spreading over all the Mediterranean world, began to take root in Palestine. It included the intellectual education of the schools, the physical education of the gymnasia, and even such things as fashions in dress, and the refined pleasures of literature and the theatre. This influence was superficial at first, but it affected those whose minds were most active and most liberal, those whose rank and circumstances gave them the greatest degree of independence. There is no doubt that it soon became widespread and profound, not only because the common people naturally ape the great, but because Hellenization brought its own rewards. If Antiochus Epiphanes had not shown such ill-timed

---

[1] CCCVIII, 190–1 ; CCLXVI, i, 44 ; CCLXV, 34 ; CCLV, 92.
[2] LXXV, i, 189 *ff.* ; Th. Reinach, *L'hellénisation du monde antique : l'hellénisme en Syrie*, 1914, 347 *ff.* ; CCLXXIV, 256 *ff.*

haste and had not tried to force the Hellenizing movement among his Jewish subjects, Palestine would have followed the same course as Egypt or Syria.   She already possessed the beginnings of a syncretism which was both cultural and religious, and would certainly have Hellenized the cult and the beliefs of Israel if the Maccabæan revolt had not interrupted it.[1]   The *ḥasidim*, or pietists, who resisted the infection, would have remained a mere sect.   It was only the unfortunate precipitancy of the Seleucid which transformed them into the acknowledged representatives of the true faith of Jahweh, and made possible that recoil of Jahwism upon itself which their influence, coupled with a strong nationalist reaction, brought about.[2]   Thus the direct Hellenization of Judaism failed, and even official Judaism became more strongly opposed to Hellenism than before.   But before the rupture there had been many open converts, especially among the aristocratic families, and even after the Maccabæan revolt Hellenistic influences continued to make themselves felt. Nor were their effects seen only in such peculiar communities as the Essenes.[3]   In general, however, the hearts of the Jews were imbued by a settled suspicion, hostile or contemptuous, of all Gentiles, an effect of the fear which the tyranny of Antiochus had caused in the minds of the pious.   Esther and Judith and the Second Book of Maccabees all bear witness to this mistrust and its consequences, but it was easier to shut out persons than ideas.

It is not always easy to indicate the route by which any particular influence managed to pierce the defences of Israel. Some entered by way of *popular superstition*, some through *Rabbinical ascendancy*, and some through *aristocratic laxity*, a laxity shared even by the priesthood in the days of the Seleucids. However, it is easier to define and classify these innovations than to trace their exact origin and history.   They may be divided broadly into two main groups, one concerned with God and Man, the other with the world and more particularly with the destiny of Israel.

[1] There is a good statement of this point of view in Edwyn Bevan, *Jerusalem under the High Priests*, London, 1904.
[2] **CCLII**, 149 *ff.*, 208 *ff.*
[3] On this particular point *cf.* **CCLVIII**, 60 *ff.*

II

GOD AND HIS HYPOSTASES

The post-Exilic idea of God was characterized by the attribute of unity.[1] *There is no God but God,* and paganism, with its myriads of divinities *who did not really exist,* was lost in error. This attitude represented a considerable advance, for, although monotheism is often considered today as the essential tenet and special possession of Judaism, it was by no means established in Israel before the Exile, since neither the Kings nor the people were really convinced that Jahweh was the sole God of the Universe. This deplorable state of indecision resulted in lapses into idolatry, lapses which the Prophets, and especially those of the Exile, had denounced as the real source of all the misfortunes of Israel.

Even the Prophets themselves, the most faithful of all the followers of Jahweh, had never been in the habit of inquiring very closely into the nature, being, or attributes of their God. But such unquestioning acceptance was hardly possible in the scribal schools, and the Deity did not escape their passion for discussion. Hence there emerged a genuine *theodicy,* built up on the intellectual plane, and divorced from the world of feeling and imagination to which the religion of the Prophets belonged. If the new system seemed somewhat incoherent it was because it had not entirely divested itself of the remnants of the old Prophetic religion which survived even in the schools, and which were much more vigorous among the people, who were scarcely touched by Rabbinical dialectic. Hence the idea of God presents two different aspects neither of which can be neglected.

As the subject of Rabbinical arguments and speculations, Jahweh tended to lose all traces of anthropomorphism and to become completely spiritualized and transcendent.[2] As I have already noted, the *Targums* had the same end in view. The conclusion of all such reflexions is well expressed by Ben-Sira (Ecclus. xliii. 27): " *We may speak much, and yet come short: wherefore in sum, he is all.*" The usual names for God attempt

[1] The essential bibliography and references to texts are to be found in **CCLII**, 359, and in Couard, *Die religiösen und sittlichen Anschauungen der alttestamentlichen Apocryphen und Pseudepigraphen,* 1907. *Cf.* also **LXXV**, Index, under the word *Gott*; **CCLIII**, 302 *ff.*; **LXVII**, 259, 290 *ff.*; **CCLXXII**, 288 *ff.* The reader should refer to A. Lods, *op. cit.,* pp. 248 *ff.* and 351 *ff.,* for a complete and precise statement of what is here said too briefly.

[2] **CCLII**, 363 *ff.*

to convey the idea of lofty transcendence and inexpressible majesty connected with the conception of his Being. He is called the *God of Heaven* (or of *the Heavens*), the *King*, the *Most High*, the *Almighty*, the *Lord* (*Elohim* or *Adonai*) and so forth.[1] We get the impression that the supreme God of Greek philosophy, presiding over the Universe, has taken the place of the old national Deity enthroned in the midst of his people. But let there be no mistake : transcendence is not abstraction, and Israel had never been more vividly conscious of the living presence of Jahweh than at this time. But while glorious titles were showered upon him, his own name was no longer spoken. To name him would be in a sense to limit him, and to suggest that he was known, that it was possible to form an adequate idea of him—hypotheses which were both inadmissible and inconceivable.[2] For a good Jew the act of pronouncing the *Written Name* was a real apostasy, involving the rejection of the yoke of the *Torah* and the denial of circumcision. He used instead the terms *Heaven*, the *Name*, the *Place*, the *Most High*, the *Living*, the *Eternal*, the *Compassionate*, the *Blessed*, etc.[3] But it was equally impossible that this spiritual God could ever have had any kind of contact with the material world, even in order to create it. To fill the gap, the Jews produced a system of intermediaries, the *hypostases* of God, who were his deputies and assistants in the creation and direction of the world. Such were the *Spirit of God* (*ruach Elohim*), his *Word* (*Memra*), his *Presence* (*Shechinah*, *i.e. Habitation*), his *Glory* (*Jekarah*, $\Delta\delta\xi\alpha$) and his *Wisdom* (*Hokmah*).[4] As a matter of fact, these hypos-

---

[1] **CCLII**, 372. Texts collected in **CCLXXXII**, 220 and notes, and in **CCLIII**, 312 *ff.* Cf. **CCLXXIX**, ii, 201 *ff.*, the chapter entitled *The Father in Heaven*.

[2] O. Holtzmann suggests in his Introduction to the translation of the *Mishnah* that the sacred name *Iaho, Ia* remained in private use long after its utterance was officially forbidden outside the Temple. This seems very probable, especially as the magical powers attributed to the name would have helped to keep it in circulation for practical purposes (*cf.* Lebreton, *Les origines du dogme de la Trinité* (2nd edit.), Paris, 1919, 133, which gives references and examples of the Jewish faith in its magical efficacy). **CCLIII**, 349, notes that the name of Jahweh became a kind of hypostasis with its own special powers, a conception which is current in the Psalms. However, the use of the name was most strictly forbidden by Rabbinical law, which was confirmed by custom. It was only supposed to be pronounced by the Priest when he blessed the people in the Temple, and with the destruction of the Temple even that exception disappeared. It is true that in Hadrian's reign Aquila used it instead of *Kyrios* (= *Adonai*) in his Greek translation, but he did not transcribe the Hebrew tetragrammaton. *Cf.* F. C. Burkitt, in **IV**, p. xii.

[3] **LI**, 457 *ff.*

[4] **CCXCVI**, 55 ; **CCLXVI**, i, 68 ; **CCLIII**, 314 *ff.*, 342 *ff.* ; **CCV**, ii, 302 *ff.*

tases are almost as difficult to define as God Himself, but since, as Lagrange puts it, " *their whole object is to evade definition*," it is fitting that they should remain vague and obscure. Did they represent actual persons or mere abstractions ? Probably both at once, or something between the two—a conception which is less intelligible to us than it was to those whom it satisfied.[1] In their day logic was less tyrannical in its demands. They were faced with the difficulty of reconciling the idea of an indefinable God with His apparent action on the world of matter, and they refused to see that their method of escape from this repugnant conception, a method based partly on their monotheism and partly on their belief in the divine omnipotence, led them into a very equivocal position. Christianity struggled long with the same problem and only escaped by the doubtful assistance of the dogma of the Trinity.

The opening words of Genesis (i. 2), " *and the Spirit of God moved upon the face of the waters*," provided the *Ruach Elohim* with a sound title to hypostatic existence,[2] although the word *ruach*, which means " breath " (ἄνεμος, *animus*), embodied rather the notion of a manifestation of the divine *dynamis*, ready, by a special act of grace, to assist the deserving, than that of a personification more or less distinct from God Himself. Nevertheless such a personification was not incompatible with the Scriptures, for in 1 Kings xxii. 21 we read of a *spirit* who asks Jahweh that he may be allowed to entice all the prophets of Ahab, King of Israel, so that they may launch him on an enterprise which will prove fatal to him. This is why the spirit of Jahweh appears as a person in Isaiah lxiii. 10, " *But they rebelled, and grieved his holy spirit ; therefore he was turned to be their enemy*." In fact, the *ruach hakkodeš*, as τὸ ἅγιον πνεῦμα or τὸ πνεῦμα τὸ ἅγιον, the *Holy Spirit*, was destined for a distinguished career. But the word *Pneuma* always suffered from a sort of fluidity which often made it very difficult to define its precise meaning, that is to say the kind of concept it was supposed to represent on any particular occasion, nor was the word *ruach* entirely free from the same ambiguity.[3]

There has been much discussion concerning the origin and

---

[1] **CCLIII**, 313 *ff.* ; **CCLII**, 394. Lagrange, **LI**, 436 *ff.*, tries to make out that there was no question of *persons* or even of *hypostases*, nothing more, in fact, than ways of expressing God—the kind of circumlocution that would appeal to the Rabbis—but this interpretation is certainly not adequate.

[2] On the history of the concept *cf.* **CCLIII**, 347 *ff.*, which gives the principal texts and references.

[3] **CCLXVI**, i, 71 *ff.*

nature of the *Word* (*Memra*) of God,[1] which, as the *Logos*, has played such an important part in Christian theology. Certain critics maintain that it was simply a natural product of Jewish thought, and cite as evidence various passages in which the Word presents the appearance of a real hypostasis.[2] Personally I cannot agree with their reading. The texts in question seem to me to mean no more than " *Jahweh speaks and his word is with power.*" Others are of opinion that this notion of the Word is one of the signs of the influence of Greek speculation, in both its platonic and its stoic forms. This is possible, and I am more inclined to accept it, in spite of the difficulty of proving it.[3] Such an influence, which must have worked unconsciously upon the Jewish doctors, provided them with a solution of their problem, a solution which was already a commonplace of Greek thought. To God is attributed the directing purpose in the creation of the universe and the ordering of the material world, without his being directly involved in either operation himself. It was not necessary to be a student of Greek philosophy to have a reasonably adequate idea of the Logos.

In the *Talmud* the part of intermediary between God and man is played, not by the *Memra*, but by the *Shechinah*. But already in the *Targum* of Onkelos and that of Jonathan in order to avoid anthropomorphism, the *Shechinah* itself has replaced Jahweh, and this explains the substitution in the *Talmud*.[4]

The only one of these divine abstractions which seems to have reached actual personification was *Wisdom*.[5] *Wisdom* was the first of God's creations, and dwelt with Him eternally, informing and irradiating all His works. The first chapter of the *Wisdom of Jesus, Son of Sirach* (Ecclus.), is quite definite on this point, and a later passage explains that the chosen resting-place of Wisdom is the Temple of Zion in the midst of

---

[1] **CCLII**, 395 ; **CCLIII**, 347. *Cf.* **CCCV**, ii, 302–33 ; *Exkurs über den Memra Iahves.*

[2] Isa. lv. 11 makes the Word God's workman. *Cf.* also Ps. xxxiii. 6 : " *By the word of Jahweh were the heavens made,*" and Ps. cxlvii. 15 : " *His word runneth swiftly.*"

[3] Nicolas, **CCLXXX**, 205, held that the proof was *impossible*, but this is an exaggeration. According to Lagrange (**LI**, 452), no sort of doctrine attached to the idea of the Word in Palestine : it was simply and solely a way of referring to God without speaking His name. This is too sweeping.

[4] **CCLXXX**, 156.

[5] **CCLII**, 394 ; **CCLIII**, 342 *ff.* The texts are collected in **CCLXXXII**, 222.

the people of Israel.[1] In a sense this *Ḥokmah* is the *Torah* itself. It is not probable that the conception of Wisdom had reached a more precise definition than any of the other hypostases we have mentioned, but it far exceeded them in importance in Jewish thought at the time of Jesus. To this the book known as the Wisdom of Solomon bears sufficient witness. Wisdom proved able to absorb all the other hypostases. We shall have to consider its influence on Philo, St. Paul, and the author of the Fourth Gospel, and more generally on the whole development of primitive Christianity.

We have been concerned till now with what may be called the *intellectual aspect of God*, corresponding to the *rational* religion of the Scribes, and representing, no doubt, their contamination in a greater or less degree by Greek thought, which reached them directly from Hellenized Syria, and indirectly by way of the Jewish colony in Alexandria. But God has also another aspect, corresponding to the religion of the heart, that religion of the spirit, characteristic of the Prophets, whose influence survived in Israel, as I have shown, even in the synagogue and among the doctors themselves, up to the time of the full expansion of legalism, and was still more vigorous among the common people.

While still maintaining that God was the Most High, far beyond the range of all human attempts at definition, and the awful Judge, whose power Jesus himself did not lessen or ignore, the Jews continued to think of Him as a perfectly definite person. He remained the chief actor in their history, the King and Ruler of their people, not figuratively but in the most real and immediate sense. They had only to glance back at their own recent annals to find in the epic of the Maccabees the witness of the presence and activity of Jahweh. The Rabbi might speculate as to whether God had performed the gracious miracle in person or had delegated the task to His Wisdom, His Word or His Presence, but the simple Jew had no need of such subtleties and his heart (and the heart of the Rabbi, for that matter) was filled with unbounded gratitude to Jahweh, who had proved himself not merely a just God, but a God of pity and love, the true *Father* of his people.

For Jesus did not invent the idea of the *Fatherhood of God*, though according to the Gospel tradition he emphasized it and gave it such fundamental importance as the very basis of the true relation between God and man, that it has been regarded as the most original feature of his teaching. It was living in

[1] Ben-Sira xxiv., which is in praise of Wisdom. *Cf.* especially verses 1, 8, 10, 11 and 12.

the religious circles of his youth.[1] Certainly it was not a tenet that either the Old Testament or the Scribes emphasized particularly, but it had a place both in the Scriptures [2] and in the Schools,[3] and was a source of religious poetry, as the Psalms of David and the Psalms of Solomon testify. In such passages it is no doubt the whole of Israel that is meant by the term *the son of God*, but during the post-exilic period the phrase was also used in a special sense of the godly man. This is not without its significance for the study of the career of Jesus and the beginnings of the Christian movement.[4]

Anyone who will compare such passages as the following :

(*a*) Whom have I in heaven but thee ?
And there is none upon earth that I desire beside thee.
My flesh and my heart faileth,
But God is the strength of my heart and my refuge for ever.

(Ps. lxxiii. 25 *ff*.)

(*b*) As the hart panteth
After the water brooks,
So panteth my soul
After thee, O God.

(Ps. xlii. 1.)

with the sayings of Jesus concerning the love of God and faith in Him, will find these Gospel utterances much more Jewish than they seem when compared with the complicated subtleties of the *sopherim*. The early Christians, who never held that Jesus first discovered and proclaimed the aspect of Jahweh reflected in the Psalms, showed a surer sense of reality than many of the moderns. Renan once wrote,[5] " *The direct Fatherhood of God—there you have the whole theology of Jesus* " ; but it was equally that of many a godly Jew in Jesus' day. It

---

[1] CCLXXIX, ii, 202 *ff*., gives numerous texts.

[2] *Pirké Aboth*, iii, 5, cites Deut. xiv. 1 : " *Ye are the children of Jahweh, your God.*" In 2 Sam. vii. 14 Jahweh says of David : " *I will be his father and he shall be my son.*" *Cf.* Jer. ii. 27 ; iii. 4 ; Mal. i. 6, which places the two feelings of the pious Jew for his God side by side : " *A son honoureth his father, and a servant his master : if then I be a father, where is mine honour ? and if I be a master, where is my fear ?* " *Cf.* also Ps. lxxxix. 25–6 : " *I will set his hand also on the sea, and his right hand on the rivers. He shall cry unto me, Thou art my father, my rock and my salvation.*" Isa. i. 2 ; xlv. 11 ; lxiii. 8, 16.

[3] *Pirké Aboth*, v, 20, attributes the following exhortation to Jehuda ben Tema, who lived in the second half of the second century A.D. : " *Be as strong as a leopard and as swift as an eagle, as agile as a deer and as strong as a lion, to do the will of thy father who is in heaven.*" In spite of the late date I see no reason for postulating Christian influence.

[4] CCLXVII, i, 401 *ff*., points out that the first Christians did not regard this notion of the fatherhood of God as peculiar to Jesus.

[5] CCCI, 76.

was the common custom to invoke the *Father who is in heaven*.[1]
Jesus did not instil into these words a new conception of God,
but rather a new religious attitude, which emphasized one of
the elements of the original conception and gave it first place
in the prayer.[2]

No reference has yet been made to the discussions which
have arisen concerning the problem of the *sources* of these
hypostases in which the influence of all the neighbours of Israel
has been claimed.   It is difficult to give direct proof of such
external influences because the immediate contacts which would
furnish us with the only certain proof of their existence are the
hardest to demonstrate.   Clearly the hypostases in question
were the products of the general idea of the transcendence of
God, but this idea itself was not properly Jewish, and is probably of the same origin as the method employed to reconcile
the idea of a transcendent God with the need to maintain the
reality of his activity in the world.   But the Jewish hypostases
had too much in common with those of the Greeks and the
Persians to have been completely independent of them.   Persian speculation concerning the *Amesha Spentas* (the " immortal
Spirits ")[3] led to such concepts as the *Spenta Armaiti* (the
" Holy Awe "), resembling the Jewish *Wisdom*, and the *Spenta
Mainyu* (the " Holy Spirit "), which may well have exerted
some influence on the *Ruach*[4] as did the Greek *Sophia* and
Logos.   This probability is greatly strengthened by our certain knowledge of Persian influence on the demonology and
angelology of the Jews, a case in which we can, for once,
demonstrate the actual fact of contact.

[1] **LI**, 461, owns that this is *one of the most admirable characteristics
of Rabbinical Judaism*, but at the same time insists that it is no more
than a *metaphor* or *substitution*, like the *Heavens*, the *Place*, the *Name*.
The impartial reader will find such an interpretation hard to reconcile
with the texts.
    [2] **CCLXXIX**, ii, 211.
    [3] A. Pettazzoni, *La religione di Zarathustra nella storia religiosa dell'
Iran*, Bologna, undated.   *Cf.* Index to the words *Ameshaspenta*, *Spenta
Armatay*, *Spenta Mainyu* ; Huart, *La Perse antique*, 1925, the index to
the same words.   Söderblom, *Manuel d'hist. des relig.*, 1925, 370 of the
French translation.
    [4] Volz, *Der Geist Gottes*, Tübingen, 1910, 175 ff.

CHAPTER II

ANGELS AND DEMONS

I

ANGELS

THERE were angels in Jewish belief before there were demons.[1] The early religion of Israel provided Jahweh with a following of celestial beings, ready to serve him and to carry out his commands, and these *Bene-Elohim* are referred to on several occasions in the Old Testament. Genesis (vi. 1 *ff.*) relates that some of them found the daughters of men fair, and that their unnatural union peopled the earth with giants. Isaiah (vi. 2) speaks of the six-winged seraphim who hovered above the throne of God, singing his praise. And in 1 Kings (xxii. 19) the Seer, Micaiah, has a vision of Jahweh on his throne with "*all the host of heaven*" on either side.

However, these early references are few in number. It was not until the Exile that angels acquired an increased importance and definite functions in Jewish belief. They arose in answer to the same desire for intermediaries between God and man, which we have already seen to have given rise to the hypostases. For instance, we notice that the prophets of the Exile and of the Return represent angels as intermediaries,[2] and as interpreters [3] of prophecy.

As soon as the Jews began to speculate about the nature of the angels, they gave them the general rôle of Jahweh's agents always ready to carry out his purposes. Hence they increased the number of the angels, gave them special functions, and arranged them as a hierarchy of individuals with personal names. In fact they visualized them as an immense train of servants and courtiers like those which thronged the courts of

---

[1] Bibliography : **CCLII**, 374 *ff.* ; **CCLXXXII**, 224 *ff.* ; **LXXV**, Index under *Engel* ; **CCLXVI**, i, 57 *ff.* ; **EB**, art. *Engel* ; **CCLIII**, 320 *ff.* ; **LXII** ; **LXVII**, 280 *ff.* ; **CCLXXIX**, i, 401 *ff.*

[2] Ezek. ix. 2 *ff.*

[3] Ezek. xl. 3 *ff.* ; xliii. 6 *ff.* ; Zech. i. 8 ; ii. 1 *ff.*, etc. ; many passages in Dan. : iv. 13 ; vii. 16 ; viii. 13, etc.

Oriental monarchs, such as the King of Persia. There is a passage in Daniel (vii. 10) which gives an idea of the teeming multitudes pictured by these visionaries : " *A fiery stream issued and came forth from before him : thousand thousands ministered unto him : and ten thousand times ten thousand stood before him*," which means that their numbers are beyond conception. In the same way the *twelve legions of angels* in Matthew (xxvi. 53), which God would have sent to Jesus' aid if he had asked for them, are a figure of speech standing for an innumerable host ; and the Apocryphal books of the Old Testament picture the world as full of them.[1]

The angels were only saved from appearing as a vast undistinguished mass by being divided into classes and categories, each with its special attributes. This was the real innovation of the post-exilic angelology borrowed, however, from Mazdeism. Thus the celestial army had its leaders, known to us as *archangels ;* some authorities gave their number as four, others as seven.[2] In general, opinion favoured the second hypothesis, a bias which may have had other reasons besides the special mystic significance of the figure seven. For instance, the reader may recall that according to the Book of Esther there were *seven* eunuchs who ministered before the throne of the King of Persia, and *seven* princes " *who saw the King's face.*" [3] The archangels were naturally given names, the most celebrated being *Raphael, Gabriel* and *Michael.*[4] It is Michael who seems to have held the position of Prince of the angels. But besides the archangels, who formed the staff of the angelic army, there were the inferior ranks of *Kerubim, Seraphim, Ophannim*, and the troops were further grouped according to their function under names suggesting *force, power, action*, which are more familiar to us in their Greek form. These are the *Powers, Principalities, Thrones*, etc., of the New Testament.[5]

All these angels, in their varying degrees, are the ministers

---

[1] References in **CCLII**, 374.

[2] On the number four, see Bk. of Jubilees, i, 27 and 29 ; ii, 1 and 3, etc. ; Test. of the Twelve Patriarchs : *Test. of Levi*, 3 ; *Test. of Judah*, 25 ; Enoch ix. 1 ; xl. 2, etc. *Cf*. Rev. iv. 6, the four winged beasts. On the number seven, see Tobit xii. 15 ; Enoch lxxxi. 5 ; xc. 21 ; Test. of the Twelve Patriarchs : *Test. of Levi*, 8. *Cf*. Rev. i. 4, the seven Spirits which are before God's throne ; i. 20 ; iii. 1 ; iv. 5 ; viii. 2.

[3] Esther i. 10 and 14.

[4] These names are given in Tobit and Daniel. The Apocryphal books also mention Phanuel, Uriel, Raguel, and Sariel or Sarakael. For an account of their appearance and functions, *cf*. **CCLII**, 376 and 381 *ff*.

[5] Ἀρχαί, κυριότητες, ἐξουσίαι, δυνάμεις, θρόνοι. They are frequently referred to in the Pauline Epistles. See Rom. viii. 38 ; 1 Cor. xv. 24 ; Col. i. 16 ; ii. 10 and 15, etc.

and messengers of God, the instruments of his will. The arch-angels and the higher ranks of angels form his guard of honour and his court, the priests of his celestial temple, his royal musicians and his close associates. The rest are the com-municating links between God and the world, and above all between God and man. It is their business both to convey divine revelations to human ears, and to bear the prayers of earth to the throne of Jahweh, where they sometimes even intercede for humanity. In consequence it becomes their special duty to watch over mankind. This protective vigilance is twofold. They exercise it, *firstly*, over humanity in its social group; thus each nation has its particular angel, at once patron and protector, and it may even happen that two national angels may come to blows in the interests of their respective flocks,[1] like the Homeric gods before Troy. This is because they have in fact replaced the old tribal gods, well known to early Jahwism, and that they satisfy that old polytheistic instinct which still lingers in the hearts of the Jewish people, in spite of all their professions of the purest monotheism.[2] *Secondly*, the angels watch over individuals, and the theory that this benevolent supervision is the special function of certain spirits leads naturally to the notion of the guardian angel.[3]

But man is not the only terrestrial care of the angels. They are concerned with physical phenomena, with elements and seasons, with the whole system of nature. In the picture of the Creation given in the *Book of Jubilees*,[4] God is shown creating *the angel of the spirit of fire, the angel of the spirit of wind*, those of *snow* and *hail* and *ice* and *clouds*, of *darkness*, of *thunder*, and *lightning*, and *heat*, and *cold*, of *winter*, and *spring*. Revela-tion (vii. 1) describes the angels of the winds in action, holding back the four winds of the earth; in xiv. 18 the angel " *that hath power over fire* " appears ; in xvi. 5 the voice of " *the angel of the waters* " is heard ; and in xix. 17–18 there is a reference to " *an angel standing in the sun* " who calls together the birds of prey to " *the great supper of God, to eat the flesh of Kings.*" Enoch (lxv. 5) speaks of an angel who was put in charge of the spring producing lead and tin.[5] The conception underlying all these passages combines a sort of animism with the personi-fication of the elements of the forces of nature and the seasons. It is a relic of the deification of natural phenomena, a relic

[1] Dan. x. 13 *ff.*   [2] Texts in **CCLII**, 379 *ff.*
[3] These guardian angels are called *watchers* (ἄγγελοι ἐγρηγόροι).   *Cf.* **CCLIII**, 322 and n. 2, 323 *ff.*
[4] *Cf.* **CCLXIX**, ii, 41.   [5] **CCLIII**, 380 ; **CCLXVI**, i.

which remained as a stumbling-block for the unwary, particularly, as we shall see, in the religious environment which produced Saint Paul, and in which he lived and worked.[1] There is a tendency, for instance, to identify a star with the angel of that star, a process which can be continued to the point at which a *demonistic* and *dynamistic* conception of the universe is reached. [2]

Whether these angelic nature-spirits owe anything to Greek or Egyptian influence is a question concerning which I do not care to hazard an opinion.[3]

In *orthodox Judaism* the angels remained God's ministers, his agents and ambassadors in all the multitudinous duties arising in the course of the government of the Universe. Further, it was acknowledged that these superhuman beings, created in the same way as men, were allowed some share in the secrets of the Deity, but that the ultimate mysteries remained sealed to them.[4]

Naturally the angelic characteristics remain somewhat indeterminate. They are free from the burden of human needs, they have attained immortality, they are penetrated by and suffused with the divine radiance. Sometimes they are represented as winged,[5] but as a rule they are pictured as young men in white and shining raiment. This luminosity is characteristic of them, being often the sign by which their presence is revealed. Enoch (lxi. 12) is fully justified in calling them " *spirits* of light." [6]

II

Demons

If external influences from Iran, Egypt and Greece helped to determine and to amplify the Jewish angelology, they certainly did not originate it, since it existed effectively before

---

[1] See 1 Cor. viii. 5, ὥσπερ εἰσὶν θεοὶ πολλοὶ and the account of the part played by the *elements of the world* (στοιχεῖα τοῦ κόσμου) in Gal. iv. 3 and 9 ; Col. ii. 8 and 20.

[2] **CCLII**, 381.   *Cf.* Reitzenstein, *Poimandres*, Leipzig, 1904, p. 72.

[3] **CCLV**, 92 *ff.*

[4] It may be recalled that this idea is expressed in Mark xiii. 32, the famous passage which says that God alone knows " that hour," and that the angels, in particular, do not share this knowledge.

[5] Enoch lxi. 1.

[6] In the East, divine manifestations are characterized by dazzling light : the Sanskrit *deva* means " shining."   *Cf.* Max Muller, *Essai sur l'hist. des religions* (2nd edit.) (French translation by G. Perrot), 1874, p. 33.   On the importance of light in all descriptions of supernatural phenomena, and in Jewish mystical terminology, see **CCL**, ii, 169.

these influences made themselves felt in Israel. But the same cannot be said about demonology, which achieved an almost boundless development during this time.[1]

In the early Judaism of the Old Testament there is no question of infernal powers ; *as an element of religion they did not exist.* God was the author of evil as of good. But a serious difficulty arises out of Leviticus (xvi. 7–10), where, in the cere-monial for the Day of Atonement, it says that Aaron is to take two goats and set them at the door of the tent of meeting, and then " *cast lots upon them, one lot for Jahweh, and the other lot for Azazel.*" The goat on which the lot falls for Jahweh is to be sacrificed, and the other is to be let loose in the wilderness " for Azazel." Who, or what, is Azazel ? The question has been widely discussed. Possibly he is to be looked upon as the prince of the *seirim* (= goats), spirits of the desert, to whom sacrifices were offered in the pre-exilic period.[2] If this ex-planation could be accepted, the question would arise whether the passage was interpolated later into Leviticus. But the nature of Azazel remains uncertain. Late Judaism may have identified Azazel with Satan, but such a process of assimilation throws no light on his origin, which must be connected with folklore. The *Targum of Pseudo-Jonathan* makes the name refer to some place in the desert, a view which is accepted by a number of Jewish commentators. I am inclined to regard him as the spirit or god of the desert, for, if he had been the Evil One originally, he would have been mentioned elsewhere in the *Torah* and the *Nebiim.* The serpent of Genesis, which plays such an important part in mythology and in the Christian ethic, was completely ignored by Judaism. From the point of view of folklore, the story related in Genesis iii. has nothing to do with the legend of the Evil One—the Adversary—and it is not in early Judaism that the identification of the Serpent with the Devil is to be found.[3]

It should be noted that in the passage from 1 Kings (xxii. 19 ff.) referred to above, when a spirit appears before Jahweh and suggests that he should deceive the prophets of Ahab with false messages, the spirit in question is one of God's ministers, a member of the heavenly host, not a demon. But as he is given the definite article (*ha ruach* = " the spirit ") the inference is that he was already set apart for a particular

---

[1] **CCLII**, 385 *ff.* ; **CCLXXXII**, 227 *ff.* ; **LXXV**, Index under *Engel* and *Zauberei* ; **EB**, art. *Demons* ; **CCLIII**, 331 *ff.* ; **CCLXXII**, 290 *ff.*

[2] **EB**, art. *Azazel* and *Satyrs.*

[3] **CCLXXX**, 240 *ff.* Cf. Frazer, *Folklore in the Old Testament*, London, 1919, 1, chap. ii, 45 *ff.* It is only in Rev. xii. 9 that the Devil is identified with " the old serpent, which deceiveth the whole world."

purpose, namely, that which he was prepared to do in this instance—to tell lies and do harm. In the last resort, however, the idea of forces of evil waging perpetual war against those of good presupposes a *dualism* which is entirely foreign to Jewish thought. It is Mazdean, and, in fact, the very basis of Zoroastrian Mazdeism.

Even *Satan*, when he appears in the Book of Job (i. 6 *ff.* ; ii. 1 *ff.*), is not yet a demon. His place is among the sons of God who surround the heavenly throne, and when he puts Job to the test, it is with the consent and authorization of Jahweh that he does so. Here also he is named with the article, *ha Satan*, the *Adversary*, and though he may be the common foe of mankind, it is more likely that he is merely the adversary of Job on this particular occasion. *In any case he is not the Adversary of God.* There is no essential difference at this stage between Satan and the Spirit of 1 Kings (xxii. 21). He is the *angel of Jahweh* (*maleach Jahweh*), while he is engaged in executing the divine wrath.[1]

But subsequently there appears a tendency to find a separate personification for that will to evil, which from being part of God's omnipotence, is gradually dissociated from him, and finally excluded altogether. It was natural to explain evil as the work of evil spirits, and to represent these as an army, with its own leader, arrayed against the hosts of God. And since manifestations of evil in this world are more striking and more numerous than those of good, it was also natural that this demonology should end by assuming a much greater importance in Jewish belief than the angelology. This is precisely what had happened by the time of Jesus. Everywhere the people saw indications of the work of evil spirits ; every misfortune, every illness, and particularly, under the name of *possession*, all disorders of the nervous system were ascribed to them. Josephus writes a good deal about demons, and thinks about them even more.[2] And the Apocryphal books of the Old Testament are similarly full of a demonology which, however confused and hard to unravel, is at least a proof of the power it exercised over the imaginations of the Jews about the beginning of the Christian era.

The theory that *the demons are really fallen angels* comes to our notice first in the Book of Enoch (vi. 2 *ff.*). The story of their fall is clearly based on the passage from Genesis (vi. 2–4)

---

[1] For instance, in Num. xxii. 22 and 32. *Maleach* = ἄγγελος = messenger.

[2] At the same time he knew how to drive them away : Jos., *B.J.*, vi, 3. *Cf.* CCLXXX, 249.

which speaks of the union of the *Bene-Elohim* with the daughters of men, a passage which is here re-interpreted to signify the fall of the spirits who allowed themselves to be seduced by the lure of mortal flesh. Hence the demons (*sedim*) would be originally *sons of God* who had turned to evil, unworthy offspring. There are doubtless other explanations of their origin, influenced partly by the Greek *daimones*[1] ; but such complications do not concern us here.

As for the numbers of these evil spirits, Enoch (vi. 5) tells us that there were 200 of them at first, and that they were organized in groups of ten under a single leader (vi. 7) ; but they begat many children, and their numbers soon rivalled, and even surpassed, those of the angels. Their leader is variously referred to as *Satan, Belial, Massema, Sammael, Malkira, Beelzebub*, and *Azazel*, and there is much uncertainty as to his designation.[2] Their *kingdom* is one of evil and injustice; nevertheless man owes to them some of his most useful knowledge, the art of metal-working and of forging weapons, the secrets of personal adornment, and the rules and practices of magic in all its branches,[3] that is to say, all the devices by which God's work can be undermined and his will opposed.

Satan is now God's Adversary, and the world is full of his demons, who are in ceaseless conflict with the celestial host. In the Apocryphal books he is the principle of evil, Sin personified, and therefore the Tempter, the Enemy of all human goodness, the Prince of Darkness in opposition to the God of Light.[4] He is especially dangerous by reason of his powers of transformation, and of appearing in many deceptive forms, often disguising himself, for instance, as one of the gods of the Gentiles. He is the father of death, because through his successful temptation of Eve, he was the cause of Adam's disobedience, which frustrated God's original purpose and deprived mankind of the gift of immortality intended for them. It is Wisdom (ii. 23 *ff.*) which describes this appalling calamity : " *God created man to be immortal, and made him in his own image. Nevertheless*

---

[1] For instance, E. Hommel maintains (in *Der Name und die Sagen des Jordan* . . ., in *Journal of the Society of Oriental Research*, xi, 3–4, Oct., 1927, p. 192) that the myth of the fall of Satan-Lucifer, the *bright star, son of the morning* of Isa. xiv. 12 (that is to say, the morning star), is related to the Phœnician legend, which reappears in Greece, of Phaeton-Eridanos, who fell from the sky into the land of Hermon. It is an hypothesis, but the fact that Enoch vi. 6 locates the fall of the angels in the same region does not necessarily confirm it.

[2] **CCLII**, 389.　　　　　　　　　　[3] References in **CCLII**, 387.

[4] This opposition of φῶς to σκότος is especially marked in the Testament of the Twelve Patriarchs. *Cf.* **CCLIII**, 334.

through envy of the devil came death into the world . . ." Thus
was the unfortunate serpent of the Creation story transformed
into the infamous One.

Indeed the religion of Israel develops into a thorough-going
dualism,[1] in which the forces of good and evil, darkness and
light wage a perpetual warfare. Everywhere Satan appears
opposed to God as his *adversary* and in truth his *opposite*
(ἀντικείμενος), as the Mazdean system opposes Angra-mainyu
to Ahura-Mazda. And on earth, in the world of men, it is
Satan who reigns.[2] The seed of evil which he sowed in the
heart of our first ancestor, Adam, continues to bear fruit among
Adam's sons.[3] It is true that his victims possess effective
weapons of defence against him ; namely, the whole art of
exorcism. But its use entails the knowledge and application
of the rules. Those who possessed this valuable secret were
held in great esteem about the time of Jesus, and were frequently called upon to exercise their powers.[4] From the
evidence of the Gospels we learn that evil spirits might be
subdued by threats and banished by the word of *authority* ;
the exorciser informed them, on behalf of God or some powerful
angel, of the awful punishment which would overtake them if
they did not immediately depart.[5] There was also virtue in
the name of a patriarch or in that of Solomon, who was reputed
to have been highly skilled in this salutary art. But it was
necessary first of all to identify the particular demon who was
causing the trouble, for some had greater powers of resistance
than others, and each had to be addressed by his own special
formula. There were probably collections of useful methods,
manuals for the would-be exorcist, in fact a whole mass of
literature, which would in itself be sufficient proof of the importance of the demonic element in Judaism in the time of Jesus.[6]

However, though the demons tormented mankind, and
seemed to be the triumphant rulers of the world, their empire
was destined to end. God, in his own good time, would abolish

---

[1] **CCLXXVIII,** ii, 95 ; 106.

[2] John xii. 31 ; xiv. 30 : ὁ ἄρχων τοῦ κόσμου τούτου ; 2 Cor. iv. 4 :
ὁ θεὸς τοῦ αἰῶνος τούτου.

[3] 4 Esdras iv. 27 *ff.* ; xiv. 20.

[4] Matt. xii. 27 gives the impression that the Pharisees made a speci-
ality of this kind of work, but the passage should be regarded rather as
hostile propaganda than as a piece of historical information.

[5] *Cf.* Jer. x. 11 : " *Thus shall ye say unto them, The gods that have not
made the heavens and the earth shall perish from the earth and from under
the heavens.*" This verse is in Aramaic, although the rest of the text is
Hebrew. It may very well represent part of a formula for exorcizing
demons.

[6] **CCLII,** 392 ; **LXXV,** iii, 413 *ff.*

for ever the powers of evil and of the evil ones, and establish once for all his direct dominion over the universe and all his creatures. When the time of the *coming Kingdom* was close at hand, the hosts of Satan would enjoy a period of supreme power, but their triumph would be swiftly followed by total annihilation.[1]

But the prototype of this vast drama, which unfolds itself in time till it ends on the threshold of the eternal Kingdom of God, is to be found in Mazdeism, and was borrowed from Mazdeism. The Jewish demonology described above was, as a whole and in its essence, the result of contamination during the Persian period. Those Greek elements which are conspicuous in the Judæo-Alexandrian demonology[2] remained secondary in Palestine and only affected details of the system. It is significant that the first Jewish text to give an instructive picture of demonology in Israel is the story of Tobit, which shows close connexions with Mesopotamia. It is still more striking that the name of the horrible demon who appears in this book as the murderer of the seven unfortunate husbands of Sarah, the daughter of Raguel (Tobit iii. 7–8), is called *Asmodeus*. Now this Asmodeus is the Parsee *Eshem-der*, and the Zend *Aêshma-daêva*; according to the *Avesta*,[3] he was the demon of lust and the most dangerous of all the evil ones. We have here, so to speak, one of the bridges by way of which Mesopotamian and Iranian influences made their way into Palestine.[4]

These influences were responsible for the introduction, or at least the widespread development, of beliefs and superstitions which had very important practical consequences. For the Jews of Jesus' day Palestine was a land peopled by good or evil spirits. They were constantly aware of their presence, sometimes as visible apparitions, but more often through the effects, for good or ill, of their ceaseless activity. A man who claimed to speak in God's name and to prepare his ways was known as a true recipient of the *sign of Jahweh* by his intimacy with angels, and still more by his authority over demons.

The *dynamis* or special *capacity* which Jesus was said to have bestowed on the Apostles before sending them out on their mission consisted in " *power and authority over all evil spirits, and to cure diseases* " (ἐξουσία ἐπὶ πάντα τὰ δαιμόνια καὶ

---

[1] References in **CCLII**, 393.   [2] **CCLXXX**, 351 *ff*.
[3] Max Muller, *Essais sur l'hist. des religions* (2nd edit.), p. 208.   *Cf.* **EB**, art. *Asmodeus*.
[4] **CCLXXVIII**, ii, 80.

νόσους θεραπεύειν).[1] There were doubtless still some sceptics among the Sadducees, but it was not the Sadducees who enjoyed the greatest reputation for piety in Israel, or possessed the greatest influence among the people. As for Jesus himself, there can be no doubt that he was born and bred and lived out his life in the midst of a threatening cloud of hostile spirits, and that belief in their existence and in their activities was one of the formative elements in his religious experience. And this belief has remained active during the whole development of Christianity, which may even be said, in the last analysis, to be founded on it, for what is more fundamental in the Christian life than the perpetual sense of struggle between the power of God and the power of Satan, both in man himself and in the world ? It was through the persistence of this attitude that the Christian faith, the origins of which we are about to examine, remained so essentially Jewish.

[1] Luke ix. 1. Since all illnesses are presumed to be the work of demons, the power of healing is only a special case of the first *charisma*. (The word *charisma* means a gift or privilege bestowed by God or by the Holy Spirit.)

CHAPTER III

THE NATURE AND DESTINY OF MAN [1]

THE chief prize at stake in the battle of Good and Evil is
man. He is tormented by demons who try to make him
their tool by causing him to commit wicked and sinful acts,
while the divine instruction of the *Torah*, confirmed by the
wisdom of the Masters, guide his feet in the paths of virtue.
It is necessary, therefore, that we should consider the ethical
and anthropological views, which the Jews of Jesus' day held
with regard to the nature and instincts of man and his destiny
both in this world and beyond the grave.

I

THE NATURE OF MAN

In the words of Genesis ii. 7, "*Jahweh God formed man of
the dust of the ground; he breathed into his nostrils the breath
of life, and man became a living soul.*" Thus man consists in
essence of a material body and of a spiritual element which
may be termed his vital principle and which comes to him
directly from God. It is on this premise that all Jewish theories
of man's nature are based.

A superficial view of man and his life does not suggest any
difference between his nature and origin and that of the animals.
Genesis ii. 19 makes the statement, "*Out of the ground Jahweh
God formed every beast of the field and every fowl of the air,*" and
although there is no mention of their receiving the breath of
life in their nostrils as man did, it is a not unwarrantable assumption that the redactor found it in his source and suppressed it,
in the belief that the breath of God had raised man to a special
and unique position of honour. The name of the first man,

---

[1] **CCLII,** § 34 ; *Die Vorstellung von Mensch und Sünde* and the Index
under *Auferstehung* and *Seele*; **CCLXXX,** 360 *ff.*; Charles, *A Critical
History of the Doctrine of a Future Life in Israel, in Judaism and in
Christianity*, 1899, and **EB,** art. *Eschatology*, by the same author;
CCLIII, 399 *ff.*; **LXVII,** 317–22 ; 342–50.

Adam, emphasizes his connexion with the earth from which he was formed, for *Adamah* means " cultivable soil." So that man is primarily *matter*—in this case *flesh*—and in the Bible the term *flesh* is often used to denote mankind,[1] as it is also in the later texts from which the greater part of this account is drawn.[2] And the fact that the expression *all flesh* (Gen. vi. 12 *ff*.) is often used to include all the living creatures of the animal kingdom is further evidence that *as far as his body goes* man is not essentially different from the animals. But since Jahweh summoned them all before man so that he might name them (Gen. ii. 19), man exercises a potential, if not an actual authority over them, since the giving of a name is the sign of domination.

The obvious tendency among the Jews to emphasize the view that man is *earth, matter, flesh*, is of importance on account of the special power of Satan over the material world ; the more firmly man is held in the bonds of *matter* the further he is removed from God, who is *Spirit*. However, he has also received the breath of God which made him a *living soul* (*nephesh chayyah*). The meaning is doubtless that by the will of God he became a *living being*, nevertheless the expression lays special stress on the spiritual nature of the vital principle. Besides, the word *soul* can only be used to translate *nephesh* if it is first relieved of all the metaphysical implications of the Greek *psyche* (ψυχή) and given its earlier sense of *anima animans*. The root idea is that of *breathing*. It was with respect to the analysis and definition of this non-material vital principle in the nature of man, that Jewish thought underwent the most striking development and was most affected by foreign influences, as was to be expected.

It is well established that the early Hebrews took the word *nephesh* to include both the source of *physical life* and the *principle of spiritual life*, which would not be very far from the popular conception of the *soul* today. They were *dichotomists*. In fact they seem to have carried the process so far that they saw in man two beings, a *corporal* and a *spiritual*, although the latter occasionally appeared in visible form, and constituted a sort of *double* of the former.[3] Normally the two would be so welded together that they would appear to be undifferentiated—every detail of their lives would correspond and synchronize perfectly, so that they would seem to be in a state of symbiosis. But occasionally the potential separation

---

[1] References in **CCLXXXII**, 143.

[2] Texts in **CCLII**, 407. The expression *flesh and blood* is sometimes used (Enoch xv. 4), and reappears in the New Testament (Matt. xvi. 17 ; Gal. i. 16, etc.).   [3] **LVI**, 43 *ff*.

actually took place, either finally, in death, or temporarily, as for instance in states of ecstasy and transport, which might set the *nephesh* free momentarily from its envelope of flesh. Thus whilst Ezekiel's body remained in Babylon, his double visited Jerusalem under the conduct of an angel who bore him up by a lock of his hair.[1] And thus, too, the apostle Paul was transported to the third heaven without being able to say afterwards whether or not his body accompanied his spirit in its flight (2 Cor. xii. 2–4).

The belief that under certain circumstances a living being could thus split into two led the Jews to suppose that the principle of physical life was in some way separate and distinct from the spiritual element, which is the *double*. But we must naturally not expect to find in their ideas the clarity and precision, above all the invariability, that would be demanded of a psychological or anthropological theory today. It seems, for instance, that in Jesus' time the human personality was often thought of as a *trichotomy*, in which man consisted of a *body* (*basar*), a *soul* (*nephesh*) and a *spirit*, the vital principle (*ruach*).[2] When he died the *ruach* returned to God and the *nephesh* went down into Sheol.[3]

Originally, the blood was the seat of soul, or life. Thus, in Genesis ix. 4, it is forbidden to eat the blood of animals, "*But the flesh with the life thereof shall ye not eat.*"[4] Moreover, the *double* lives in the blood. This explains Jahweh's words to Cain in Genesis iv. 10 : "*What hast thou done ? Behold the voice of thy brother's blood which crieth unto me from the ground.*" This is no mere figure of speech. The blood cries out, that is to say, the soul, or double of the victim, calls for vengeance (Job xxiv. 12) and will continue to demand it unless someone will throw earth on the spilt blood, to stifle its cries. "*O earth,*" we read in Job xvi. 18, "*cover not thou my blood, and let my cry have no resting place.*"

There are other words besides *nephesh* which are sometimes used to designate both the vital principle and at the same time the seat of all the functions and emotions of the spiritual being in man. It may be called *ruach*, the *spirit*, the *breath* ; or *neshamah*, the *respiration* or *breath* in a more physical sense ; or *lêb*, *lêbab*, the *heart*. In time the terms developed slight differences of meaning, but these do not concern us here.[5] The

---

[1] Ezek. viii. 3 *ff.*

[2] This conception is supported by the second version of the Creation Story, which occurs in Gen. ii. 7 ; vi. 17 ; vii. 15. *Cf.* Ps. civ. 29–30.

[3] **EB**, art. *Eschatology*, § 20.

[4] *Cf.* Lev. xvii. 11 and 14.   [5] Texts in **CCLXXXII**, 145 *ff.*

important point is that they all referred to man's spiritual self
in contrast with the *body*, to that vital principle with which
God had endowed Adam by breathing into his nostrils, and
which was the source of his whole spiritual and affective life.
It was only the *trichotomic* view which divided man into *body*,
soul and *breath*. The distinction is not generally very clear.

The only way in which the Jews could think of man was
as a union of these two principles, the material and the spiritual.
For them human life was necessarily and essentially *twofold*.
That is to say, that as God created Adam *complete* in his own
image, so the sons of Adam's seed were complete beings in their
father's image. The notion of the pre-existence of the soul,
of a reservoir of souls awaiting the moment of their incarnation,
was quite alien to the thought of ancient Israel. The Jews
could only conceive of man in his totality, as the vital union
of flesh and soul.

It is none the less easy to see how the influence of Persian
theories of good and evil and of the distinction between *matter*,
which was bad, and *spirit*, which was fundamentally good, and
of the Greek anthropologists with their discourse of a soul
whose fate was independent of the body that had housed it,
led the Jews to think of the *nephesh* as a more definite entity,
incorporating all that was divine and eternal in man. Indeed,
to reach such a standpoint they had to do little more than
clarify and develop the ideas which they already held. It was
a view which certainly did not find favour with all the Jews
of Jesus' day, but there were many among them who believed
that the soul, individualized and regarded as a responsible
moral agent, had its own independent existence and destiny.
Josephus [1] says of the Pharisees : " *They believe that souls are
endowed with immortal power* (ἀθανατον τε ἰσχὺν ταὶς ψυχαίς)
*and that somewhere under the earth rewards and punishments will
be meted out to them, according to whether they have loved vice or
virtue. The former will be condemned to perpetual imprisonment,
but the others will be allowed to return to life.*" The last sentence
does not refer to metempsychosis, as might be supposed, but
to the resurrection. [2] The same writer says elsewhere [3] that

---

[1] Jos., *Ant.*, xviii, 1, 3.

[2] However, CCLXXVII, 255, suggests that the Jewish belief in the
resurrection may have been based on the doctrine of metempsychosis.
The author submits that instead of accepting metempsychosis in its usual
form, as a general law by which the soul, passing from body to body,
perpetually begins its life afresh, the Jews interpreted it as *a unique event
which would occur once for all* in the life history of every man. It is an
ingenious theory, and not to be regarded as more than an hypothesis.

[3] Jos., *B.J.*, ii, 8, 14.

the Pharisees hold that the souls of all the dead will return to earth in another body. That is to say, that the soul is the permanent element in man, which survives bodily death, and which will some day form the centre and reason for the reconstitution of the personality which will therefore still be the same, though clothed in other flesh. But the wicked souls will remain imprisoned in Gehenna. Josephus adds [1] that the Sadducees do not share these beliefs, denying both the survival of souls and the retribution which they will undergo in the next life. They hold that the soul comes to an end with the body.[2]

The same authority states [3] that it is the Essenes who have given this doctrine (at once Greek and Persian in tendency) its clearest and most complete form. The soul is immortal (τὰς δὲ ψυχὰς ἀθανάτους ἀεί), and had its pre-existence in the most tenuous region of the ether (ἐκ τοῦ λεπτοτάτου φοιτώσας αἰθέρος). The souls are united with the flesh by the power of sensual love, and are there held imprisoned; but as soon as they are freed from the fetters of desire they joyfully take flight back to the heights of heaven. When the doctrine reaches this stage of development, the soul does really become the important and permanent element in man, and its destiny alone is of importance. Though, as I have said, this idea was not fundamentally Jewish, it was nevertheless one which the Jews could accept without hesitation.

The fact that man was made in the image of God (Gen. i. 26–7; ix. 6) gave him a great advantage; and the Creation stories suggest that the redactors are careful to emphasize the unique dignity conferred on man by this signal privilege. It raises him so far above all other creatures that God is forced to acknowledge that the animal kingdom cannot provide Adam with a help meet for him (Gen. ii. 20). That is why Eve is created from Adam's own body (Gen. ii. 21 *ff.*). No one doubts that man is superior to God's other creatures, or that the world was made for his use [4]; but it is not easy to find a satisfactory interpretation of man's likeness to God.

According to Wisdom ii. 23, " *God created man to be immortal,*

---

[1] Jos., *B.J.*, loc. cit.

[2] Jos., *Ant.*, xviii, 1, 4. New Testament references to the Sadducees give the same impression of their views. *Cf.* Mark xii. 18; Matt. xxii. 23; Luke xx. 27; Acts xxiii. 8.

[3] Jos., *B.J.*, ii, 8, 11.

[4] Wisdom ix. 1 *ff.* : " *Thou who hast made all things with thy word, and ordained man through thy wisdom, that he should have dominion over the creatures which thou hast made.*" *Cf.* x. 12; Ecclus. xvii. 2 : " *He . . . gave him power over the things that are in the earth.*"

and made him in his own image."   This explanation, which may
very well have been influenced by Greek spiritualism, argues
that it is man's immortal soul which makes him godlike.   But
his gratifying resemblance to the Creator could also be explained
by his authority over the animals, or again by his capacity for
thinking and knowing, and above all by his power to distinguish
between good and evil [1] ; supposing these characteristics to be
peculiar to the human species.   However, these various points
of view are not necessarily incompatible.   Taken together, they
afford a general explanation, namely, that God has endowed
man with exceptional qualities as compared with those which
distinguish his other creatures, and that these divine gifts are
the proof of his resemblance to his Creator.

But as the conception of God becomes more transcendental,
the conception of man is correspondingly lowered, and the
doctrine gathers strength that man is irrevocably doomed to
sin, or as Saint Paul puts it, that man dwells in *sinful flesh*,[2]
so that even though God has enabled him to distinguish between
good and evil, and endowed him with a will, which is free, at
least in theory, to choose between them, and though it may
be true that he has within him two tendencies (*yetzer*) which
urge him in opposite directions,[3] yet in reality it is his passions
which control him, inclining his will towards evil almost in
spite of himself.   Ben-Sira makes a vigorous attack on the
excuse that man is predestined to sin : " *Say not thou, my sin
cometh from God ; for he doeth not the thing that he hateth.   Say
not thou, He hath caused me to err ; for he hath no need of the
sinful man.*" [4]   No doubt this doctrine, with its encouragement
of irresponsibility, did not lack adherents in the days of Jesus
Ben-Sira.[5]   Josephus goes so far as to claim that the Pharisees
accepted it, though in the absence of any supporting evidence,
his statement cannot be considered conclusive.   But he can
scarcely have been mistaken about the existence of such an
attitude, even if he is mistaken in his attribution of it.   It is
only the outcome and logical conclusion of the observation
recorded in Wisdom (iv. 12) which appears to be quite in keeping
with current opinion : " *The bewitching of naughtiness doth
obscure that which is honest ; and the frenzy of concupiscence
doth undermine the simple mind.*"   Man's soul is depicted as
the scene of a battle between good and evil spirits, a battle in
which the latter are generally victorious.[6]

[1] Ecclus. xvii. 7 : " *He filled them with knowledge and understanding,
and shewed them good and evil.*"

[2] *Cf.* Rom. vii. 20, 23–5 ; viii. 1–4.   [3] **IX**, 94.

[4] Ecclus. xv. 11–17.   [5] **CCLXXX**, 366 *ff.*   [6] **CCLII**, 409.

Ultimately the whole of Adam's race is affected by the consequences of the ancestral fault.[1] It is not a question of original sin, as Catholic theology understands it, but rather of a kind of *congenital disposition*, a sinful inclination which has its roots deep in the hearts of all Adam's descendants.   To the anxious inquiry : " *Who is there who has not sinned ?* " the answer is always " *No man*," for none is pure in the eyes of the Lord [2] ; and reflexion on this fact leads to the conclusion that it would have been better not to have been born, or to have been like the beasts, which have no reason to fear what comes after death.[3]

Only by the help of God, given in answer to fervent prayer, can man hope to be delivered from the bondage of sin.[4] A frail hope, indeed, for although to its possessors the Law offers a sure guide to the good (according to the will of God), the Law is hard to know and still harder to obey. How many can honestly say that they have succeeded in this difficult task ? [5] We are reminded of that famous passage from Saint Paul (Rom. vii. 7 *ff.*), which describes the Law, holy and righteous in itself, as a constant source of sin, because by defining every occasion for sin it increases the sinfulness of the wretched man who is unable to keep the whole of it. In spite of the Law, and almost by reason of it, Paul felt himself sinking into the dark night of sin and perdition, and there were probably many among his contemporaries who shared his pessimism.

II

Man's Destiny [6]

What, then, does *perdition* imply ? First, that the Jew who feared it no longer limited the destiny of man to this life, and that he looked forward to a life beyond the grave, a future state which would be favourable or fatal according to his conduct during his life on earth. Such an idea did not spring full fledged and spontaneously from the Jewish mind.

The general Jewish belief accepted the obvious interpretation of the Old Testament account of the creation and the fall of Adam, namely, that, if God's original design had not mis-

---

[1] **CCLXXX**, 370 *ff.* ; **LXXV**, iii, 228.

[2] 4 Esdras vii. 46, 48 ; Enoch xv. 4 : Apoc. Baruch xlviii. 42 *ff.*

[3] 4 Esdras viii. 116–26.   [4] Wisdom vii. 7.

[5] Tixeront, *Hist. des dogmes*, Paris, 1905, i, 39 *ff.*, makes the mistake of relying exclusively on 4 Esdras, which is under suspicion of Christian influence.

[6] On the idea of *retribution*, *cf.* Lods, *The Prophets of Israel*, book iii, chap. i, § 2.

carried, man would never have experienced want or suffering or death.[1]   The error of Adam, or rather the act of Eve, made it necessary for God to alter his scheme, and to bring death into the world.   " *The woman was the first sinner,*" says Ben-Sira, " *and through her we all die.*"   Man was cast out of Paradise and deprived of the fruit of the Tree of Life ;   therefore he became mortal.   It was long before the imagination of Israel could conceive of any remedy for this disaster.

The early Israelites [2] before the Jahwism of the Old Testament had been established, believed in the survival of the *double*, either in the tomb or in the land of *Sheol* ;   or rather, they believed, fantastic and contradictory as it may appear, that it survived in both places at once.[3]   Even in the period of Jahwism the Jewish conception of *Sheol* never became very clear or consistent.[4]   Men knew only that it was a region under the earth, deeper even than the ocean-bed, among the roots of the mountains ;   and also that it was not a pleasant dwelling-place, at least from the point of view of the living.   Job (x. 20-2), for instance, describes it thus : " *Are not my days few ?   Grant me then a little breathing space before I go whence I shall not return, even to the land of darkness and the shadow of death ;   a land of darkness and desolation, and of the shadow of death, without any order, and where the very light is as utter darkness.*"   It was an abode of *night* and *silence*, according to the Psalmist (Ps. xciv. 17) [5] : " *Unless the Lord had been my help, my soul had quickly dwelt in silence.*"   And Daniel (xii. 21) describes it as the land of *dust* : " *And many of them that sleep in the dust of the earth shall awake.*"   Sometimes *Sheol* is imagined as an immense necropolis in which each of the dead has his tomb, and where every dead monarch in his royal sepulchre is surrounded by his silent subjects.[6]   At other times the image seems to be that of a city or palace lying behind locked gates [7] —perhaps those *gates of hell* which shall not prevail against the Church (Matt. xvi. 18)—where each retains his rank on

---

[1] On the other hand, when God is supposed to be talking to Adam in Gen. iii. 9, he presents death rather as the necessary consequence of man's origin—he came out of the dust, and to dust must he return.   The two theories can be reconciled by the belief that by absolute obedience man is able to triumph over his nature.   Moreover, the Scriptures offer examples of men who did not die, such as Enoch and Elijah (Gen. v. 24 ; 2 Kings ii.).

[2] For ideas of a *future life* in Semitic religions, see bibliography in **CCXCVIII**, 190, n. 2.

[3] **LVI**, Index under *Sheol*.   [4] **LVI**, 205.

[5] *Cf.* Ps. cxv. 17.   [6] Ezek. xxxii. 18–32 ; Isa. xiv. 11.

[7] Isa. xxxviii. 10 ; Ps. ix. 14 ; Job xxxviii. 17 ; Wisdom xvi. 13 ; **Psalms** of Solomon, xvi. 2.

earth. Such divergences and contradictions should not be judged severely, since even today current opinions about the survival of the dead man in the grave, or the immortality of his soul, or the double judgment, individual and general, which he will undergo, and his resurrection, are not very coherent, or capable of rational conception. However, reason has but little sway in these matters.

It is impossible to say when Israel first conceived the idea of *Sheol*. It was doubtless preceded by that of the continued existence of the double in the tomb, but scholars like Marti and Gunkel are probably mistaken in dating it as late as the establishment of Jahwism in the land of Canaan. Gunkel maintains that the concept was imported from Babylon. But the Babylonians were not the only people who believed in a land of the dead, and the fact that the descriptions of *Sheol* and of *Aralu*, its Babylonian equivalent, correspond more and more closely as time goes on, proves that the former was influenced by the latter, but not that it was derived from it. Besides, the descriptions found in the earliest texts suggest that the Jews were familiar with the idea of *Sheol* before the conquest of Canaan.[1]

However obscure the origin of *Sheol* may be, there is general agreement on one point. Jahweh had nothing to do with the land of the dead ; souls entering it were outside his knowledge, and they themselves knew him no more.[2] The reason for this may be [3] that in ancient belief, the dead became *elohim* in their own right, and were worshipped by descendants, to whom they in their turn rendered various supernatural services, such as oracular responses.[4] It was thus that the ancient Greeks and Romans regarded their relations with their dead ancestors. Hence Jahweh took no part in the affairs of *Sheol*, though he would intervene when the occasion required it, as he did when his adversaries took refuge there in a vain attempt to escape his wrath (Amos ix. 2). There is no suggestion that when he created the world he also created *Sheol*.

The *Sheol* of the Jews is thus not unlike that desolate region to which Ulysses descended in search of Tiresias, and of which Achilles, then an inmate of it, gave him such a sorry account.

---

[1] **LVI,** 108 *ff.*, treats the subject fully, giving arguments and sources.
[2] Ps. cxv. 17 : " *The dead praise not Jahweh, neither any that go down into silence.*" Ps. lxxxviii. 10–11 : " *Will thou shew wonders to the dead ? Shall the dead arise and praise thee ? Shall thy lovingkindness be declared in the grave? or thy faithfulness in destruction?* " Isa. xxxviii. 18: " *For Sheol cannot praise thee ; death cannot celebrate thee. They that go down into the pit cannot hope for thy truth.*"
[3] **LVI,** 225.
[4] Lods, *Le Culte des ancêtres dans l'antiquité hébraïque* . . ., Paris, 1906.

But in certain respects Jahwism modified the prevailing notion of the land of the dead. Hitherto the lives of the departed had been largely modelled on ordinary human existence ; the supposed survival of social distinctions has already been mentioned, and other human institutions were presumed to be equally characteristic of the nether world. But Job, who was a good Jahwist, speaks longingly of the peace of *Sheol* where all men are equal because all are nothing. "*There*," he says (Job iii. 17–19), "*the wicked cease from troubling ; and there the weary be at rest. There the prisoners rest together ; they hear not the voice of the oppressor. The small and the great are there and the slave is free from his master.*" It was probably because Jahwism put an end to the cult of the dead among the Hebrews that it had the effect of sterilizing (as it were) their conception of *Sheol*, and reducing its inhabitants to an inert state in which they barely survived, without energy and almost without memory. This torpid condition was characteristic of them, according to the latest Biblical sources.[1] Scholars have pointed out that in Greece the triumph of the great Olympian deities had similar results. On the one hand it put an end to the ancestor worship which had held such a prominent place in the religion of the Mycenæan age, and at the same time it reduced the shades to a state of semi-consciousness.[2]

The souls in *Sheol* were shades ; that is the meaning of their Hebrew designation, *rephaîm*. They were described as sleeping : "*So man lieth down, and riseth not again ; till the heavens be no more, they shall not awake, nor be raised out of their sleep*" (Job xiv. 12). Indeed death was regarded as an everlasting sleep. Jeremiah (li. 39 and 57) says, "*They shall sleep a perpetual sleep, and not wake.*" They did not suffer annihilation, but their survival was only partial, for they were left to stagnate in a lethargy of half-awareness untroubled by any kind of retribution for the vices or virtues of their previous existence. As Ecclesiastes (ix. 5) puts it, "*the dead know not anything, neither have they any more a reward, for the memory of them is forgotten.*" For the Jahwist the only real life was the life of this world, which might, with God's blessing, be both long and happy. Death he regarded as not merely a calamity, but also a punishment. The righteous man rejoiced in the knowledge that he would live on in his children, and did not pin his faith to survival in " another world."[3] This is not difficult to understand, for there was nothing particularly attractive in the prospect of his shade descending to that bleak and negative

---

[1] **LVI**, 214.   [2] Rohde, *Psyche* (2nd edit.), 341.
[3] A long list of texts is given in **CCLXXXII**, 237.

abode in the bowels of the earth, and a future life of this type did not harmonize well with a moral and religious attitude to existence in this world. When the Prophets threatened their people with well-deserved retribution, they were clearly anticipating human catastrophes, which were to overtake the culprits in the course of their earthly lives. Even the Jews of early times were convinced that any tribulations a man might endure were necessarily the result of his sins and the penalty exacted for them. Thus when Job's three friends visited him in the midst of his afflictions, they came with the fixed intention of proving to him that he had deserved his misfortunes, although Job himself assured them of his innocence (Job iii.–xxxi.). In the end God vindicated Job by announcing that his trials had only been a test of his devotion (xlii. 7 *ff.*), a conclusion which shows that the doctrine of retribution in this life was beginning to be severely shaken.

An attempt has been made to use certain scriptural passages [1] as evidence for a belief in, or at least a hope of, *eternal life* ; but the whole sense of the Old Testament is adverse to such an interpretation, and the student has only to examine the passages themselves to realize that they do not support the argument based on them.[2] The idea of eternal life, in which

---

[1] Job xix. 25–7 ; Prov. xiv. 32 and xv. 24 ; Ps. xvi. 10.

[2] Job xix. 25 : " *I know that my vindicator liveth and that at the last he shall stand upon the dust. And though after my skin this body be destroyed, yet without my flesh I shall see God : I shall see on my side and mine eyes shall behold, and not another.*" When Job speaks here of seeing God, he may of course mean after his death and resurrection, but a simpler interpretation would be that he is comforting himself with the hope of a divine revelation when he has recovered from the disease which has reduced him to a skeleton. The point is settled by xiv. 14, when his exclamation, " *O that a man might die and live again!* " clearly expresses his regret that his wish cannot be fulfilled. Prov. xiv. 32 : " *The wicked is overthrown by his own wickedness ; the righteous hath faith even in his death.*" xv. 24 : " *The wise man follows a way of life that leads upwards, that he may depart from the place of the dead which is below.*" The meaning of the first quotation is very doubtful, because the Hebrew may be read in various ways. Kautzsch takes *bethummô* to mean *Redlichkeit* and renders it : " *aber der Fromme findet Zuflucht in seiner Redlichkeit,*" that is to say, " *but the pious man finds refuge in his uprightness.*" The second passage may very well mean that by his prudence the wise man is able to avoid death, and only a reader in search of evidence for a particular theory would be likely to find in it a reference to the raising of the souls of the just. Ps. xvi. 10 : " *For thou wilt not leave my soul to Sheol ; neither wilt thou suffer thy godly one to see the pit.*" In its context this can only mean, " *thou wilt not cause me to die ; thou wilt keep me from death.*" Verse 9 runs : " *Therefore my heart is glad, and my glory rejoiceth ; my flesh also shall dwell in safety.*" The Psalmist speaks only of men's earthly life. It is thus clear that none of these three passages can be used as authority for a belief in eternal life.

the righteous would find bliss, and sinners torment, was a late development, which is first vouched for by Daniel [1] (xii. 2 *ff.*) : "*And many of them that sleep in the dust of the earth shall awake, some to everlasting life, and some to shame and everlasting contempt.*" The Jews had not yet evolved the belief that each shade would be judged when it entered *Sheol* and allotted immediate punishment or reward. The passage refers to a *future* state in which the soul, *returning to the earth in a renewed body*, should be given its deserts. The ultimate fate of man was therefore not decided until after his resurrection.

III
THE RESURRECTION

This belief in a resurrection was of primary importance in the religious beliefs of the Jews in Jesus' day [2] ; so much so that it may be said to have transformed the old Jahwism into a new religion. Both its logical grounds and its moral basis are fairly obvious. In the old days when Israel was at the height of its prosperity, the lives of the majority of the pious might well have been sufficiently happy to be regarded as the material evidence of God's favour, and an occasional exception to this rule could be overlooked. But there was no room for such a theory during the period of humiliation and distress which began with the Exile and culminated in the Seleucid tyranny. Men whose piety and uprightness were unimpeachable might suffer the most cruel fate ; and indeed, under the yoke of the *goyim*, piety was only an additional cause of persecution. In order to justify this seeming contradiction and to maintain their faith in God's righteousness, the Jews had to fall back on the hope of some compensation in another life. The Alexandrian Jews, who were in contact with the spiritualism of the Greeks, accepted the doctrine of the immortality of the soul, and so, apparently, did the Essenes in Palestine,[3] possibly under Greek influence. Clear statements on this point

---

[1] There is some doubt, too, as to whether this famous passage belongs to the same period as the context in which it appears, namely, about the year 165. **CCLXXVII**, 247–9, makes out a strong case against the likelihood of any reference being made in such veiled terms to a doctrine which must have been almost unknown at the time, since neither Ben-Sira nor 1 Maccabees nor any of the Jewish writings of the second century alludes to it. If this is true, the verse might be an interpolation of a later date than its context. It is a somewhat disquieting suggestion.

[2] **CCLXXIX**, ii, 295 *ff.*

[3] Jos., *B.J.*, ii, 8, 11. *Cf.* **LXXV**, iii, 380 ; **CCLXXVII**, 286 *ff.*

are to be found in the works of Philo, who was strongly influenced by Plato and neo-Pythagorism,[1] and in the Book of Wisdom. Nevertheless the Jews of Palestine had no liking for this way of solving the problem of man's destiny. Their anthropological *dichotomy* [2] was not *dualistic*, and they held to their conviction that a truly living being was always an *embodied spirit*, soul and body having been created by God for a mutual interdependence and being therefore equally incapable of genuine life apart from one another. This explains the Jewish preference for belief in the resurrection, which is fundamentally different. It also gives a clue to the distaste and resistance that Christianity, preaching the doctrine of the resurrection, was later to encounter among peoples in contact with Hellenic culture. But the Christian attitude, by a remarkable effort of syncretism, managed to ignore the contradiction between these two eschatological beliefs, and to retain both of them, welding them into one coherent whole. It must be added that the Jews never reached complete agreement as to physical conditions or the material realization of the resurrection. The schools of Hillel and Shammaï believed in the restoration of the original body, but it is by no means certain that they did not regard this return to the flesh as a kind of intermediate stage between terrestrial life and immortality.[3]

Certain writers [4] claim to have established the possibility that the idea of the resurrection arose spontaneously in Israel. They base their arguments on passages like Isaiah xxvi. 19, which runs : " *Thy dead shall live ; my dead bodies shall arise ! Awake and sing, ye that dwell in the dust : for thy dew is as the dew of light, and the earth shall cast forth the shades.*" But what proof is there that this verse represents a spontaneous creation of the spirit of Israel, and that it owes nothing to Persian influences ? [5] Such passages certainly seem to echo Persian

---

[1] **CCLXXX**, 318 *ff.* ; **LXXV**, iii, 561 ; **CCLXXVII**, 225.

[2] Even those Jews who were *trichotomists*, making a threefold division of the human being, did not subscribe to the idea of a spirit capable of a separate existence.

[3] **CCL**, i, 168 *ff.*   [4] **CCLXXXII**, 241.

[5] *Cf.* **CCLV**, 416, which makes a comparison between the Persian ideas concerning the condition of the soul after death, and those contained in the Testament of the Twelve Patriarchs, Asher, 6. On the other hand, **CCLXXVII**, 255 and n. 3, considers it impossible that Persia should have had any considerable influence over Israel during the last 200 years before the Christian era. This author believes external influences to have been wholly Greek (Pythagorean), reaching Palestine through the Jews of Alexandria (p. 342). His arguments are not entirely convincing, but it is possible that the Iranian idea was later subjected to a Hellenistic interpretation. The same is true in the case of Josephus.

thought, though it is true that this influence could only really affect the eschatological beliefs of the Jews when they had modified their conception of Jahweh and admitted that he ruled the dead as well as the living, and that the souls of the departed could not possibly dwell for ever out of his sight and beyond the scope of his justice.[1]

Faith in the resurrection appears to have taken root among the Jews of Palestine at the time of the Maccabees.[2] For instance, the Second Book of Maccabees relates that Judas commanded a sacrifice for the sins of the dead, in the belief that they would one day be restored to life. For, as the author says, " *It would be a difficult and vain thing to pray for the dead*," if they were not to rise again. There was still some doubt as to how general this re-awakening of the *rephaïm* was to be, but the most usual opinion was that only the righteous would rise again. The *Mishnah* tractate *Sanhedrin* still retains this idea of a restricted resurrection. It claims that " *The generation of the Flood will have no part in the next world, and will not be raised for the judgment*," [3] and then enumerates other classes of sinners, including the people of Sodom, who will share the same fate. In fact, the old Jewish idea that there was no retribution for the dead in *Sheol* still persisted, with the difference that a small minority—the righteous—were to be delivered from the cheerless oblivion of their subterranean existence and allowed to see the light again.

At the same time this very limited kind of resurrection could not be reconciled with the Persian belief in universal judgment, which required that all the dead should rise again before the terrible reckoning took place. Moreover, it ignored the logical conclusion that if the pious were to be rewarded, sinners should also be punished. The author of the passage from Daniel (ii. 12) quoted above, evidently had this in mind, yet even he was only prepared for the resurrection of *many of the dead*, not of all. It seemed more just that after their apparent victory in this world Israel's persecutors should be penalized in the next ; and this opinion, which Christianity adopted, did finally oust the belief that resurrection was a privilege reserved for the elect. In Jesus' lifetime Jewish allegiance was divided between the two possibilities.[4] In those

---

[1] **LIX**, 271.

[2] 2 Macc. vii. 9–11 ; xii. 43–5 ; xiv. 36 ; xiv. 46. *Cf.* **CCLXXVIII**, ii, 174 *ff.*

[3] *Sanhedrin*, xi, 3 (Hoelscher, p. 105).

[4] **LXXV**, ii, 542 *ff.*, n. 52, and above all 547 *ff.* ; **CCLV**, 84, which points out the two ideas in the Jewish *Apocalypses* of Jesus' day.

Apocalyptic books in which the influence of the Pharisees is marked, there are already evidences of a tendency to turn *Sheol* into *hell*, the abode of sinners, while the spirits of the just ascend to heaven where, among the angelic host, the Messiah awaits his hour, and where they themselves await their resurrection.[1] Opinion on these subjects was as yet far from uniform.[2]

Nevertheless, hope in the resurrection was gaining ground. Pharisaic circles accepted it, and spread it among the populace through the agency of the synagogues. Yet it encountered a certain amount of resistance. Josephus tells us [3] that the Sadducees would not countenance it ; and it was also rejected by the Samaritans and, in general, by the priesthood. The authors of the earlier Apocryphal books (Ecclesiasticus, Judith, Tobit, and the First Book of the Maccabees) appear to have had no knowledge of it, and are content with the old notion of *Sheol* as the abode of the dead.[4] But this does not apply to later Apocryphal works like Daniel, 2 Maccabees, Enoch, the Apocalypse of Baruch and the Testament of the Twelve Patriarchs.[5] Hence the opinion must be rejected that the idea of the resurrection was unknown to the majority of Jews in the time of Jesus.[6] I believe, on the contrary, that the great mass of the Jewish population already adhered strongly to it, and that only the somewhat sceptical aristocrats of the Temple staff, who professed to hold strictly to the teachings of the *Torah*, openly denied it.[7] The fact that the later Apocryphal books are well aware of the resurrection idea while the earlier ones are silent on the subject proves that it was about the time of the birth of Jesus that the new teaching came into its own.

Indeed, the resurrection was not preached for its own sake, as a single, unrelated fact, but as an integral part of a system which considered man's fate as bound up with the fate of the world, and connected the future of humanity with the eschatological transformation of the world. And this Jewish conception of a transformed world had an even more profound effect on the early history of Christianity than the ideas outlined in this chapter concerning the future destiny of man.

---

[1] **CCLV**, 83 and 92. *Gehenna* appears in the *Ascension of Moses*, 10.
[2] **CCLV**, 109.   [3] Jos., *B.J.*, ii, 8, 14.
[4] **LXXV**, ii, 508.
[5] **LXXV**, ii, 547—Loisy (**LIX**, 270) notes that 2 Maccabees speaks of the resurrection as though he were upholding it against the attacks of an opposition.
[6] **CCLXXX**, 314 *ff.*   [7] **LXXV**, ii, 547.

NOTE

The first suggestion of a system of classifying the dead according to their merits, and of distributing them in different departments of *Sheol*, where they received preliminary rewards and punishments, apparently occurs in Enoch xx. ; that is to say, probably in the second century B.C., before the year 170. Unfortunately, however, the Book of Enoch is composite, and there is great uncertainty as to the dates of its component parts (**XLVIII,** 224 *ff.* ; 230 *ff.*). Moreover, the text of the chapter in question is so corrupt that the interpretation of certain passages in it remains doubtful. See Ad. Lods, *Le Livre d'Hénoch. Fragments grecs découverts a Akhmim*, Paris, 1892, 173 *ff.* ; Lagrange (**LI,** 112). On the Ethiopian text, *cf.* Fr. Martin, *Le Livre d'Hénoch*, Paris, 1906.

CHAPTER IV

ESCHATOLOGY AND MESSIANISM [1]

IN approaching this subject it is necessary to resist the temptation of making definite statements and of over-systematization. For the contemporaries of Jesus had neither evolved a fixed eschatological doctrine nor systematized the various beliefs that were current among them. Different writers would uphold different theories, according to the particular influences to which they had been subjected, but the theories themselves were not well established. If passages dealing with the subject seem vague and hesitant, it is because they reflect a real vagueness and hesitancy in the thought of the time. There was as much confusion concerning the destiny of the world as concerning that of man. Another temptation is to assume *a priori* that the lines of thought which prevailed later because they had the force of Christianity behind them, were already in control at the time of Jesus' birth. It would be quite misleading to suppose that Jewish thought and Jewish literature viewed the coming of the Messiah in just the same way as the New Testament.

[1] *Cf.* Lods, *The Prophets of Israel*, book iii, chap. i, § 3. On *Eschatology* see **CCLXXXIV** ; **CCLX** ; **CCLXXIX**, ii, 377–95 ; Charles, *A Critical History of a Future Life in Israel, in Judaism and in Christianity*, 1899 ; *Eschatology* in **EB** (by the same author) ; **CCLV**, parts i and ii ; **CCLXXX**, 266 *ff*. ; **CCLII**, § 36, 435 *ff*. ; **CCLXVI**, i, 44–7 ; **CCLXV**, 69 *ff*. ; **CCLIII**, chap. xvi ; **CCLX**, chap. vii ; **LXVII**, 342–53. On *Messianism* see **LXXV**, ii, 496 *ff*., bibliography, 496 *ff*. ; **CCLXXIX**, ii, 323–76 ; Baldensperger, *Die Messianisch-apokalyptischen Hoffnungen des Judentums* (2nd edit.), Strasburg, 1903 ; Boehmer, *Der Alttestamentliche Unterbau des Reiches Gottes*, Leipzig, 1902 ; Oesterley, *The Evolution of the Messianic Idea, a Study in Comparative Religion*, London, 1908 ; **CCLXXV** ; **CCLXVI** ; Duhm, *Das Kommende Reich Gottes*, Tübingen, 1910 ; **LXIII** ; **CCLXXIV**, chap. viii ; **CCLIII**, chaps. xii–xiii ; **CCLXX**, 219 ; above all **CCLIX** (see the analytical table for the various aspects of the subject), and **CCLXXXIII**, which deals primarily with the question of the false hopes of a Messiah which were constantly arising among the Jews of the Dispersion.

I

THE FOUNDATIONS OF JEWISH ESCHATOLOGY

What may be termed *classical* Jahwism, that is to say the Jahwism which finds its expression in the prophetic books, was faced with two really important problems. Firstly, it was clear that the world fell far short of God's just requirements, and it was essential that something should be done to bridge this gulf. Men who flouted God's commands, whether they did so wantonly or in ignorance, must sooner or later repent and enter the fold, or else be punished for their misdeeds. Secondly, although God, had chosen Israel from among the nations, his people had not always behaved in a very exemplary way towards him, and they themselves could scarcely consider their normal condition as a proof of divine favour, for instead of ruling the world they had often to suffer tyranny and defeat. How could their continued misfortunes be explained unless Jahweh had deliberately broken the oath which he had sworn to Abraham and to Jacob and to Moses ? Yet such a betrayal of faith was utterly impossible. As Micah declares in vii. 20, " *Thou wilt perform the truth to Jacob, and the mercy to Abraham, which thou hast sworn to our fathers from the days of old.*"

This twofold problem, which arose out of historical circumstances, formed a basis for various views concerning the future of the world and of the Jewish people. They are distinct from the opinions on the same subjects which were current about the time of Jesus' birth, but they helped to determine the direction and scope of the later views. These are the essential facts.

The world might be openly flaunting its ungodliness, the Jews might be glaringly oblivious of their covenant obligations, nevertheless *the day of Jahweh* would come.[1] The first allusion to it appears in Amos, about the middle of the eighth century : " *Woe unto you that desire the day of Jahweh.*" " *Wherefore would ye have the day of Jahweh ? . . . It is darkness and no light ? even very dark, and no brightness in it ?* " (v. 18 and 20). Two facts emerge from this passage ; first that Amos was not the originator of *the day of Jahweh*, since his contemporaries were also familiar with it, and secondly, that he differed from those contemporaries in the meaning he attached to it.[2] The others, skilfully identifying the cause of Jahweh with that of

---

[1] A. Causse, *Le jour de Iahvé et la fête de l'avènement de Iahvé*, in **RHP**, 1923.

[2] For the way in which they probably pictured it, see Lods, *The Prophets of Israel*, book ii, chap. i, § iii, 4.

Israel, and happening also to live at a time when the Jews held a fairly strong position with regard to neighbouring peoples,[1] were confident that *the day of Jahweh* would mean the final triumph of the chosen people, and the due subjugation of the godless. But for Amos the *day* stood for the victory of divine justice which would involve terrible retribution for Israel.

The two aspects persisted side by side in the imagination of the Prophets, and the *day of Jahweh* became a favourite theme of their meditations, predictions and threats. They often proclaimed its dread approach. Isaiah (xiii. 6–9) gives warning of it, with the words, " *Howl ye, for the day of Jahweh is at hand; it shall come as a destruction from the Almighty. . . . Behold the day of Jahweh cometh, cruel both with wrath and fierce anger, to lay the land desolate, and to destroy the sinners thereof out of it.*" [2] No doubt these alarming predictions of the imminent arrival of the *acharith-hayyamim*, the *end of the days*, which were never fulfilled, were the object of a certain amount of ridicule among the more sceptical Israelites. Such an attitude seems to be reflected in Ezekiel (xii. 21 ff.), " *The word of Jahweh came to me, saying, Son of man, what is that proverb that ye have in the land of Israel, saying, The days are prolonged and every vision faileth?* " Needless to say, Jahweh then announced, through the mouth of his prophet, that this time the warning was no mere figure of speech, and his *day* would come indeed.

It would be a day of dread, heralded by fearful portents. Earth and heaven would be subjected to an appalling upheaval, and the Prophets allowed their imaginations free rein in picturing the horrors of the catastrophe.[3] But after the day of terror and judgment, the world, cleansed and regenerated, would enter upon a new era. And when the divine wrath should smite the *nations* who had given cause for it, those neighbouring peoples with whom the Jews were continually at loggerheads would naturally, according to these alarming predictions, be singled out for a particularly dire vengeance. Syria and Phœnicia,

---

[1] It was during the reign of Jeroboam II, King of Israel (783?–743?) that the people of Damascus, who had long threatened his kingdom, were brought to heel. This and other military victories tended to give Israel the illusion of a strength it did not really possess.

[2] *Cf.* Zeph. i. 7 and 14 : " *The great day of Jahweh is near, it is near and hasteth greatly* " ; Zech. iii. 10 ; Ezek. xiii. 5 ; xxx, 3 ; Joel, i. 15 : " *For the day of Jahweh is at hand : it cometh as a destruction from the Almighty* " ; ii. 1 ; ii. 11 ; ii. 31 ; iii. 14 ; Obad. 15 : " *For the day of Jahweh is near upon all the nations.*"

[3] *Cf.* in particular Amos viii. 8 *ff.* ; Isa. ii. 9 *ff.* ; xiii. 6 *ff.* ; xxiv. 17 *ff.* ; Hab. iii. 3 *ff.* ; Ezek. xxxii. 7 *ff.* ; xxxviii. 18 *ff.* ; etc.

Edom and Moab, Philistines and Ammonites, would be all but annihilated in the explosion of God's righteous wrath. Amos kindly warns them of their fate (i. 3–ii. 3), and most of the other Prophets derive comfort from these agreeable expectations.[1] Moreover, God would not spare any nation which had grown too great. Isaiah makes this clear, " *For the day of Jahweh shall be upon every one that is lifted up, and he shall be brought low* (ii. 12). . . . *And Jahweh alone shall be exalted in that day* " (ii. 17).[2] In particular, those haughty nations, the Assyrians and the Babylonians, who had been rendered yet more arrogant by being so often used as rods with which Jahweh scourged his guilty people, would now be humbled before his majesty.[3] And all the heathen and idolators would be banished from his sight : " *For the nation and the kingdom that will not serve thee shall perish ; yea, those nations shall be utterly wasted* " (Isa. lx. 12).[4]

If it had been only the idolatrous peoples who were to feel God's just anger and to suffer for the wrongs they had inflicted on Israel, the Jews would have seen in this the fulfilment of all their desires, and the contemplation of such a future would have partially assuaged their bitterness. But they had reason to fear that on the Great Day divine justice would exact from them also the penalty of their breaches of the covenant between themselves and Jahweh. The Prophets are as insistent on this as on the punishment of the heathen, and never suggest that it is only the *goyim* who will be judged. Theoretically, Israel was to be smitten and utterly destroyed.[5] Of course the threat was not taken quite literally, and it was understood that a *remnant* of God's people would survive : " *It shall be as when the harvest man gathereth the sheaves, and reapeth the ears with his arm ; and it shall be as he that gathereth ears in the valley of Rephaim. Yet a gleaning shall be left in it, as at the shaking of the olive tree ; two or three berries in the top of the uppermost bough, four or five in the branches thereof, saith the Lord God of Israel* " (Isa. xvii. 5 *ff.*). The passage implies that in the ordeal of the judgment day the wicked, forming the bulk of the people, would perish, while the chosen few would survive

[1] Isa. xiii.–xxi. ; xxiii.–xxvii. ; Jer. xxv. 9–38 ; xxvii. 2–11 ; xliii. 8–13 ; xlvi.–li. ; Ezek. xxv.–xxxii. ; xxxv. ; xxxviii. ; etc.

[2] *Cf.* Isa. v. 15 *ff.* ; xxxiii. 10.

[3] Isa. x. 5 *ff.* ; xxxvii. 21–9 ; xlvii.

[4] *Cf.* Zech. ix. 1–6 ; Hab. ii. 4 *ff.* ; Obad. 3 *ff.* ; Isa. xiv. 13 *ff.* ; xvi. 6 ; xxiii. 9 ; xxv. 11, etc. ; Jer. xlviii. 29 *ff.* ; xlix. 16 *ff.* ; li. 31 *ff.* ; Ezek. xxvii. 1 *ff.* ; xxviii. 1 *ff.* ; xxix. 2 *ff.*, etc.

[5] The appendix to Amos ix. 8 *ff.* states this clearly. *Cf.* also Isa. vi. 11–13.

and triumph. From these survivors would spring a new generation which would be pleasing to God,[1] and would make a new
Covenant with him, which would be good, true, and final.

It may not be superfluous to explain that when Old Testament writers speak of the *day* or of the *judgment of Jahweh* they
are not thinking of the appointed day of judgment with which
Christianity has made us familiar, when a formal sentence would
be pronounced. All they meant was that a time would come
when God's patience would at length be exhausted, and when
his anger would descend on those who had provoked it. First
he would unloose the shafts of war against his people. No
doubt the Assyrians and the Egyptians would be the instruments of his wrath, as they had been so often in the past.
Other scourges, such as plagues and famines, would follow.
Hosea (viii. 13 ; ix. 3 and 6, etc.) prophesies a *return to Egypt* ;
Isaiah (vii. 17 *ff*.) and Jeremiah (xx. 4 ; xxii. 25 *ff*.) threaten an
Assyrian invasion ; Micah (vii. 12) combines both these threats,
foretelling trouble from the south and from the east. They all
vied with one another in the invention and description of the
most frightful calamities. Obviously, the wretched instruments of punishment would not receive their own retribution
till later. Here also God's methods would be neither summary
nor direct. The nations who had first trodden Israel underfoot
would then either fall upon one another, or be torn by civil
wars, or suffer from various destroying scourges.[2] It was only
occasionally that one of these writers visualized Israel itself as
becoming God's ultimate agent and crushing the nations by
whom it had been crushed. The hope of such a revenge comforted Jewish nationalism with agreeable anticipation, a form
of encouragement which was not the less effective for being
somewhat puerile.[3]

Even the total destruction of the *goyim* cannot be too
strictly interpreted, for those very Prophets who affirm that
they will be wiped off the face of the earth give them a place
in their descriptions of the future under the new Covenant.

---

[1] Most of the prophetic books contain many texts supporting this
view. *Cf.* Isa. i. 9 ; iv. 3 ; x. 20–2 ; xi. 16, etc. ; Jer. iv. 27 ; v. 10 and
18 ; vi. 9 ; xxiii. 3, etc. ; Ezek. vi. 8 *ff*. ; xii. 16 ; xiv. 22, etc.
[2] References are collected in **CCLXXXII**, 184 *ff*.
[3] Mic. iv. 13 ; Zeph. ii. 9 ; Zech. xii. 6 ; ii. 8 ; Joel iii. 8 ; Obad. 18.

II

THE NEW COVENANT AFTER THE DAY OF JAHWEH [1]

Jahweh was thus to enter into a new Covenant with that
remnant of the people which had escaped destruction, a covenant
which would in future be faithfully kept ; and upon his chosen
people, now regenerated and truly worthy of his favour, he
would pour out of his Spirit.[2] Jerusalem would become a
peerless city, where God would be worshipped with splendour
of ritual and in purity of heart ; and Jahweh would indeed
make Mount Zion his dwelling-place. The Israelites who had
been scattered over the face of the earth would be reunited
there [3] ; old hatreds would be forgotten, and the new Israel,
ruled by a king of the lineage of David, would know a prosperity
hitherto undreamed of. The people would multiply exceedingly,
and no nation would be able to withstand their might. Indeed
their neighbours might of their own will become vassals of the
elect ; they might draw near to the Holy Mountain and beg
to be admitted to the Covenant. Then all men would live by
the light of Jahweh's Law ; this at least was the view of Micah
and Isaiah and a number of other Prophets. Peace and happiness would be diffused over the whole world. The earth would
bring forth more abundantly ; beasts of prey would grow harm-
less or disappear. Every man would attain the extreme limits
of human longevity ; perhaps even death itself would perish.[4]
Certainly there would be no more disease or infirmity and men
would enjoy perfect health under the rays of a sun seven times
more powerful than of old, and of a moon which would turn
night into day. Such was the *kingdom* of the Messiah, which
would be in truth the *reign of God* on earth. The Rabbis
conceived of it metaphorically as a banquet at which the
righteous sat enthroned in light, with crowns upon their
heads.[5]

The Prophets were thus contemplating a genuine
palingenesia, the rebirth both of the world and of mankind.
The new order would persist for as long as the Covenant itself

---

[1] Jer. xxxi. 31–4. *Cf.* **CCLIX**, 160 *ff.*
[2] For the whole of the following description, *cf.* **CCLIII**, 236 *ff.*
[3] Isa. xxvii. 12.
[4] Isa. xxv. 8 : " *He shall destroy death for ever.*"
[5] **CCL**, i, 168 *ff.* The word *malkuth*, which is rendered by the Greek
βασιλεία, can mean *kingdom*, but its primary sense is *royalty*, the *exercise
of the royal power*, hence *reign*. *Cf.* Barth, *Die Hauptprobleme des Lebens
Jesu*, Gütersloh, 1911, 39 ; **XXXIII**, 106 *ff.*

should last, that is to say eternally. " *I will build them up and not pull them down; I will plant them and not pluck them up.*" [1]

The foregoing paragraphs present a brief summary of the affirmations, not always consistent, which constantly recur in the works of the Prophets both of the Exile and of the Return. In them Israel found consolation for its fallen state in the contemplation of future triumph, and a spur to zeal in God's service, by which it might hasten the advent of the promised paradisal age. There was not the slightest doubt that this blissful existence *would take place on the earth*, and that the new bond of union with Jahweh, which would be the precious reward of his restored favour, would result merely in human happiness. It was true that this happiness would reach a degree of intensity hitherto unknown among men, but it would none the less be moulded by the aspirations, the prejudices and the passions of the Jews who were anticipating it.

A narrow and bitter nationalism, a jealous theocracy, and the desire for full material satisfaction, united to create this alluring dream of a renewed world, born out of desolation and dismay. The Græco-Romans would have thought of a revival of this kind as a return to the Golden Age, but for the Jews it meant rather a reversion to that life of innocence and bliss which Adam and Eve led in Eden when the world was young, a time when man and beast should once more lie side by side in perfect amity and peace as they did of old (Isa. xi. 6–8 ; ii. 4). [2] Ultimately the pagan and the Jewish visions merge in a common desire for a life of unalloyed happiness in a world for ever young, beneficent and fruitful :

> Ver erat aeternum, placidique tepentibus auris
> Mulcebant Zephyri natos sine semine flores.
> Ovid, *Metamorphoses*, i, 107 *ff.*

In theory it was Jahweh himself who was to establish and maintain the new order. [3] The elect who were to take part in it were to assemble either on *the mountain* of Jahweh or in *his city* or *his garden*, [4] and he was to be in their midst. Since he was the undisputed ruler of the present world, it was only natural that he should also rule the world to come, a conclusion which was reinforced by the tendency to heighten the idea of his sovereignty. The Second Isaiah is really the first Old

[1] Jer. xxiv. 6. *Cf.* xxxi. 36 *ff.*
[2] CCLIX, 152 *ff.*
[3] Mic. iv. ; Ps. xlvii. 9 ; xcvi.–xcix. *Cf.* CCLIX, 209 *ff.*
[4] CCLIX, 164 *ff.* ; 171 *ff.* ; 179 *ff.*

Testament writer to base the eschatological character of the kingdom of Jahweh [1] on the conception contained in the words: " *I the Lord, I am the first, and I also am the last* " (Isa. xli. 4 ; xliv. 6 ; xlviii. 12). The earlier writers rarely suggest that the national God is to be attended by an *Anointed One* or *Messiah*,[2] to whom he will delegate all or part of his power for the execution of his purposes. It has been said with justice that the Jews of the post-exilic period looked forward to the Messianic Kingdom before they came to expect the Messiah.[3] Israel was perfectly familiar with the idea of a symbolic ceremony in which Jahweh, by the anointing of his chosen servant with holy oil, conferred on him his special grace ; since the king, the High Priests, and indeed the nation itself as a whole were all *anointed ones*, or *Messiahs*.[4] It was only rather late, though the exact date is not known, that the word took on the eschatological sense in which it is now used ; namely, as applied to the individual who would put an end to the *old dispensation* and usher in the *new*.[5]

In the whole of the Pentateuch, despite its editorial changes, there are only two possible allusions to the Messiah. The first occurs in Genesis xlix. 10, in the blessing of Judah by Jacob, a passage whose text is somewhat doubtful : " *The sceptre shall not depart from Judah nor the ruler's staff from between his knees until his lord (?) shall come,*[6] *and him will the peoples obey.*" The other reference is to be found in Numbers xxiv. 17 : " *I see him, but not now ; I behold him, but not nigh. A star cometh out of Jacob, and a sceptre riseth out of Israel.*" In both cases the reference is most probably to an *ideal monarch* whom Jahweh is holding in reserve so that he may govern the chosen people in the *last days*. Perhaps it is David himself to whom God has entrusted the great work of vengeance, or one of that hero's descendants, for the Jewish imagination was always ready to

[1] Isa. xli. 1–13 ; xxi.–xxix. ; xliii. 8–13 ; xliv. 6–20 ; xlv. 20–1 ; xlviii. 12–16.

[2] The word is the Aramaic *meshiḥa* (Hebrew *mâshiaḥ*), which is exactly rendered by the Greek *Christos*.

[3] Max Dienemann, *Judentum und Christentum* (2nd edit.), Frankfort-am-Main, 1919, chap. iv. : *Der Messias und die messianische Zeit*.

[4] In the coronation ceremony of a Jewish king the essential feature is not the crowning, but the *anointing*. *Cf.* 1 Kings xix. 15.

[5] **CCLIX**, 1 *ff.*

[6] This is the key word, and the meaning is doubtful because the Hebrew is corrupt. The translation given here is based on the reading *môšelô*, which does mean *overlord*, but another possible reading would be *šâlêv*, which would be rendered by the *peaceful one*. One can only say that the passage *very probably* refers to the Messiah. *Cf.* v. 67.

evoke that glorious figure from its past.[1]   The final vision of Amos (ix. 11) contains the words : " *In that day will I raise up the tabernacle of David which is fallen, and close up the breaches thereof ; and I will raise up his ruins, and build it as in the days of old.*"   And Hosea (iii. 5) runs, " *Afterwards shall the children of Israel return, and seek once more the Lord their God, and David their king.*"   And both Jeremiah and Ezekiel agree in representing a long line of regenerated princes of the house of David ruling over Israel.[2]

The prophets then saw that future with which each of them was occupied, in terms of *the restoration of the reign of Jahweh on earth, the restoration of the chosen people*, and *the restoration of the house of David*.   The *Messianic expectation* did not as yet enter into their scheme, for although they might speak now and then of the Messiah, this Messiah was not a single, unique individual, but a kind of collective personality composed of the endless line of Davidic kings who were to be the future rulers of Israel.   As such he would be the perfect servant of Jahweh : " *The spirit of Jahweh shall rest upon him, and his delight shall be in the fear of the Lord* " (Isa. xi. 2–3).   He was invested with every regal attribute of wisdom and magnificence ;   he would be the father of his people, striking terror into the hearts of their foes.[3]   But there was as yet no suggestion of the apocalyptic figure of the heavenly hero with whom we are familiar from later writings.   He only held a secondary place in the scheme of the New Covenant.   Even after the return from Exile the Jews centred all their hopes on the full realization, *on this earth*, of the promises made by Jahweh to their ancestors.   This may, if desired, be regarded as the Messianic Kingdom ;   but only as set up by Jahweh, and not, as yet, by the Messiah.[4]

[1] **CCLIX**, 230 *ff*.   The Jews have always shown a marked inclination to see all their national leaders as *sons of David*.   When they were later under Roman rule, after the destruction of Jerusalem, they attributed this descent to their *patriarch* (*cf*. **XLVII**, i, 395 and n. 8–9) and even to the *exilarch* who lived in Babylonia (**XLVII**, i, 400, n. 3).   The Jews came to use David almost as the Romans used *Cæsar*, simply as a title of honour.

[2] Jer. xvii. 25 ;   xxii. 4 ;   xxxiii. 17–26 ;   Ezek. xliii. 7 ;   xlv. 8 ; xlvi. 16–18, etc.

[3] Passages are collected in **CCLXXXII**, 198–201.   It is necessary to guard against the false interpretations which Christian theology has given to many of them, by transferring them to an order of ideas alien to them, that is to say by adapting them forcibly to its own conceptions.

[4] Max Dienemann, *Judentum und Christentum* (2nd edit.), pp. 58–63 ; **CCXCII**, 19 *ff*.   Note that neither the Second Isaiah (lvi.–lxvii.) nor Malachi speaks of the Messiah.   And according to Matt. iv. 5–6 Elijah's return will herald, not the advent of the Messiah, but the *day of Jahweh*.

It was the successive disappointments of the Return which gradually forced Israel to modify its conception of the future which God had in store for his chosen people and for the world. It is not easy to trace the origin of the eschatological element which is to be found in the Jewish conception of the Messiah as soon as that conception took definite form ; namely, the conviction, which later on became essential, that the Messiah would play the leading part in the tremendous drama in which the *present age* would be superseded by the *age to come*. It was perhaps natural that the idea of the *age to come*, which was to be a return to the earthly Paradise, should be completed by the idea of an ideal king, a *King of Paradise*. But it was useless to search Jewish tradition for such a king. Foreign influences have been suggested from the land of Amurru in the north, or from Phœnicia in the west, but these districts, with their migrant populations, are much more likely to have served as channels for the thought and mythology of the countries beyond Egypt and Persia. The latter may very well have been responsible for the general form in which the eschatological visions of the Jews were cast, while Egypt may have given them their first notion of a Messiah.[1]

Certainly the Persian conception of the *last things* was sufficiently striking.[2] They imagined a time when the perpetual struggle between good and evil would be further intensified in a crisis which would be, in a sense, decisive. First, terrible *portents* would appear ; nature would be convulsed, and the foes of Iran would hurl themselves madly upon her, countless destroying hosts of men and demons. Then, at the crucial moment, *Hushêdar*, son of Zarathustra, would be born out of Lake Frazdân. He would assemble the warriors of Iran, and there would follow a thousand years of appalling strife and bloodshed, in which the angels of Ahura-Mazda would take part, and which would end in victory for the forces of *good*. Then under the rule of Hushêdar Mâh, another son of Zarathustra, a second millennium would ensue, during which happiness would be the lot of mankind. But since there would be nothing left to desire, its faith would grow weak and die, and Angramainyu, the Evil One, seeing his opportunity, would loose the dragon *Azhi Dahâka* upon the world. The monster would devour a third of all mankind. It would defile water and fire, destroy all plant life, and cause man to commit unspeakable

---

[1] **CCLIX**, 230 *ff*.

[2] There is a good account by Ed. Lehmann in Chantepie de la Saussaye, *Manuel d'hist. des religions*, 474 *ff*., of the French translation, or better in ii, 248 *ff*., of the second German edition (1924).

sins, so that Ahura-Mazda would be obliged to send the hero *Keresâspa* to quell the dragon and restore order on the earth.

The world would grow calm again, and one day a young girl would go to bathe in Lake Kâsava, and, from the seed which Zarathustra had once let fall in its waters, would bear the infant *Saoshyant*, the *Saviour*. He would bring the universe to an end. He would preside over the resurrection and judgment of the dead, and would separate the good, who would enter into heaven, from the wicked who would be swallowed up in hell, but only for three days. After this the mountains would crumble and men would be confronted by the purifying fire : having passed through it they would all be united in perfect love and with one accord would sing the praises of Ahura-Mazda. There would be one final conflict, in which the good angels, headed by Ahura-Mazda and *Sraosha*, would triumph over Angra-mainyu, Azhi Dahâka, and the hosts of evil, who would be cast into the river of fire. And at length all things, living and inanimate, would rest for ever in deathless perfection.

I have given a somewhat simplified version of this eschatological fantasy, but the probability is that the Jews themselves took over even less than this.[1] The features which specially attracted their attention were the conflicts, horrors and catastrophes, the battle between good and evil, the war of angels and demons, the intervention of one or more heroes with supernatural powers, the millennium followed by resurrection, judgment and retribution, and the idea of a tremendous cataclysm which was to mark the downfall of this imperfect world and the dawning splendours of the *Kingdom of God* which was to take its place.[2] In any case, there is reason to think that Persia was not the only source of Jewish apocalyptic. Thus in the Book of the Secrets of Enoch, or the Slavonic Enoch, the idea that souls were created before the world seems to be due to *Hellenic* influence.[3]

The suggestion that the actual idea of a Messiah was derived from Egypt may be substantiated as follows. In the valley of the Nile the legend ran that once, before the beginning of time, there had been an age of joy and prosperity under the sceptre of Osiris, the ideal king, son of Earth and Heaven, the

[1] Böcklein, *Die Verwandschaft der jüdisch-christlichen mit der parsischen Eschatologie*, Göttingen, 1902.

[2] For an account of the transformation of the Persian Saviour into the Jewish Messiah, and of his general importance, *cf.* Reitzenstein, *Das iranische Erlösung-Mysterium*, Bonn, 1921, 116.

[3] **CCLV**, 104. Other borrowings from the same source have been noted by I. Lévy, **CCLXXVII**, 160 *ff.*, but are of minor importance.

Good Being who had redeemed mankind from barbarism.   So far as we know, the Egyptians were not expecting their king to return *at the end of time* ; but among all the themes for medita- tion which Egyptian religion and philosophy presented to the Jewish imagination, was this important conception of the *ideal king*.   It was only necessary for the Jews to transfer him from the past and invest him with the Messianic functions, and then to find for him a name which would link him with David.[1]

III

Predominance of Eschatology about the Time of Jesus

During the period preceding the birth of Jesus, eschatological ideas were prominent in Jewish speculations and preoccupa- tions.   The Roman domination no doubt heightened and sharpened these ideas,[2] because it emphasized the contrast between the present state of Israel and the comforting promises of the prophets of the Exile.   But from that time the Jews lived in a constant state of anxiety or even worse, which lasted more than a century, with the result that the literature of the period was very largely apocalyptic.   Of this literature little remains, but the fragments which have survived, mutilated and inadequate as they are, are evidence of a religious movement of great intensity and importance.[3]   Most of these writings seem to have been produced between 168 and 135, or thereabouts ; but the same themes were constantly reverted to and elaborated in the years which followed.   Moreover, although they were the direct outcome of the times and expressed the fundamental needs of the men of that day, they were usually attributed to celebrities of a far-distant past to Enoch, the son of Jared and father of Methuselah, to the twelve sons of Jacob, to Moses or Solomon, or even to more recent celebrities such as Ezra.

Naturally these Apocalypses varied a good deal in their descriptions of the *last things*, but they were all closely allied in spirit and aim, and in their fundamental ideas.   They all exemplified a new form of prophecy, very different from the old,[4] for, whereas the prophets of former times had thought only of the present and of the world of living men, these Seers

[1] CCLIX, 232.   [2] CCLXXVII, 332.
[3] CCLXXVI, 163 *ff.*, gives the bibliography.   *Cf.* CCLXVI, i, 44–7 ; CCLXV, 70, n. 1 and 2 ; CCLIII, 242–86.   Sanday, CCCIII, 49, reviews the controversy of the last thirty years regarding the status of apocalyptic writings in the Jewish world just before the Christian era.   *Cf.* in addi- tion CCLXXIX, i, 127 *ff.* ; ii, 279 *ff.*
[4] CCLXXIX, ii, 343 *ff.*

turned their eyes to the future and to a realization of the divine Promises which would be dependent on a complete transformation of the world and of the conditions of human life. This world was evil, therefore it must vanish; this life was wretched, hence it must be replaced by a better. But since Jahweh had ceased to be an anthropomorphic God and was now all spirit, he could no longer accomplish such a mundane task himself, and hence the notion of the *Intermediary*, the agent of God, the Messiah, now absolutely necessary for the carrying out of his programme, grew rapidly in precision and importance.

As I have said, there was no fundamentally necessary connexion between the predicted dissolution of the present world and its regeneration, and the Messianic expectation; which explains why some of the Apocalypses seem to ignore Messianic ideas. But actually the two strands of thought became so closely entwined as to be inseparable. Exactly in what order they appeared it would be hard to say, and at this point the matter is not of much importance. If this world was controlled by the forces of evil, led by Satan, then presumably it could only be freed by means of a struggle between the Adversary and some divine envoy. Several of the Apocalypses describe this conflict, which affords the authors an excellent opportunity for venting their bitterness against the oppressors of Israel. As the Jews saw their last hopes vanish, as they were plunged deeper and deeper into helpless wretchedness, these visionaries, their hearts already poisoned by an implacable hate, were aroused to a frenzy of denunciation. Moreover, they castigated with invectives the godless whose impiety retarded the fulfilment of God's promises.[1] The greater part of these Apocalypses appear to emanate from Pharisaic centres [2]; they are filled with the characteristic legalism of the sect, and also with their fervent piety and ardent faith that Jahweh would fulfil his promises. Even at this later period there was still no fixed and definite doctrine with regard to these subjects, and we must beware of trying to make clear and systematic that which often remains vague and obscure. It is a temptation which has not always been resisted; and yet it is only necessary to glance at the more detailed descriptions of such major events as the fate of the dead while awaiting judgment, the coming of the Messiah, and the final destiny of the wicked, to discover many diverse conceptions and even speculations. No doubt all these variations were equally acceptable so long as they could find a place in the general programme which proved to be extremely comprehensive.[3] Possibly the only thing which all

[1] CCLV, 82.   [2] CCLV, 93.   [3] CCLV, 108.

these Messianic writers had in common was the liveliness of their hope and the eagerness with which they awaited its fulfilment.

I have spoken above of a programme, but in reality there were two,[1] corresponding to two different but equally popular types of eschatological thought.

According to the first, God would manifest the Messiah, and the wicked, who would rise up against him in a general revolt, would suffer defeat and annihilation. Then would follow a long period of peace and happiness, during which the earth, thus purged of its evil elements, would be under the reign of the Messiah. Persian influence ultimately fixed the length of his reign at *a thousand years*. It would be terminated by the resurrection of the dead and the last judgment, after which the eternal reign of God would begin.

The alternative plan was simpler and kept closer to the old idea of the kingdom. After the advent of the Messiah and the revolt and destruction of the wicked, the dead would at once be raised ; the judgment would decide their destiny, and the eternal reign of the Messiah would begin.

The Jewish apocalyptic writers developed numerous variations on these two eschatological themes, all tending to dramatize the central situation. In all these variations different elements would be selected and combined, and even when two presentations were essentially the same, some internal transposition would generally give an appearance of difference.[2] The most characteristic lines of thought producing these variants may be described as follows :

(1) The Messiah doubtless would not come unheralded. Warning of his approach would be given by wars, famines and calamities of every kind. In the upheaval, nature would forget her laws ; the world would throw off all constraint, whether of reason, piety or common sense, till the condition of the living would be more pitiable than that of the dead.[3]

(2) But the Messiah could not make his appearance in the midst of this anarchy, so he would be preceded by Elijah, of whom Ben-Sira says, " *Thou who art ready for the time, as it is written to still wrath before the fierce anger of God, to turn the hearts of the fathers unto the children, and to restore the tribes of Israel* " (Ecclus. xlviii. 10).[4] That Prophet who had been caught up to heaven without dying would now return, and would restore

---

[1] *Cf*. Tixeront, *Hist. des. dogmes*, i, 43, which gives a list of references.
[2] For details, *cf*. **CCLXXV**, 186 *ff*.
[3] Apoc. Baruch xlviii. 41.
[4] The same idea occurs in Mal. iv. 5 *ff*., which probably influenced Ecclesiasticus.

order on earth, redress the balance which had been lost,[1] and prepare the way of the Messiah.

(3) Since the figure of this envoy from Jahweh held the very centre of the eschatological picture, and since his activity sets the final drama in motion, the Jews naturally produced a number of accounts both of his person and of his activities, which did not all tally with one another. To this point, and to the further discrepancies which appeared in their attempts to link up Elijah and his activities with the judgment, the resurrection and the end of the world, we shall return shortly.

(4) The coming of the Messiah would provoke a coalition of the wicked under the command of a leader, as to whose identity opinion seems to have remained vague.[2] It was left for Christian apocalyptic to fill in the uncertain outline and give this figure the name of *Antechrist*, or rather *Antichrist*.

(5) The hosts of evil would be defeated ; but opinions varied as to the identity of the victor. Some said that God himself would thus irresistibly demonstrate his power,[3] but the greater number believed that the Messiah, invested by Jahweh with supernatural might, would be the actual conqueror. This second theory is more in line with the general development of Jewish eschatology.[4]

(6) The overthrow of the wicked would be followed by the establishment of the blessed Messianic Kingdom. The Messiah, prince of peace,[5] would be enthroned at Jerusalem ; but the holy city would be renewed and purged of idolatry, or even replaced by a celestial city sent down fully fashioned from on high.[6] In and around this city the chosen people, now no longer scattered, would dwell in all their ancient glory. This point of time was sometimes chosen for the resurrection of the righteous of Israel. The *Kingdom of God* would bring about a peace untroubled by fear, a prosperity which no chance could destroy, an inalienable bliss. It would be the true Golden Age. Jewish imagination warmed to the task of depicting this era of unparalleled happiness, in which Jahweh and his people would at length be united in that perfect and unclouded harmony which the Covenant had promised and must eventually bring forth.[7]

[1] Mark ix. 12 : Ἡλείας μὲν ἐλθὼν πρῶτον ἀποκαθιστάνει πάντα.

[2] Enoch xc. ; Apoc. Baruch xl. *Cf.* M. Friedländer, *Der Antichrist*, Göttingen, 1901.

[3] Asc. Mos. x. 7.   [4] Apoc. Baruch xxxix. 7 *ff.*

[5] This seems to have been his true character, rather than that of warrior hero, or conqueror. *Cf.* **CCLX**, 286.

[6] Enoch xc. 28–30.

[7] Enoch x. 16 *ff.* ; Apoc. Baruch xxix. 5–8 ; lxxiii. 2–7.

(7) This Messianic reign was sometimes thought of as eternal[1] ; but it was more usual to suppose that after a long period of years, *e.g.*, a thousand, the scene of the Kingdom would undergo a further transformation, in which all its perishable and corruptible elements would be destroyed in a vast and purifying fire.[2]

(8) It was then that the dead would arise. For a long time, as we have seen, this was held to apply only to the righteous, the sinners remaining in perpetual oblivion in the dust of *Sheol* ; but at last it was felt that the logic of retribution demanded the punishment of the wicked as well as the reward of the righteous and hence a universal resurrection.[3] " *For all men shall rise again, some to be exalted and some to be humbled and put to shame.*"[4] This resurrection is usually interpreted as meaning a restoration of the body which had been laid in the grave, but there may be also a suggestion that the righteous will undergo a kind of spiritual transformation. This is, at any rate, plausible in those cases where their resurrection was anticipated before the reign of the Messiah.[5]

(9) Opinions differed widely with regard to the last judgment. Some supposed that there would be two such judgments, one when the Messiah had overthrown his enemies, and one after the general resurrection at the end of the millennium. Theoretically Jahweh himself was to be the judge and to pronounce sentence, yet in Enoch lxix. 27, and possibly also in xli. 9, this function is attributed to the *Son of Man*, who has the rôle of the angel of the Lord, giving judgment in God's presence and in his name. It should be noted, however, that chapters xxxvii. to lxxi. of Enoch were written after the Christian era had begun, and are even alleged by some to be of Christian authorship. They may well have been influenced by Christian accounts of the last day and of the part which Christ was to play in it.

(10) At the judgment mankind would be divided. The righteous would be privileged to enter God's kingdom, where they would dwell in his divine presence, among the angelic host, gazing upon his countenance, and sharing in his *glory*, that is to say, they would shine with a radiance like the sun ; and they would live for ever.[6] It must be confessed that the description of heavenly joys is somewhat vague. As for the wicked, they would share the fate of the demons, being cast into *Gehenna*

---

[1] Enoch lxii. 14 ; Ps. Solomon xvii. 4 ; Sib. Oracles iii. 49–50 ; 766.
[2] Apoc. Baruch lxxiv. 2 *ff.*   [3] Apoc. Baruch l. 2 *ff.*
[4] Test. of the Twelve Patriarchs, Benj. 10.
[5] **CCLV**, 84.   [6] **CCLV**, 92.

for eternity. It was only very much later, in the *Zohar*,[1] that Jewish thought showed any sign of being influenced by the idea which was the climax of Persian eschatology, that of a renewed universe, in which all creation, even the evil spirits themselves, would enjoy happiness and peace.

Such, then, are the main features of the picture of the last things. The angle of vision differed with each observer, for on this subject there was no authoritative teaching. Some of the documents in question, with their more or less marked peculiarities, may derive from some special sect or circle of Messianic believers, and may represent merely the opinions of a small group of Jews. This accounts for the seemingly, and actually, vague, confused and cloudy effect produced by the description as a whole. But it also bears witness to the keen interest of the pious Jews in these visions and meditations, which comforted them in their misfortunes. It is unnecessary to show that such dreams had nothing in common with the ancient Jahwism. In form and frequently in content, this popular literature, with its emotional appeal, is as far removed from the *Tannaïm*, with their exegesis and legalistic studies, as the professional theologian of the present day is from the mazes of the Cabbala or the calculations of millennial enthusiasts.[2]

IV

CHARACTER OF THE MESSIAH

For us the most interesting of all these fantasies are those which are concerned with the Messianic expectation, and these therefore deserve somewhat closer attention.[3] The first impression which we get from the sources is that this Messianic hope, under the guise of a belief in a Davidic king, who would restore the glories of Israel, was almost entirely a popular one, being in reality a survival of the hopes which had been awakened, and afterwards disappointed by the Return. In more or less enlightened circles, it was very much less widespread than the expectation of the end of the world and resurrection of the dead [4]; but those who supported it did so most energetically and with important results. It has even been suggested as the motive power in the evolution of Judaism, but this is clearly an exaggeration.[5] It undoubtedly was the impulse behind the

---

[1] Franck, *La Kabbale* (2nd edit.), Paris, 1889, 217, n. 2.

[2] **CCLXXIX**, i, 127.

[3] **CCLXXII**, 294 *ff.* ; **CCLIX**, *Erstes Buch.*   [4] **CCXCII**, 22.

[5] **CCLVIII**, 157, " *Die Messiasidee ist die triebende Kraft in der Entwicklung des Judentums.*"

constant state of unrest in Palestine, the inspiration of the
great rebellions against the power of Rome, and in consequence
the cause of the ruin of the Jewish people ; but that is quite
another matter.

The expectation of a Messiah first arose,[1] as we have seen,
out of the impossibility of reconciling God's promises of prosperity for his people, with the wretched conditions in which he
allowed them to linger. As the conception of the power of God was
heightened and extended, the more impossible it became to accept
as final the humiliation of Israel, which could only be explained
by the weakness of Israel's Lord, or his failure to keep his
promise. On the other hand, the Jewish national fortunes were
at such a low ebb that it seemed impossible for them to be
restored save by some divine miracle, some direct intervention
on the part of God. And the further they got from anthropomorphism, and the more familiar they became with Persian
eschatology, the stronger grew the idea of an instrument of
Jahweh, of an *Intermediary*.

At the outset they hoped for a restoration of the House of
David in some such fashion as the Prophets had conceived of
it ; but the destruction of the Persian Empire was followed by
such a series of troubles and disasters, that Israel turned more
and more towards some wholly supernatural revival of the
national glory. In particular, the violent attack of the Seleucid
Antiochus Epiphanes (175–164 B.C.) which endangered their
very religion, and the unexpected check which that attack
received at the hands of the Maccabees, encouraged the devout to
put their trust for the future in the direct intervention of God.

It was at this time that the Book of Daniel, which was

[1] I use the term *expectation*, a hope which became increasingly im-
patient, rather than *idea*, because the Messianic idea came into existence
long before this period. Some scholars would even have us believe that
it dates back to the time of Moses, at least in the sense that men looked
forward to the direct *reign* of Jahweh which would come to pass in the
future, as the direct reign of Osiris had shed its light on the dawn of
Egypt. The theory is ill-founded and unsupported by documentary
evidence, but nevertheless the tenth-century court poets who hailed
David as the Messiah during his own lifetime must have had some
grounds for this form of flattery. It seems extremely likely that the
same idea was exploited for the benefit of subsequent sovereigns even
more frequently than reliable documents suggest (**CCLIX**, 277). In
reality we can trace neither its origin nor its earlier forms. In all probability it only became definite and of practical importance as a reaction
against the misfortunes which overwhelmed Israel in the sixth century.
In the old days it was the king who was the Anointed or *Mashiah* of
Jahweh ; in post-exilic literature this rôle was ordinarily attributed to
the High Priest, heir of the priest-kings who ruled before the Captivity
(**CCLIX**, 4).

later to become at once the basis and the justification of the Messianic hope, appeared.[1] Chapter vii. (13 ff.) contains the following passage : " *I saw in the night visions, and behold, one like the Son of Man came with the clouds of heaven, and came to the Ancient of days, and they brought him near before him. And there was given him dominion, and glory, and a kingdom, that all people, nations and languages should serve him ; his dominion is an everlasting dominion which shall not pass away, and his kingdom shall never be destroyed.*" When the author spoke of this figure who was *like a son of man* (which simply means like a *man*) he was certainly not thinking of the Messiah. The figure may have been merely a symbol of the chosen people who were destined to supersede the four monstrous beasts described in the beginning of the chapter (vii. 3), and which probably represent the Empires of the Babylonians, Medes, Persians, and Macedonians. But the identification of the figure with the Messiah was tempting. To bring it about, it was only necessary to imagine that the symbolic figure was a heavenly person, sent by God, and invested with his power, bearing the name of the *Son of Man*, to say that the Messiah would appear in such a form. The identification is actually effected in the Book of Enoch, at least in its later parts, which represent the Messiah as the heavenly Man, a miraculous being, created by God before time began and reserved in heaven till his appointed hour.[2] It should be noted, moreover, that this victorious Messiah was not necessarily foreseen as the warrior of popular imagination, adorned with the spoils of conquest.[3]

The old conception of the Davidic king, destined to bring in the Kingdom of God for Israel, had to be transformed before the conception of the Messiah could be arrived at. The transformation was the result of foreign influence, of contact with some myth describing the accession of a new god to the throne of the world.[4] The fact that the Messiah was represented as having to take the field against a host which included demons as well as the wicked, and as triumphing over the world of

---

[1] There is an interesting examination of the passage in **CCLIX**, 341 ff.
[2] **CCLX**, 286.
[3] Enoch xxxix. 6 ; xlvi. 1, 2 ; xlviii. 3–6 ; lxvii. 7 ; lxx. 1 ; 4 Esdras xii. 32 ; xiii. 26, 52. *Cf.* **LIX**, 275 ; **CCLXXXVIII**, 40 ff. ; **CCLIX**, 373 ff., 379 ff. Note that the expression *Son of Man* (*bar-enosh* or *bar-nasha*) stresses the *humanity* of the Messiah, like the Greek υἱὸς τοῦ ἀνθρώπου, as opposed to *Son of God* (*ben-elohim* or *bar-ilaha* = υἱὸς τοῦ Θεοῦ). **CCXCVIII**, 383.
[4] **CCLXI**, 25. It has been suggested that (**CCLXXXVIII**, *loc. cit.*) we have here the transformation of a sun-god, but no convincing proof of this has been brought forward.

fallen angels and their leader, makes it clear that the myth in question had its source in the Persian idea of the final struggle between Good and Evil. It is to be noted, however, that the expectation of an ideal king, ruling over the universe, was common to the Semitic peoples. It represents the particular pattern of the reorganization of the world peculiar to the Semitic imagination.[1] Even in Assyro-Babylonian religion, the expectation of a Messianic kingdom seems to be an anticipation of the myth as it was later developed by Jewish Christianity. It already contains the Messiah, who is both god and man, the supernatural birth, the miraculous resurrection, the hope of a return, and other elements.[2]

The apocalyptic visions of Enoch and 4 Esdras did not gain general acceptance in Israel, and even those who did accept them did so with reservations. The Sibylline Oracles, for instance, still preserved the notion of an invincible king who would come to reign over the renewed world, and would convert the Gentiles by the splendour of his glory.[3] Moreover, the Psalms of Solomon, which belong to the time of Pompey (about 63 B.C.), maintain the same attitude, as the following passages show : " *It is thou, O Lord, who hast chosen David to be king over Israel, and thou hast made a covenant with him regarding his seed for ever, that his kingdom shall not pass away from before thy presence* " (xvii. 4) ; " *Hearken, Lord, and raise up for them their king, of the house of David, at the hour which thou hast appointed, O God, to rule over thy servant, Israel ; and gird him with strength that he may bring low the unjust rulers and purge Jerusalem of the nations who throng her streets, bringing her to ruin. Give him wisdom and justice, and let him drive out sinners from the heritage. . . .*" (xvii. 21), and again in xvii. 30: " *And he will bring all the heathen under his yoke, and they will serve him.*" These quotations obviously represent the earlier belief, and it is hard to say whether, in the time of Jesus, it still predominated. I am inclined to think so, because, in the first place, the various Messianic claimants known to us had nothing celestial about their origins, and in the second place, the Pharisaic schools do not seem to have represented the appearance and birth of the Messiah as differing at all from those of any ordinary man.[4] Justin Martyr attributes to the Jew Trypho the saying, " *We all await a Messiah who shall be a man born of men,*" [5] and

---

[1] **CCXCVII**, 303.
[2] *Cf.* Dhorme, *La Religion Assyro-Babylonienne*, Paris, 1910, 171 *ff.*
[3] *Sib. Oracles* iii. 652 *ff.*   [4] **CCLXXV**, 223.
[5] *Dial.*, xlix, 1, καὶ γὰρ πάντες ἡμεῖς τὸν χριστὸν ἄνθρωπον ἐξ ἀνθρώπων προσδοκῶμεν γενήσεσθαι. The idea of a Messiah already existing in

this was probably the current idea. It seemed likely that the Messiah had already been born somewhere, unknown to men, and that at any moment he might manifest himself. In Jesus' day there was a widespread belief that this Messiah was not to be found among kings and the mighty of this world, but among the men of God, inspired by the spirit of the Prophets.[1] It should be noted, moreover, that it was only about this time that the word *Messiah* (Anointed) came into general use to designate God's deputy in the last great crisis, and that it did not come into general use among the Rabbis until after the destruction of the Temple, in A.D. 70. This should be borne in mind.[2]

The Rabbis seem to have been in doubt as to the nature of the coming Messiah, wavering between the passage from Daniel (vii. 13) which states that the Son of Man will make his appearance upon the clouds of heaven, and Zechariah, ix. 9, which shows him riding meekly on an ass.[3] The Christians managed to reconcile and combine these two aspects, but for the Jews they remained distinct, and no doubt each man chose between them according to his temperament and inclinations.[4] However, all the evidence goes to prove that as yet it was only a small group of enthusiasts who responded to Daniel's vision, though that vision was ultimately to prevail. Meanwhile the devout Jew, accustomed as he was to apocalypses of all sorts, was quite ready to accept any and every manifestation of Jahweh that had to do with the establishment of that kingdom which was a centre of his hopes.

It cannot be too strongly stressed that we no longer possess the data which would enable us to disentangle and date accurately all the eschatological and Messianic conceptions contained in our sources. We can conclude, however, that before the first century A.D. the Jews were much more deeply concerned with the *Kingdom of God*, that reign of bliss under the perfected Covenant, than with the figure of the Messiah ; and that during that century, on the other hand, the Messianic expectation became increasingly prominent up to the time of the Great Revolt. The cause of this movement lay not so much in the added disasters which fell on Israel, as in those calculations,

---

heaven, whence Jahweh would send him at the appointed hour, an hour whose arrival might be hastened by the piety of the faithful, was, however, already familiar in certain quarters. *Cf.* Enoch xxxix. 6 ; xlvi. 1, 2 ; xlviii. 3–6 ; lxii. 7 ; lxx. 1 ; 4 Esdras xii. 32 ; xiii. 26, etc. But 4 Esdras is under suspicion of Christian influence.

[1] CCXCVIII, 399.　　　　　　　　　　　[2] CCL, i, 136 *ff.*
[3] CCLXXV, 227 *ff.*　　　　　　　　　　[4] CCLXXVIII, ii, 330.

widely accepted among the common people, which claimed to establish a date for the inauguration of the long-desired *Kingdom of God* (ἡ βασιλεία τοῦ Θεὸν). Apparently one such estimate fixed the Great Day about the year A.D. 30, and it may be that even then popular imagination still concentrated on the *coming Kingdom* rather than on the Messiah : it was the Kingdom which was preached both by John the Baptist and by Jesus.[1]

In the circles where Pharisaic teaching predominated, it was held that the Messiah would be the *son of David*, as the Prophets had foretold. The expression *the reign of the house of David* was commonly used to denote the Messianic era.[2] But it is not certain that the Rabbis believed in a secret survival of the *house of David* somewhere, awaiting the hour of manifestation ; the term *the house of David* probably meant *God's chosen race*, whom he would consider *worthy to reign*. The common people, on the contrary, took the words literally, and so did the compilers of the genealogies in Matthew and Luke. Their only object was to link the son of Joseph the Carpenter with David. The drastic precautionary measures which the Flavians and the Antonines apparently took against the *house of David* imply that they, too, took the words literally.[3]

There are hints, however, of other conceptions of Jahweh's Anointed, which must be briefly examined. It may have been during the rule of the Priestly family of the Hasmonæans that the idea arose that the Messiah would spring from their house, or at least from the tribe of Levi and not from that of Judah from which David sprang. Certainly, whatever the date and circumstances of its origin, the idea of the advent of a Messiah of the *tribe of Levi* gained adherents in Israel, and no doubt those of the priestly caste who were sympathetic to Messianism found it most acceptable.

A curious document, published in 1910,[4] relating to a Jewish sect established at Damascus, which will form the subject of a later chapter, contains the definite statement that the Messiah will not be a scion of the house of David, but " *a priest of the race of Aaron and of Israel, who shall chastise all those who rebel against the authority of the priesthood.*"[5] This

---

[1] **CCLXXXIII,** 5 *ff.*   [2] **CCLXXV,** 216.

[3] Eusebius, *H.E.,* iii. 12, tells of Vespasian's search for members of the house of David ; Domitian seems to have followed his example (iii. 19–20), and later Trajan (iii. 32). *Cf.* Michael the Syrian, vi. 3 (Chabot's edit., i, 169*a*), on the searches and executions attributed to Vespasian.

[4] Schechter, *Documents of Jewish Sectaries,* vol. i. *Fragments of a Zadokite work,* Cambridge, 1910.

[5] Israel Lévy, *Un écrit sadducéen antérieur à la destruction du Temple,* **REJ,** April 1, 1911, 167.

document alone might be set aside as merely expressing the opinion of a few schismatics, but its evidence is confirmed by the Testament of the Twelve Patriarchs.[1] It was probably because of this second opinion as to the derivation of the Messiah, which was fairly widespread and which contradicted the first, that it was considered necessary to blend the two theories by saying that *He who was to come* would be descended both from Levi and from Judah, from Levi inasmuch as he would be High Priest, from Judah in his capacity of King.[2]

There is no need to enlarge on the view that a Messiah might come who would be a *son of Joseph*, also called a *son of Ephraim* ; doubtless a Messiah of a lower rank, whose nature and relation to the other Messiah is hard to define. We only know that he was destined to perish in the fight against the powers of evil and that it was the son of David who would assume the kingdom.[3] We have no means of dating the appearance of this concept of a Messiah who would be a *son of Joseph*, or of tracing its development. It may be that Dalman is right in claiming that it originated in the blessing pronounced by the dying Moses in Deuteronomy, xxxiii. 16–17 [4] : " *Let the blessing of him that dwelt in the bush come upon the head of Joseph, and upon the forehead of him that was made ruler over his brothers. His glory is like the firstling of his bullock. His horns are like the horns of the buffalo ; with them he shall push the people together to the ends of the earth.*" The most probable source for the belief that this Messiah was doomed to perish in the final conflict is an obscure passage from Zechariah (xii. 10) : " *They shall mourn*

[1] Levi xviii. 1, which says that the Lord will raise up a priest who will accomplish all his designs.

[2] Test. of the Twelve Patriarchs, Levi ii. : Διὰ σοῦ καὶ Ἰούδα ὀφθήσεται κύριος ἐν ανθρώποις, and other passages. Schürer, **LXXV**, iii, 257, n. 64, has collected some of them (Simeon, 7 ; Dan. 5 ; Gad. 8 ; Joseph, 19), but rightly suspects them of Christian influence. The evidence of Simeon, 7, alone suffices : ἀναστήσει γὰρ κύριος ἐκ τοῦ Λευὶ ὡς ἀρχιερεα καὶ ἐκ τοῦ Ἰούδα ὡς βασιλέα, θεὸν καὶ ἄνθρωπον. A fragment of Irenæus, taken from a *catena* on Deuteronomy (*P.G.*, vol. vii, col. 1240, no. xvii) confirms the hypothesis that the Christians accepted the twofold origin of the Messiah : ἐκ δὲ τοῦ Λευὶ καὶ τοῦ Ἰούδα τὸ κατὰ σαρκὰ, ὡς βασιλεὺς καὶ ἱερεὺς ἐγεννήθη. The Epistle to the Hebrews discusses the thesis of the High-priesthood of the Lord Jesus.

[3] *Talmud Bab., Sukkah*, 52[a], in **LXXV**, ii, 535, n. 34. The *son of Joseph* is introduced as a familiar figure in Rab. Dosa's discussion of Zech. xii. 10. There were two Rabbis of this name, one belonging to the latter part of the first century, and the other to Hadrian's reign ; and the passage may refer equally well to either of them.

[4] It is in reference to this passage that the *Babylonian Talmud* calls the Messiah the son of Joseph. The *Jerusalem Talmud* does not mention him. *Cf.* **CCLXXV**, 252.

*for him, as one mourneth for his only son. They shall weep
bitterly for him, as one weepeth for his firstborn."*

This belief in a Messianic " son of Joseph," which might be
more valuable if it could be accurately dated, is interesting
chiefly because it raises for the first time the question of a
suffering Messiah, which is so important and has been so much
discussed in connexion with the Christian interpretation of
the death of Jesus.[1] But the *son of Joseph* or *Ephraim* of
whom the *Talmud* speaks [2] was not really a suffering *Messiah*
in the strict sense ; he was to die in battle, which is quite a
different matter. Students have long been divided on the
subject, some maintaining that Jesus' contemporaries were
already quite convinced of the possible, or even the inevitable,
suffering and death in store for the Messiah, while others deny
it.[3] The evidence seems to favour the second view.

This is not the place to go into the question in detail, but
it may be worth considering the passage which the partisans
of the theory that the Messiah was destined to suffer consider
decisive, namely chapters lii. and liii. of Deutero-Isaiah,[4] which
deal with the *Servant of Jahweh (Ebed-Jahweh)*. It is easy to
imagine the relief with which Christians faced with the task
of removing the *stumbling-block of the Cross* (1 Cor. i. 23), a task
which could only be accomplished by proving that, *according
to the Scriptures* themselves, Jesus, the Messiah, had to suffer
agony and death in order to take away the sins of the world,
must have welcomed the discovery of the following passage
(Isa. liii. 3 *ff.*) :

> He was despised and rejected of men,
> A man of sorrows and acquainted with grief ;
> And we hid as it were our faces from him ;
> He was despised, and we esteemed him not.

> 4. Surely he hath borne our griefs,
> And carried our sorrows :
> Yet we did esteem him stricken,
> Smitten of God, and afflicted.

---

[1] Dalman, *Der leidende und der sterbende Messias der Synagoge in
ersten nachchristlichen Jahrtausend*, Berlin, 1888 ; **CCLXXV**, 236 *ff.* ;
LXXV, ii, 553 *ff.* ; **LI**, 386.

[2] **CCCV**, ii, 273 *ff.*, 363 *ff.*

[3] Bibliography in Goguel, *Jésus de Nazareth*, Paris, 1925, 199, n. 2,
and in Odeberg, *III Enoch, or the Hebrew Book of Enoch*, Cambridge, 1928,
144, n. 5, who would like to see in the suffering Messiah the figure of Bar-
Cochba, who was overthrown in Hadrian's reign, after a period of
triumph.

[4] On this passage see **CCXXIII**, 64 *ff.*, 102 *ff.*, 122 *ff.* ; **CCLIX**, 316 *ff.*,
337.

5. But he was wounded for our transgressions,
He was bruised for our iniquities ;
The chastisement of our peace was upon him ;
And with his stripes we are healed.

.   .   .   .

7. He was oppressed, and he was afflicted,
Yet he opened not his mouth :
He is brought as a lamb to the slaughter,
And as a sheep before her shearers is dumb,
So he opened not his mouth.

The temptation to regard the tragic fate of the Nazarene as the necessary fulfilment of this prophecy, and to use the vivid images of these superb lines to eke out their perhaps rather hazy recollections of the traditional accounts of the Passion, was one which the Christians could scarcely be expected to resist. But the naturalness of their action is not a justification of it, or a proof that Deutero-Isaiah really intended the words in question to refer to the Messiah.

While the whole poem is permeated by the myth of the *servant of Jahweh*,[1] it is not surprising that it contains no explicit statement calculated to establish the precise meaning of that myth. On the whole the critics are agreed in viewing this *Ebed-Jahweh* as a personification of the chosen people, Israel,[2] and in taking the following chapters as an account of the trials of the Jewish nation at the hands of the *goyim*, who enjoy their brief hour of triumph, till the repentance of the Exiles prepares the way for the new Covenant (lix.) and the victorious establishment of the New Jerusalem (lx.),

Arise, O Jerusalem, and shine ; for thy light is come,
And the glory of the Lord is risen upon thee.

This interpretation is extremely plausible, but it has been challenged none the less, even by those who are not bound by credal considerations. Hugo Gressmann, for instance, to whom theology is indebted for so many valuable suggestions, has pointed out that the *Servant* "*undergoes suffering and trial with his people, but cannot be identified with them.*"[3] And since in his opinion there can be no question here of a historical figure (for, as he points out, Isaiah's description falls altogether outside actuality, and has nothing personal or specific about it [4]), he assumes that the Prophet is thinking of an ideal Servant, the Messianic King. He qualifies this general conclusion, however, by making it clear that Deutero-Isaiah has created a

[1] Isa. xlii. 1–4 ; xlix. 1–6 *ff.* ; l. 4, 4–10 ; lii. 13–liii. 12. On these passages see **CCLIX**, 287 *ff.*
[2] **CCXXIII**, 18 *ff.*   [3] **CCLIX**, 317.   [4] **CCLIX**, 219–23.

new and important variant of the Messianic figure, namely, the *Messiah of the Exile,* who fits easily into the Prophet's vision of Jahwism as a universal religion.[1]

If Gressmann is right, Christians had some justification for seeing in the passage in question a reference to their own Messiah, Jesus. But it is only an apparent justification, and from the genuine Palestinian point of view they were wrong, because there is no evidence that the Jews of the pre-Christian era regarded this mysterious *Ebed-Jahweh* as the Messiah, and we never find him playing the part which popular belief assigned to the Messiah. Of course, no one can say with certainty that there were not some Jews, most likely those belonging to small groups more or less on the fringes of the general belief, who, thinking on relatively original lines, anticipated the Christian exegesis by giving Isaiah lii.–liii. a Messianic interpretation,[2] but I repeat there is not the slightest evidence for such a hypothesis. For us the main fact is that the *Ebed-Jahweh* of Deutero-Isaiah was outside the range of the current conceptions of the Saviour of Israel. It may be observed that it would have been easy enough to make use of the trials of Job, for instance, in support of the tendentious and forced exegesis of the Deutero-Isaiah passage put forward by Christian apologetic.[3] But this was not done till after the death of Jesus, and by the Christians themselves. It was not until the end of the second century A.D., or even the beginning of the third, that the Rabbis began to realize its significance, and the possibility of turning it to account for their own purposes.[4] To suppose that while the

[1] CCLIX, 339.

[2] LXXV, 175 *ff.*, and CCLXXXVIII, 41, who strongly favours this view, and compares the two Messiahs with the dying Tammuz and the victorious Marduk, or with Adonis and Melkart. In particular, see Gressmann, CCLX, 317 *ff.*, who sees in Isaiah's description of the sad fate of the *Ebed-Jahweh* a return to the great Semitic myth of the dying and rising god, a god, that is to say, of the same type as Tammuz-Adonis. Since every phenomenon must have its cause, it is quite permissible to suppose that the Semitic myth in question influenced the form of the passage from Isaiah, or even helped to inspire it, but to go further than this is to read more into the text than it warrants, and to be led astray by a desire for a well-rounded system.

[3] Spitta, *Zur. Gesch. und Liter. des Urchristentums,* Göttingen, 1901, iii, 2.

[4] CCLII, 450 ; CCLVII, 151 ; CCLXXV, 236 *ff.* ; LXXV, ii, 648 *ff.* P. de Grandmaison (*Jésus-Christ,* Paris, 1928, ii, 259, n. 1) expresses surprise at this long silence in Rabbinic writings, and cannot understand why such " obvious " passages as Isa. liii. and Zech. xiv. 1 *ff.* were not taken up and expounded. He attempts to discover " one or two allusions " in the Apocryphal books (Similitudes of Enoch xlvi. 4 *ff.* ; Test. of the Twelve Patriarchs, Benj. iii. 8), but he is obliged to admit that they

people as a whole went on looking for the King of Glory, there
were Jews, of whom nothing positive is known, but necessarily
far above the general level, who, shortly before the Christian
era, had adopted a conception of the Messiah in harmony with
the character of the *Ebed-Jahweh*,[1] is only, I think, to explain
the obscure by the still more obscure.

One essential fact calls for special note : there is no doubt
that Judaism was well acquainted with the idea of voluntary
expiatory suffering,[2] and that it also recognized the redemptive
efficacy, under certain circumstances, of the shedding of blood [3] ;
the question is whether these ideas really underlie Isaiah
lii.–liii., or even Wisdom ii. 12–20, which takes up and develops
more fully than Deutero-Isaiah the theme of the Righteous
One persecuted and finally vindicated by God against His
adversaries. It seems extremely doubtful. There is nothing
in the passage from Wisdom to suggest such an interpretation,
and since the author appears to have been familiar with Isaiah
in its present form,[4] he cannot have known what seems so
obvious to some modern scholars. The original idea was that
the Servant of Jahweh would suffer and die for the sins of the
people (liii. 5–6) ; Jahweh who had afflicted him would be
appeased by the severity of the ordeal which he had imposed,
and would raise him up with honour and glory (liii. 10) to be
the restorer of Israel and the light of the Gentiles (Loisy).
This is the essential point which the Prophet, whose aim is
above all the *consolation of Israel,* chiefly wishes to impress
on his readers. The Servant has somewhat the character of the
scapegoat laden with the sins of the people, rather than that of

are " highly questionable," as indeed they are. For the attempts that
have been made to prove that the Christian interpretation of Isa. lii.–liii.
was already current in Israel in the time of Jesus, *cf.* **CCLXXIX,** i, 551,
and iii, 166, n. 255. On the Rabbinical passages cited, see Montefiore,
Rabbinic Literature and Gospel Teachings, London, 1930, 305 *ff.*

[1] I. Lévy, *Le sacrifice d'Isaac*, 184. The passages from Justin Martyr
(*Dial.*, lxxxix, 2 ; xci, 1 ; xciii, 2) adduced by Schürer in support of his
argument (**LXXV,** ii, 555) do seem capable of such an interpretation,
and the Catholic writer J. Bonsirven, S.J., is fully justified in referring
to them, in his recent work, *Les idées juives au temps de Notre Seigneur*
(Paris, 1934, 161), as " *rather remarkable admissions*," and although
Justin Martyr attributes them to the Jew Trypho, I am inclined to
think that the Christian apologist was responsible for them himself,
being already convinced that the Scriptures must necessarily have foretold the sufferings of Christ.

[2] **CCLXXV,** 236.

[3] *Cf.* Windisch, *Die Sühnkraft des Blutes*, Excursus in Hebrews,
pp. 77 *ff.*, in Lietzmann, *Hdb. zum N. T.*, Tübingen, 1913, and p. 82 of the
2nd edit. (1931).

[4] *Cf.* Wisdom ii. 12 and Isa. iii. 2.

the *Redeemer* sent by Jahweh, which is the rôle attributed to Jesus by Christianity. Moreover, a close examination of the original passage, in which both the text and its interpretation are uncertain,[1] leaves a strong impression that Christian exegesis has read into the passage the meaning which it desired to extract from it.

The silence which was preserved by the early Rabbis on the subject of the Messiah's sufferings is an unanswerable argument. In their teaching concerning the Anointed of Jahweh, the early rabbis laid emphasis chiefly on an idea which is the very opposite of the one for which Deutero-Isaiah is supposed to provide evidence. They affirmed the complete and inevitable triumph of the Blessed One, and the future glory of his reign. Thus as Fr. Lagrange puts it, the Rabbis as a whole " *shut their eyes to those texts which predicted the sufferings of the Messiah.*" In particular, they did not realize until the second half of the second century A.D., or even later, that Isaiah lii. 13–liii. 12 foretold them. The author of the *Targum of Jonathan* exercises remarkable exegetical ingenuity with regard to Isaiah lii.–liii., in order to refer anything unfortunate in the prophecy to the people, the Temple, and so on, leaving the glory for the Messiah. Even when the Rabbis did begin to acknowledge the possible sufferings of the Messiah, they relegated his ordeal to the period of his life before his glorification. The point is that in early Rabbinical teaching the death of the Messiah, son of David, was never expiatory. Where it is mentioned, as in the passage from 4 Esdras (vii. 29) which runs, " *After these years* "—the 400 years of the Messianic reign of bliss—" *shall my son, the Messiah, die, and all in whom is the breath of life,*" [2] it is a natural death, and, so to speak, neutral : it emphasizes the humanity of the Messiah, and is without special significance either with regard to salvation or forgiveness.[3] In other words, the Christian interpretation of Christ's death is not based on the traditions of Israel, and the difficulty with which (on the evidence of the Synoptic Gospels [4]) Jesus' disciples accepted his future sufferings, as well as the dislike shown by the Jews, in the cause of subsequent polemics, to the idea of the Passion, is of great evidential importance.

The fact is that, as Fr. Lagrange rightly points out,[5] as

---

[1] **CCXXIII**, 122 *ff.*

[2] I know of no other passage of similar tenor and this dates from after the destruction of Jerusalem in A.D. 70. *Cf.* Gunkel, in **CCLXIX**, ii, 352.

[3] **CCLXXV**, 245.

[4] Mark viii. 31 *ff.* ; Matt. xvi. 21 *ff.* ; Luke ix. 22 *ff.*

[5] **CCLXXV**, 251.

long as the Jews believed that salvation lay in exact observance of the *Torah*, it was inconceivable that they should accept the idea of the sacrificial death or expiatory sufferings of the Messiah. This was quite clear to Saint Paul. For Israel the Messianic hope constituted a natural sequel to the Law, not an obstacle to it, and implied not its abolition, but its complete fulfilment. That is why we now recognize that the Christian doctrine of the Messiah is no mere extension of Jewish Messianism, but the natural consequence of Jesus' fate and the fruit of the meditations of his disciples after his death, and on the subject of that death.[1]

V

THE PLACE OF MESSIANISM IN JEWISH LIFE

Finally, it is clear that in practice, eschatological and Messianic speculation led to beliefs that varied widely as between different circles, groups, or even individuals.[2] Each formed conclusions determined by his temperament or culture. To the Zealot the Messiah appeared as a kind of glorified Judas Maccabees. To the Pharisee he was the righteous ruler over God's people, freed at last from the yoke of the *goyim*. For the pious Essene he was God's envoy, invested with supernatural power. Apparently the only opponents of these comforting speculations were the priests of Jerusalem and the aristocracy of the Holy City. Those in office, who found it more profitable to maintain an attitude of compromise towards foreigners and unbelievers, had good reason to fear the unrest and disturbance that Messianism might kindle among those who were less contented with their lot and more spiritually minded than themselves. The politicians of Palestine were prudently opposed to hopes which they knew to be deceptive and to a faith pregnant with disastrous enterprise. The Romans shared this distrust and were for ever on the alert with regard to this Jewish illusion.

It is obvious, from the way in which Josephus avoids the question of the eschatological expectations of Israel, that the Jewish teachers attached the utmost importance to it. It is possible that sober-minded men like himself sought to neutralize Messianic enthusiasm by producing a contemporary Messiah.

---

[1] *Cf.* **CCLXXVIII**, i, 118, which urges in proof of this the probability that the disciples did not understand what Jesus told them of his predestined passion (Mark ix. 10 ; ix. 30 *ff.*).

[2] On the history of the belief, see **LXXV**, ii, 505 *ff.* ; **XXXIII**, 218.

We know that there was a time when the returned exiles were fully convinced that Zerubbabel was the Blessed One of Jahweh. At the same time Cyrus,[1] and even Alexander,[2] were suspected of being the Messiah, and Josephus has the incredible effrontery to claim that the Promises found their fulfilment in Vespasian.[3] Suetonius and Tacitus naturally echo the Jewish historian [4] and allege that Vespasian and Titus are indeed the objects of the prophecies which promised that the world should be ruled by " *certain men coming out of Judæa*." [5]   It need hardly be said that the Jewish people were not affected by such interpretations.

It is no exaggeration to say that just before the birth of Jesus, speculations as to the date and duration of the Messianic reign, the coming of the Messiah, the Day of Jahweh, the Resurrection and the Last Judgment, were central in Jewish thought, and occupied the chief place among the politico-religious questions which engrossed the inhabitants of Palestine. The Scribes discussed them in their schools, they were the inspiration of the synagogues, and the common people found in their expectation of *what was to come* consolation and stimulus, not unmixed with anxiety.   Up till this time interest in the coming of the Messiah does not seem to have been keen, and the Messiah finds no great place in the texts, but this can no longer be said of Jesus' contemporaries or of the following generation.   Interest and enthusiasm increased till the time of the Great Revolt ; a crop of prophets and Messiahs arose,[6] and there were numerous incidents portending an imminent divine manifestation.

I have spoken above of arithmetical calculations. Such reckonings, which claim to give a date for the coming of the Messiah, may be found in the apocalyptic books.[7]   The announcement that " the Kingdom was at hand," which is the essence of Jesus' teaching (Matt. i. 14–15 ; ix. 1 ; xiii. 30),

---

[1] At any rate, **LXXV**, ii, 508, is prepared to apply Sib. Oracles iii. 286 *ff.* to him :

καὶ τότε δὴ Θεὸς οὐρανόθεν πέμψει βασιλέα
κρινεῖ δ'ἄνδρα ἔκαστον ἐν αἵματι καὶ πυρὸς αὐγῇ

—*Then God will send a king from heaven to judge all men with blood and flaming fire.*

[2] Kampers, *Alexander der Grosse und die Idee der Weltimperiums in Prophetie und Saga*, Friburg, 1901.

[3] Jos., *B.J.*, vi, 5, 4.

[4] **LXXV**, ii, 518.

[5] Tacitus, *Hist.*, v, 13.   *Cf.* Suetonius, *Vesp.*, 4.

[6] Jos., *B.J.*, ii, 13, 4 ; vi, 5, 2 ; *Ant.*, xx, 8, 6.   *Cf.* **XLVIII**, 5 *ff.*

[7] **CCLXXX**, 273 ; **CCLXXXIII**, 6.

no doubt depended on a current belief that the Kingdom would be inaugurated 5,000 years after the Creation. This date referred only to the *millennium*, the thousand years of earthly bliss which were to precede the *Day of Jahweh*.[1] This parlour game of arithmetical prophecy has exercised its fascination in many ages, and can count its enthusiasts even today. There were those who based their hopes on religious or moral grounds, believing that their expectation would be fulfilled when the virtue and piety of the chosen people should warrant such a reward. The wisest and no doubt the most numerous held that the hour appointed by God's will was a divine secret.[2]

The most convincing proof of the practical importance of Messianism about the time of Jesus is the state of emotional upheaval persisting in Israel, a state which would otherwise be quite unmotivated, and which can only be explained by the Messianic hope.[3] During the century which preceded the birth of Jesus, and still more during the two centuries which followed, this state of unrest gave rise to various popular movements of more or less importance, which did serious harm to the Jewish nation, and led at last to its final downfall. Each visionary who arose, each rebel who incited Israel to take arms, could count on a following who would be ready to hail him as the long-awaited Messiah. We have not even a glimpse of many of the Jewish insurgents belonging to this period ; but by reading between the lines we can gather a certain amount from Josephus, in spite of his cautious reticence. At Herod's death, for instance, there was a reaction against his tyranny, in which various popular leaders were particularly active.[4] There was also a certain Judas who took up arms in Galilee after the deposition of Archelaus in A.D. 6, when the Roman administrators were trying to get some idea of the resources of the country by means of a census.[5] This man declared that he owed allegiance to no lord or master but God (μόνον ἡγεμόνα καὶ δεσπότην τὸν Θεόν). A little later there are hints of two pretenders, Theudas and an Egyptian (probably an Alexandrian

---

[1] Assumpt. Mos. i. 17–18. *Cf.* **CCLXXXIII.**

[2] This is the idea expressed in the famous passage from Mark (xiii. 32) : " *But of that day or that hour knoweth no man . . . but only the Father.*"

[3] Friedländer, *Die religiösen Bewegungen des Judentums im Zeitalter Jesu*, Berlin, 1905 ; **CCXCVIII,** 409 *ff.*

[4] Jos., *Ant.*, xvii, 8, 3–17, 9, 2 ; xvii, 10, 2. Josephus sagely remarks that these were all movements of minor importance, led by men with a passion for innovations (xvii, 9, 1, συνελθόντες νεωτέρων ἐπιθυμίᾳ πραγμάτων).

[5] Jos., *Ant.*, xviii, 1, 6.

Jew), who declared that God had sent them to fulfil his divine plan.[1] Theudas gave himself out to be a prophet, or even the Messiah himself, and announced that he had power over the waters of Jordan, which would draw back to let him pass. It is quite possible that John the Baptist was also looked upon as the Blessed One.[2] The only way to understand Jesus' own career as Messiah is to restore it to its proper background and surroundings : the historical development that led up to it and in a very real sense conditioned it.

[1] On the first, see Jos., *Ant.*, xx, 5, 1, γόης τις ἀνὴρ Θευδᾶς ὀνόματι, and Acts v. 36 ; on the second, Eusebius, *H.E.*, ii, 21, 1 *ff.* ; Jos., *Ant.*, xx, 8, 6, and Acts xxi. 38.

[2] Mark vi. 14–16 ; viii. 28. *Cf.* Klostermann, *Mark* (2nd edit.), p. 66.

CHAPTER V

THE PROBLEM OF UNIVERSALISM [1]

THE RESULT OF THE INNOVATIONS

I

THE SUBJECTS OF THE KINGDOM

WHO was to inherit this Kingdom of God, which the Jews of Jesus' day pictured as including both the earthly reign of the Messiah, and the eternal reign of Jahweh after the dissolution of the material world ? Was it to be the heritage of Israel alone, or did the Jews still hold to their earlier eschatological traditions, which said that it might (or even must) be shared ultimately with some or all of the *goyim* ? In a word, were they particularists or universalists ? The question is complicated by the fact that no fixed or orthodox view controlled the variety of private opinions in the period under discussion.

We may recall the fact that the early Jews always took it for granted that, if the *nations* were to have any part in Jahweh's beneficence, they must first recognize his power and conform to his Law. In other words, they must themselves become Jews. Every individual has the right to seek the Truth, to discover it and to confess it, and therefore become a convert to Israel ; and there is nothing to prevent such a conversion from extending to a whole nation. In fact, something of the sort took place in Palestine itself at the beginning of the Christian era, when a considerable section of the Jewish population of Galilee consisted of recent converts, ancient settlers in the district, whom the Jewish colonists, under the Hasmonæans, had prevailed on to accept the *Torah* and submit to circumcision. In the ordinary way, the *chosen people* could not admit that the heathen could achieve salvation by any other means. From being a deity responsible for the welfare of a dozen

[1] *Cf.* **CCLIII**, 53–86, which goes into the question much more fully, including its relation to the Judaism of the *Diaspora* ; **CXCVI**.

tribes, Jahweh had become the ruler of the world, and that world and its inhabitants had only to be made aware of this truth and accept its consequences in order to join the ranks of his worshippers. For the present *Israel alone had this knowledge,* and thus held a unique and privileged position in relation to God ; but this did not preclude the possibility that the time would come when the nations, in their turn, might see the light. On the other hand, there was nothing to forbid the belief that they might not, and that God might finally lose patience with them and annihilate them. In the first case either Israel would reign over the converted Gentiles as subjects, or else they would be assimilated—it was a matter of personal opinion. In the other case, Israel would remain the sole witness and beneficiary of the Truth.

These two streams of thought ran side by side in Roman Palestine.[1] Jews living on Gentile soil would naturally tend to " denationalize " their religion ; and we shall soon see that this actually happened. Hence they would also be likely to preach their faith to those around them, and in doing so they would urge its superiority over the Gentile cults. A considerable proportion of Judæo-Hellenistic literature was produced with the object of healing the blindness of the Gentiles.[2] The apostle Paul, addressing the hypothetical Jew of the Epistle to the Romans, says (ii. 19–20) : " *(Thou) art confident that thou thyself art a guide of the blind, a light of them which are in darkness, an instructor of the foolish, a teacher of babes, which hast the form of knowledge and of the truth in the Law.*" [3] The Jews of Palestine found this rôle less attractive, but succumbed to it partially. They could not fail to be influenced by the Hellenized Jews, whose example led them to generalize and universalize their religion.[4] But this tendency met with opposition, with the result that a number of contradictory passages are to be found, directly opposed to one another.

First of all, there is nothing easier than to find definite statements of universalism in the Scriptures. Take for instance Jeremiah xxxi. 33–4 : " *I will be their God, and they shall be my people. And they shall teach no more every man his neighbour, and every man his brother, saying, Know Jahweh ; for they shall*

---

[1] **CCLXV**, 33. [2] **LXXV**, iii, 114.
[3] **LXXV**, iii, 550 *ff.* Philo was to teach that God made no difference between man and man, and that nobility did not depend on birth but on wisdom and virtue. All those who forsook idolatry and turned to the true God were members of the authentic Israel which was not *that according to the flesh.* It was this sort of cosmopolitan attitude which proved that Judaism was truly the best of all religions.
[4] **CCLXV**, 75.

know me." It is true that the context refers not to the *nations* but rather to a regenerated Israel ; but the quotation itself might very well mean that all mankind would one day be brought into the fold of the true God. Isaiah ii. 2–4 describes this universal reconciliation, which would lead to the conversion of all weapons of war into agricultural instruments : " *And they shall not learn war any more.*" [1] The Book of Psalms, that great monument which enshrines so much of the impassioned piety of Israel, contains many echoes of what might be called the *spirit of universalism*, representing Jahweh again and again as ruler of the whole earth, a God within all men's reach. Thus we find in Psalm xxii. 27 *ff.* the statement : " *Then* " (that is to say, when Jahweh has delivered Israel and so convinced all men of his sovereign power) " *all the ends of the earth shall remember and turn to Jahweh ; and all the kindreds of the nations shall bow down before him. For the kingdom is Jahweh's ; and he is the governor among the nations.*" Other psalms express the universality, not only of God's reign but also of his benevolence. " *O Jahweh, thou preservest man and beast. How excellent is thy lovingkindness, O God ! The children of men take refuge under the shadow of thy wings* " (Ps. xxxvi. 7 *ff.*). " *Jahweh is good to all and his tender mercies are over all his works* " (Ps. cxlv. 9). The Book of Jonah is particularly striking from this point of view.[2] It describes how a crew of heathen sailors call upon Jahweh for help (i. 14) and how a heathen population (the Ninevites) believed in him and entreated his mercy (iii. 5) until " *God repented him of the evil that he had said that he would do unto them, and did it not* " (iii. 10). He reflected that the proportion of those who were not responsible for their actions was too great, for the city contained " *more than twenty thousand persons that cannot discern between their right hand and their left hand, and also much cattle* " (iv. 11).

In the second place, Rabbinical literature abounds in exhortations to love at the same time, both God, and all mankind considered as God's creatures,[3] an idea which occurs at least three times in the Testament of the Twelve Patriarchs, more or less clearly expressed.[4] What more convincing proof of love to mankind can be given than the attempt to open their eyes to the truth by which they may be saved ? If Matthew xxiii. 15 is to be believed, the Pharisees were at great pains to secure

---

[1] The same picture occurs in Mic. iv. 1–5.
[2] **CCLII**, 149 *ff.*
[3] **CCLXV**, 57–8 and n. 1 ; **CCL**, i, 18 *ff.*, on the Great Commandment.
[4] Issachar v. and vii. ; Dan. v. *Cf.* also Levi xiv. 4 : " *The Light of the Torah was given to enlighten all mankind.*"

converts. " *Woe unto you,*" he says, " *scribes and Pharisees, hypocrites! for ye compass sea and land to make one proselyte.*" The Rabbis delighted to think of Abraham, the father of the race and the recipient of the divine promises, as the model proselyte and the supreme proselytizer, and his example naturally carried weight.[1]

Our evidence, however, for the alleged zeal of the Pharisees is very slight, and it is probable that the Palestinian Jews of that day, even the least bigoted of them, could only conceive of a *universalism* which was compatible with their own deep-rooted *particularism*.[2] Jahweh was certainly the creator of the world ; but he was first the father of Israel ; undoubtedly he was the God of all mankind, but his chosen people had the first claim on him, and his law remained indefeasible.   Circumcision, the distinctive mark of the Jew, was to be just as rigorously imposed on all the faithful, whatever their origin, and nonconformity in this respect was always a disgrace.   On the other hand, even where Messianism tended towards universalism, it gained nothing in spirituality.   Its fundamental idea was still the restoration of Israel, that is to say, the triumph of Jewish nationalism.   In every case it was in Palestine and for Palestine that the Messianic Kingdom was to be instituted, and in Palestine that the great eschatological drama was to be staged.

It can thus be said with perfect truth that in Palestine universalism was nothing more than an extension of particularism, implying the absorption of the Gentile world by the chosen people.   There was as yet no place in Israel for Paul's declared attitude, " *There is neither Jew nor Greek* " (Gal. iii. 28) ; and indeed there is even reason to believe that the spirit of exclusive nationalism was a more vital force among the common people than our documentary evidence suggests.[3]

II

THE IMPORTANCE OF THE INNOVATIONS

If the foregoing sketch of Jewish religious thought in Palestine just before the Christian era be compared with earlier

---

[1] Montefiore, in **CCLXVII**, i, 43, cites characteristic passages illustrating this point.

[2] **CCLXV**, 76, gives a good account of the process by which this apparent contradiction was overcome.   The Rabbis of the first century took the laws of the *Pentateuch* on the obligation to love the *stranger* (the *ger* = the foreign colonist) and made them refer to the necessity of loving the proselyte : *cf.* Montefiore, *loc. cit.*

[3] **CCLXV**, *loc cit.* ;   **CCXCIV**, i, 228.

phases of development as deduced from documents dating from the Exile or before it, the conclusion cannot be avoided that in the interval Israel had been vitally affected by foreign influences.[1] Undoubtedly these influences were most effective where they corresponded with the main lines of Jewish thought, feeling and tradition, which merely means that the Jews borrowed from their neighbours whatever they had most need of. The task of assigning these borrowings to their proper sources, and still more that of calculating the extent of the influence in each case, is full of difficulties, and much must always remain uncertain. The fundamental influence seems to be that of *Babylonia*, with its peculiar cosmological, astrological and gnostic systems. *Persia* [2] follows, with important contributions in the field of angelology, demonology and eschatology ; and finally we can perceive the result of contact with the *Hellenistic world* in the evolution of the idea of God, in the building up of a belief in the immortality of the soul, and in something new in the Jewish attitude to the *Torah* and its interpretation—a development which will be referred to again. This subtle and pervasive influence of the Greek genius, which was constantly reinforced by the traffic between the colonies of the *Diaspora* on the one hand and Jerusalem and Judæa on the other, is particularly hard to detect, because it is so diffused, but it may well be more important than it appears.[3]

There is never any question of deliberate, premeditated and conscious borrowing ; what confronts us is the result of a gradual contamination, a natural responsiveness to contact with foreign patterns of thought, followed by a process of adaptation, which may be quick or slow, but which is essentially spon-

---

[1] On this conclusion see **CCLIII**, chap. xxv (the last in the book). Lagrange (**LI**, 388), who denies the possibility of pagan influences acting on God's people or on his Book, attributes the growing popularity of this kind of explanation in connection with the undeniable *innovations* that have formed the subject of this section, to the increasing obsession with the comparative study of religion. Naturally as long as Judaism was regarded as a religion which God had set apart from the rest and above them, it could not be studied as it can now that it is at length restored to its proper historical setting.

[2] I. Scheftelvowitz, *Die Altpersische Religion und das Judentum*, Giessen, 1920.

[3] I. Lévy's book (**CCLXXVII**, book iv) contains a number of statements as to the extent and intensity of this influence. They do not carry conviction, but they are enough to show the need for a complete re-examination of the problem. Nielsen (**CCXCVIII**, 31 *ff.*) was already convinced of Hellenic influences in the more northerly Semitic countries, Syria, Palestine, even northern Arabia, and as far as the Euphrates, about the beginning of the Christian era.

taneous and automatic.   The phenomenon is not in the least unusual or surprising, and in fact coincides completely with the normal developments among neighbouring peoples ; but just because it happens to apply to the *people of God*, religious prejudice—Christian more than Jewish—has long stood in the way of its recognition.   It is impossible for anyone who still denies it to understand the historical process which led up to the birth of Christianity.

BOOK III

THE REAL NATURE OF JEWISH RELIGIOUS LIFE IN PALESTINE

CHAPTER I

THE MAIN CURRENTS OF ORTHODOX RELIGION: THE SADDUCEES, THE PHARISEES AND THE ZEALOTS

DOCUMENTS cannot always be translated into terms of real life, because they cannot make clear to us the true importance and the extent of the influence of the facts which they contain. The task of setting these facts in their true perspective is often exceedingly difficult, and it is even more difficult to get the various perspectives properly related to each other. Moreover, the period of Jewish life just before the Christian era was undoubtedly one of complexity and confusion, containing cross-currents which cannot be brought within a single definition and which no general formula will cover. All we can do is to attempt a brief analysis of the period, pointing out its main tendencies and noting its characteristic manifestations in their most obvious forms.

Even such a general account, however, must not be too rigidly systematized, or forced into over-precise categories. There is good reason to fear that the sharp outlines of Josephus' descriptions were by no means warranted by the reality. For example, when he tries to assist the imagination of his Greek and Roman readers by likening the *Sadducees* to the Epicureans, the *Pharisees* to the Stoics, and the *Essenes* to the Pythagoreans, he is guilty of exaggeration or even invention. There is a further danger of using certain superficially arresting words in too rigid a sense. The term *Pharisee* is of little value as a description, for there were various types of Pharisees.

There is no doubt that in its approach to all the problems set by public, religious and moral life, Israel was at this time

161

characterized by a variety of divergent tendencies,[1] four of which are evident even within the orthodox Judaism of the *Torah* and the *Temple*. These are represented by the groups known as the *Sadducees*, the *Pharisees*, the *Zealots* and the *Essenes*.[2]

I

THE SADDUCEES

No exact account can be given of the meaning or origin of the word *Sadducee*.[3] Attempts have been made to derive it from Zadok, the High Priest in Solomon's day, but this etymology can hardly be taken seriously, for apart from the difficulty of the double *d* in *saddukim*, which is well vouched for, there is the surprising fact that the Sadducees never laid any claim to such a connexion, by calling themselves, for example, the *sons of Zadok*. It seems more probable that the name of this sect was in some way linked with the ideas and beliefs which current opinion imputed, rightly or wrongly, to its adherents, and that their designation, like nearly everything else we know of them, may be due to their opponents.[4] In the literature of the *Talmud*, Sadduceeism ultimately finds expression in the curious epithet *epicurean*, used to denote those who reject the resurrection and despise the oral Law, or Tradition.[5] This is no doubt the real clue to the meaning of the term [6]; but our concern here is rather with the Sadducean tendency itself than with the term.[7]

This tendency involves three main points. (1) The Sadducees denied the resurrection, personal immortality, the future life, and retribution. (2) They denied the existence of angels or demons. (3) They rejected the supremacy of *fate* (εἱμαρμένη), or determinism, and believed in the freedom of the will.[8] That is to say, they adopted the rôle of orthodox believers of the old school, holding fast to the spirit and the principles of

---

[1] Josephus calls them αἱρέσεις (*cf. Ant.*, xiii, 5, 9 : κατὰ δὲ τὸν χρόνον τοῦτον τρεῖς αἱρέσεις τῶν Ἰουδαίων ἦσαν) or φιλοσοφίαι (*cf. Ant.*, xviii, 1, 2 : Ἰουδαίοις φιλοσοφίαι τρεῖς ἦσαν. . . .).

[2] General bibliography in **CCLII**, 294 *ff.* ; **LXXV**, ii, 447–9 ; **CCLIII**, chaps. ix and xxiv ; **CCLXXXIV**, 31 ; **LI**, chap. xii.

[3] **EB**, art. *Sadducees*, §§ 1 and 2 ; **CCLIII**, 185, n. 1 ; **CCLXXVIII**, 290 *ff*.

[4] **CCLXXII**, 319.   [5] Jos., *Ant.*, xiii, 10, 6.

[6] Cowley, in **EB**, § 2 of the article quoted, recalls the Persian *zindik*, which is used of a *manichee*, or more generally of any *unbeliever* ; but the hypothesis is weak.

[7] **CCLXXVIII**, ii, 291 *ff.* ; **LXXV**, ii, 406 *ff*.

[8] Jos., *Ant.*, xv, 5, 9 ; *B.J.*, ii, 8, 14.

genuine Jahwism as expressed in the *Torah*, and rejecting the innovations which we have just discussed. With regard to religion, they give the impression of being strict conservatives, refusing, according to Origen and Jerome, to regard as sacred any books not included in the *Torah*.[1] This may not be strictly true, but their extreme exclusiveness caused such exaggerated statements to be made about them.

They were also conservatives in politics. There is no reason to think that they refused to believe in a future manifestation of the Messiah, but the Messianism which served to stir up unrest among the people did not find favour with them. They maintained an attitude of cautious reserve towards dangerous enthusiasms and ill-advised illusions, and any disturbance among the people put them on their guard.[2] They would, and in fact they did, readily uphold the existing order, whatever it happened to be, as long as the religion of Israel as a whole was respected and maintained; but even on this point they may have been ready to compromise, and even on occasion to identify the rights of Jahweh with their own privileges.[3] They knew that wisdom counselled acceptance of the inevitable.

They were drawn from the Jerusalem aristocracy, the wealthy, and the priests and officers of the Temple, people of rank and importance.[4] It is therefore more accurate to think of them as a *party* than as a religious sect or a school of philosophy. And indeed it is very probable that their enemies exaggerated their laxity and that they were on the whole better Jews than modern writers, judging them by the apparent ease with which they seem to have adapted themselves to the political enslavement of Israel, sometimes give them credit for. It has been suggested [5] that Jesus had some sympathy with them, since he spoke ill of the Pharisees and appeared to accept the authority of the Roman Cæsar. But we must remember that the sentiments of the gospel writers were not necessarily those of Jesus himself, and that the meaning of the familiar exhortation, " *Render unto Cæsar the things which are Cæsar's* " (Mark xii. 17), may well have been very different from that usually attributed to it.

---

[1] Origen, *C. Celsum*, i, 49 ; Jerome, *Comm. in Mt.*, xx, 31–2. *Cf.* **LXXV**, ii, 411, n. 25.

[2] **CCLXXVIII**, ii, 293, compares them to the English *High Church* as opposed to the Methodists.

[3] **CCXCIV**, i, 205.

[4] Jos., *Ant.*, xiii, 10, 6, insists on their *cult of aristocracy*. He says that only the rich followed them.

[5] R. Leszyuski, *Die Sadducaër*, Berlin, 1912, chap. iii.

II

THE PHARISEES

Over against the Sadducees stand the *Pharisees*.[1] The meaning of the word is clear.[2] The *parushim* (φαρισαῖοι) are *the separated ones* (οἱ ἀφωρισμένοι),[3] those who are separated from the common herd or *am-haareṣ* (" people of the land "), whose laxity in observing the Law rendered any contact with them defiling. They spoke of themselves as the *ḥaberim,* or " brethren," and possibly as the *ḥasidim,* or " godly ones ".[4] It was their enemies who gave the term *Pharisee* a derogatory, or even insulting, meaning. The word itself simply indicates their religious standpoint. Lagrange defines them [5] rightly enough as " *a fraternity boasting a unique acquaintance with the Law of God, both written and oral, and organized for the purposes of observing this Law with even greater exactitude, and of imposing it on others.*"

Like the Sadducees, they did not constitute a genuine sect, for the word *sect* usually implies a difference of *creed* between the group in question and the rest of the adherents of their own religion.[6] And the Pharisees were not by any means opposed to what may be termed normal Judaism. They aimed at the most rigid observance of the Law. They professed exactly the same veneration for the *Torah* as every other Israelite, but they introduced new subtleties of interpretation, analysing and commenting, extending its scope and increasing its rigour by their glosses. Even while they threw in the added weight of their own scruples, they never regarded the Law as a burden. On the contrary, they welcomed it as the gracious gift of Jahweh, a perpetual source of delight. In their view it was " *the perfect expression of what man himself would choose, if he had perfect knowledge.*" [7] Further, they saw no essential difference between the *Torah* and the *Haggadah* or even the free *Halachah,* seeing only in these the *Torah* itself enlarged, expounded and fructified ; for they were unanimous in their conviction that neither the

---

[1] Bibliography in **LXXV,** ii, 380 *ff.*

[2] **LXXV,** iii, 397 ; **EB,** art. *Scribes,* § 3 ; **CCLXXVIII,** ii, 283 ; **CCLXXXIX,** i, 57 *ff.*

[3] Jos., *B.J.,* i, 3, 5 ; *Ant.,* xiii, 11, 2.

[4] **LXXVI,** 132 ; **CCLXXVII,** 235.

[5] **LI,** 272.

[6] **EB,** art. *Scribes,* § 5. This conclusion is emphasized in S. Zeitlin, *The History of the Second Jewish Commonwealth,* Philadelphia, 1933, xi, 43 *ff.,* and the whole of chap. viii.

[7] **CCXCII,** 16.

harshness nor the extreme minuteness of the prescriptions resulting from their exegesis of the written Word would discourage
any but those conventional minds which were content with the
outward form.[1]

The rigours so long attributed to the Pharisees by scholars
like Nicolas, Renan, Albert Réville and de Pressensé in France,
Schürer in Germany, and Charles in England, are the result of
too much reliance on the statements of the Gospels ; but the
labours of eminent Jewish scholars have at last given us a just
critical estimate.[2]   The Pharisees are no longer accused of crushing spiritual religion under a load of minute observances, of
losing themselves in a waste of puerile and wearisome detail, or
of losing the essential spirit of the Law in their attachment to a
formal and hypocritical devotion.[3]   It is interesting to observe
the extent to which Nicolas was governed by prejudice. He
was too profound a scholar not to be aware of the discrepancies
between the statements of the Gospels and the evidence afforded
by the most reliable Jewish documents ; hence he persuaded
himself that all the praiseworthy Pharisees lived *before the time of
Jesus* and that those who are supposed to have hindered his
work by their hostility had "*fallen away from the virtues of their
fathers.*" It is only fair to add that Nicolas admitted the
existence of many honourable exceptions, but the general opinion
today is that it was rather the type of Pharisee caricatured in
the Gospels which was exceptional.

In fact, it is increasingly clear that the long-established
habit of looking upon the religion of Jesus as a reaction against
Pharisaism is erroneous. It was in reality the Christians who
edited the Gospel stories, who conceived the idea of setting up
the " hypocritical " Pharisees in such strong contrast to Jesus,
and their attitude is explained by the resistance which they
had encountered from Pharisaic orthodoxy in their own efforts
to win the support of the Jews.[4] We shall see that, so far as
we can judge, the religion of Jesus appears to be consistent with
the general lines and even the spirit of Pharisaic religion, though
not with its outward form. No doubt their strict legalism and
the laboured casuistry which enforced it by which it was imposed

[1] J. Weill, *L'essence du pharisaïsme*, in **REJ**, 1913, 9.

[2] **CCLXII** ; **CCLXIII** ; **CCL** ; Elbogen, *Die Religionsanschauungen der
Pharisäer*, Berlin, 1904, and the same author's *Einige neuere Theorien
über Ursprung der Pharisäer und Sadduzäer*, in *Jewish Studies in memory
of I. Abrahams*, New York, 1927, 135 *ff.*

[3] *Cf.* particularly **CCC**, i, 88 *ff.* ; **CCLXXX**, 74.

[4] **CCCII**, i, 119, does admit that the Pharisees' opposition to Jesus was
not as intense or as unanimous as that of the Sadducees, but he nevertheless
insists that their *outlook* was thoroughly hostile.

may appear to us somewhat childish and ridiculous. But, to say nothing of the fact that not all Pharisees indulged in the absurdities in which the Talmudic literature abounds, we have no right to judge them from our point of view, since it prevents us from seeing them in their true light. The meaning of their behaviour and its religious value must have been something very different for the people of Palestine from what we have accustomed ourselves to think. There is no aspect of the question which ought not to be approached with caution, not even the intellectual pedantry which flourished so richly in the schools, causing teachers and pupils alike to despise the unlearned. Such an attitude undoubtedly reveals the arrogance of learning, and pride in the observance of the *Torah*, but it is no evidence whatever of the absence of religious feeling or sincere piety. On the contrary, we find the proof of the triumphant persistence of these life-giving and inspiring sentiments in the numerous passages with a Christian ring about them which the earliest parts of the *Talmud* attribute to the *Fathers* of Pharisaic Rabbinism.

Let us consider for a moment their conception of sin.[1] For them sin meant transgressing, deliberately or otherwise, against the will of Jahweh. Its effect was to destroy the harmony that should exist between man and God. In any case, *since no sin was unforgivable*, this happy relationship could always be restored through repentance (*teshubah = metanoia*), by a changed life or an altered behaviour, to which divine forgiveness was never refused. Since sin was always attributed to the responsibility of the individual, *reparation* could only be made by the action of individual repentance, and the Pharisees had no notion of any redemption from without, through vicarious self-sacrifice. Redemption was in fact present in essence in the conscience and the will of every sinner. This is surely not far removed from the teaching of Jesus.

In spite of their legalism, the Pharisees were quite ready to welcome religious innovations, and Josephus (*Ant.*, xiii, 10, 6) makes the positive statement that they imposed on the people ordinances not contained in the Law of Moses. The reason for this is that their religion was a living thing, so that they were peculiarly conscious of the need for expanding the old Jahwism and incorporating whatever additions the religious needs of their time demanded. No doubt, too, they regarded all such additions as an integral part of the heritage of Israel, accepting them as issuing from the ancestral tradition which they undertook to express in the language of the *Torah* and to bring under

[1] **XXXIII**, 102 *ff.* ; **CCLXXIX**, i, 460–72 ; 507–34.

its authority.[1] This is the persistent illusion of all religions,
which continually progress while they imagine themselves to
be immovable. It has long been fashionable to represent the
Pharisees as obstructing the true religious life of Israel, but it
was really from them that the future of the people was to
develop.[2] They resolutely confronted the dangers of absorption
which, even up to the present time, have threatened the Jewish
faith. They are the true begetters of the *Talmud*, which has
been, in the striking words of Nicolas, " *the spiritual Palestine of
the Jews* " ever since their disappearance as a nation. Involuntarily and even unawares, they displayed a deep and instinctive
sense of continuity in change, that is to say of true evolution, by
which alone religions are vital and enduring.

The Pharisees believed in angels and demons. They shared
the general hope of a resurrection and looked for the imminent
advent of the Kingdom of God. Their close adherence to the
Torah, their disciplined lives, the breadth of their creed and the
pious zeal with which they taught and encouraged their brethren
in the synagogues, all served to ensure for them both the respect
of the people and a considerable measure of influence over them.[3]

They shared the illusions of the Jewish nationalist movement ; that is to say, they believed in the survival of the Jewish
State and in its triumphant return to power at some future
date. As a rule they linked up this improbable event more or
less closely with the great Messianic drama. Like their probable
ancestors, the *ḥasidim*, who, since the days of Seleucid domination, had resisted Greek influence and the impolitic attempts
to absorb them made by Antiochus Epiphanes,[4] they remained

---

[1] Jos., *Ant.*, xiii, 10, 6 : νόμιμα πολλά τινα παρέδοσαν τῷ δήμῳ οἱ
Φαρισαῖοι ἐκ πατέρων διαδοχῆς ; **XXXIII**, 179 *ff*.

[2] **CCLXVII**, i, 136 ; **XXXIII**, 118 ; 248.

[3] Jos., *Ant.*, xiii, 10, 16 : τῶν δὲ Φαρισαίων τὸ πλῆθος σύμμαχον ἐχόντων.

[4] **CCLXXIII**, chap. xxiv. This generally accepted view of the origin
of the Pharisees has lately been strongly disputed by Isidore Lévy.
According to this author the sect was of Hellenic origin and was the result
of the influence of the Jewish colony at Alexandria, which was saturated
with Pythagorean ideas. He dates its first appearance about the year
6 B.C. (*cf.* Jos., *Ant.*, xvii, 2, 4) and assigns its formation to Herod's reign.
In that case the passages from Josephus which trace it back to Hyrcanus I
(135–105) and depict it as intimately bound up with the history of the
Hasmonæans could have no basis of fact. (*Cf.* **CCLXXVII**, 211, 236 *ff*.,
247, 253 *ff*.) It is not necessary for me to discuss Lévy's arguments
here, for the question of the origin of Pharisaism has no direct bearing on
our subject ; but I must confess that, cogent though these arguments are,
they have failed to convince me. For one thing, they are dependent on a
general theory which is too absolute to harmonize readily with the infinite
complexities of the true development of myths and beliefs, namely, that
of the sovereign influence of the Pythagorean legend over the religious

implacable in their hatred of foreign overlords ; but clearly their chief concern was to preserve their religion inviolate, and it is probably no exaggeration to say that they looked upon political independence primarily as the best means of realizing their religious ideals. Josephus relates an incident which is illuminating in this regard.[1] Petronius, Governor of Syria under Caligula, once asked certain Pharisees why they sought to make war on Cæsar, regardless of his power and their own weakness. They replied that they had no intention of making war (οὐδαμῶς πολεμήσομεν), but that they would rather perish then and there than disobey one jot of the Law. Thereupon they threw themselves on the ground, bared their necks and declared their willingness to die. Such an attitude seems the natural expression of their real feelings. They may not have goaded on the Messianic agitators, but neither did they discourage them, and quite frequently they gave them support, they fervently longed for *the Coming One*. They were easily persuaded that the hour of his advent was at hand, and welcomed suffering for the triumph of the *Torah*.

They had little in common with the conservative Sadducees,[2] who were only too ready to represent them as revolutionaries and fomenters of dangerous ideas. Their ideas and the influence which they had over the common people rendered them equally unpopular with the established authorities. Perhaps most of the Hasmonæans,[3] and certainly the Herods and the Roman governors, were already suspicious of them and viewed their tendencies with alarm.[4] But whether they were liked or loathed they occupied an important place in Palestine in the time of Jesus ; and, although they were doubtless less numerous and less solidly entrenched in Galilee than in Judæa, there also they acted as leaven in the religious life lived according to the *Torah*. In my opinion Jesus cannot be explained if this is ignored. There is every probability that his Messianic hope, his belief in the imminence of the Kingdom, his filial trust in God, and his moral ideals all came to him from the very people whom the Evangelists have painted as his chief enemies.

Since the Pharisees were necessarily occupied in the study of the *Torah*, they were the chief clients of the Scribes, and often

life of ancient times ; and secondly, I can scarcely believe that Josephus really invented a whole century of Pharisaic history. Moreover, Lévy's ingenious argument is too neat to be convincing. The problem demands close examination. *Cf.* **CCLXXIX**, i, 59 ; **LI**, 271 *ff.*

[1] Jos., *Ant.*, xviii, 8, 3.
[2] **CCLXXVIII**, ii, 293 *ff.*, defines the relation between the two groups.
[3] **CCLXV**, 37.   [4] **CCLV**, 80.

became Scribes themselves. The schools seemed to be their natural sphere, although the study of the Law was not in the least dependent on Pharisaic interests. The reason was rather that the schools provided all possible opportunities for discussing, probing and commenting on the precious sacred books whose remote immobility they sought to bring to life. The curriculum of every Jewish school was based on the canon of the Scriptures. Moreover, the Pharisees were so essentially scholastic in their outlook that they preferred speculation to action, and easily mistook the former for the latter. Whenever we get a glimpse of the Pharisees they appear as interpreters and jurists, rather than as men of action.[1] Thus they were usually more inclined to talk about the Messiah, and to define his place in the world to come, than to risk their lives in support of the claimants, of varying degrees of importance, who arose at intervals and presented themselves for Israel's acceptance.

III

THE ZEALOTS

Meanwhile there was a large body of men in Palestine who, while they were closely akin to the Pharisees, being, like them, legalists, pietists, Messianists and nationalists, were intolerant of the double scandal of the godlessness of many of their compatriots, and the subjugation of God's people to the yoke of the *goyim*. These people certainly counted on Jahweh's aid to deliver them from their troubles, but they were also determined to make use of every opportunity to help heaven by means of their own efforts. They were known as *Zealots* or *Canancæans*.[2] They formed what may be termed the extreme left wing of the Pharisees, and Josephus exactly expresses this relationship when he says [3] that on the whole members of this party shared the doctrines of the Pharisees, but that they had an invincible love of liberty and " *acknowledged no leader or master but God* " (μόνον ἡγεμόνα καὶ δεσπότην τὸν θεὸν ὑπειληφόσι). They preferred death, for themselves and their families, to the necessity of owing obedience to any man. Consequently they deplored the passive attitude of the Pharisees and extolled

[1] CCLXXVII, 243, and CCLXXVIII, ii, 309.
[2] Καναναῖοι, the Greek transliteration of *qan'anaija*, meaning *zealot*. *Cf.* LXXV, i, 486 and n. 138 ; CCLII, 309 ; CCXCII, i, appendix i, 421 *ff.* ; CCLXXVIII, ii, 402 ; CCLXXII, 300.
[3] Jos., *Ant.*, xviii, 1, 6 ; *cf. B.J.*, ii, 8, 1.

action.[1] Josephus connects the appearance of the Zealots as a party with a movement that followed the deposition of Archelaus and the reduction of Judæa to the status of a Roman province, about A.D. 6 or 7, a movement probably provoked by the census which Quirinius ordered at that time. A certain Galilean named *Judas of Gamala* [2] joined forces with a Pharisee called *Sadduk* and rose in revolt. He tried to stir the people to an insurrection, but only succeeded in mustering a few armed bands. The Romans dealt drastically with them and speedily suppressed the revolt, whose leaders were slain in battle [3] ; but the feelings and the attitude of mind that lay behind their rising seems to have persisted after their deaths, and to have given birth to the Zealot faction. Josephus classifies it as the fourth aspect or category of Jewish philosophy [4] ; and he describes Judas, the leader of this particular school, as a notable sophist.[5]

I have no great faith in this account, which is characterized by a very widespread tendency among classical authors, that of making a single individual responsible for a collective movement. The probability is that the establishment of direct Roman rule on Jewish territory brought nationalist feeling in Palestine to boiling-point and set up the state of permanent unrest which characterized the Zealots and made them ready for any sort of headstrong action. Not long afterwards the Zealots, who, like the other groups mentioned in this chapter, must have represented rather an attitude of mind than an organized faction, began to employ terrorist methods against the adherents of Rome and all those suspected of laxity in religion, going so far as to stab openly in the streets anyone whom they thought it expedient to remove.[6] This is why they are also known as *sicarii*, or " assassins." [7] Later on their fervour played a leading part in the Great Revolt, and in the meantime it fostered banditry in the parts of the country which favoured it, and gave the Roman police much trouble.[8] Thus, although

---

[1] **CCLXXVIII**, *loc. cit.* : *die Männer der Praxis.*

[2] **EB**, art. *Judas of Galilee.*

[3] Such are the feeble glimmerings which seem to emerge from *B.J.*, ii, 8, 1 ; ii. 17, 8 ; vii, 8, 1, and from *Ant.*, xviii, 1, 1 ; xviii, 1, 6 ; xx, 5, 2, etc.

[4] Jos., *Ant.*, xviii, 1, 1 : εἴ γε καὶ ᾿Ιουδας καὶ Σάδδονκος τετάρτην φιλοσοφίαν ἐπείσακτον ἡμῖν ἐγείραντες.

[5] Jos., *B.J.*, ii, 8, 1 : σοφιστὴς ἰδίας αἱρέσεως . . . σοφιστὴς δεινότατος.

[6] Jos., *Ant.*, xx, 8, 10.

[7] **LXXV**, i, 574.

[8] **CCLXXVIII**, ii, 404, seems to connect them with all the movements of which we have any knowledge about the time of the birth of Christianity and during the years before it.

their behaviour sprang from a fundamentally religious impulse and was directed towards religious ends—as shown by their use of prophetic enthusiasm [1]—it frequently took the form of political agitation.

[1] There are also grounds for believing that they both inspired and used a good deal of the apocalyptic literature which is so alien to the *Halachah* of the Pharisees (*cf.* **XXXIII,** 123).   This characteristic distinguishes the Zealots from those who may, nevertheless, be called their masters.   They followed out the teachings of the School to their logical conclusion in action.

CHAPTER II

THE ESSENES

I

What We Know of Them. The Name

IT is clear, at the outset, that the position of the Essenes is quite different from that of the three groups dealt with in the previous chapter.[1]

Although our information concerning them is neither complete nor satisfactory,[2] we have enough evidence to be able to draw certain useful conclusions. Our sources are limited to a score of passages from Josephus,[3] a brief mention by the Elder Pliny,[4] and a short work generally attributed to Philo and known as *Quod omnis probus liber*.[5] What may be gathered from Christian literature adds little to the knowledge gained from these three groups of documents,[6] and, strangely enough, there is no mention of the Essenes either in the Jewish canonical or Deuterocanonical writings, or in the Biblical apocrypha, or in Rabbinical literature.[7] Careful examination of these various

[1] Bibliography in **LXXV**, ii, 556 *ff.*, and in **DACL**, art. *Cénobitisme*, col. 3059 *ff.* See in particular **LXXV**, ii, 556–84 ; **CCLII**, 311 *ff.* ; **CCLXXVI**, i, 149–71 ; Kaufmann, *Esseni*, in **JE**, v (1903) ; Chr. Bugge, *Zum Essäerproblem*, in **ZNW**, xiv (1913), 135 *ff.* ; W. Bauer, *Essener* in *Pauly-Wissowa-Kroll* ; **HRE**, supplement iv, 386–440 ; **CCLXXVIII**, ii, 393 *ff.* ; **CCLXXVII**, 264–93 ; **CCLIII**, chap. xxiv ; **CCLXXIII**, 116–33 ; **LI**, 307 *ff.*, which gives a translation of the texts ; **CCLXXII**, 297 *ff.*

[2] **EB**, art. *Essenes* (Jülicher), § 1 ; **CCLXXVII**, 264 *ff.*

[3] Especially *B.J.*, ii, 8, 2–13 ; *Ant.*, xviii, 1, 5, though there are some discrepancies.   [4] *Hist. Nat.*, v, 17, 4.

[5] *Quod omnis*, 12–13 ; §§ 75–91 of Cohn's edition, vi. Josephus and Philo appear to have used the same source. For the place occupied by the *Quod omnis* in Philo's works, *cf.* **CCLXXVII**, 264, n. 3. The authenticity of the work is discussed in **CCLXXVI**, i, 154.

[6] Eusebius, *Praepar. Evangel.*, viii, 11, probably owes something to Philo's lost *Apologia*. The testimony of *Philosophumena*, 9, and Epiphanius, *Haeres*, 19, is second or even third hand.

[7] There is one exception : one of the tractates of the *Mishnah* (*Sheqalim*, v, 6) mentions among the buildings formerly attached to the Temple the Hall of the *Hassaïm* ('Εσσαῖοι, 'Εσσενοί). *Cf.* **CCLXXVII**, 267 and n. 5.

testimonies does not convince us that what they tell us is true, still less that it is the whole truth.[1] We lack the means of testing their assertions, so that the answers to many important questions can only be given in terms of probability. The unusual character of the religion of the Essenes, of whom Pliny says, " *Gens sola et in toto orbe praeter ceteras mira*," might be a temptation to mendacity and offer an excuse for more or less elaborate embellishments, just as it might attract the attention of a conscientious observer. It is thus impossible to give a precise estimate of the trustworthiness of all the details which our sources contain.[2]

It is unfortunate that the secret books of the Essenes, mentioned by Josephus,[3] have perished, leaving no trace. The likeness of the eschatological views of the Essenes, as reported by Josephus, to Enoch's version of Paradise, has led to the suggestion that their books were of an apocalyptic nature. It has even been claimed that this sect is responsible for all the apocryphal writings which pass under the name of Enoch, a view which has found some favour among scholars.[4] The Assumption of Moses, which dates from about Jesus' lifetime has also been attributed to them. Charles, who has recently taken up the problem again, only admits this view in the case of the end of the Book of Enoch (Enoch cxviii. 1–15), which bears witness to a very highly developed angelology. Perhaps some chance discovery may add to the documentation of the subject.

There is some doubt as to the meaning of the word Essene.[5] Philo calls them θεραπευταί θεοῦ, which could mean either *cultores Dei* or else *medici Dei* (" God's physicians "), and this has led to the suggestion that the word comes from *'asi*, meaning " physician." Others have derived it from *ḥaseh* (meaning " holy " or " pure "), an etymology which is supported by the fact that Philo apparently identifies ᾿Εσσαῖοι with the Greek ὅσιοι, " saints," or " pious ones," but which is open to the

---

[1] **CCLXVI,** i, 139.

[2] Josephus (*Vita*, ii) certainly claims to have made a special study of the Essenes in order to enlighten himself as to the true nature of their rule, but that is no reason for believing him.

[3] *B.J.*, ii, 8, 7. *Cf.* **XLVII,** i, 25.

[4] Lightfoot and Kohler, for instance. *Cf.* Lightfoot, *Epistles to the Colossians and to Philemon*, 1876, 82–98, 349–419 ; Kohler, *The Essenes and the Apocalyptic Literature*, in *J.Q.R.*, xi, 145–68. Kohler attributes Enoch, the Book of Jubilees, the Testament of the Twelve Patriarchs and the Testament of Job to the Essenes.

[5] **LXXV,** ii, 559 *ff.* ; **DACL,** art. *Cénobitisme*, col. 3059 ; **CCLXXXVII,** 32.

objection [1] that *hasé* is an Eastern Aramaic word, which would have been unfamiliar to the people of Palestine. I confess that this argument does not seem to me to be final. Lastly, the word is traced back to *hassaim* (" the silent "), which would be readily explained by the rule of silence which was imposed on the members of the sect, as we shall see later. Even Josephus is uncertain as to the Greek form of the name ; writing it sometimes as ʼΕσσηνοί, and sometimes as ʼΕσσαῖοι. The first form occurs fourteen times, the second, six. Philo has ʼΕσαῖοι and Pliny *Esseni*. The question is not one of vital importance, and we may content ourselves with the very probable statement that the name Essene had some sort of connexion with the religious vocation of those who bore it.

II

ORIGIN OF THE SECT

The origin of the Essenes has been the subject of endless discussion and has given rise to the greatest diversity of opinion. Judging from their most obvious external characteristic—namely, their withdrawal from the stream of daily life—it might most naturally be supposed that they aimed at a strict expression of the Pharisaic ideal, a Pharisaism pushed to its logical extreme.[2] Nevertheless, the singular features presented not only by their discipline, but also by their beliefs, renders it difficult to follow the more conservative of modern scholars in their endeavour to bring both within the confines of pure Jahwism. Accordingly, the great majority of modern critics now admit that in point of origin, Essenism was largely indebted to foreign influence. The question is, which ? and it is not easy to give a decisive answer.[3]

Parseeism and Buddhism have both been suggested, on inconclusive grounds. Similarly, the *Therapeutae*, described by Philo in his treatise *De Vita Contemplativa*, have been suggested. To this, however, two objections may be raised. Firstly, we do not know at what precise date the Alexandrian community of recluses, known to Philo, was formed, hence

[1] **CCLXXVII**, 267, n. 3.
[2] **LXXV**, ii, 577 ; Dom Leclercq, *Cénobitisme*, col. 3059. This is essentially Duchesne's idea, who thinks of them (in *H.A.*, i, 12) as men who, abandoning the life of the world and of the Temple in disgust, sought refuge in the strict observance of the Law.
[3] **LXXV**, ii, 573 *ff.*, summarizes and discusses various hypotheses. *Cf.* **CCLXXVI**, i, 155.
[4] **CCLXXXVII**, 33. *Cf.* **CCLXVI**, i, 113, n. 3.

it is impossible to establish its priority to the Essene community. Secondly, it is difficult to see how an institution, intelligible only against a background of Greek culture, could ever have been transported to and taken root in Palestinian soil.[1] Again, certain scholars of note have taken the view that only a foreign influence acting *directly* upon Palestinian Judaism could have given rise to the Essene movement, and it is in the Greek world that resemblances have usually been sought. The suggestion here is that Essenism might have been produced simply by the " synthetic " influence of Hellenistic Judaism, and might be a kind of reaction on the part of the country's higher elements to the influence of Jewish communities living on Greek soil. It is in this sense, for instance, that Friedländer [2] understands the matter when he writes that the Synagogue of the Essenes was the " *beloved daughter of the Synagogue of the Diaspora.*" In point of fact, however, this view assumes a total misunderstanding of the way in which such a reaction might work and of the results it might produce, and it involves the further objection that we have no texts by which to determine with certainty the antecedent conditions in the Synagogues of the Dispersion.

Such light as Philo casts upon some aspects of Alexandrian Jewish thought scarcely illumines for us the life of *all* Jewish centres of the Diaspora. Moreover, how can we explain the fact that this Judaized Hellenism, transported into Judah, should have so spontaneously " pushed ahead," in the philosophic sense, as Friedländer maintains it did ?

In view of this objection, it becomes necessary to seek an influence at once less complex and more precise. Following Josephus, who actually identifies their mode of life with that of the Pythagoreans,[3] the attempt has been made to prove that the essential customs and beliefs of the Essenes derived directly either from Pythagoreanism, or from Orphism, or from both, at a time when they were apparently fused together. Scholars of repute, such as Döllinger, Zeller, Schürer, Dietrich, Pfleiderer and Legge, have, from different points of view and for different reasons, each maintained this view.[4] In recent years it has been vigorously upheld by M. Isidore Lévy, who has striven to show [5] that all the seemingly essential elements of

---

[1] **CCLXVI**, i, 138.   [2] **CCLVIII**, 60 *ff.*

[3] *Ant.*, xv, 10, 4 : Γένος δὲ τοῦτ᾽ ἐστὶ διαίτῃ χρώμενον τῇ παρ᾽ Ἕλλησιν ὑπὸ Πυθαγόρου καταδεδειγμένη.

[4] **LXXV**, *loc. cit.* ; Döllinger, *Heidenthum und Judenthum*, Ratisbon, 1857, 755 *ff.* ; **CCLXXVI**, i, 155 ; **CCLXXVII**, 369 and n. 10.

[5] **CCLXXVII**, 268 *ff.* ; Cumont, *Esséniens et Pythagoriciens*, in *Contes rendus de L'Acad. des Inscript.*, April–June, 1930, 99 *ff.*

Essenism correspond exactly to the obligations imposed upon themselves by the Pythagoreans, whose school presents the characteristics of a church. These essential elements included the original beliefs, the conception of the world and of life, the determination of cardinal virtues, the principles of fraternal solidarity within a closed community, rules of conduct for an ascetic society, religious rituals and ceremonies of purification, as well as certain peculiar customs such as the objection to the oath and the rule of silence. Hence a Pythagorean community at Alexandria might have furnished the model which, transported to Palestine about a half-century before the Christian era, might there have been adopted to Jahwism in the form of the Essene movement. It may be admitted that the points of resemblance stressed by Lévy are beyond dispute. Nevertheless, the dogmatic conclusion which he deduces from them by no means follows so obviously as he would have us suppose. Granting that Pythagoreanism was indeed the ultimate source whence Essenism substantially developed, there is nothing to prove that it was the immediate one, nor that the stream flowed into Palestine through an Alexandrian channel. Several Essene customs, whether derived or not in the first place from Pythagorean usages, which must themselves have had an origin, recur in other Oriental cults. Thus, the veneration paid by the Essenes to the sun [1] suggests the influence of some syncretistic solar cult.[2] At the same time it should not be forgotten that scholars of the first rank have not only denied the direct influence of Pythagoreanism upon Essene doctrine,[3] but have regarded as improbable, even unthinkable, any direct influence of Greek philosophy and theology on Palestine.[4]

Neither the variety of aspects under which Essenism can be considered, nor the very diversity of its points of contact with other religious organizations, which the study of it shows to exist, favours a simple explanation of its origin. I have the impression that we are here concerned rather with a spontaneous combination of several influences emanating from different quarters and operating essentially on the level of popular life,

[1] Jos., *B.J.*, ii, 8, 5 ; ii, 8, 9.
[2] This is Dölger's hypothesis in *Sol Salutis*, Munster, 1920, 36, and *Der Heilige Fisch*, Munster, 1922, 97. He tries to explain the resemblances between neo-Pythagoreanism and the cult of the Essenes by reference to a *Sonnenkult* that exerted an influence on both.
[3] CCLIII, 458 *ff*.
[4] CCLXXVIII, ii, 399 ; CCCVIII, 191, n. 2. The former believes that the cult developed spontaneously in this direction on Jewish soil ; the latter suggests rather that Josephus has arbitrarily Hellenized the Essenes.

even in Palestine,[1] than with the mere diffusion of any single one of them. I have already pointed out that at the time in question Palestine was swept by many varied currents of thought.

If, for instance, we stress the resemblances between Essenism and Parseeism, viz. the frequent baptisms, the white garments, the veneration—if not worship—of the sun, the rejection of bloody sacrifices and the practice of magic, it must be remembered, before we draw conclusions from them, that the whole of Judaism had been under Persian influence at the time when Israel was under the domination of the Great King. Hence, such Persian influence as appears may be purely secondary in character, amounting to no more than a further development confined to certain specific points.[2] Similarly, even if we are prepared to admit the influence of the Pythagorean rule, it is not necessary to suppose that this was direct.

Reuss and Nicholas, who reject any explanation of Essenism as due to the penetration of foreign ideas, see in it a phenomenon sufficiently explained by the usual considerations of religious psychology.[3] For them the Essenes were Jews whose fervent piety could not be satisfied by the national religion, even supplemented by the teaching of the Synagogue. Certain of the devout would at first have formed groups, and cultivating together a mystical discipline, would have constituted a kind of *collegium pietatis*. The form of life thus established would gradually have expanded, become more comprehensive and regularized. Thus we come back to the point of view already described, which regards the Essenes simply as extreme Pharisees, at once more mystical and more logical than the generality of their brethren, more deeply rooted than they in the prejudices of their religion and race, and who anticipated exactly the famous *secessi de populo* of Tertullian.

Such considerations are by no means unreasonable, and may, indeed, contain a large measure of truth. At the same time, they scarcely take sufficient account of the form which the Essene reaction took, the organization which it adopted, and the extraneous ideas and practices into which it seems to have settled down. It is more probable that these men, so strangely

[1] Jülicher, in **EB**, *Essenes*, § 7. *Contra*, Lagrange, in **LI**, 323, who cannot believe that " *a sect is . . . formed by collecting and combining elements from different sources.*" But this is not quite what is suggested, and in any case P. Lagrange accepts Pythagorean influence, *cf.* 325 *ff.*

[2] **LXXV,** ii, 582. This author believes in a basic Greek influence, and attaches great importance to the *Lebensideal* of the followers of Pythagoras.

[3] See in particular **CCLXXX,** 80.

isolated from their brethren, assimilated, spontaneously and without deliberate choice, out of the confused mass of influences at work around them, those which best suited their own aspirations and needs. They allowed themselves to be contaminated, so to speak, by those ideas which fell into line with their own, or, in other words, yielded naturally to the spirit of syncretism which prevailed around them.

This explanation, doubtless more elaborate than that which would see in Essenism the mere Jewish transformation of a foreign belief and cult, appears to me to take more adequate account of a phenomenon which analysis shows to have been far more complex in character.

I frankly agree that recent historical and archæological studies have lent probability to the theory of a strong Pythagorean influence on the Essene movement by throwing into relief the cardinal part played by Orphic Pythagoreanism in Græco-Roman life during the last century of the Republic and the first century of the Empire. Such influence I would not deny, but I do not think that it was the only influence at work. Moreover, I regard it as probable that the source of this influence was Alexandria, since certain curious texts and a number of very significant monuments from Rome and Pompeii alike reveal the fact that the neo-Pythagoreanism which flourished in the century during which Christianity arose, had its origin in Egypt.[1]

Essenism dates, in fact, from a time when Israel was subjected to strong foreign influences. We cannot, so to speak, produce its birth-certificate, nevertheless we have at our disposal a number of valuable indications. In the first place, if what I have just said is true, there is reason to believe that the Essenes were later than the Pharisees.[2] In the second place, it is to be noted that Josephus mentions them for the first time [3] in recounting the history of the reign of Jonathan (161–148 B.C.). Admittedly, his expression " at that time " (κατὰ δὲ τὸν χρόνον τοῦτον) remains somewhat vague, and the fact that he deals with all three Jewish sects (τρεῖς αἱρέσεις τῶν Ἰουδαίων) as being *on the same level* leaves open the possibility that Essenism was not necessarily born during the reign of Jonathan. Josephus may perhaps have thought that it originated at the time of the Maccabees, and this view gains probability from the fact that it was precisely at that period

---

[1] Carcopino, *La basilique pythagoricienne de la Porte Majeure*, Paris, 1927 ; Rostovtzeff, *Mystic Italy*, New York, 1927 ; Gernet and Boulanger, *Le Génie grec dans la religion*, 1932, 393–481.
[2] **CCLXXX**, 90.   [3] *Ant.*, xiii, 5, 9.

that the conscientious scruples which may have produced the movement first became active, when the Hasmonæans, having usurped the High-Priesthood, for Jonathan was the first king to become High Priest, forsook those ancient paths which the community of the faithful had hitherto followed. If this argument be accepted, it will perhaps be necessary to put the date as late as the reign of John Hyrcanus (d. 105), or of his son Aristobulus (105–104).[1] In any case, the first express allusion to an Essene has reference to the year 105, for it is in that year that " *a certain Judas the Essene* " is said to have gained a reputation as a prophet by predicting the death of Aristobulus.[2] It is reasonable to refer to the latter part of the second century that feeling of world-weariness which seems to have produced the Essene movement. The most interesting feature of Pliny's allusion to the sects is precisely his reference to this characteristic. Pliny has just remarked that the Essenes do not have wives, and are therefore recruited from the ranks of men who are tired of life.[3] And indeed, at the first glance, they appear, both by their spirit and their organization, as a sort of earlier anticipation of Christian monasticism and of our own " *tertiary orders* " living during the present century under a rule and a religious discipline. There is in the Essene something both of the monk and of the friar.

III

The Essene Community. Its Mode of Life

There is no reason for believing that there ever existed such a thing as an actual order of Essenes,[4] uniform in character and everywhere subject to the same rule and to a central authority. Were such the case, it would be a fact of paramount importance, but in point of fact we find no trace of it.

In order to gain a proper picture of the Essenes, it is necessary

---

[1] **CCLXXX**, 90 ; **CCCIX**, i, 147 ; **CCLXXVII**, 266 *ff.* ; comes to the conclusion that " *the beginnings of the society were not earlier than the reign of the last Hasmonæans.*" **CCLXXVIII**, ii, 395, says it began " *towards the end of the second century, during the disturbances which marked the reign of John Hyrcanus.*"

[2] Jos., *Ant.*, xiii, 11, 2 : . . . Ἰούδαν τινὰ Ἐσσηνὸν τὸ γένος. . . .

[3] Pliny, *H.N.*, v, 17, 4 : " *quos vita fessos ad mores eorum fortunae fluctus agitat.*"

[4] This is not Bousset's opinion (see **CCLIII**, 457), *Die Essener waren in ersten Linie ein Orden,* or that of Eduard Meyer (**CCLXXVIII**, ii, 393), who speaks of them as an *order of monks* ; in my opinion this is merely an anticipation.

to think, not of the mediæval monastic orders but rather of the earlier type of monasticism, prior to them all, where a common tendency towards asceticism and renunciation of the world found expression at one and the same time, in a variety of forms. Thus, some of its adherents devoted themselves to the life of the hermit, whilst others preferred the monastery, with its adjoining cells, or the convent in which life was run upon communal lines, and yet others formed small groups in the town, or wandered alone over the countryside.[1]

The thing about the Essenes which at once struck eye-witnesses as singular and curious was the practice of the communal life, and the monastic house, constituting what we should call today *houses of regulars*, that is, dwellings possessing a certain religious status, and not open to all and sundry.[2] At the head of each such house was a *chief*, or *superior*, to whom all owed obedience.[3]

Some kind of initiation was obviously necessary in order to become a member of the community, and there were certain rites and regulations, observance of which was considered necessary in order to gain admittance. The existence of these, however, at present rests upon supposition rather than on knowledge. We do not know, for instance, at what age postulants were admitted. Philo says [4] that they had to be adults, whilst Josephus asserts, on the contrary, that children could equally be received with a view to training for the ascetic life.[5] This divergence may perhaps be explained simply as due to variations of custom in each group. It is, however, a point on which we have really no knowledge. On the other hand, we have definite information that there was a novitiate comprising two stages, the first of a year and the second of two years,[6] the transition from the one to the other being marked by a ritual bath.

According to Josephus,[7] the Essenes were divided into four classes (εἰς μοίρας τέσσαρας), though he does not tell us how. Schürer, however, has supposed with considerable probability that the classes consist of *children*, the two stages of *novices* and the *brethren* proper. The latter considered themselves so different from the novices that they purified themselves after contact with them, as after contact with a stranger.[8]

[1] There is a good collection of characteristic facts and references in **DACL**, art. *Cénobitisme*, col. 3061.
[2] Thus the refectory was reserved for the sole use of the members. (Jos., *B.J.*, ii, 8, 5.)
[3] Jos., *B.J.*, ii, 8, 6. He calls this official the ἐπιμελητής, or *curator*.
[4] Philo, *Quod omnis*, 12. *Cf.* Eusebius, *Praepar. evangel.*, viii, 11, 3.
[5] *B.J.*, ii, 8, 2.   [6] **LXXV**, ii, 563.   [7] *B.J.*, ii, 8, 10.
[8] Jos., *B.J.*, ii, 8, 10; Eusebius, *Praepar. evangel.*, viii, 11, 3.

Entrance to the fourth degree, *i.e.*, the attainment of the full rank of an Essene, was also accompanied by characteristic rites. Firstly, the initiate took an oath, the terms of which embraced the obligations which he accepted, *viz.*: to worship God, to fulfil his duty towards his fellow-men, to practise justice, to refrain from rash judgments. Secondly, he received certain objects to which a symbolic value was attached and of which henceforth he was not to lose hold. They were (*a*) a blue garment,[1] (*b*) a girdle, and (*c*) an axe.

The life of the brethren was controlled by a strict discipline, and for any serious breach of it a jury of not less than a hundred members could, if necessary, pronounce sentence of expulsion upon the accused, or even, in cases of blasphemy against God and the Lawgiver, condemn him to death.[2] The fundamental principle of the brotherhood was the renunciation of personal property on the part of its members and the practice of communism. Those who entered the Essene community forthwith made over all their possessions to the common stock.[3] Brethren were chosen to look after the needs of the brotherhood and to prepare the food. This was partaken of in common, in an attitude of grave and reverent silence, accompanied by prayers, so that the meal assumed the form of a ritual repast.[4]

The daily life of the community was sober, chaste, and well-ordered—the life of men who regarded earthly life as a prison and who eschewed pleasure as evil. Beginning and ending with prayer, each day was filled with work. In practice, this consisted almost exclusively in agricultural labour,[5] for the Essenes did not engage in commerce and placed a ban upon certain crafts, such as that of the armourer, as being unclean.[6] Indeed, the main concern of the Essenes was to avoid impurity, and it is for this reason that baths and purificatory ablutions occupied so large a place in their routine. To the same end, they took great care to reduce to a minimum the uncleanness consequent upon the discharge of natural functions.[7]

[1] Actually it seems likely that postulants were dressed in blue from the beginning of their novitiate. *Cf.* Jos., *B.J.*, ii, 8, 3 and 7.

[2] Jos., *B.J.*, ii, 8, 9.

[3] Jos., *B.J.*, ii, 8, 3. This idea of having all things in common, θαυμάσιον αὐτοῖς τὸ κοινωνικόν, seems to have made a particularly deep impression on Josephus. It is by no means characteristic of the Jewish tradition and savours of Pythagorean influence.

[4] Described in Jos., *B.J.*, ii, 8, 5. Schürer (**LXXV**, ii, 568) says of them : " *die den Character von Opfermahlen hatten.*" *Cf.* **CCLII**, 317.

[5] Jos., *Ant.*, xviii, 1, 5.

[6] Philo, *Quod omnis*, 12 ; Eusebius, *Praepar. evangel.*, viii, 11, 8–9.

[7] Jos., *B.J.*, ii, 8, 5 ; ii, 8, 9 ; ii, 8, 10 ; **LXXV**, ii, 567.

The Essenes submitted to a number of rules which struck their contemporaries as strange. Thus, they rejected slavery [1] and banned marriage.[2] On this last point, however, there does not seem to have been complete agreement among them, and from this we may perhaps infer that their various congregations were not, in fact, subjected to that uniformity of practice which we might have been led to believe. Josephus tells us, with a clarity leaving no room for doubt, that there were among the Essenes some who, for the purpose of begetting children, accepted marriage and sexual intercourse with women carefully chosen and purified by appropriate lustrations.[3] On the other hand, if we connect Pliny's statement quoted above with that of Philo,[4] that " no Essene takes a wife," we may well believe that celibacy was the more usual practice among them. This, however, is not a Jewish trait and is rather to be classed among those which at once suggest a Pythagorean influence. At the same time, it must not be forgotten that the precept of sexual abstinence can indeed be derived from certain passages of the Bible, where the exercise of bodily functions is associated with the idea of ritual impurity. Thus, Exodus xix. 15 reads categorically, " *And he (Moses) said unto the people, Be ready against the third day : come not near a woman,*" whilst in 1 Samuel xxi. 4–5, David, in order to obtain permission to eat consecrated bread, declares : " *Of a truth, women have been kept from us these three days ; . . . and my men are holy.*"

Apart from the oath which they took on joining the brotherhood, the Essenes placed a ban upon all oaths, because they thought that the man who is unable to keep his word without immediately invoking the Deity already stands condemned.[5] Here again we have a typical Pythagorean characteristic.[6] It recurs in the New Testament, perhaps indeed under Essene influence.[7] The same basic idea may perhaps also explain the law of silence which the brethren accepted and which obliged them to restrict to the indispensable minimum all occasions of conversation.[8]

They rejected the sacrifice of animals, and for this reason, so it would appear, took no part in the temple worship.[9] Nevertheless, they were accustomed to send offerings to the Sanctuary, and there is reason to believe that they frequented it, though

[1] Jos., *Ant.*, xviii, 1, 5 ; Philo, *Quod omnis*, 12.
[2] Pliny, *H.N.*, v, 17 : " *sine ulla femina, omne venere abdicata.*"
[3] *B.J.*, ii, 8, 13 ; *cf.* CCLXXCII, 286.
[4] *Quod omnis*, 12.   [5] Jos., *B.J.*, ii, 8, 6 ; *Ant.*, xv, 10, 4.
[6] CCLXXVII, 278.   [7] Matt. v. 34 *ff.* ; Jas. v. 12.
[8] Jos., *B.J.*, ii, 8, 5 *ff.*
[9] Jos., *Ant.*, xviii, 1, 5 ; Philo, *Quod omnis*, 12.

assembling in a special quarter which bore their name, and which is mentioned in the *Mishnah* as the Chamber of the *Hassaim*.[1] If it could be proved that their objection to the sacrifice of animals was the result of a ban upon eating flesh, and the consequent obligation of a vegetarian diet, the probability of Pythagorean influence on this point also would be considerably increased. As it is, however, there is nothing to this effect in any of our early sources, and those modern scholars who attribute this form of asceticism to the Essenes are only drawing a possible conclusion from the fact that they eschewed bloody sacrifices.[2] Recently, Eduard Meyer has maintained [3] that there is no need to go beyond the limits of Judaism itself in order to explain this abstention, and he draws attention to a passage in Amos (v. 21–5) where Jahweh rejects sacrifices offered to him and claims in their place the exercise of justice. Meyer affirms [4] that the attitude of the Law towards sacrifices is throughout one of toleration rather than of injunction, and he points out that this is, in fact, the interpretation which the Rabbis gave to the opening chapters of Leviticus when they stressed the words " *he whose heart prompteth him to offer a sacrifice.*" Unfortunately, there is nothing to prove that an interpretation suggested, in all likelihood, by the very disappearance of the Temple actually obtained in Israel at a time when it still claimed to be with its elaborate sacrificial ritual, the religious centre of the nation.

IV

DOCTRINES

However much they may have separated themselves from their fellow-countrymen, *the Essenes were and remained Jews*. So far as we know, they never regarded themselves as heretics. Indeed, Josephus tells us [5] that he spent three whole years among them for the purpose of perfecting his Jewish education !

Their essential Judaism is further attested by their scrupulous regard for the Law, and more particularly by their constant

---

[1] *Sheqalim*, v, 6 ; **CCLXXVII,** 267 *ff.*

[2] **LXXV,** ii, 569 ; **CCLXXVII,** 285 ; **CCLII,** 317. *Contra,* **CCLXXVIII,** 11, 397, who still maintains that the Essenes, *in besonderem Masse,* looked upon the consumption of the flesh of animals, or of any once living creatures, as a sin. The reasons given are not very convincing.

[3] **CCLXXVIII,** ii, 398.

[4] Relying on **LXXXVIII,** 260, n. 4.

[5] **CCLXXVIII,** ii, 394, compares the three groups (Sadducees, Pharisees and Essenes) with the schools of the scholastic philosophers or with the *vier orthodoxen Rechtssysteme des Islâms.*

precautions against ritual impurity and their strict observance of the Sabbath. On that day, not only did they forbid the kindling of fire and the cooking of food, but they even went so far as to deny to their bodies the gratification of their natural demands.[1]

Their devotion to the *Torah* could at times reach the point of martyrdom. Thus, Josephus tells us [2] that at the time of the great war, when the Romans sought to compel them to blaspheme the Lawgiver and eat forbidden food, they refused with indomitable courage, cheerfully preferring death to surrender. Nevertheless, their respect for the Law did not prevent their adopting sundry practices which not only lacked its authority, but were actually in violation of its precepts.[3]

It is even more difficult to form an idea of their doctrines than of their practices.

Philo and Josephus both deal with the subject in some detail, but little reliance can be placed on either, for they both seem to have interpreted and hence to have modified their facts. Philo, for his part, might well have given us the Essene beliefs, not as they were, but as he wished them to be, namely, as useful rules of practical wisdom. Josephus, on the other hand, true to the basic purpose of his work, seeks to clothe them in Hellenic garb, describing Essene views of the soul in terms derived from Homer and Plato. Nevertheless, by carefully assembling and sifting our evidence, certain probable conclusions emerge, in the light of which the Essenes are revealed as no less singular in their ideas than they were in their conduct.

It is probable, though not certain, that they shared, at least in principle, the common Messianic hope while adapting it to their own views.

According to the author of the *Philosophumena*, they believed in a Final Judgment and a conflagration of the universe, to be followed in turn by the everlasting damnation of the wicked.[4] Not impossibly, it is to this belief that Josephus alludes when he says [5] that the Essenes, like the Greeks, believed in an Abode of the Blessed, situated beyond the ocean, and likewise in a Hell, gloomy and full of torment.[6] Be this as it may, there can be no doubt that they were far more concerned with the destiny of the soul, on the nature of which they were wont

---

[1] Jos., *B.J.*, ii, 8, 9.　　　　　　　　　[2] *B.J.*, ii, 8, 10.

[3] **CCLXXXVII**, 33. They probably harmonized these discrepancies by means of allegorical interpretations. *Cf.* Philo, *Quod omnis*, 22–3.

[4] *Philos.*, ix, 27.　　　　　　　　　[5] *B.J.*, ii, 8, 11.

[6] **CCLXXVIII**, ii, 402, very justly observes that these are also Persian ideas.

to reflect, than with any materialistic realization of Israel's eschatological hopes.

It may be suspected [1] that they professed a dualistic system of philosophy, according to which God was the personification of Good and matter was Evil. The soul, they thought, was immortal, having its origin in the most rarefied portion of the ether, and was imprisoned in the body until such time as being released it would soar once more into the heavenly heights.[2] This doctrine was, of course, in flat contradiction to the monistic teaching of orthodox Jahwism, which held that, since the soul existed before the body, it necessarily survived it, having its own life independent of its fleshly vesture.

Unfortunately, we do not understand how the Essenes conceived of the soul. To what degree, for instance, did they hold it responsible for human actions, and to what extent was it self-determined ? Again, when they spoke of future retribution, did they believe that it was only the soul which would receive it ? It is idle to speculate on such questions, for they can but lead us into darkness and confusion.

According to Josephus,[3] the brethren were strict fatalists, whereas the Pharisees were only partly so, and the Sadducees not at all. If this is so, how, we may ask, did they conceive of human responsibility and just retribution ? How, again, did they reconcile such fatalism with belief in God ? How did they explain the relation between matter as the principle of Evil and God as the principle of Good ? Was there no way of breaking the circle of determinism ? Moreover, what purpose was served by these sacraments of baptism and communion of which we hear ?

To questions such as these there is at present no answer. We do not know even whether the Essenes believed in the resurrection.[4] Some of our modern historians deny it, others affirm it, proving only that our texts are as yet inconclusive and ambiguous. Similarly, if they believed in the return of the dead to life, a view which is intelligible enough on the basis of Monism, it would still be necessary to explain how such a view could be reconciled with their dualism.

It would appear that they attached great importance to curative magic, that is, to the mysterious properties of plants and stones, beneficial alike to body and soul.[5] It is natural to ask whether they made use of such magical lore in attempts to control the workings of fate, and whether they knew of any

[1] *Cf.* Philo, *Quod omnis*, 12.
[2] Jos., *B.J.*, ii, 8, 11.
[3] *Ant.*, xiii, 5, 9.
[4] **CCLXXVII**, 288, n. 1.
[5] Jos., *B.J.*, ii, 8, 6 ; **CCLII**, 318 *ff*.

means by which its will might be thwarted by invoking the omnipotent names of certain angels.[1] Here again, however, we have to confess our ignorance. Nevertheless, we may regard it as probable that they practically dispensed with fate, or εἱμαρμένη, just as Paul managed to ignore the implications of predestination in order to safeguard moral obligation and individual responsibility.

Angelology, to which allusion has been made in the preceding paragraph, occupied a due place in the beliefs and sacred books of the Essenes.[2] In all likelihood, it incorporated a large number of current Palestinian ideas on the subject of good and evil spirits, but they belonged to a different circle of ideas from those usually held by the Jews. Their angelology was, no doubt, an integral part of a cosmology, dominated by speculations concerning God and His name, the divine essence, and the creation of the world, visible and invisible.[3] We may take it that it assumed the form of a kind of theory of cosmic powers. Here, of course, we touch upon a point of cardinal importance, and it is unfortunate that our understanding of it is so imperfect.

Josephus asserts that, among other duties undertaken by initiates, they were pledged to guard the sacred writings of the sect, and the *names of the angels*.[4] This may refer to certain prescribed formulæ of invocation or adjuration by the names of angels, and may be compared with those " *elements of the world* " (στοιχεῖα τοῦ κόσμου) which were also cosmic angels whose worship among the Galatians and Colossians caused Paul so much anxiety.[5]

Josephus represents the Essenes as awaiting the rising of the sun in an attitude of religious devotion, and as addressing to it certain traditional prayers (πατρίους δέ τινας εἰς αυτὸν εὐχάς) as if to hasten its appearance (ὥσπερ ἱκετεύοντες ἀνατεῖλαι).[6]

This is extremely interesting : Schürer, however, remarks [7] that it is not an act of *worship*, but rather of *invocation* pure and simple. It may be so : nevertheless, it should be observed that such invocation, standing thus alone and by itself, surely presupposes that in the belief of the people concerned the sun was not merely the luminary of day, but a conscious cosmic

---

[1] This is what Reitzenstein (*Poimandres*, 75) believes, but I can find no reference which would justify his opinion.

[2] Jos., *B.J.*, ii, 8.　　　　　　　　　　　　　　　　[3] **CCLXXX**, 172 *ff*.

[4] *B.J.*, ii, 8. I may point out, without offering an explanation, the fact that *Philosophumena*, ix, 24, which follows Josephus so closely in the main, omits all mention of this recommendation concerning the Books and the angelic names.

[5] Gal. iv. 3 and 9 ; Col. ii. 8 and 20.

[6] *B.J.*, ii, 8, 5.　　　　　　　　　　　　　　　　[7] **LXXV**, ii, 571.

power, and it is on just such a belief that the entire religion of the στοιχεῖα, or *elements of the world*, rests. Certain critics,[1] embarrassed by this kind of sun-worship, have endeavoured to connect the rite with the Jewish practice of prayer at dawn. This, however, is a waste of time : for if the Essenes had followed common Jewish practice, Josephus would have had no occasion to remark it. On the contrary, the very fact that he does so proves that it was unusual. Nor should we forget the constant care which the Essenes took not to defile the holy light of the sun.[2] Accordingly, there is at least a presumption in favour of the existence among them of—I will not say *worship*, because saints are not worshipped, and yet they have their place in the Catholic cult—but rather of an *invocation*, a *cult* of the cosmic powers.

In this we come very close to gnosticism with its *œons*, or stages, which reach from Man creeping upon the earth to God enthroned in the *plērōma*. Similarly, we are not far from the *Sephiroth* of the Kabbalah, who are akin to the gnostic *œons*.[3]

Nor is it only in its angelology that the teaching of the Essenes possesses points of affinity with gnosticism. The fact, for instance, that certain of the brethren seem to have been released from that law of celibacy which bound the rest, might well be explained in the light of the gnostic distinction between the *child* (νήπιος) and the *full-grown* (τέλειος). Similarly, the obligation of secrecy imposed upon neophytes no doubt implies the existence of certain esoteric interpretations of Scripture,[4] evidently based upon some form of higher knowledge, or *epignōsis*, such as that which Paul boasted had been revealed to him. Again, the idea that the body, fashioned out of matter corruptible and perishable, is but the prison of the incorruptible immortal, if not eternal, soul, is likewise familiar in gnosticism. If we could be sure that the Testament of Job was really of Essene origin,[5] there would be reason to believe also that initiates of the sect were taught that the *Cosmocrator* was identical with Satan himself, and that the ritual girdle which each of the brethren wore constituted a kind of prophylactic amulet against

---

[1] CCLXXVI, 8, 154, n. 3, based on Jülicher, EB, art. *Essenes*, and Cheyne, *Jewish Religious Life after the Exile*, New York, 1898, 251.

[2] *B.J.*, ii, 8, 9.

[3] CCLXXX, 233 *ff.*, has apprehended this relationship perfectly.

[4] CCLXXVI, i, 157.

[5] See Kohler, *Kohut's Semitic Studies*, Berlin, 1897, 265 *ff.* ; and CCLXXIII, 238 *ff.*. Similar arguments are applied to the Book of Jubilees, the Testament of the Twelve Patriarchs and the Wisdom of Enoch in LI, 121 *ff.*, LI, 130, and LI, 263 *ff.* respectively. It would be rash to make any definite assertions.

the Adversary. At the same time it imparted the gift of understanding the marvels of the angelic world. Unfortunately, however, it is impossible with any degree of certainty to attribute the work in question to an Essene origin.[1] Nevertheless, without relying on this source, I do not think it rash to assume the existence of gnostic ideas among the Essenes. Astrological gnosticism is the offspring of Babylon and Iran, and it is thence that Essenism probably derived it.

In order to estimate the influence of the Essenes, it is necessary to know the total strength of their several communities. Philo and Josephus—the one, no doubt, depending on the other—agree on the small figure of 4,000.[2] They do not, however, agree on the subject of their distribution. Pliny is the sole authority for the statement that their *gens* is the *socia palmarum* and that their settlement was in the desert of Engedi, while John Chrysostom represents them [3] as wandering in the region of the Dead Sea. Against this is the statement of Josephus and Philo that they were to be found in the cities of Judæa,[4] and we know that in Jerusalem they gave their name to one of the city gates.[5] Nevertheless, these various statements are not really irreconcilable. Pliny may only have been speaking of those Essenes whom he happened to have seen in the desert, without excluding the possibility that he had met others elsewhere. Moreover, those of the brethren who married probably ceased to share the communal existence. Accordingly, there may have been some variation both in their distribution and in their organization.

Were the Essenes to be found outside Palestine ? Certain scholars have been tempted to suspect their existence in Syria and Egypt.[6] There is, however, no positive evidence in support of such a view.[7] It has been claimed that the Christian ascetics

[1] **CCLXXVI**, i, 153, n. 4. In its original form this apocrypha is a *midrash* on the Book of Job, consisting of his story as told by his brother Nahor (*Νηρεύς*). Only the Greek version is extant, and it shows signs of Christian editing. *Cf.* M. R. James, *Apocrypha anecdota*, 1897, ii. Migne, *Dict. des Apocryphes*, gives a translation.

[2] *Quod omnis*, 12 ; *Ant.*, xviii, 1, 5. Schürer, *op. cit.*, ii, 561, n. 1, thinks that Josephus took his facts from Philo, but if it was not Philo who wrote *Quod omnis*, perhaps the process should be reversed.

[3] **LXXV**, ii, 563.

[4] *B.J.*, ii. 8, 4. In point of fact, the *Quod omnis* begins by saying that they fled the cities because of the immorality of the urban population, and then affirms later (*cf.* Eusebius, *Praepar. evangel.*, viii, 11, 1) that many of them lived in the towns and villages of Judæa.

[5] *B.J.*, v, 4, 2 : ἐπὶ τὴν Ἐσσηνῶν πύλην.   [6] **XLVII**, i, 488.

[7] **LXXV**, ii, 561, n. 2 ; F. Martinez, *L'Ascétisme chrétien pendant les trois premier siècles de l'Église*, Paris, 1913, 10. Friedländer makes much

at Rome, of whom the Epistle to the Romans (xiv.–xv.) appears to speak, were Essenes, and the same claim has been advanced in respect of the men mentioned in the Epistle to the Colossians (ii. 16) as judging " *in respect of meat and of drink.*" But such theories lack solid foundation. In point of fact, we have no evidence of the brethren except in Palestine. The life which they led in that country earned for them tributes of the warmest admiration from early writers.[1] Nevertheless, it is impossible at present to estimate their influence, and it is surprising to find that they are not mentioned in the Synoptic Gospels or the *Talmud.*

It is true that the question has been raised long ago whether Jesus himself might not have been an Essene, and his preaching simply a popularization of Essene doctrine. Such a view, however, rests upon no documentary evidence, and at present it is very difficult to believe it. For Essenism seeks to flee from the world, whereas Christianity (even in the narrower sense of the teaching of Jesus) seeks essentially to convert it. Moreover, the Jesus of the Gospels possesses not a single trait which recalls the Essene described in our sources. Admittedly, there are certain points of similarity between the spirit of Essenism and certain ascetic tendencies which appeared later in Christianity. Similarly, there are passages in the New Testament, which might be thought to reflect Essene ideas, *e.g.* the second chapter of Colossians, where Paul thunders against an astrological gnosis, which, however, is by no means proved to be really Essene. Such superficial and uncertain parallels furnish no convincing proof of the Essenism of Jesus. In any case, the Nazarene would represent an Essene of a unique kind, whose originality would consist in the absence of any resemblance to any standard type.

Much the same might be said about John the Baptist, who has also been claimed as an Essene. As Jülicher rightly remarks, if Philo is correct in his statement [2] that the brethren never had difficulties with the successive rulers of Palestine, it is plain that the history of the Baptist cannot be a chapter of theirs. Neither his personal traits, the character of his asceticism, nor the form and aim of his activity, favour such a view.

of the phrase found in *Quod omnis*, 12 : ἡ Παλαιστίνη καὶ Συρία, as opposed to the corrected form : ἡ Παλαιστίνη Συρία, meaning Palestinian Syria. However, there seems little doubt that the correction should be accepted. *Cf.* **LXXV**, *loc. cit.* **LIX**, ii, 399, narrows the issue to one salient fact, namely, that there is no trace whatever of the Essenes outside Palestine.

[1] **DACL**, art. *Cénobitisme*, col. 3061 *ff.*

[2] **EB**, art. *Essenes*, § 8 ; *Quod omnis*, 12.

It is not impossible that the Essene movement finally merged with and was absorbed into Christianity. If so [1] the fusion left no perceptible trace. The dissolution of the brotherhood is wrapt in obscurity ; perhaps it was consummated as the result of that tempest which swept the Palestinian world in the time of Hadrian.[2]

The question has been raised whether the Ossæans, Sampsæans and Elkesaites mentioned by Epiphanius [3] may not represent a survival of the three higher classes of the Essenes, lingering on into Christian times.[4] Epiphanius seems to believe it, but there is a measure of uncertainty in his convictions, and still more in his information. The whole subject is veiled in darkness, nor does it bear directly upon our present theme.

What really concerns us in Essenism is not only the fact that it has sometimes been thought to have produced Jesus, but rather that it reveals to us, within the compass of orthodox Judaism, a society which supplemented the *Torah* with a rule of life, a discipline, speculations, and ritual practices which were foreign to the tradition of Jahwism, but which rendered possible the interpenetration of the national religion by the spirit and ideas of a cosmological gnosis. Moreover, it furnishes a remarkable example of the strange religious growths which could flourish on the ancient Jewish soil.

---

[1] This is Kohler's position in **CCLXXIII**, 238 *ff.*, where he makes the Essenes responsible for everything of an apocalpytic nature in Jesus' teaching and for all the apocalpytic literature of the Church. This is an opinion for which I see no proof.

[2] **CCLXXVI**, i, 170.   [3] *Haer.*, xix, 5 ; xxx, 3 ; liii, 2.

[4] **CCLXV**, 235 *ff.*, which supports this hypothesis.

CHAPTER III

THE SECTS. THE PEOPLE

I

ACTUAL EXISTENCE OF SECTS. SOURCES OF INFORMATION

THE existence of sects in Judaism at the beginning of the Christian era has long been suspected.[1] Nevertheless, historians who have endeavoured to describe the life of the Jews in that epoch have almost invariably ignored them. Moreover, the serious study of the Apocrypha, or books excluded from the two canons, has had to wait so long for recognition that it is not yet sufficiently advanced to enable us to draw from those documents all the information which they may contain. As the result of impressions derived from the Epistles of Paul, the Acts of the Apostles and, more generally, the later history of Jewish-Christian contacts, there has been a tendency to exaggerate Jewish intolerance, and it has not been sufficiently observed that throughout their history the Jews have never shown themselves really bigoted except on one point : the observance of the Law. On the contrary, what we should call philosophic thought, that is, speculation about the Law, and as a supplement to it, has always been tolerated, among them.[2] Today the existence of sects is recognized even by the most cautious historians who are not attracted by rash theories.[3] At the same time it will be understood that we are very poorly informed concerning these various religious organizations ; we catch glimpses of them and we divine their existence, but we do not see them in a full light.[4]

Nevertheless, our sources enable us to establish certain

---

[1] M. Jost, *Gesch. des Judentums und seiner Sekten*, ii, 1858 ; Fr. Oehler, *Corpus haeresiologicum*, Berlin, 3 vols., 1858–61 ; B. Lipsius, *Zur Quellenkritik des Epiphanius*, 1865 ; *id., Die Quellen der ältesten Ketzergeschichtes neu untersucht*, 1875.—The most recent treatment of the material is that of Ed. Meyer, in **CCLXXV**, ii, 402 *ff.* *Cf.* also **CCLIII**, 461, n. 1, on Jewish sects resembling the Essenes in their rites of ablution.

[2] **CCCVII**, 210.

[3] J. Case, *The Historicity of Jesus*, Chicago, 1912, 119 ; **CCLXV**, 233.

[4] **XLVII**, i, 488.

useful conclusions. They show, for instance, that there existed
even in Palestine a current of asceticism of which the Essenes
are far from being the only example, and which could at all
times find striking expression, in the realm of practical religion,
in the life of some outstanding personality. I only mention
the Nazirites to put them on record,[1] because their asceticism,
the result of a vow, was at first purely temporary. Nevertheless, it is not impossible that at the time of Jesus the term
Nazirite had come to denote a permanent dedication to a
religious life.[2] In that case, the *Nazirs* would carry on the
tradition of the Rechabites. We know from 2 Kings x. 15 *ff.*
that about B.C. 900, when Jehu was king of Israel, a certain
Jonadab, son of Rechab, established a rule of ascetic life for
himself and his descendants : they were not to dwell under
a roof, to possess no property, and to drink no wine. Three
centuries later, Jeremiah (xxxv. 1–10) knew of Rechabites who
still remained faithful to the ancestral vow. Is it not therefore
possible that by a process of evolution not clear to us this
institution continued to exist in later Judaism in the form of
the Nazirate ? That we should be able to put the question
marks an advance ; unfortunately, however, there is no evidence which enables us to answer it.

On the other hand, there are other ascetics concerning whom
we possess a good deal of information. Such, for instance, is
Banos, with whom Josephus says that he spent three years
in his youth.[3] Banos lived in the desert, without any concern
for what might befall him, living on such food as chance provided, and washing himself several times a day in cold water.
It may be supposed that Josephus was not his only disciple
($\zeta\eta\lambda\omega\tau\dot\eta\varsigma$), and he himself was certainly not alone of his kind
in the country, for the whole account which Josephus gives
of him is intended to show that the discipline adopted by this
famous anchorite represented one of the aspects of religious
life in Palestine. Hence a conscientious young man would
need to acquaint himself similarly with the aspects represented
by the Sadducees, the Pharisees, and the Essenes, if he wished
to perfect his education. In all likelihood, three years would

---

[1] The *nazir* is, in essence, one who is *consecrated* and thereby *separated*
from the life of the community, being dedicated by vow to the service
of Jahweh. The law governing the Nazirate is set forth in Num. vi.
The chapter is undoubtedly post-exilic, but this does not imply that the
institution itself may not have been of higher antiquity. *Cf.* **EB**, art.
Nazirite.

[2] Salvatorelli, *Il significato di " Nazareno,"* Rome, 1911 ; Schiwirtz,
Morgenl. Mönchtum, i, 3.

[3] *Vita,* 2.

not have been necessary for Josephus to assimilate a simple practice of asceticism, and it may therefore be supposed that Banos professed a doctrine which his mode of life expressed, or at least a certain manner of regarding and interpreting the Law, which required some study on the part of his pupils.

Evidently John the Baptist bears a great resemblance to Banos.[1] The Gospels stress the Messianic teaching of this forerunner of Christ, and they have reasons for doing so which are perfectly clear. Nevertheless, " the voice of him who cried in the wilderness " may have dealt with other subjects than those to which, rightly or wrongly, the Synoptic tradition has given currency.[2] He also had disciples, distinct from the passing multitudes who thronged to receive his baptism of purification and to tremble at his threats of doom. These disciples are mentioned in several passages of the Gospels,[3] and are distinct both from the mass of pious Jews and from the little flock of the Nazarene.[4]

About fifteen years ago certain scholars arrived at the belief that the line of descent from the Baptist's disciples was not extinct, and this led many to indulge in extravagant hopes on the following grounds. A religion known as Mandæism,[5] still surviving in a fragmentary form in Mesopotamia, has produced a sacred literature with which scholars are now becoming familiar.[6] A characteristic of it is a doctrine of salvation, the roots of which, it is claimed, lie in Iranian soil,[7] and which assumes the form of a revelation, or gnosis. It has been observed that this gnosis possesses undeniable [8] points of affinity with

[1] **CCLXXII**, 352.

[2] **CCLXXXVIII**, 66 *ff.* All available information concerning the Baptist has recently been assembled in **CCXC**.

[3] Mark ii. 18 ; Matt. ii. 2 ; Mark vi. 29 ; *cf.* **EB,** art. *John the Baptist* ; **CCLXXXV**, 417 *ff.*

[4] Bultmann, *Die Geschichte der Synoptischen tradition*, Göttingen, 1921, 101.

[5] Brandt, *Die Mandäische Religion*, Leipzig, 1889 ; **EB**, art. *Mandeans* ; Kessler, *Mandäer*, in **HRE** ; Lidzbarski, *Mandäische Fragen*, in ZNTW, xxvi (1917), 70 *ff.* ; *id., Alter und Heimat der mandäischen Religion, ibid.*, xxvii (1918), 321 *ff.* [The fullest and most recent study is by E. S. Drower, The *Mandæans*, Oxford, 1938.]

[6] Translations of the *Sidra d'Yahya* (*The Book of John*), the *Qolasta* (*Liturgy*) and the *Ginza* (*Treasure*) have been published by Lidzbarski (1915–25). On their contents, see H. Gressmann in *Zeitschr. f. Kirchl. Gesch.*, 1922 and 1923 ; G. R. S. Mead, *The Gnostic John the Baptizer. Selections from the Mandæan John-Book*, London, **1924.**

[7] Reitzenstein, *Das iranische Erlösungsmysterium*, Bonn, 1921, chap. vi. Bibliography in **CCLXXXV**, 25 and 173.

[8] W. Bauer, *Jn.*, 2nd edit., Tübingen, 1925 ; Lohmeyer, *Apoc.*, Tübingen, 1926. *Cf.* also J. Behm, *Die mandäische Religion und das*

the teaching of the Fourth Gospel, the Apocalypse, and the Odes of Solomon, although the direction of the influence is a question upon which it is wiser not to dogmatize.

Moreover, these Mandæans show points of resemblance to the Baptist,[1] observing a rite of Baptism comparable with his. In point of fact, they used to administer it in the Euphrates, but at the outset they accepted the fiction that it was done in the Jordan. It is but a step from this to the supposition that one or two at least of the main tendencies of the earliest Christian thought came from John the Baptist, who might himself have been imbued with a syncretism combining the Jewish Messianic hope and the soteriological ideas of the Persians. This step has indeed been taken, but in spite of prolonged discussions the proof of the theory has not yet been established. The more closely they are examined, the less convincing and important do these points of comparison become. Mandæism resumes its real character as an incoherent mass of diverse elements, none of which, probably, ever possessed the importance somewhat light-heartedly attributed to it.[2] The door through which certain scholars dreamed of seeing new vistas has been closed again, and the pre-Christian pseudo-syncretism of the Baptist, which would have given him a unique place among the founders or leaders of Jewish sects, has vanished. We only discern dimly, in the shadow of the *Torah*, the figure of an ascetic and harbinger of the Kingdom of God, seen through a distorting mist of late and confused speculations none of which could by any possible chance be attributed to him.

Asceticism, indeed, does not correspond to any natural tendency in Judaism. It represents a source of religious life very different from legalism. Its basis is essentially individualistic, since it derives its authority from the conscience of the man who practises it, and since it fosters mysticism, which is still more personal and anti-social. Moreover, it may be observed that asceticism is specially opposed to the whole spirit of the *Torah* and to the orthodoxy based upon its precepts ; for the religion of the Prophets would have found itself in harmony with it, and the early church-fathers, who were not far wrong, regarded the great Prophets along with John

---

Christentum ; Lagrange, *La gnose mandéenne et la tradition synoptique*, in **RB**, 1927-8, and **LI**, 422 and Index ; **CCXC**, 113 *ff.* ; Lietzmann, *Ein Beitrag zur Mandäerfrage*, Berlin, 1930, **SBA**, xxvii ; F. C. Burkitt, *The Mandeans*, **JTS**, xxix (1928), 292 *ff.*

[1] For the contrary view, see **CCLXVII**, i, 108.

[2] Loisy, *Le Mandéisme et les origines chrétiennes*, Paris, 1934. This work would seem to refute and dispose of the so-called " Mandæan theory " once and for all.

the Baptist as the models and guides of Christian monasticism.[1]
The monastic life is, indeed, such as Elijah or Elisha might
have led,[2] and in some of the prophets there is a touch of the
Hindu *fakir*.[3]

II

SAMARIA AND SAMARITAN DOCTRINES

In speaking of Palestinian Judaism we nearly always have
in mind the Judaism which was centred in Jerusalem. It is
necessary, however, to take into account also that interesting
aspect which found its focal point in Samaria.[4] Here, where
schism had provided a refuge from the theocratic tyranny of
the Return, and among a population far more mixed than
that of Judæa, an atmosphere developed which was favourable
to foreign influences, and to new forms of religious syncretism.[5]
Here, no doubt, was rich soil for speculations of a mystical,
gnostic and magical type. Such, at least, is the impression
conveyed by the stories, legendary in form, but perhaps less
devoid of historical elements than is generally believed, concerning Simon, "the Father of all the Heresies," Dositheus
and Menander, all of whom are reputed to have been Samaritans.[6] The Christian historians of the heresies regard them
as responsible for the Christian gnosis of the second century,
which may simply mean that the heretics in question adopted
those current gnostic ideas whose potent influence a growing
Christianity could not avoid, and which were in fact carried
to insane lengths by certain Syrian and Egyptian Christians
of the second century.[7] The stimulus which inspired the first
of these heresiarchs, namely Simon, must have been of pre-
Christian origin, and for this reason is especially worthy of
attention.

So far as we can judge, the teaching of the Samaritans at
the first excluded a belief in the Resurrection, and it is for

---

[1] **CCCIV**, i, 2.

[2] 2 Kings ii. 1–25 ; iv. 25, 38 *ff.* ; vi. 1 *ff.*

[3] Sanday, **CCCIII**, 6, draws attention to the manner in which the
prophet Ezekiel is said likewise to have lain prostrate upon his couch for
some 190 (or possibly 390) days, " bearing the iniquity of the house of
Israel " (Ezek. iv. 4–8).

[4] **CCLXXVIII**, ii, 409.

[5] **CCLXVI**, i, 151 ; J. A. Montgomery, *The Samaritans, the earliest
Jewish sect*, 1907. [M. Gaster, *The Samaritans, Schweich Lectures*, 1924.]

[6] Duchesne, *Hist. ancienne de l'Église*, i, 156 *ff.* ; on Simon, see
CCLXXVI, i, chap. vi *ff.*

[7] Alfaric, *Christianisme et Gnosticisme*, in *Rev. Hist.*, CXLV, 1924.

this reason that early Christian writers compare them with the Sadducees.[1] Later on, however, they came to accept it.[2] The Samaritans also expected a Messiah, whom they called *Taheb*, that is, *he who returns*, or *restores*.[3] This belief was based on the passage of Deuteronomy, xviii. 18 : " *I will raise them up a prophet from among their brethren like unto thee ; and I will put my words in his mouth, and he shall speak unto them all that I shall command him.*" This expectation produced risings among the Samaritans analogous to the Messianic crises in Palestine.[4] Origen places [5] in the time of Jesus the attempt of Dositheus, who, it seems, sought to pass himself off as the One whom Moses had foretold, and claimed to be the Son of God (υἱὸς τοῦ Θεου). He preached an ascetic doctrine which took such deep root that survivals of it could still be observed as late as the fifth century and even in the Middle Ages, in the twelfth century.[6] The Dositheans are still represented as denying the future life, but in point of fact we are far from being clear about the founder or his sect. If we may believe Epiphanius, the Dositheans perhaps had some resemblance to the Essenes,[7] and there can be no doubt that they did indeed rally to Simon, who is variously made out to be the master or pupil of Dositheus.[8]

It is also possible that tradition has confused under one name two very different sects, the one ascetic and character-ized by a strict observance of the Pentateuch, the other gnostic and syncretistic.[9] Clearly, it is wiser not to be dogmatic on this question. Furthermore, Epiphanius (i, 10–12) had heard of other sects among the Samaritans, and gives us their names together with a number of unequally attested details. It is enough for us to note the fact that such sects existed, and bore witness to the presence in Samaria of an intensive religious life very similar to that found in Judæa.

---

[1] *Philos.*, ix, 29 ; Origen, *C. Celsum*, i, 49 ; Epiph., *Haer.*, i, 14. Origen stresses the fact that the Samaritans, like the Sadducees, accept no Scriptures other than the Pentateuch.

[2] **CCLXXVIII**, 409, n. 4.

[3] **LXXV**, ii, 522 ; Montgomery, *op. cit.*, 241 *ff*. He was possibly regarded as *Moses redivivus*.

[4] **CCLXXVIII**, 410. [5] Origen, *C. Celsum*, i, 57.

[6] Montgomery, *op. cit.*, 259.

[7] Epiph., *Haer.*, xiii, 1. Isidore Lévy (**CCLXXVII**, 292) concludes from this resemblance, and from the legend which makes Dositheus die voluntarily of hunger in a cavern, the influence of the legend of Pytha-goras.

[8] Montgomery, *op. cit.*, 252 *ff.* ; **REJ**, xlii, 27 *ff.* ; 220 *ff.* ; xliii, 50 *ff*.

[9] **CCLXVII**, i, 101, n. 1.

III

DISTINCTIVELY JEWISH SECTS

Concerning sects which may properly be termed Jewish, we are not altogether without direct information.

A curious document discovered at Cairo and published in 1910 [1] acquaints us with a religious body known as *the New Covenant of Damascus*, and which seems to have been a Jewish sectarian group. These people, however, were not heretics, like the Samaritans, banned from the community of Israel. Rather were they schismatics, who turned their back upon the Temple and rejected the belief in a Messiah from the tribe of Judah. At that time the members of this Covenant still remained attached to the Law. Moreover, they did not constitute a fraternity separated by a special rule of life from the Jewish community, nor were they a secret religious society, bound by the discipline of a Mystery. On the contrary, they are presented to us simply as an association of pious legalists who interpreted the Law after their own manner. At the same time, they accepted, together with the Law, the authority of certain apocryphal writings, such as the Book of Jubilees, the Testament of the Twelve Patriarchs and the Hegu, of which last we know nothing. They believed in a Messiah sprung from Aaron and Israel, who would therefore be neither Davidic nor Judæan. Possibly it is in the different orientation of the Messianic hope that the basis of their separation is to be found. Nevertheless, the cause of the movement itself remains obscure, if we accept the view that the sect was born at Jerusalem, and that its faith grew up as the result of serious disagreements with the Temple or the Schools.[2]

Adherents of this sect styled themselves " *The Community* (*sc.* of the *Righteous*) " and " *The Sons of the New Covenant.*" The latter name suggests that they may have been inspired by

---

[1] S. Schechter, *Documents of Jewish Sectaries*, vol. i ; *Fragments of a Zadokite Work*, Cambridge, 1901. The text is badly preserved and full of obscurities. Schechter's edition contains an English translation and commentary. A French version has been published by Lagrange, under the title of *La Secte juive de la Nouvelle Alliance au pays de Damas*, **RB**, 1912, 213 *ff.* ; *cf.* **XLVII**, 26, n. 1, 492 *ff.*, and **LI**, 331 *ff.* *Cf.* also **CCLXVII**, i, 97, n. 1, and *id.*, Index, s.v. *Covenanters* ; **CCLXXVIII**, ii, 47 and n. 2 ; **CCLXXIX**, i, 201 *ff.* ; Israel Lévy, *Un écrit Sadducéen antérieur à la destruction du Temple*, **REJ**, 1st April, 1911.

[2] **LI, 332.**

that passage of Jeremiah [1] which the Epistle to the Hebrews also makes use of to justify the New Covenant of Christianity.

In order to gain admission, the candidate had to apply, after promising to renounce the life of corruption. He had also to be approved by a duly appointed " inspector " (*mebaqqer*), who held a preliminary inquiry concerning his mode of life and personal worth. If the verdict was favourable, he was then required to take an oath of obedience to the Law of Moses and the rules of the Community. A monthly subscription supplied the funds necessary for defraying the cost of charitable works and communal expenses. Like the Jewish community itself, the *Covenant* comprised priests, Levites, lay members and proselytes. All were duly inscribed in the roll and were organized in groups or *camps*, of from ten to a thousand persons. At the head of each group were a priest, and an inspector who fulfilled the functions of overseer and administrator. He was required to be versed in the Law and in its interpretation according to the *Covenant*; one of his duties was to provide instruction for his flock. A tribunal of ten members exercised supreme judicial authority over the Community, having power to inflict various punishments, especially that of excommunication and, in certain cases, of death. As a whole, the rules of the sect convey the impression of a *rule of life* according to the Law rather than a body of doctrine. Nevertheless, it is not unlikely that a body of doctrine did exist side by side with the rule of life, consisting probably in an original *Mishnah*, that is, in a more or less distinctive interpretation of the *Torah*. [2]

There are reasons for believing that the sect goes back to the middle of the third century B.C. [3] It was the result of a *desire for righteousness*, that is, a desire for a stricter observance of the Law, whereby its adherents might distinguish themselves from the mass of Jews who were considered to have become lax. These sectaries therefore made a new Covenant with God, through the intermediary of a Lawgiver, or Preacher

---

[1] Jer. xxxi. 31–4 : " *Behold, the days come, saith the Lord, when I will make a new covenant with the house of Israel and with the house of Judah*," etc.

[2] **XLVII**, i, 495, n.

[3] This dating has given rise to heated controversy. The most moderate and widespread view is that (*cf.* **CCLXXVII**, 290, n. 6) which places the origin of the sect (which may well have survived into the Middle Ages) in the period before the destruction of the Temple. It would therefore be all but contemporary with Christianity. Some (*cf.* **LI**, 331) would even push it back to a date near 170 B.C., *i.e.* in the Maccabæan age.

of Righteousness, whom they also called *The Star*. The evidence of the document under discussion would suggest that this figure belonged to the past, though there is one passage where he is spoken of as "*The Coming One.*" Perhaps it is not too rash to suppose that his votaries placed him in the past, but yet awaited his return. Certain it is that they believed the last days to be near at hand and the appearance of the Messiah imminent.

The true origin and nature of these sectaries has long remained a problem. In the absence of sources we have to fall back on hypotheses. It has not been proved that they are the same as the Dositheans, or that they were Christians.[1] The probability is that they belonged to a Jewish movement hitherto unknown,[2] and it is for this reason that they interest us.

Christian writers, especially the historians of heresy, knew of a certain number of Jewish sects.[3] They even knew, or thought they knew, that these were imbued with gnostic ideas, since they regarded them as the prime source of the Christian gnosis.[4] Unfortunately, the names mentioned by these writers are not as a rule accompanied by any information : we perceive much unconvincing confusion and an even more irritating vagueness concerning the localization and date of origin of the various sects. Often we are left without an answer to the questions whether they emanated from Palestine or from the *Diaspora*, or whether they were anterior to the birth of Jesus.

Justin, for instance, writing in the second century, with a good knowledge of the Palestinian world, since he was born at Flavia Neapolis, the ancient Shechem (modern Nablus), lived there for some time, and regarded himself as of Samaritan descent,[5] mentions seven sects (αἱρέσεις). Yet the very number *seven*, which recurs in Hegesippus (second half of the second century A.D.) attached to quite different names, excites suspicion ; while the names themselves—Sadducees, Genists, Merists, Galileans, Helenians, Pharisees and Baptists—mean little. The Merists and Genists do not appear elsewhere ; the Sadducees, Galileans, Pharisees and Baptists recur in Hegesippus, who adds the Essenes, Samaritans and Masbotheans. Epiphanius, in the fourth century, likewise holds the strictly Jewish

[1] The former view is maintained by Schechter, *op. cit.*, p. xxi; the latter by Margoliouth, *Expositor*, 1911, 499 *ff.* ; 1912, 213 *ff.*
[2] **CCLXVII**, i, 101.
[3] Justin, *Dial.*, 80, 4 *ff.* ; Hegesippus in Eus., *H.E.*, iv, 22, 5 *ff.* ; Epiph., *Haer.*, chap. i, 18, 19, 30 and 53 ; *Constit. apost.*, vi, 6 (pp. 313 *ff.*, ed. Funk) ; Isidore of Seville, *Etymol.*, viii, 4.
[4] Hegesippus, *loc. cit.*, says this categorically.
[5] *Dial.*, 100, 6 : ἀπὸ τοῦ γένους τοῦ ἐμοῦ, λέγω δὲ τῶν Σαμαρέων.

sects to have been seven in number, enumerating the Sadducees, Scribes, Pharisees, Hemerobaptists, Nazareans, Ossenians and Herodians. To these he adds the Essenes, Sabneans, Gorthenians (Hegesippus knows of a Gorthaios) and Dositheans. We may go to the trouble of identifying the Galileans of Justin with the Nazareans of Epiphanius, the Baptists and Hemerobaptists with the disciples of John or the Essenes, the Helenians with the followers of Simon (who may have taken their name from his consort Helena); we may suppose that Epiphanius arbitrarily distinguished between Ossenes and Essenes, and we may identify Sadducees, Pharisees, Essenes, Scribes and Herodians. But we shall be little the wiser for guessing, in the absence of sources, at the exact identity of the other alleged sects.[1]

No useful purpose can be served by such futile guessing, and we shall therefore confine our attention to the Nazareans mentioned by Epiphanius (xix, 1 ; xxix, 6). These have been the subject of prolonged discussion.[2] They seem to have dwelt on the east of the Jordan, in the region of Gilead and Bashan, and to have preserved the outward appearance of Judaism. They practised circumcision, observed the Sabbath, submitted to the Law of Moses and paid due honour to the Patriarchs. At the same time, they would not so much as hear of animal sacrifices, and remained strict vegetarians. Moreover, they rejected the authority of the Pentateuch and refused to recognize the divine inspiration of Moses. They did not believe in predestination, and placed no confidence in astrology. Accordingly, in certain points they resembled the Essenes, and in others differed widely from them. Indeed, the whole subject bristles with questions. If they rejected the *Torah*, where did they find the true Law of Moses ? Did they believe in a specific revelation, and if so, what did it contain ? Did they possess Scriptures of their own ? How could they pass for Jews, if they repudiated the *Torah* ? To all these questions no answer seems at present possible.

The followers of the " mythological " school,[3] especially Benjamin Smith, have distorted the passages of Epiphanius under discussion in order to find in these Nazareans the true " inventors " of Jesus the Saviour and, so to speak, Christians before Christianity. Without attaching further importance here to a theory which we shall encounter again later on, it is

---

[1] CCLXV, 233 *ff.*
[2] CCLVIII, 99 *ff.*; XLVII, i, 287 and n. 1 ; CCLXXVIII, i, 408 *ff.*; CCLXXVII, 289 *ff.*; CCLIII, 456–61.
[3] *I.e.* those who refer the existence of Jesus to the realm of mythology.

clearly of interest to our present inquiry to ascertain the real character of these sectaries and to find out whether they professed any special doctrine concerning the realization of the Messianic hope, and whether they played a part in the shaping of John the Baptist and of Jesus.[1]

In this connexion the vital question has been raised whether we have here actually a pre-Christian sect.[2] There are obvious limits to our reliance on the information, and especially on the chronology of Epiphanius. Moreover, our distrust is increased by the fact that, in another passage, the same writer speaks of a sect of Nazoreans (Ναζωραῖοι), whom he derives from the gnostic Cerinthus, an Alexandrian Jew of the second or third generation after Christ. The two names, viz. Nazorean and Nazarean, resemble each other so closely that we can scarcely resist suspecting a confusion, and the pains which Epiphanius has taken to convince us that he is not guilty in this respect have not appeared to scholars a sufficient guarantee. Accordingly many authorities take the view that there was no such thing as a pre-Christian sect of Nazareans.[3] But since, on the contrary, others are prepared to admit it,[4] it is permissible to conclude that our information is at present ambiguous and does not allow of any definite solution of the problem. Nevertheless, despite the uncertainty of our sources, the conviction, shared by their authors, seems to be justified, namely, that at the beginning of the Christian era there indeed existed in Israel, and even in Palestine, sundry sects, varying in number and peculiarity, who claimed at first to be Jewish, inasmuch as their members were recruited among Jews and remained attached by various ties to authentic Judaism, but who later

---

[1] This is the view of Friedländer (**CCLVIII**, 131 *ff.* ; 130 *ff.* ; 148 ; 150), who further maintains (*ibid.*, 142) that they derived their name from the word *neṣer*, " offshoot," which denoted the expected Scion of David (*cf.* Isa. ii. 1).

[2] *Haer.*, xxix, 6 : ἦν γὰρ ἡ αἵρεσις τῶν Ναζαραίων πρὸ Χριστοῦ καὶ Χριστὸν οὐκ ᾔδει.

[3] So Bousset, Goguel, Israel Lévy and several more recent writers.

[4] So Juster and Ed. Meyer, who explains the name from the root *n-ṣ-r*, " to guard, observe," so that the Naṣoreans would be " the observant." Juster, following Friedländer, bases his view on a passage in Jerome, *Epist.*, cxii, 13, *ad* Augustinum, which states that even in his day there existed in all the synagogues of the East a class of heretics condemned by the Pharisees under the name of *minim*, but popularly called Nazareans. Jerome adds, however, that these believed in Christ, desiring to be both Jews and Christians at the same time, when they were actually neither. It is plain, therefore, that the passage treats of a post-Christian syncretistic sect, and thus scarcely accords with the description given by Epiphanius.

professed distinctive doctrines in which orthodox Christian teachers recognized the germs of those gnostic heresies which developed in the Church during the second century. From this it follows that there is nothing rash in attributing to them a certain share in the birth of Christianity, even if we cannot tell what it may have been. These sects made their appearance on the fringe of orthodox Jahwism, just as Christianity did when it assumed a definite form.

IV

JUDAISM AS A SYNCRETISTIC RELIGION

It has long been acknowledged [1] that in the time of Jesus Judaism had already become a syncretistic religion. It was syncretistic in the sense that, even within the framework of orthodoxy (more elastic than might be supposed), elements had been admitted and absorbed which were really foreign to its basic character. It was syncretistic in the further sense that it recognized, on the confines of its orthodoxy, religious forms characterized and dominated by tendencies even more at variance with the *Torah*.

The most powerful and, so to speak, the most fertile of these tendencies was that which is commonly called *gnostic*. Gnosis is divinely revealed knowledge as opposed to knowledge gained by reason and experience, the product of the human mind. In other words, gnosis is knowledge *per se* ; complete and absolute, liberated from reason and human control.[2] With the supreme revelation of metaphysical Truth it combines cosmological ideas, speculations concerning matter, and the nature of the forces (*dynameis*) which called it into being and control it, and concerning the origin and destiny of living creatures, especially of man. Its principal adjunct is mystical astrology.

It is possible that Gnosticism had its origin in Mesopotamia

---

[1] **CCLXI**, 34 *ff.*

[2] Perception through the senses is called αἴσθησις ; knowledge based on reason is called ἐπιστήμη. In contrast to these, γνῶσις is revelation vouchsafed from God (γνῶσις θεοῦ) concerning ways and means necessary for salvation (σωτηρία). *Cf. Corpus Hermeticum, Poim.*, viii, 1 *ff.* ; x, 15 ; xi, 21 : ἡ γὰρ τελεία κακία τὸ ἀγνοεῖν τὸ θεῖον ; *Asclep.*, lxxxi, 8. It is essentially an illumination (φῶς τῆς γνώσεως), and does not lend itself to rational proof, being a mystic gift (λόγος ἀπόρρητοςϰ αἱ μυστικός, *Philos.*, v, 7). *Cf.* Brandt, *Die mand. Rel.*, 170 *f.* ; J. Kroll, *Lehre d. Herm.*, 375. On gnosticism in general, see the clear and concise article, with full Bibliography, in **RGG**, ii, col. 1272 *ff.*

and was a product of Babylon,[1] but it was probably further developed by Persian thought at the time when the empire of the Achæmenids threw open to it the world of Western Asia, Syria and Egypt. It would have been a miracle, had later Judaism been able to entrench itself against the assaults of an influence which beset it on all sides.

Nor, in fact, did it so entrench itself, for we can now no longer doubt that there actually existed a Jewish gnosis from which the various sects drew their nourishment. In all probability, these sects sincerely believed themselves to be entirely orthodox with regard to the *Torah*; nevertheless, they occupied themselves with esoteric doctrines which fostered their illusion[2] by seeming to be in accord with a genuine legalism, while they falsified its spirit by interpretations wholly alien to it. Moreover, in addition to the sects proper, all the great movements of contemporary Jewish thought, whether Pharisaism or Essenism, owed something to this gnosis,[3] which had come, indeed, to be the essence and mainstay of all religious speculation in the East.

Concerning the nature of this Jewish gnosis, its content and composition, we are reduced to hazardous deductions, such, for instance, as may be drawn from Galatians and Colossians, and hypotheses. There is something surprising in this lack of material, for, while we can understand the disappearance of that literature, esoteric if not actually hermetic, in which the thought of these closed sects must doubtless have found expression, it is not so easy to understand the silence of those Christian writers who fought against the Christianizing gnosis, yet seem forsooth to have preserved no accurate remembrance of it, except of Simon the Samaritan and Dositheus. It may be said, in fact, that to these two names they have attributed almost everything of Palestinian gnosis which survived the destruction of the Jewish nation.

The basic myth of all gnostic teaching concerning the nature and destiny of man is always as follows : Man is formed out of a fusion of matter, which is the corporeal flesh, with a life-principle, which is the spiritual soul. The latter is of divine origin ; by accident it has fallen into the bondage of matter from which it longs to be freed that it may return to its source, to

---

[1] **ANZ**, *Zur Frage nach dem Ursprung des Gnostizismus*, in *Texte und Untersuchungen*, 1897.

[2] For references and discussion, see Toussaint, **CCCVI**, 72 *ff*. *Cf*. **CCLXV**, 240 ; Friedländer, *Der vorchristliche jüdische Gnostizismus*, 1898.

[3] On gnostic tendencies among the Rabbis of the first century, see **CCCXXVII**, 33 and n.

the abode of God. Matter is not the creation of the supreme God but of an inferior divinity by whose Law the world is bound. Hence the liberation of the *spirit*—that is, of the spiritual principle in man—is his emancipation from the evil bondage occasioned by this law of the Demiurge. At a later date, within the framework of Christian belief, the gnostics came to identify the Demiurge with Jahweh and his law with the *Torah*. It is, however, highly improbable that the Jews themselves ever reached this daring pitch of impiety. The case of Saint Paul, who respects the Law while at the same time maintaining its inadequacy to give salvation to mankind, is convincing evidence on this point ; moreover, the reconciliation effected by Philo of Alexandria between his syncretistic philosophy, with its marked gnostic tendency, and orthodox legalism, points in the same direction. Moreover, they probably brought back the old Iranian dualism, opposing to Jahweh and his Law, bringing salvation to him who understands it aright, Satan, master of the material world and his Law of destruction. It is, moreover, some such conception as this which, as we shall see, dominates the spirit of the Evangelists.

But the release of the divine spark, imprisoned in the corruption of matter, cannot be accomplished of its own initiative. There is need for the help of an Intermediary. Perhaps certain sects of Ophite origin, such as the Sethites,[1] expected the decisive aid of a divine being, a heavenly messenger, if you will, a *Christ*, who would combine within himself in a more or less distorted form the ideas of Persian eschatology and the Messianic visions of Daniel.[2]

Thus, it was the spirit of syncretism which was responsible for the rise of Jewish sects even in Palestine. That spirit pervaded the entire Orient at the beginning of the Christian era.[3] Through it divergent beliefs tended to be reconciled and combined, to supplement one another, and to become subordinated to a few general but powerful motives which we may, without attempting for the present to deal with them in detail, connect with the idea of, and desire for, *salvation*. The effect of this syncretism has been detected even in certain Rabbinical speculations,[4] and it must have operated to an even greater degree in Jewish circles less immune from it than the Schools. It is to be

[1] See, on the Sethites, **CCLXXVI**, i, 175.

[2] **CCLVIII**, 88 *ff.* ; 93 *ff.* seeks to invest these possibilities with the aura of certainty. This is going too far, though on several points the comparisons and conclusions advanced are suggestive.

[3] H. Schaeder, *Studien zum antiken Synkretismus*, 1926.

[4] **CCLXV**, 38 : Simeon ben Azzai held theosophical speculation in esteem ; Simeon ben Soma believed in the pre-existence of matter ;

regretted that concerning the forms of religion produced in Palestine by this syncretistic tendency, our information is too meagre and scattered to provide an adequate basis for scientific study or analysis.[1] Nevertheless, our sources are at least sufficient to justify the conclusion towards which the whole of our inquiry in this chapter has been tending, namely, to show that in practical life Palestinian Judaism largely escaped from the rigid legalism, the simple monotheism and the strict observance of the Law, within whose limits it has so long been supposed to have been confined.[2]

As has been very properly observed,[3] Jahwism in the classical period was mainly characterized by monotheism and the fear of mysticism. Yet, when later Judaism is subjected to analysis, far more numerous and varied elements, and even tendencies in the opposite direction, make their appearance. Once exposed to foreign influences the traditional faith proved receptive to actively polytheistic ideas. These, no doubt, were adapted and accommodated as far as possible to its own ways of thought, that is to say, they were brought within the framework of its own monotheism. Nevertheless, they contributed to the

---

Elisha ben Abuya premised two powers in the Godhead, and regarded all outward observance of the Law as superfluous. These teachers are all later than the beginning of the Christian era, but it is hardly likely that just at the time when Israel was tending to narrow the boundaries of her thought, they would have created that movement of speculation to which they belong and which seems at first sight so foreign to the Jewish spirit.

[1] CCLXV, 36, n. 1 ; 233. Cf. Epiphanius, *Haer.*, xviii, 19 (29), 30, 53, and Hegesippus (in Eus., *H.E.*, iv, 21, 5), where there is mention of seven sects, or heretical schisms (τῶν ἑπτὰ αἱρέσεων). Unfortunately, we know nothing about them, and Epiphanius is none too trustworthy. We may perhaps await further light on the subject from future excavations in Palestine, for on one point such light has already been granted. Twenty-three years ago G. F. Hill, in his *Catalogue of the Greek Coins of Palestine*, xix, 29, published a silver coin, dated by him in the Fifth century B.C., on one side of which is shown a bearded head and on the other a bearded person seated in a winged chariot and accompanied by the name Jahweh in Hebrew characters. It has been suggested that this is a representation of Dionysus (H. Gressmann, **ZATW**, *Neue Folge*, ii, 1925, 16 ff.). If so, we should have here a syncretistic fusion of Jahweh and Dionysus. Though not definite enough, this example is nevertheless of great interest. Better examples may yet be discovered. In the meanwhile, a further instance may be cited. A gem, now in the Berlin Museum (de Haas, *Bilderatlas, Die Religion i.d. Umwelt des Christentums*, Leipzig, 1926, No. 79), depicts on the obverse the dog-headed Anubis, together with palm and purse, and on the reverse an archangel with the superscription ΓΑΒΡΙΗΡΣΑΒΑΩ = Gabriel Sabaoth. Here likewise we have an instructive case of syncretism.

[2] CCLXV, 37 and n. ; 240.   [3] CCLXI, 37.

weakening of its former rigidity. Moreover, later Judaism also came under the influence of gnostic dogma and mystical asceticism, by which it was unconsciously assimilated to those ardently soteriological religions which were its neighbours on all sides. If its development had taken any other course, the birth of Christianity could only have been explained as a miracle. To those, however, who bear in mind the conclusions adduced in the preceding pages, the alleged miracle is reduced to the proportions of a readily intelligible historical phenomenon.

V

THE PEOPLE

So far we have considered only the upper and educated classes, or the recognized religious groups, in the Palestinian world. But we have yet to inquire, what was the religion of the lesser folk of the towns and countryside, the labourers and peasants, who occupy so large a place among this agricultural people, and what they were thinking and feeling, and the impulses which moved *them* ? It is highly important that we should know the answers to these questions, for it is from this environment that Jesus himself sprang, and it was to people of this type that he preached. Unfortunately, however, the sources which might here afford us light are few and late, and of very doubtful interpretation.[1]

In Rabbinic literature there occurs an expression ʿam ha-areṣ (pl. ʿamê ha-areṣ),[2] which means literally " the people of the land." Taken in its primary sense, the expression clearly has no depreciatory meaning, nor, indeed, could it have had in the mouth of Pharisaic sages who never professed any *à priori* contempt for the working classes and who, according to Josephus (*Ant.*, xviii, 18), actually enjoyed a great reputation among them.[3] Nevertheless, in process of time, the expression came

---

[1] A number of Rabbinic texts are given in **LXXV**, ii, 387 *ff.*, and a bibliography will be found *ibid.*, 400, n. 54. *Cf.* also **CCLXV**, 43 and n. 1. For an idea of the divergence in interpretation, contrast G. F. Moore, The *Am-haareṣ*, in **CCLXVII**, i, 439 *ff.* and appendix E, with Abraham's study of the same subject in Montefiore, *The Synoptic Gospels*, London, 1927, ii, 647 *ff.*, and with Montefiore's own observations in the same vein, *op. cit.*, i, p. lxxvi ; *id.*, *Rabbinic Literature*, 3–15.

[2] **LXXV**, ii, 468 *ff.*

[3] *Talmud, Berachoth* 17a, shows clearly that certain of the Rabbis indeed subscribed to the idea that every man serves God according to his means, the scribe in the city and by study of the *Torah*, the peasant in the country and labouring in the field. *Cf.* **CCL**, i, 57.

to denote the bad Jew, the man who could not recite the *Shema*, nor the morning and evening prayers, who did not wear the ritual fringes (*zizith*) on his garment, who omitted to don the phylacteries (*tefillim*) necessary to proper devotion, who ate without first washing his hands ; the man who, having a son, neglected to teach him the Law, or, having property, did not pay his tithe to Jahweh—in a word, the non-practising Jew. The scrupulous observers of the Law, who banded themselves together in small societies (*chaburah*) for mutual edification, and called themselves *chaberim*, came to regard such a man as unclean. Moreover, the term ʿ*am ha-areş* also developed the meaning of unlearned, as contrasted with the man who had attended the Schools and was instructed in the Law. Since, then, we find that the unlearned, the non-practising Jew, and the plebeian are all comprehended under the same term, it is tempting to conclude that among the lower orders, hindered already in the strict observance of the Law by the limitations of their lives of toil, there were many lax, and even indifferent, with regard to religion. It was in these " sinners " (ἁμαρτωλοί), as the Gospels suggest,[1] that Jesus was principally interested, and whom he found among the lower orders with whom he consorted. It is to these also that reference is made in the passage in John vii. 49, " *this people which knoweth not the law.*"

Prudence, however, would counsel us to resist the temptation of such deductions and to avoid the conclusion they suggest. In the first place, it is far more likely that persons lax through indifference were to be found among the rich than among the poor. It is pre-eminently the publicans to whom the term ʿ*am ha-areş* applies, and they were certainly not afflicted with poverty.[2] In the second place, an unlearned person, astray in belief and practice from the point of view of a scribe of the period after the fall of Jerusalem, need not have been a non-practising Jew.[3] The force and depth of the popular movement which produced the Great Rebellion prove that the common folk of Palestine sincerely believed in their religion

---

[1] Mark ii. 15–17 ; Matt. ix. 10–12 ; xi. 19 ; Luke xv. 2 ; xviii. 13–14 ; xix. 7, etc. The question has been raised whether the *babes* (νήπιοι) who, according to Matt. xi. 25 (*cf.* 21, 15) and Luke x. 21, received the revelation denied to the *wise and prudent* (ἀπὸ σοφῶν καὶ συνετῶν), might not be identified with the ʿ*am ha-areş*. The same question has also been raised in respect of the *little ones* (μικροί), for whom Jesus shows such solicitude (Mark ix. 42 ; Matt. x. 42 ; Luke xvii. 2, etc.). In neither case is it possible to give a definite answer.

[2] Büchler, *Der galiläische Am-haaretz des zweiten Jahrhunderts*, Vienna, 1906 ; Montefiore, *Syn. Gospels*, i, p. cviii.

[3] **CCLV**, i, 655 *ff.* ; 659 *ff.*

and lived by it.   Their credulity and their superstitions increased
rather than diminished their faith in it.   The real essence of
their belief lies beyond our reach.

Abrahams has gone to considerable trouble [1] to prove that
the contempt of the rabbis for the ʿam ha-areṣ had nothing to do
with the latter's poverty—when they were poor—nor was it
based upon any class hatred or social motive.   This we may well
accept, even though the term does sometimes mean *poor*.[2]
But there were *poor* (ʿanavim) in Palestine of whom mention
should be made.[3]   In all probability, it is to them that the
famous, but so often misunderstood, utterance of Matthew v. 3
really refers :   " *Blessed are the poor in spirit*," by which is meant,
" *Blessed are they who have the true spirit of poverty*."   It is not
necessarily a question of the indigent, but of men whose piety
lifts them above material circumstance.   In this sense, even the
rich might be poor, though undoubtedly the ʿanavim were not
as a rule to be found among Jews on whom Fortune had smiled.
Rather were they recruited from the middle and lower classes.
Their legalism was, no doubt, not very strict, nor their formalism
very exacting.   None the less, they were sustained by an intense
mysticism, and their hearts belonged wholly to Jahweh.   The
Psalter was their book and reflects the nature of their piety.
They believed unshakeably in the future of Israel and awaited
unmoved the full realization of the divine promises.[4]   Their
ideas and their beliefs no doubt scarcely differed from those
of the Pharisees, but they were set in a different perspective, namely, that of mysticism.   In the eyes of a strict scribe,
they too might be numbered among the ʿam ha-ares.

In the light of these considerations, it would seem that two
distinct classes of ʿam ha-areṣ may be recognized.   The first
consisting of the common folk, full of good intentions, thoroughly
devoted to Jahweh, but ignorant and lax in the practice of their
religion : credulous, naïve, trusting and superstitious, at home
in a supernatural and miraculous world.   To the second class
would belong the ʿanavim, neither ignorant, nor deterred from

[1] **CCLV**, ii, 656.   For the opposite view, see L. de Grandmaison,
Jésus Christ, Paris, 1928, ii, 10 and n. 1, where the famous utterance of
Hillel is quoted : an ʿam-ha-areṣ cannot be pious (ḥasid); *Pirké Abôth*. ii, 6.

[2] The point is surely proved by a comparison of two texts quoted by
Abrahams himself, *viz.* (1) *Talm. Bab., Nedarim*, 81a :   " Pay special
heed unto a poor man, for from such doth the Torah issue forth " ; (ii)
Talmud Bab., Sanhedrin, 96a :   " Pay special heed unto the ʿam ha-areṣ,
for from such doth the Torah issue forth."

[3] **IX** ;   *cf.* Walter Sattler, *Die Anavim im Zeitalter Jesu Christi*, in
Festgabe für Ad. Jülicher, Tübingen, 1907.

[4] **IX**, 105 ;   112.

strict observance by care for their daily bread, but alien to the spirit of the Schools, if not to their doctrines, intensely religious, more inclined to trust Jahweh than to fear him, guided rather by impulse than by scruple.[1]

This distinction may be an artificial one, and I admit that, though it may be true in principle, it was not so sharp in reality. Be this as it may, it is clear that none in Israel hoped or yearned for the coming of the Man of God with more eager faith than did the 'am ha-areṣ. The tradition of their people, apart from the Messianic hope proper, had rendered them familiar with the expectation of a Divine Message embodied in a person. The Spirit of Jahweh had long been accustomed to take hold of a man and make him a mouthpiece and an instrument. We know that already towards the time of Jesus there were many mystics who believed themselves to be *the Coming One*, or imagined at least that they had received authority (ἐξουσία) to prepare the way for his coming. The oppressed had little to lose if they lent a willing ear to such men or pursued the will o' the wisp of their illusions ; and the 'anavim, having once believed that these fanatics were sent by God, had no further fears. The dis-illusionments, occasionally disastrous, which these unfortunate people had already experienced did not kill their conviction that a decisive intervention was at hand, and might even now be presenting itself.

If a *nabi* of the political type arose preaching a holy war against the foreign oppressor, and obtained a following, the result was a bloody revolt with all its consequences. In the first two centuries of the Christian era, Israel had several times known the depths of such disturbance and disaster, and between the great crises we hear of a number of such attempts, either abortive or promptly strangled. They explain and justify the distrust of his subjects entertained by the Roman procurator. But if, however, the prophet in question, renouncing the appeal to force, claimed to be wholly concerned with religion, what would happen ? He might announce the advent of the Blessed of Jahweh, and raise still higher the faith of the 'anavim disposed to believe in him. But the mere prolongation of a vain hope should tend to allay the unrest accompanying it. Again, he might bring them a doctrine more or less novel and a revelation more or less original, but he could scarcely hope for its accept-ance in the face of the hostility of the Sadducees or the dialectic of the Pharisees. He had no chance of success within the circle

---

[1] W. Sattler, *op. cit.* The author attaches great importance to these people, whom he connects with John the Baptist and Jesus, detecting further reference to them in the Epistle of James.

of legalistic orthodoxy. The only people whom he could hope to win over, within the limits of the true Israel, would be the members of those largely syncretistic circles from which the sects were recruited. It is probable that, at the time of the Herodians enthusiasts, abounded in Syria and Palestine popular preachers, agitators of every kind, magicians and wonder-workers, all more or less prophets of the Messiah and harbingers of deliverance.[1]

[1] Gillis Wetter, *Der Sohn Gottes*, Göttingen, 1916 ; **CCXCVIII**, 409 *ff.*

BOOK IV

HELLENISTIC JUDAISM

CHAPTER I

THE DIASPORA [1]

I

ORIGIN AND DISTRIBUTION

A LARGE number of Jews lived outside Palestine and constituted the *Diaspora*, or *Dispersion*. As we already know, various causes had contributed to drive them out of their country at different periods of their history, *e.g.* foreign rule, so frequently imposed upon Israel; the revolts which had so often rent the nation; the desire which seized many of its children to go and seek their fortune on soil less ungrateful than the stony tracts of Judah; the lure of trade and the thirst for gain.

When, in 537 B.C., the Persian monarch permitted the rebuilding of the Holy City, many of those who had been deported in 588 did not return. They remained " beside the waters of Babylon," and there built up a large and affluent colony.

So much is well known. But even before this colony arose, more or less numerous groups of Jews had already settled round the eastern Mediterranean,[2] and it has been suspected, not without some reason, that these had on several occasions established connexions with their brothers and neighbours, the Phœnicians.[3]

[1] **LXXV**, Index, s.v. *Diaspora, Proselyten, Synagogen*; **XLVII**, analytical tables and especially i, 243–53 (Jewish worship and the religious policy of the Empire); 255–90 (Proselytism); **CCCXXIX**; **CCVIII**, 192–211 (Hellenistic Judaism); **CLII**, 432–7 (Relation of the Diaspora to Palestinian Judaism); **CCLXXIX**, Index to vol. ii, s.v. *Synagogue*; **CCCXIX** (Jewish life at Rome).

[2] **VIII**.

[3] G. Rosen, *Juden und Phönizier. Das antike Judentum als Mission-religion und die Entstehung d. jüdischen Diaspora*, Tübingen, 1929.

211

Difficult as it may be to assess today the full importance of these migrations, they prove at least that the Jewish habit of leaving the mother-country had already existed for some time before they were compelled to do so.

After the Macedonian conquest in 330 B.C., the succession of wars waged in Palestine caused many of its inhabitants to be transplanted to Egyptian or Syrian soil whence they did not return. According to Josephus (*Ant.*, xii, 1), the Jewish community in Alexandria owed its origin to the capture of Jerusalem by Ptolemy Soter in 319. The Egyptian king carried away with him a large number of Jewish families whom he settled in Egypt. These he took from almost all parts of the country, from the Judæan hills around Jerusalem and from the district of Gerizim in Samaria. His father, Ptolemy Lagos, had previously installed Jews in Cyrenaica,[1] and tradition puts their number at no less than 100,000 souls.[2]

Similarly, Antiochus the Great (223–188 B.C.) drew upon the Jewish communities of Mesopotamia in order to found colonies in Phrygia and Lydia (Jos., *Ant.*, xii, 8, 4).

Again, during the course of the Maccabæan revolt, which began in 166, and later in the ceaseless wars waged at the beginning of the first century by Alexander Jannæus, from 79 and onwards, against his Syrian, Arabian and Egyptian neighbours, large batches of Jewish soldiers and of the inhabitants of the ravaged country were taken captive and sold as slaves in the markets of Asia Minor and Egypt.[3] Even when they were redeemed later through their own work or through the help of their brethren, they remained of their own accord in the land to which they had by then become accustomed, and, forming themselves into groups, sought to establish there a community formally recognized by the local authorities. Thus, the nucleus of the Jewish community in Rome seems to have been a band of prisoners, captured in Asia during the war against Antiochus the Great (192–188), and released later, prior to the capture of Jerusalem by Pompey.[4] In 139, a decree of the *praetor peregrinus* ordered those Jews who had admitted Italian proselytes to the celebration of their sabbath to leave Rome and Italy within ten days, and from this it is plain that the colony had by that time already acquired a certain degree of importance.[5]

On the other hand, many of the political movements in Judæa, notably the civil wars and the bitter struggles for power which ensued in the age of Hasmonæan decadence, resulted in

---

[1] Jos., *C. Ap.*, ii, 4, 44. [2] *Letter of Aristeas*, 12 (ed. Wendland).
[3] **XLVII**, ii, 17, where references to texts are given.
[4] Philo, *Legatio*, 23. [5] **LV**, vi, 65.

the more or less voluntary exile of the vanquished,[1] and the same is true of those Jews who had lent support to one or other of the foreign princes (such as the king of Egypt in the third century) during the brief spell of his domination of the country, but who, on his departure, feared the vengeance of their opponents.[2]

The Greek, and later the Roman, conquest of Palestine, also produced an inevitable emigration. Jews who found themselves ill at ease at home would migrate to the land of their conqueror in search of better conditions, their own country being no longer able to maintain a large population in plenty.[3] Nor was the movement confined to the Jews ; it pervaded the entire Orient. Any family which prospered in a place would attract others to it, since the Jew, unless he became altogether indigent, never lost touch with his homeland and especially with Jerusalem.[4] About 88 B.C. Mithridates carried off from Cos a sum of 800 talents (roughly £38,000) amassed by the Jews of the island,[5] and this affords an interesting indication of the prosperity to which they had attained in their new surroundings.[6] They were, as a rule, hard-working and industrious, and for this reason several of the contemporary princes, such as Ptolemy Philadelphus in Egypt and several of the Seleucids in Syria, held them in special esteem, and readily invited them to their countries. The celebrated Jewish community of Antioch was the result of such a policy.

According to Strabo, quoted with pride by Josephus (*Ant.* xiv, 7, 2), the *Diaspora* had by this time extended to *every city* (εἰς πᾶσαν πόλιν ἤδη παρεληλύθει) and it was not easy to find a place on earth which was free of Jews (καὶ τόπον οὐκ ἔστι ʽ ϱᾳδίως εὑϱεῖν τῆς οἰκουμένης ὅς οὐ παραδεδέκται τοῦτο τὸ φῦλον). This exaggeration is not without parallels.[7] There is the often-quoted line of the Sibylline Oracles [8] :

> Every land and sea is full of thee,
>
> (πᾶσα δὲ γαῖα σέθεν πλήϱης καὶ πᾶσα θάλασσα)

---

[1] CCCXXIX, 620.

[2] In the reign of Ptolemy VI Philomator, the son of the High Priest Onias, frustrated in his ambitions, retired to Egypt with a large number of his followers and founded at Leontopolis a rival Temple to that in Jerusalem. *Cf.* CCCXXIX, 620.

[3] CCCXXIX, 621.   [4] CCLXV, 27.

[5] LXV, v, 284 ; *cf.* Jos., *Ant.*, xiv, 7, 2, which is based on Strabo.

[6] On the prosperity of the Jews at Cyrene and Alexandria during the same epoch, *cf.* Jos., *loc. cit.*

[7] Passages are collected in CCCXXII, i, 2 n.

[8] *Or. Sib.*, iii, 271. This text, of Jewish origin, may be dated in the second century B.C.

or that of Seneca, recorded by Saint Augustine, according to which " the manners and customs of this vile race are already implanted in every land, so that the vanquished have imposed their laws on the victors." [1]   Similarly, we may recall in this connexion the confused but significant list of peoples in Acts ii. 9–11 : " *Parthians and Medes and Edomites and the dwellers in Mesopotamia, Judæa and Cappadocia, Pontus and Asia, Phrygia and Pamphylia, Egypt and the parts of Lybia about Cyrene, sojourners from Rome both Jews and proselytes, Cretans and Arabians.*" [2]

The description of this geographical expansion has been supplemented by the evidence of literary and epigraphic sources. Naturally, it is impossible to arrive at complete certainty, but the resultant impression is that the passages quoted are but exaggerating what was more or less the truth.

Thus, it is possible to state that, from the first century B.C. Jews were to be found in most of the provinces of the Roman Empire, especially in those which surrounded the Mediterranean, or bordered on the Black Sea.   In Armenia, for instance, the upper classes traced their descent to Biblical characters. [3]   To the east of Palestine, beyond Syria, Jewish colonies grew up on a large scale throughout Babylonia, Mesopotamia and Media. They were also plentiful in Syria and Egypt (where they had settled in all the nomes as far as Upper Egypt), [4] in Rome and in the provinces of Asia Minor. [5]   Throughout the whole of the west and in Africa, with the exception of Cyrenaica, they were far more sparsely scattered. [6]

This widespread dispersion of the emigrants does not imply a small handful of scattered settlers.   On the contrary, certain communities seem to have been very well populated : the race was prolific.   No doubt, we need not take too literally the statement of Philo that throughout the Diaspora the Jewish nation bid fair to equal the native population in number, [7] so that they would have comprised half of the human race. [8]   Nevertheless,

---

[1] *Civ. Dei*, vii, 11.

[2] The passage has been compared with the letter of Agrippa to Caligula (*apud* Philo, *Leg.*, 36), which likewise enumerates the countries where Jews were to be found.   The two lists resemble each other.

[3] **XLVII**, i, 199, n. 2.

[4] **LXXV**, iii, 499 ; **CCCVIII**, 192.—Philo, *In Flac.*, 6, says that between Catabathmos in Lybia and the frontiers of Ethiopia there dwelt a million Jews.

[5] Philo, *Leg.*, 33.

[6] **CCCXXII**, i, 2 *ff.*, where it is observed that there is no mention of the West either in the passage of Acts or in the letter of Agrippa.

[7] Philo, *Vita Mos.*, ii, 27.   [8] Philo, *Leg.*, 31.

it is hard to see how the Alexandrian philosopher could ever
have ventured such a statement had not the facts appeared to
have warranted it, at least on a broad view.

There are approximate figures available. At Rome, in
4 B.C., when a deputation arrived from Palestine, no less than
8,000 Jews went out to meet it.[1] In A.D. 19, Tiberius deported
to Sardinia nearly 4,000 members of the Jewish community
capable of bearing arms.[2] In the second century, Jewish
uprisings in Cyrene, Alexandria and Cyprus claimed victims
estimated by ancient writers at hundreds of thousands.[3] These
figures cannot, of course, be pressed too closely, and there is no
contemporary census to check them. Nevertheless, they permit
the rough calculation that at the commencement of the current
era the Diaspora numbered between 4,000,000 and 6,000,000,
perhaps even 7,000,000, souls.[4] We do not know whether this
total includes proselytes, but it is probable. Accepting Philo's
statement that there were 1,000,000 Jews in Egypt, their proportion in that country would have been one seventh or one
eighth of the total population.[5] It is, however, the extent
rather than the numerical strength of the Dispersion which is
of interest to us, since wherever there was a Jewish nucleus,
there was also a centre for the further spread of Judaism.

II

THE JEWISH COMMUNITIES OF THE DIASPORA

Uprooted from their native soil, the Jews of the Diaspora
regarded as their fatherland the country in which they were
born. Nevertheless, they did not merge into the surrounding
population. Religion and pride alike forbade them to do so,
and they never ceased to belong to the Jewish nation. It has
been observed [6] that on their tombs the particular community
in which they were enrolled is never stated, unless they occupied
an official position in it. The word used to denote their mutual
relationship is συγγενής (*of the same race*). A deep-seated sense
of brotherhood united them, expressed, so to speak, in their
common respect for the *Torah*.

[1] Jos., *Ant.*, xvii, 11, 1 ; *B.J.*, ii, 6 1.

[2] Jos., *Ant.*, xviii, 3, 5 ; Tacitus, *Ann.*, ii, 85 ; Suetonius, *Tiberius*, 36.

[3] Dio Cassius, lxviii, 32, gives the number as 220,000 in Cyrenaica
and 240,000 at Cyprus, during the reign of Trajan. Eusebius, *H.E.*, iv, 2,
adds that in the suppression of the insurrection *several myriads* of Jews
lost their lives.

[4] J. Beloch, *Die Bevölkerung d. griechisch-röm.*, Welt, 1886, 246 ;
XLVII, i, 209.

[5] CCCXXII, i, 3. [6] XLVII, i, 418, n. 1.

They often lived in a separate quarter of the town in which they had received formal permission to settle. The reason for this was not compulsion,[1] but a desire for close union and companionship. In every case they formed on foreign soil what was, so to speak, a cell in the Jewish organism, a petty state with its own organization, administrative, financial, judicial and religious. Subject to the general rules of the city, they yet enjoyed certain privileges, necessitated by their special situation.

The Jewish community is known to us under a variety of names,[2] *viz.* the *thiasos, the assembly, the synagogue, the people, the body, the totality,* etc., or, simply, *the Jews* or *the Hebrews.*

The term most in use in modern times is *the synagogue,* but this was by no means the dominant one in antiquity.[3] The groups in question did not answer exactly to what the Gentiles called *colleges* or *thiasoi* or *eranoi.* They were not modelled upon those organizations, and were distinguished from them by special features. Admission to them was by right of birth; the non-Jew could never belong. In complexity of function and life, far deeper than any which existed among the pagan associations, they resembled a small city set in the midst of another, rather than a *college.* Finally, since they were, legally, part of the Jewish nation, they remained subject in matters of law to the central Jewish authority.

Possibly, the different names by which these groups were known correspond to differences in constitution which distinguished them from one another. Concerning these, however, we have no information.[4] Moreover, it is not these certain, though elusive, differences so much as the common traits which, taken together, give us a clear idea of the organization of these colonies.

(1) The Jewish community was not controlled by a *lex,* or specific statute, as was the pagan *college,* but merely by administrative rules. Not one of these has come down to us, though we may safely assume that they were more elaborate in the large communities than in the small.

(2) The community was of the democratic type. Its members formed an assembly, which elected its officials and which tendered advice in all matters of importance, whether they

---

[1] At Alexandria they lived in the Delta quarter, but not all of them were settled there, being found also in almost every part of the city.

[2] **XLVII,** i, 414 *ff.,* gives a complete list of such terms : πολίτευμα, πολιτεία, κατοικία, θίασος, προσευχή, σύνοδος, συναγωγή, στῆμα, ἔθνος, λαός, *universitas, corpus.*

[3] **XLVII,** i, 417, n. 3 ; *contra,* Schürer, **DB,** v, 100ᵃ (s.v. *Diaspora*).

[4] All available knowledge on the subject is collected in **XLVII,** i, 438–50.

concerned religion and worship or administration and policy. Cicero (*Pro Flacco*, 28) describes a demonstration organized by the Jews of Rome and of a political character.[1]

(3) The government of the community, in the strict sense of the word, was in the hands of a Council (*gerousia*), whose members were called the Elders (*gerontes* or *presbyteroi*) and the president the *Gerousiarch* (γερουσιαρχῶν, or ἐπιστάτης τῶν παλαίων, or προστάτης). We do not know what conditions were attached to the tenure of these offices. Age was not enough, and the term *Elder* was, of course, no more to be taken literally than is the French *Senator*. Sometimes, it represents a title conferred by way of honour upon a distinguished member of the community, even upon a woman.[2] It was the business of the *gerousia* to look after the general interests of the community.

(4) Strictly administrative duties were entrusted to another Council consisting of several members, called *Archontes*, and sometimes even to a single person called an *Archon*. These officials were elected by the community, usually for a year, but sometimes for life, and were chosen in the *gerousia*, whose executive officers they became. Along with them we find a General Secretary, or Registrar, the *Grammateus*. The archonship was a coveted distinction, and it, too, was sometimes conferred as a title of honour in recognition of benefactions.

(5) There was also, apparently, a kind of committee composed of influential persons who were regarded as the protectors and benefactors of the community—*patres et matres synagogae*, but we do not know what it did or how it was elected.

In large cities, where the Jews were numerous and lived in different quarters, their union into a single body might present difficulties, and the local authorities, becoming uneasy, may have endeavoured more or less to obstruct it.[3] In such cases, the Jews formed themselves into what may be described as *parishes*, each preserving in miniature the organization described above, but subjected to a central *gerousia* which exercised authority over them all and maintained their unity. Even in Rome, as we know from epigraphic evidence, there existed a kind of General President of the whole community called the Exarch, while, according to Acts xxviii. 17, when Paul arrived

---

[1] Further examples will be found in **XLVII**, i, 440, n. 6.
[2] **XLVII**, i, 441, n. 8.
[3] Schürer stresses this aspect of the problem. *Cf.* **XLVII**, i, 420, n. 4 ; **DACL**, s.v. *Monteverde*, col. 2565, on the synagogues of Rome : seven are quoted from the cemetery of Monteverde, and three from that of **Vigna Randanini**.

at that city he called together the chiefs of the Jewish community regarded as a whole (τοὺς ὄντας τῶν Ἰουδαίων πρώτους).

Every group of Orientals settled in a foreign city established there a place of prayer. The Jews, for their part, made the *synagogue* the centre of their community. In point of *law*, the synagogue had its own administrative machinery, quite distinct from that described above. In point of fact, however, the distinction between the officials of the synagogue and those of the colony is often difficult to apprehend, since their titles are often the same and of uncertain meaning.[1] Apparently, each synagogue possessed, at first, its own *archisynagogos*, also called *rabbi*, *didaskalos*, or *princeps synagogae*, *i.e.* chief, and religious director. It was the duty of this official to see that the *Torah* was observed, to preside over meetings and to organize divine worship. Anyone chosen for this position of trust had to give proof of unquestionable competence in theology, law and medicine. The *archisynagogos* was also charged with supervising the collection of taxes due both to the Temple at Jerusalem and to the State. He is not to be confused with the *archon*, though the two offices do not seem to have been mutually incompatible. Subordinate to the *archisynagogos* were the following officials: (*a*) the *priests* (ἱεροί), whose functions elude us; (*b*) a *sacristan* (the *hazzan*, ὑπηρέτης, νεόκορος), who was the factotum of the chief; (*c*) a *reader* of the Scriptures; (*d*) a *translator*, whose duty it was to render the Hebrew text intelligible to an audience ignorant of the sacred tongue.

The synagogue constituted the true centre and focus of Jewish life in its entirety.[2] Sermons were delivered there, the Law was read there, prayers offered, and classes held. It was also a court of justice, and a place where sentences were carried out, as well as being a rendezvous for the discussion of the whole community's varied interests. The law of the State afforded it protection as a religious building.

The synagogue building (οἶκος τῆς συναγωγῆς) was not constructed according to an invariable pattern. Certainly, the Rabbis endeavoured to lay down definite rules, prescribing, for instance, that the building should be erected in the highest part of the city, with its entrance facing the east.[3] Nevertheless, the numerous remains of synagogues discovered in the Holy Land and elsewhere show clearly that these injunctions were not always followed.[4] On pagan soil, the synagogue was, as a rule, outside the city-complex, and corresponded, both in style and

[1] XLVII, i, 450 *ff.*; CCCXXXVI, i, 105 *ff.*
[2] XLVII, i, 456 *ff.*   [3] *Megillah*, iv, 22.
[4] EB, s.v. *Synagogue*, §§ 5–7.

appearance, to the usage and taste of the country. Even in Galilee, the synagogue of Capernaum (Tell Hum), excavated by the Franciscans,[1] gives the appearance of a Græco-Roman edifice, while that of Dura-Europus, recently disinterred, recalls in its frescoed walls the same æsthetic canons as the pagan buildings of that place. And the same is true also of mediæval synagogues; here they may be Gothic and there Moorish.

Nevertheless, it is not difficult to trace a real uniformity in the arrangement of the interior. There was a court, or *atrium*, enclosed by walls, and a portico (ἐξέδρα) giving access, with or without a vestibule (πρόναος), to a large rectangular room, often furnished with benches, at least round the sides. At the far end, facing the entrance, was an *ark*, *i.e.* a chest or cupboard, containing the scrolls of the Law and all the Holy Books. In the middle of the room there was a sort of platform, on which stands the reading desk, also used as a pulpit for the delivery of sermons. The room was occupied by the Jews seated, it would seem, according to their profession. Proselytes remained outside in the courtyard, before the open door, or under the porch.

III

The Status of the Jews in the Empire

The community, considered as a corporate body, enjoyed under the Roman Empire a certain number of legally guaranteed rights.[2] Such were the right of association and convocation *ipso jure*, of discharging religious duties and celebrating worship, and of duly observing the Sabbath. It was forbidden to summon a Jew to Court on the Sabbath, to exact labour from him, or even to compel him to indulge in free amusements.[3] Similarly, the community enjoyed the right of collecting money and organizing a common fund, and consequently also of taxing its members at need and inflicting fines upon them. It possessed full property rights in its own communal buildings and cemeteries. It could make contracts, buy, sell, give and receive gifts. It could not inherit in the strict sense, but it could accept legacies,

---

[1] R. P. G. Orfali, *Capharnaum et ses ruines*, Paris, 1912.

[2] **XLVII**, i, 409 *ff.*; 424 *ff.*—In those parts of the Hellenistic world where Jews had been settled for some time—in Egypt, for example—they naturally enjoyed privileges granted originally by the local monarchs which remained in force under Roman rule (Jos., *Ant.*, xix, 5, 2; *B.J.*, ii, 18, 7; *C. Ap.*, ii, 4). The retention or increase of these privileges was the cause, or perhaps the excuse, of a formidable agitation, especially at Alexandria, during the entire period with which we are here concerned.

[3] **XLVII**, i, 355 *ff.*

plead in court, send deputations to lay its petitions before the Roman authorities, confer by decree honours, titles, distinctions and official marks of recognition. Finally, it could, at least, in religious matters, administer justice to its members.[1]

Thus, as was said above, the community constituted a kind of miniature city, set in the midst of another and protected by it. In return for this protection the Jews made certain concessions.[2] The State did not compel them to style the Emperor a god, but they agreed to take oaths by his name, accommodating the usual formula to their own beliefs. They celebrated the festivals. of his birth (*dies natalis*) and accession. They joined in the various commemorations of victories and occasions of public mourning, observing them, however, in their own way, and abstaining from any outward demonstration which appeared to them to savour of paganism. The State was satisfied with this degree of loyalty. They had to pray for the welfare of the Empire and the prosperity of the Emperor. This they did, just as at Jerusalem they had offered sacrifices with the same intent. Thus, thanks to the privileges accorded them, they were able, while preserving a kind of autonomy, to seem perfectly loyal subjects, which is, as we shall see, a fact of great importance.[3]

The social condition of these settlers [4] presents a considerable inequality. Side by side with the fortunate were many who were far from prosperous. The synagogues were surrounded with beggars, of whom a large part must have been Jews. Indeed, there are not wanting sources which represent the Jews, even at Rome, as largely destitute,[5] and the cheapness of so many of their sarcophagi confirms this impression. Nevertheless, there are grounds for doubt, for it is not easy to understand how that close solidarity which the ancients regarded as a distinctive virtue of the Jews and which formed indeed one of the major charges against them,[6] that exclusive fraternity which involved them in the charge of hatred of the human race (*odium generis humani*), and provided an excuse for the prevalent anti-Semitism, could ever have countenanced the hopeless destitution in which so many of their race were sunk. In view of this, it has been suggested [7] that these Jews, so despised by

---

[1] **XLVII**, ii, 153.   [2] **XLVII**, i, 342 ff.

[3] On Roman policy towards the Jews—usually very benevolent—see **CCLXVII**, v, 377 *ff.* (by V. M. Scramuzza).

[4] **XLVII**, ii, 291 *ff.* ; 305 *ff.* (classes) ; 315 (wealth) ; **CCCXXVII**, part 3.

[5] **XLVII**, ii, 319.

[6] Cicero, *Pro Flacco*, 28 : *Quanta concordia !* Passages are collected in **XLVII**, ii, 166, n. 3.

[7] **XLVII**, ii, 159.

Juvenal [1] for instance, were really men banished from the synagogue, suffering the penalty of excommunication, and therefore merely on the fringe of the community proper. This is perhaps supported by the fact that within the community itself there existed certain societies for mutual assistance in which men of the same profession were banded together, so much so that, whenever a Jewish traveller presented himself at the synagogue, he was at once asked his trade and was then referred to the professional association which was responsible for him. Here we may indeed detect an analogy to the pagan colleges, and at the same time one of the most characteristic traits of Jewish solidarity.

As for the maintenance of national unity, this was achieved in the following manner :

(1) Jerusalem remained an object of reverence, and frequent pilgrimages secured contact with it on the part of the community living in the Diaspora. Josephus (*B.J.*, vi, 9, 3) speaks of some two and a half million pilgrims, and even of three millions (*B.J.*, ii, 14, 3), gathered together for the Passover in the Holy City, shortly before the Great Rebellion of A.D. 66. The figure is certainly exaggerated, but at least suggests an imposing multitude. Philo [2] says that thousands of Jews flocked to the Temple from thousands of cities.

(2) Every Jew from the age of twenty and upwards paid an annual tax to the Temple. A special delegation, rigorously protected by Roman Law, carried this *holy money* ($\iota\varepsilon\varrho\grave{\alpha}$ $\chi\varrho\acute{\eta}\mu\alpha\tau\alpha$) to Jerusalem year by year.[3]

(3) All the Jews owed submission and obedience, in theory, to the head of the nation in Palestine. The Roman State assented to this.[4] The Jewish population of Babylon and Persia likewise acknowledged this obligation.[5]

By these means, then, constant contact was maintained between the utmost bounds of the Jewish world and its centre. After the destruction of Jerusalem, the link was forged once more in the person of the *Nasi'*, or *Patriarch* of Tiberias, the religious head of Israel, and by the institution of apostles (*apostoli*), or regular envoys, who represented him throughout the Diaspora, and acted on his behalf as overseers of the religious life, watching over the regular observance of the ritual and collecting taxes, etc.[6] At the time with which we are concerned it was the Sanhedrin which was recognized by the Jews of the Dispersion as the principal symbol of their unity.

[1] *Sat.*, iii, 13 *ff.*
[2] *De Spec. Leg.*, i, 69.
[3] **XLVII**, i, 377 *ff.*
[4] **XLVII**, i, 391.
[5] **CCLXV**, 28.
[6] **XLVII**, i, 388 *ff.*

IV

INFLUENCE OF THE GREEK ENVIRONMENT

The charter of liberty granted to the Jews under the Roman Empire permitted them, at least in theory and in law, to preserve their religion uncontaminated by contacts with paganism. In fact, however, it did not protect the Jewish spirit against the powerful influences of the Hellenistic environment. Through daily contact with men possessing a higher culture than their own, the traditional Jewish fear of an alien culture gradually diminished and ultimately left no adequate defence against the influences of the surrounding world.

This cardinal fact involved three principal consequences:

(1) There grew up a Hellenized Judaism favourable to Greek philosophy.

(2) As the result of this internal transformation, *a spirit of propaganda* developed among the Hellenized Jews.

(3) A syncretism, at once intellectual and religious, gradually developed, resulting, after various vicissitudes, in the creation of *sects*, and fostered the establishment of a Jewish *gnosis*.

The Jews who had immigrated to Greek territory found themselves obliged by the actual necessities of life to learn the language of the country, and thus came to forget their own tongue, so that even the Bible had to be translated into Greek for their benefit. Of these translations—for there were several of them—the most famous saw the light of day at Alexandria, where the Jewish community kept an annual festival in honour of its publication. Legend referred its compilation to the time of Ptolemy Philadelphus (285–246 B.C.). This monarch was said to have asked the High Priest at Jerusalem to assemble seventy-two learned elders who translated the Pentateuch in seventy-two days (Josephus, *Ant.*, xii, 2, 2 *ff.*). Actually, the task was a long and laborious one, begun in all likelihood towards the middle of the third century and finished in the last third of the second century B.C., if not somewhat later. This translation is called the Septuagint, in reference to the seventy or seventy-two translators mentioned above.

The Septuagint spread through all the Greek-speaking Jewish colonies, and, though far from perfect, was commonly regarded as inspired, and shared the respect granted to the original text.[1] Moreover, it afforded an opportunity for interested pagans to obtain information concerning Judaism, and exerted great influence over the whole of the religious literature

[1] Philo, *Vit. Mos.*, ii, 6.

published at the beginning of the Christian era.[1] The Jews, for their part, came into contact with Greek letters and Greek thought, and this placed them in a delicate position with regard to the *Torah* similar to that occupied by many educated religious persons today with regard to science and dogma. They, too, managed to convince themselves that there could not be any real contradiction between their knowledge and their faith, and sought to reconcile them. Accordingly, they laid down the principle that anything of merit in Greek wisdom came from the Bible, and they imagined that there had existed in Egypt a translation of it, much earlier than the Septuagint, of which the Greek philosophers had availed themselves. A certain Aristobulus gave substance to this legend by dint of anachronisms, daring interpretations and interpolations. Once having taken root in Alexandria, it spread throughout the entire Jewish world of the Diaspora, and was later adopted in turn by Christian writers.[2]

Subsequently, the demand arose among the Jews for the application to the Bible of a form of exegesis which enjoyed great popularity at that period [3] and which owed its existence to the daring use of symbolism and allegory, producing an interpretation, which made it possible to harmonize the sacred text with Greek speculation. In a sense, the Septuagint already represented the application of this extraordinary method [4]; and certain of the Biblical Apocrypha, such as the Wisdom of Solomon, 2 Maccabees, 3 and 4 Maccabees, and the Sibylline Oracles, provide even better examples. Most typical of all, however, are the writings of Philo of Alexandria.

This man, who occupies a place of his own in the history of Greek philosophy,[5] was born at Alexandria *c.* B.C. 30 and died there *c.* A.D. 54. He was the *ethnarch*, hence the judge and general administrator, of his community. Having studied with equal diligence both the *Torah* and the philosophy of the Gentiles, he felt himself sufficiently attached to both to be unwilling to sacrifice the one to the other. He therefore introduced his metaphysical ideas into the Bible, and found them there without difficulty. An extravagant exegesis, which no obstacle could deflect from its goal, established at all

---

[1] **CCCXV**, 206 ; **CCCVIII**, 196.

[2] Michel Nicolas, *Études sur Philon d'Alexandrie*, **RHR**, v, 321. On Aristobulus, see **LXXV**, iii, 384 *ff.* ; **CCCXXIII**, 861 *ff.* ; **CCCXXIV**, 66 *ff.*

[3] **CCCXI**, 35 *ff.*

[4] **CCCXIV**, 61, where the Septuagint Version is described as " a . . . material Hellenization of Jewish monotheism."

[5] On Philo, see **CCCXI** ; **CCCXL**, iii, part 5, 338 *ff.* ; **LXXV**, iii, 487 *ff.* ; 542 *ff.*

costs a harmony which was indispensable to him. A few words
may here be devoted to it, because at a later date Christian
teachers were to find in it an example, an encouragement and
a model.

The point of departure for this method is the following : *Fact*
must be ignored, as being merely contingent and unimportant.
What matters is the *idea* which a fact expresses. This expression is, however, necessarily incomplete, because true and
absolute reality is, by its very nature, transcendental, so that
it can only be perceived on earth as a reflection and a symbol.
Hence, to resolve a problem of exegesis, it is only necessary to
discover the appropriate symbol and the idea which that symbol
conceals. For instance, at the beginning of the book of Genesis
there is to be found the story of Adam and Eve. At first sight,
the philosophic meaning escapes notice, but it becomes clear the
moment the story is seen as a symbol of the essential duality
of human nature and of the relation between the intelligence
and the senses.

This method leads to a system of which the broad outlines
may here be stated, in view of the Christian use of it later,
keeping in mind also that neither the method, the tendencies
which gave it its direction, nor the conclusions drawn from it
were the invention of Philo. The special importance of the
Alexandrian lies in the fact that he is the typical example of a
spirit and a method of interpretation.

Above the universe there is God, in Himself indefinable, and
of whom it can only be said that he is ($ὁ$ $ὤν$). He is absolute
being ($τὸ$ $ὄν$), without qualities and without attributes ($ἄποιος$).
We should have no conception of him, had he not deigned to
reveal himself to us in *the Law*, which is *his word*, and which
has taught us that he is the supreme creator of all things. But,
it may be asked, how could he, a being without form and limit,
have acted upon matter whose nature is only form and limit ?
How could he establish relations with it ? Philo's idea is that
he could not do so directly, but had to resort to the medium of
his *ideas* (*logoi*). It was easy to identify the *logoi*, issuing from
God, with the biblical *bene-Elohim*, or " Sons of God," that is,
with the angels and demons whom we shall presently meet
again in pagan philosophy. As a matter of fact, there is a
certain fluidity in Philo's thought concerning the exact relationship of these *logoi* to God. When he wished to explain the
origin of evil, he attributed to the *logoi* a quality of imperfection,
which implied that, after they had emanated from God, they
became actually independent of him and thus able to act upon
the world in ways not in harmony with the plan of the divine

perfection. But when he wished to establish a close connexion between God and the finished work of creation, he represented the *logoi* as remaining with him, and as being, so to speak, nothing more than temporary expressions of his will.

The source of these *logoi*, including them all and, as it were, absorbing them, is the Logos itself.[1] This again is not the invention of Philo. He had found it in the writings of the Stoics, or in the concepts of that syncretistic philosophy which gathered and combined, around the name of Plato, the essential dogmas of all the great Schools. Behind the Philonian conception we recognize at once the Platonic Theory of Ideas,[2] side by side with Stoic speculations concerning the *spermatikos logos*, or " seminal reason " of things—the principle of universal causality.[3] All this had to be given a Jewish colour; the Logos therefore became the necessary intermediary between God and Man,[4] the great agent of God in the moral and material worlds, the sole form in which God revealed himself to men. It is through, by and in the Logos that man feels after God and raises himself Godwards.

The Philonian Logos presents two aspects of especial interest : (a) It emanates from God and in order to express this fact in terms of the Palestinian tendency to withdraw God from the world of action in order to avoid limiting and defining him, Philo indulges in a veritable orgy of metaphors, foreshadowing those employed by Christian theologians when they attempted to define the relationship between the natures of the Father and the Son.[5] Many of the terms characteristic of fourth century polemics are already in use here, *e.g.* the Logos is *the firstborn son of God* (υἱὸς πρωτόγονος), his *image* (εἰκων), his *impress* (χαρακτήρ), his *likeness* (ἀπεικόνισμα), *a second God* (ἕτερος θεός), and *a replica of God* (δεύτερος θεός, lit. " second God "). He is to be regarded as the mouthpiece and messenger of the Most High.

(b) The Logos is also the Mediator between God and men, the High Priest and *Intercessor* (ἱκέτης) for the world, and appears before God in this capacity. He is also Man *per se*, Man *par excellence*, made in the image of God (ὁ κατ᾽ εἰκόνα ἄνθρωπος, ὁ ἀρχέτυπος τοῦ αἰτίου).[6] Analogous ideas recur in the Christological thought of Paul and the Paulines, and this affords the best possible proof of the success which they attained and of the interest which they possess for our own study.

It is remarkable that Philo failed to take the step which

---

[1] CCCXI, 83–112; CCCXXXV; CCCXXXVII, 75 *ff.*
[2] CCCXIX, ii, 414 *ff.*   [3] CCCXIII, 267.   [4] CCCXI, 98 *ff.*
[5] CCCXXXVII, 92 *ff.*   [6] τὸ αἴτιον = " cause, form."

Christian theology later succeeded in taking, *viz.* the identification of the Logos — or *Pneuma* — of God with *Christ*. He expected the Messiah—though with less impatience than the Palestinians—but he never connected the Messiah with the Logos. Moreover, he remained undecided concerning the relationship of the nature of the Logos to God. Such a definition of the nature of the Logos as the following leaves us bewildered : "It is not unbegotten (ἀγέννητος), like God, nor begotten (γεννητός), like ourselves, but stands midway between these two extremes" (ἀλλὰ μέσος τῶν ἄκρων).[1] Here, indeed, is a language which Patristic Theology soon learned to speak.

On the other hand, Philo expresses definite ideas on the subject of sin. In the hands of Paul and of the Christians who came under Alexandrian influence, they became the basis of the theology of repentance. The essentials are these : evil does not come from God, but from matter or from inferior powers, the imperfect *logoi* who work upon matter at the order of God.[2] It is they who have introduced into matter, which is co-eternal with God, though formless and inert, the spirit of life (νοῦς) to bring about creation. The opening words of Genesis, if pressed, could bear such an interpretation, for it is not incompatible with the priority of matter.[3] The chaos of Genesis is not the same as non-existence.

Philo thinks of Man in terms of Greek dualism. He therefore distinguishes the soul from the body, holding that the one might exist without the other. Souls which are not burdened with the flesh fill the space between the world and God, and only when they come too near the earth do they take a body, whereupon sin enters into them along with the imperfection of matter. By their own power alone they are unable to escape the consequences of this fall, and it is only the grace (χάρις) of God which permits them to perform any good deed. Accordingly, all their efforts must be directed towards liberation from the shackles of matter, and to the recovery of their original purity by rising once more to their source in the Godhead. Thus the aim and science of life is "the good life," by which is meant the attainment of *askesis* (ἄσκησις), or detachment from matter, leading in turn to *ecstasy*,[4] or full understanding of the divine, apprehended directly and by *evidence* (ἐναργείᾳ). "*The*

---

[1] *Quis rerum divin. haeres*, 42.
[2] **LXXI**, v, 357 *ff.* ; **CCCXI**, 250 *ff.*
[3] Gen. i. 1–2 might actually be translated, "When God began to create the heavens and earth, the earth was without form and void . . ." *Cf.* **V**, i.
[4] **CCCXI**, 196–205.

prime happiness and the most perfect, the acme of bliss and felicity, is the knowledge of God." [1]

All this is presented to us under the strange guise of a medley of Biblical texts and philosophic *dogmata*, brought together and blended by somewhat rash dialectical methods. In other words, we are in a region of pure metaphysics. Today, Philo's dialectical edifice, reared upon a foundation of purely verbal dexterity, seems to us wholly arbitrary. But it satisfied him, and his methods were in keeping with the spirit of his environment and of his age. Moreover, this type of metaphysic resulted in very interesting consequences.

(1) The Bible, interpreted by Philo, was far more convincing and intelligible to the educated pagan, than the genuine Jewish Bible.

(2) Philo, and the Jews who thought like him, had divested themselves of nationalism, and had come to believe that divine bliss is the lot of *all* the righteous, irrespective of race, who keep the Law during their earthly life.

(3) They had also freed themselves from ritualism. Doubtless, they did not reject the observances of the Law, but they gave them a much smaller place in religion, and attached far less importance to them, than did the Rabbis of Palestine.

(4) They did not reject the Messianic ideas of Palestine, but they diluted them. It is true that the Sibylline Oracles are the expression of a very eager expectation of the Deliverer,[2] but in their Greek literary form they represent a tendency which is scarcely Hellenistic, and is quite secondary in Alexandrian Judaism. The Philonians, having blended their Judaism with the fertile dualism of Greek thought,[3] were more interested in the destiny of the soul than in the Messianic regeneration.

In all this there are ideas, tendencies, a method and conclusions which, it must be repeated, are not peculiar to Philo. They became the common heritage of enlightened Jews throughout the Diaspora. They were, in course of time, to exercise a profound and lasting influence upon the structure of Christianity; meanwhile they explain both the possibility and the success of Jewish propaganda.

[1] *De Decal.*, 81.
[2] *Cf. Or. Sib.*, iii, 632 *ff*.
[3] *Cf.* Wisdom iii. 1–8 ; v. 1 *ff*. ; viii. 19 *ff*. ; ix. 15.

V

JEWISH PROPAGANDA [1]; ITS CAUSES

Philo asserts [2] that the Bible was translated into Greek with the aim of propaganda, and, indeed, it is not impossible that this motive was present in the minds of the authors of the Septuagint.[3] Be this as it may, however, there can be no doubt that Hellenistic Judaism was thoroughly imbued with the missionary spirit.

Indeed, this was not altogether a new thing. There are passages in the Old Testament [4] which speak of " *spreading righteousness among the nations* " and even " *among the peoples afar off,*" whilst there are others which give encouragement to " *the stranger who cleaves unto Jahweh,*" so that he shall not say, " *Jahweh will separate me from His people.*" [5] The Maccabæan leaders, John Hyrcanus, Aristobulus and Alexander Jannæus, in waging their wars, paid as much attention to propaganda as to conquest. For them, at least, the two went together.[6] The Pharisees of the time of Jesus were distinguished, according to Matthew xxiii. 15, by the zeal with which they sought proselytes. Nevertheless, it would appear that there were two tendencies in Israel, as regards missionary propaganda [7]: the one favoured missions to the Gentiles and proselytism, while the other was hostile to them. The more generous attitude towards proselytes was certainly not the more widespread, and as a rule the Palestinians regarded converts as Jews of second rank. In the Diaspora, however, the movement assumed quite a different complexion, both in the eyes of the Jews and of the Gentiles.

In freeing themselves from the shackles of a narrow nationalism, the Jews arrived at the idea that they had received from God the deposit of divine truth and that it was their mission to propagate it. Each of them became, according to his means, " *an agent for monotheism and the Last Judgment.*" [8] They no longer offered to the Gentiles an exclusive and unfriendly

[1] Bibliography in **XLVII,** i, 253, n. 10 ; **LXXV,** iii, 150–88 (102–25, 3rd edit.) ; **CCCXXIX,** 628 ; **CCLXVII,** v, n. viii, 74–96 (by Kirsopp Lake).
[2] *Vita Mosis,* 2.   [3] **XLVII,** i, 253 *ff.*
[4] Isa. xlii. 1–4 ; xlix. 1–6.   [5] Isa. lvi. 3.
[6] **XLVII,** i, 253, n. 11, where references are given.
[7] Israel Lévy, in **REJ,** 1905, 28 *ff.* ; *cf.* **CCLXV,** 30, n. 1.
[8] **LXXI,** v, 441.—On the evolution of the *Gottes-Idee,* as an instrument of propaganda, *cf.* **LXXV,** iii, 114 : " The one and only God, Lord of heaven and earth, cannot be the God and Father of but one people, preferring it to all others."

Judaism, utterly distasteful to them, but a lofty religion and a religious philosophy embodying an attractive syncretism whose artificiality and weakness were not apparent to the men of that age. " It can readily be imagined that this religion, in which were combined, under the auspices of Platonic speculation, the teachings of the prophets and the noblest precepts of Stoic morality, exercised a lively attraction upon those minds for whom philosophy alone was not sufficient and to whom the pagan cults did not afford that moral sustenance which they needed." [1] The Jews themselves, living in daily contact with all classes of Gentile society, no longer seemed to them to be segregating themselves from the rest of mankind, or to constitute a *tertium genus*, as they seemed to do in Palestine.

At first, the Græco-Romans had not evinced very much sympathy for the Jews and their beliefs.[2] To Cicero (*Pro Flacco*, 28) their religion still appeared a *barbara superstitio*. Their customs were derided, they themselves were the theme of malicious gossip ; their origin was the subject of humiliating jests, and the origin of their rites was treated in the same way.[3] Because " *they hung their Temple with ivy*," and because, according to rumour, a golden vine had been found in that building, it was supposed by some that they worshipped Bacchus, the conqueror of the East ; but they were accused of turning the smiling and joyous rites instituted by Liber into a sad and gloomy business. Their religious practices and domestic customs were said to be strange and repellent. Such is the verdict of Tacitus at the end of one of the chapters of his *History* (v, 5) where he describes Judaism in the most scornful terms. Moreover, in Alexandria, where a virulent anti-Semitism raged, there sprang up a polemical literature full of insults, calumny and varied accusations, of which Josephus gives us some idea in his *Contra Apionem*. The main charges of this polemic, such as the accusation that the Jews worshipped an ass's head, or practised ritual murder, spread throughout the whole Roman world.[4]

Apart from these absurdities, harmful though they must have been, current anti-Semitism was confined to three principal charges, *viz.* (1) that the Jews were forbidden to eat pork [5] ; (2) that they observed the Sabbath (with which was coupled,

---

[1] **CCCXXXVI**, 91.
[2] Bibliography in **LXXV**, iii, 102 and n. 1 ; *cf.* also H. I. Bell, *Juden und Griechen im römischen Alexandria*, Leipzig, 1926.
[3] Tacitus, *Hist.*, v, 2.
[4] **LXXV**, iii[3], 104 *ff.*
[5] Juvenal, *Sat.*, vi, 160 : " *Et vetus indulget senibus clementia porcis* " ; xiv, 98 : " *nec distare putant humana carne suillam.*"

incidentally, the fact that they practised circumcision),[1] and (3) that they did not use images in their worship.[2] In the general attitude of Gentiles to Jews contempt was more marked than hatred.

Under such circumstances the question arises how Jewish propaganda could have begun and why it succeeded. Here, in brief, are the reasons [3]:

(1) The propaganda of the Diaspora sought above all to present Judaism to the outer world in a form which would not repel it. Laying little stress on those customs at which the anti-Semites gibed, it insisted rather on Jahwistic monotheism and ethics, presenting Judaism as *the one pure religion*, a religion without images, or, as we should say, " a worship in spirit and in truth." Viewed in another light, it presented Judaism as the perfect philosophy. A Jew who borrowed the name of Phocylides, and who lived towards the middle of the first century A.D., wrote a manual of Jewish morality for the use of pagans.[4] He confined it to the essential teachings of religion, to certain rules of common morality and to a small number of exceedingly mild observances. The endeavour of Josephus (*Ant.*, xx, 11 ; *Vita*, xxiii) to render Judaism acceptable as a religious philosophy, and that to which the whole work of Philo bears witness, were directed towards the same end. If Strabo (xvi, 2, 35) speaks with a certain sympathy of Moses, it is because the Jewish source upon which he draws portrayed the Lawgiver under the guise of a genuine Stoic philosopher. Similarly, Varro, who saw in imageless worship the appropriate form of *casta religio*, cites with approval the example of the Jews.[5]

(2) Outside Jerusalem Judaism practised no cult in the strict sense of the word, but was confined entirely to a form of life which it imposed on its adherents. It offered itself as the supreme way of life, justified by the oldest book in the world, and expressing itself in a practical discipline of moral and holy living superior to anything offered by the other ancient religions, because no other had sought to the same extent to free mankind from the bondage of sin.

(3) The religious needs of the pagan world at this period no longer found satisfaction in the ancient national religions, and they turned with an ever-growing determination to the

---

[1] Juvenal, *Sat.*, xiv, 96 *ff.*

[2] Juvenal, *Sat.*, xiv, 97 : " *Nihil praeter nubes et caeli numen adorant.*" Pliny, *Hist. Nat.*, xiii, 4, 46 : " *Gens contumelia numinum insignis.*" *Cf.* Tacitus, *Hist.*, v, 5.

[3] **LXXV**, iii, 107 ff.   [4] **CCCIX.**

[5] Augustine, *Civ. Dei*, iv, 31.

beliefs and cults of the East. This tendency proved of great advantage to Judaism, itself also an Eastern religion, but purer and freer from a tormented ritualism and an obsolete mythology.

Actually, those who proved susceptible to the religious influence of Israel were not of the same type as those who abandoned themselves to anti-Semitism, nor of those who revelled in the violent emotionalism and phantasmagoria of the Mysteries. In the assemblies wherein the votaries of Isis or of the Great Phrygian Mother forgathered, a certain amount of imagination was required in order to attain the state of mind necessary for religious ecstasy ; while the synagogue made no such demands. Nevertheless, the chances of success of its propaganda increased in proportion as the conviction grew that a single God governed the world, though worshipped under different names in respect of his different functions, and that the necessary condition of effective participation in any religious life was the acceptance of a moral law.

Jewish propaganda varied in intensity in different periods. It probably reached its highest peak and met with its greatest success towards the middle of the first century A.D.[1] The Great Rebellion, followed by the capture of Jerusalem (66–70), brought to Rome, and dispersed throughout the Empire, large numbers of Jews who might potentially have swelled the ranks of the missionaries. These, however, sore at heart at the misfortunes of Israel, and embittered by the destruction of the Temple, were more prone to take up an attitude of intolerant and exclusive opposition to the Gentiles than to assist their brethren in converting them. The disastrous revolts of the second century and the terrible repressions which followed conduced to the same end. The Jews, even those of the Diaspora, withdrew into themselves, and their line of action contributed materially to create that bitter and uncompromising character which is reflected in contemporary apocalyptic writings. They finally reached the point of asserting that the proselytes were a canker in the body of Israel, and that an attitude of distrust towards those who sought entry should rightly be maintained to the twenty-fourth generation.[2] It should be added that the Jews already had a correct suspicion that their missionary efforts had been surpassed and rendered fruitless by those of the Christians. Nevertheless, these efforts were never to be given up so long as the Roman Empire endured, so much so that under the Christian Emperors conversion to

---

[1] **CCCXXXVIII**, 117 ; **CCCXXXII**, 253 *ff*.
[2] Renan, *Égl. chrét.*, 25 ; Duchesne, *H.A.*, i, 215.

Judaism became a crime, and the Church never ceased to complain of the rival attraction of the synagogue.[1]

VI
METHODS AND SUCCESS OF JEWISH PROPAGANDA

Various indeed were the methods employed by Jewish propaganda.

First there was *individual influence*. As soon as a Jew believed in the value of spreading his religion, he began working in his own circle. This was the method adopted by the devotees of Oriental cults, and later by the Christians when first they made their appearance in the Gentile world.

Then there was the method of *literary propaganda* which gave rise to an extensive literature, often wearing a pagan mask in order the better to attract the attention of men who would not have opened a Jewish book.[2] Differing in form, these writings nevertheless possessed one common feature[3]: they presented themselves either under cover of a legendary authority, such as that of the Sibyl,[4] or else under the names of historical figures, such as Aristeas, an alleged official at the court of Ptolemy II Philadelphus,[5] or Hecatæus of Abdera, the philosopher and historian of the time of Alexander.[6] The city of Alexandria was the great workshop for the production of such works, each of which has its own definite purpose. Thus, the Sibylline Oracles are direct propaganda, stressing the folly of idolatrous cults and exalting the eternal bliss which is the promised reward of conversion. The others prefer indirect methods, seeking rather to bring honour and respect to the Jewish name and to the Jewish Law. This, for instance, is the object of Pseudo-Aristeas. Indeed, it may be said that, in a sense, all the Jews who wrote in Greek were apologists, and therefore propagandists, for Judaism.

Lastly, there was the propaganda carried on *by the synagogues*, which strove to interest well-disposed pagans, admitting them at least to their precincts, and instructing them in the truth.

All these methods appear to have met with considerable success. Josephus, exaggerating as usual, writes as follows:[7] " There is no city among the Greeks, nor any people among

---

[1] Commodian, *Instr.*, i, 28, 11 *ff.* ; i, 37, especially vv. 8 *ff.* Juridical texts in **XLVII**, i, 260.

[2] **XLVII**, i, 254 n.   [3] **LXXV**, iii, 420 *ff.*   [4] **LXXV**, iii, 421.

[5] On the Letter of Aristeas, see **LXXV**, iii, 466.

[6] He was the author of a work entitled *On the Jews*. *Cf.* **LXXV**, iii, 461.   [7] *C. Ap.*, ii, 29 ; **XLVII**, i, 276 and note ; **LXXV**, iii, 115 *ff.*

the barbarians, whither our custom of sabbatical rest has not spread, and where our fasts, our kindling of lights, and many of our dietary laws are not observed." [1] We may at least believe that these various Jewish customs were known and practised, either in their entirety, or separately, in a large number of cities, and that proselytes were to be found among all the Jewish settlements of the Græco-Roman world.[2] Unfortunately, it is impossible to estimate their number. To say as Theodore Reinach does [3] that they were " numerous " is not saying much.

The Latin poets, Horace, Martial, Juvenal and Persius, attest the fact that there was many a non-Jew at Rome who kept the sabbath and followed the practices of the synagogue.[4] Tacitus bears evidence to the same effect when (*Hist.*, v, 5) he censures those bad citizens who scorn the religion of their fathers and do not blush to traffic with Jews. Converts were actually recruited from the ranks of the aristocracy, and even from the imperial family, in the time of Nero, since Poppæa was a proselyte ; [5] and under the Flavians it seems probable that Flavius Clemens, first-cousin of Domitian, and his wife Flavia Domitilla, granddaughter of Vespasian, were among the number. *Judaicam vivere vitam*, " to live the Jewish life," was true of several eminent Romans at this time.[6]

In the East, the success of Jewish missionary activity was greater still, if we may trust such information as we possess concerning the state of affairs at Antioch (Antioch on the Orontes and Antioch in Pisidia), Thessalonica, etc.[7] A certain king of Adiabene, a state on the border of the Roman Empire and Parthia, became converted to Judaism along with his family, and Josephus speaks of this pious royal household with a certain excusable pride.[8]

It must, however, be observed that there were different degrees of conversion. Full proselytes were those who accepted the three essential obligations of Judaism,[9] *viz.* (*a*) circumcision,

---

[1] Tertullian, *Ad Nat.*, i, 13 : " *Judaei enim fasti, Sabbata et coena pura et judaici ritus lucernarum et jejunia cum azymis et orationes litorales quae utique aliena sunt a diis vestris.*"

[2] Seneca, in Augustine, *Civ. Dei*, vi, 11, quoted from a lost treatise, *De Superstitione.*

[3] **CCCXXIX**, 629.   [4] **CCLXV**, 29 ; **CCCXXVIII**, 12 *ff.*

[5] Tacitus, *Ann.*, xiv, 6.

[6] Suetonius, *Dom.*, 12. *Cf.* **CCCXXXIV**, 227.

[7] Passages are collected in **LXXV**, iii, 117 *ff.* ; *cf.* Acts xiii. 16, 26, 43, 50, etc.

[8] *Ant.*, xx, 2–4 ; *B.J.*, ii, 19, 2 ; iv. 9, 11 ; v, 2, 2, etc. *Cf.* **LXXV**, iii, 119.

[9] **LXXV**, iii, 129 ; **XLVII**, i, 274 ; **CCLXVII**, v, 77 *ff.*

(b) the ritual bath, and (c) sacrifice at the Temple. The second of these obligations was a ceremony of some importance, possessing points of affinity with the Christian rite of baptism, whilst the third naturally fell out of use when the sacred edifice was destroyed. Proselytes of this type conformed to all the requirements of the Law. Doubtless, they counted more women than men among their numbers, since the obligation of circumcision would often deter the latter. But there must have been cases where the father was content to keep the Sabbath and observe some of the injunctions of the Law, while the son went a step further and resigned himself to the decisive operation.[1]

Side by side with these " proselytes of righteousness," who could scarcely have been the most numerous, were the half-proselytes who recoiled from circumcision and from the exigencies of strict conformity to the Law, and who refused also to change their manner of life, but who nevertheless accepted monotheism and, to a greater or less extent, the moral precepts of the *Torah*. These were called the " *God-fearers* " or " *worshippers of God*." [2] Among these also there may have been varying degrees, and the religious characteristic common to most of them was the worship of the one God. It should be noted, in fact, that the chief impediment to complete conversion was always the legalism of the Jewish religion. As we shall see, Christianity profited greatly by this aversion.

In point of law, full proselytes were regarded as genuine Israelites. In point of fact, however, they occupied an inferior position in the main body of the Chosen People. The decisions of the Rabbis placed them under a number of disabilities of which one was actually humiliating : they were not allowed to say that Abraham was their *father*.[3] On the whole the great mass of converts, especially those known as " Proselytes of the Gate," and who did not really accept either the full obligations of Judaism or Jewish nationalism, remained indifferent to these restrictions. What these men sought in the company of the

---

[1] Juvenal, *Sat.*, xiv, 96 *ff*. : " . . . *carne suillam qua pater abstinuit ; mox et praeputia ponunt. Cf.* **CCLXVII**, v, 88 *ff*.

[2] Φοβούμενοι τὸν Θεόν, σεβόμενοι τὸν Θεόν, or simply σεβόμενοι, or Ἰουδαΐζοντες. Other less frequent terms also occur. A study of them, both Hebrew and Greek, will be found in **CCLXVII**, v, 80–8. It should be observed that the titles φοβούμενοι (or, σεβόμενοι) τὸν θεὸν (Latin, *metuentes*) do not define in any precise manner the persons to whom they are applied. They remain vague and elastic, referring more to general tendency than to any clearly determined category.

[3] Rabbinical passages are collected in **LXXV**, iii, 133. Their true meaning was possibly only perceived after the upheavals of the second century.

synagogue and in the faith of Israel was a religious satisfaction which they could not find elsewhere. It would appear that, in general, the synagogues of the Diaspora gave a warm welcome to their proselytes and to converts of every type. Nevertheless, Philo in his day found reason to complain of the pride which held the pure Jew aloof from these newcomers. This feeling is, however, perfectly understandable, even apart from any prejudices of birth, since the growing number of proselytes might readily appear to threaten the purity of the Jewish religion and the legitimate influence of the true children of Abraham.

Roman law did not categorically forbid such proselytism in itself,[1] but it refused to accept certain of its consequences. For example, if a proselyte were confronted with any of the legal obligations from which persons of Jewish race were exempted, he might not avail himself of the same privilege. Similarly, he could not refuse to worship the Gods of the Empire without exposing himself to a charge of atheism. A female convert could always fall under an accusation of impiety in regard to the household gods ; under Tiberius, a certain Fulvia was convicted of this crime by her husband Saturninus [2] ; under Nero a woman called Pomponia Graecina was accused before a domestic tribunal on the same charge.[3] Domitian roused the activity of informers against the proselytes, whom he ordered to sacrifice to the national gods ; if they refused, they were charged with atheism. These various examples lead to the conclusion that proselytism was always open to the charge of atheism ; it depended on the public authorities whether they took action or not.[4] Nerva forbade the denunciations which his predecessor had encouraged.[5] On the other hand, if we follow Spartianus, we must attribute to Hadrian a measure of great severity and likely to prove extremely detrimental to Jewish propaganda ; he is said to have forbidden circumcision and to have put it on the same level as castration,[6] punishable by a severe law (*Lex Cornelia de Sicariis et Veneficis*). This restriction, restored from others made by Antiochus Epiphanes (1 Macc. i. 63 ; 2 Macc. vi. 4–11), was, it is further stated, one

---

[1] **XLVII,** i, 255 *ff*. [2] **XLVII,** i, 256, n. 3.

[3] Tacitus, *Ann.*, xiii, 32 : She was accused of *superstitio externa*. There are reasons for thinking that this refers to Judaism ; see Mommsen, *Droit pénal*, ii, 278, n. 2 (in the French translation).

[4] **XLVII,** i, 257, n. 1.

[5] *Dio Cass.*, lxviii, 1, 2.

[6] *Hist. Aug., Had.*, xiv, 2. Spartianus is a somewhat inferior authority, and it may well be that there is a certain degree of confusion regarding persons or dates in his statement.

of the causes of the great revolt of Bar Cochba.[1] Be this as it
may, Antoninus Pius modified the law of Hadrian by restoring
circumcision as one of the Jewish privileges, but he confirmed
that law by continuing the prohibition in the case of non-Jews.[2]
If a Jew performed the operation upon a proselyte, he exposed
himself to a severe punishment, *viz.* deportation or death,
according to social rank.[3] Various penalties, such as banish-
ment, confiscation of property, or even execution, threatened
any freeman who allowed himself to be circumcised ; on the
other hand, a slave *ipso facto* obtained his freedom, the law
presuming in his case that he had been subjected to constraint.[4]
At the time when the Christian hope spread among the Jewish
settlements of the eastern Mediterranean, the legislation sum-
marized above no longer existed. Nevertheless, in popular
opinion circumcision continued to be in bad odour.

Thus, Jewish propaganda had planted the religion of Israel
or, at least, its more essential ideas in the pagan world. This
does not mean merely the accession of proselytes and God-
fearers, but also the spread of Jewish influence among men of
education and inquiring spirit on the one hand, and also among
the lower classes in a more elementary form, not unmixed with
superstition. The idea of the Most High God ($\delta\ \Theta\varepsilon\grave{o}\varsigma\ \delta\ \H{v}\psi\iota\sigma\tau o\varsigma$)
and a certain respect for the Sabbatical rest found a response
even among those who did not become converts.[5] Jewish words
and expressions came into current use, especially in the realm
of magic,[6] carrying with them notions and suggestions, by no
means to be ignored by those who wish to understand how the
way was paved for Christianity.

Certainly, this influence of Israel under all its aspects can
only be regarded as a thin veneer spread over the surface of the
Græco-Roman religious world. This remains true, even though
it prepared the way for a religion which, itself issuing out of
Judaism, freed itself from the defects which Gentiles as a
whole had found a hindrance in Judaism. It remains for us to
inquire whether the influence of Jewish propaganda did not
last to a later date than we might at first sight be inclined to
believe, and if strange patterns were not produced from the
syncretistic tendencies of the time, which, in the end, led to
interesting expressions, both on the Jewish and on the pagan
side. It has been maintained that the synagogue of the
Diaspora was definitely heretical.[7] If this be true, what
contribution did that heretical tendency bring to the syncretism ?

[1] **XLVII**, i, 165, n. 1.   [2] Modestinus, in *Dig.*, xlviii, 8, 11.
[3] Paul, *Sent.*, v, 22, 4.   [4] **XLVII**, i, 269.
[5] **CCCXXII**, 2.   [6] **CCCVIII**, 194.   [7] **CCLVIII**.

And what did those pagans who merely skimmed the surface of Judaism do with the ideas which they borrowed from it ? How did they combine those ideas with their own stock of prior beliefs ? These questions are of primary importance for us, but the answers are unfortunately shrouded in obscurity.

CHAPTER II

THE JUDÆO-PAGAN SYNCRETISM

I

THE RECIPROCAL INFLUENCE OF JUDAISM AND PAGANISM

Primary Aspects

THE real question is this : Could the Jews of the Diaspora
have lived in constant contact with the foreign religions
around them, without in some measure becoming subject to
their influence ? To this, the example of Philo has already
given us an answer.

Conversely, could Gentiles, consorting daily with Jews, and
to some extent interested in their beliefs, even if they did not
go so far as to adopt them, have succeeded in keeping those
beliefs entirely separate from their own religious ideas ? This
would seem, *à priori*, unlikely.

It is true that stress [1] is usually laid on the exclusiveness
of the Jewish brotherhood which characterized the communities
of the Diaspora, and also on the persistent hatred of the Jews
towards the Gentiles. These two attitudes, no matter whence
they came or where they were found, must have produced in the
Israelite mistrust and hostility towards everything that came
from without. Similarly, emphasis is commonly laid on the
anti-Semitism of the Gentiles. All this is, no doubt, true, but
we are not concerned with voluntary and conscious borrowings
on either side. We can only speak in the one case of slow
penetration by the environment, and in the other of a gradual
contamination. To influences of this type the Jews, even those
of Palestine, never offered appreciable resistance, even allowing
their ritual to be affected, although ritual offers more resistance
to such encroachments than religious emotions and impressions.
The Prophets had often reproached their people for this very
tendency. [2]

The pagans of Asia Minor and Syria, on the other hand,
had long been accustomed to combine myths of diverse origin,

[1] CCLXV, 31   [2] Ezek. viii. 14 ; Jer. vii. 18 ; xliv. 17–19.

the process known as *syncretism*. It is therefore by no means a paradox to take for granted the existence of such reciprocal influences and more or less interesting combinations, even before we have established their existence.

There are certain facts which immediately leap to the eye and confirm this first induction.

(1) The synagogue was not only a house of prayer ; it was also a meeting-place for men of different minds and outlook, as well as a centre of instruction [1] frequented alike by Jews and by proselytes of different degrees. The latter did not leave their knowledge or their ideas at the door before entering. They could not live their normal customary life, unless they adapted the Torah and the Jewish religion in general, to their own mental outlook and to the demands of their own culture. They could not possibly keep those who had converted them in ignorance of this process of adaptation.

(2) We must also take into account the question of mixed marriages. Unfortunately, we have no certain information concerning their number.[2] The Law forbade them, and so, too, did orthodox tradition,[3] but we know that in fact the prohibition was not always observed [4] ; moreover, quality made up for quantity, for these marriages were usually contracted among the higher orders of society. It would be, perhaps, more cautious to say that our sources only refer to these more notable instances.[5] It is difficult to believe that a mixed marriage did not promote a constant interchange of opinions, beliefs and impressions between the parties concerned.

(3) Philo, the Essenes, the Therapeutae, and the authors of the Alexandrian Apocrypha [6] in their several degree give proof of this process of permeation both among individuals and among groups. Along with a clear basis of apparently predominant Jewish doctrine, there appears among them all the influence of Greek philosophic thought, and even of a Helleno-Egyptian syncretism which had already reached a high stage of development.

[1] **CCLVIII**, 64.

[2] **CCCXXXIX**, 10, says they were fairly frequent, but his statements are based entirely on the single passage, Acts xvi. 1, and that refers only to one definite case.

[3] Passages are collected in **XLVII**, ii, 45, n. 4.

[4] Test. of the Twelve Patriarchs, Levi xiv. 5–8, rebukes the Jews, even of priestly rank, for marrying heathen women.

[5] References will be found in **XLVII**, ii, 45, n. 5, where it is pointed out that, according to Jerome (*Ep.*, xxxix, 1), the mother of Origen was a Jewess.

[6] **CCCX**, 482, where Philo is actually regarded as the *culmination* of Judæo-Hellenistic syncretism.

(4) It can be shown that throughout the Orient the practice of keeping the Sabbath was already observed on a wide scale and in a variety of forms.[1] This, however, may not be entirely due to a mere borrowing from Judaism, but speculations concerning the number 7 may have had more to do with it than any recollection of the divine rest upon the seventh day.[2] Nevertheless, it was Judaism which laid down the principle, provided an explanation of it, and furnished the most complete example of its application. External influences are apparent in many cases, but contact with Jewish ideas is none the less clear.

(5) If at present we are forced to proceed in darkness, it is because the literary sources which might have given us light no longer exist. Once, however, they did exist. In 4 Esdras xiv. 45–6 we find a clear distinction between the canonical books, of which there are twenty-four, and the others, of which there are seventy. The former may be read by everyone, the latter only by the learned : " . . . *the Most High spake and said, The first which thou hast written do thou publish, so that they which are worthy and they which are unworthy may read therein ; howbeit, the seventy which are more recent do thou keep, that thou mayest deliver them to such as be wise among thy people.*" From this it follows that there was once a Jewish hermeneutic literature. That it was more recent and more abundant than the other need not surprise us.

(6) Lastly, a number of magical texts have come down to us which show us the syncretistic process at work in a limited but none the less genuine form, and their mere existence proves, in my opinion, that there must also have been other more elaborate and complicated forms. The names Iao, Sabaoth, Michael, Raphael and other Jewish angels are there to be found side by side with those of Egyptian or Greek divinities.[3] Moreover, the Jews were renowned throughout the Roman world for their skill in magic arts,[4] and here again we may recognize the influence of syncretism, for this knowledge must have come to them principally through contact with the Chaldæans. " After the Jews," says Cumont, " had been initiated into the secret lore and practices of the Persians and the Chaldæans, they served as the indirect means by which knowledge of certain formulæ spread throughout the area of the Dispersion." [5]

---

[1] CCLVIII, 14–52.   [2] CCLVIII, 45.
[3] CCCXII, 96. *Cf.* Deissmann, *Licht vom Osten*, 2nd edit., Tübingen, 1909, 186 ; CCLXXVI, ii, 32 *ff.*
[4] Blau, *Das altjüdische Zauberwesen*, 1898.   [5] CCCXII, 281.

II

Syncretistic Conceptions of God

Scholars are today generally agreed that a culture-mixture of the type described really took place in the area of the Diaspora, and that both individual types of syncretism and completely composite cults came into existence there. Epigraphic discoveries have enabled us, though as yet but rarely, to catch a glimpse of or to understand a few examples of the former. As to the latter, various monuments reveal their existence, but give us no knowledge of them. Thus there now lies open to the inquiry and research of scholars an entirely new field, difficult enough to explore, but certainly rich in prospects.[1]

Of the indications, or positive evidence, still elusive and slender, at present available, two groups may be mentioned. The first relates to the use of the title *Hypsistos*, or *Most High*, a Jewish epithet of Jahweh in the Diaspora, to designate pagan deities.[2] The second reveals the existence of a Judaizing gnosis.

Many of the pagan *thiasoi*, without adhering to the synagogue, worshipped the supreme God, the Most High, the Eternal, the Creator. Nevertheless, even if all these are perfectly suitable epithets for the God of the Jews, it is by no means certain that they were always addressed to Him, for other divinities, foremost of whom was Zeus, also bore the title of *Hypsistos*[3] and might fittingly be addressed by any of the titles just mentioned. We must, therefore, beware of facile identifications, though the establishment of a few really certain cases would warrant the conclusion which we seek to draw. It is not without significance that the pagans, even in cases where there is no proof of Judaizing, called the God of the Jews by the title *Hypsistos*.[4]

We get an instructive glimpse of at least one of these composite cults, the cult of *Sabazios*, an ancient Thracian form of Dionysos, whom a fanciful etymology, significant in its tendency, connected with *Sabaoth*, the *Kyrios Sabaoth* of the Septuagint.[5] In the *Questions* of Plutarch,[6] we read how one of the guests

[1] **CCCXII**, xx and p. 96.

[2] **CIL**, vi, 50 (from Rome): " Ἄττει ὑψίστῳ καὶ συνέχοντι τὸ πᾶν. Both title and description are Jewish; *cf.* **CCCXII**, 94.

[3] **CCCXII**, 368; on the inscriptions from the kingdom of the Bosphorus, originally published by Latyschev, in 1890, wherein ὕψιστος is applied to Zeus, Gê and Hêlios, see **CCLXVII**, v, 90 *ff.*

[4] Philo, *Leg.*, xxiii, 40; *In Flacc.*, 7.

[5] **CCCXII**, 97.   [6] *Quaest. conviv.*, iv, 6.

maintained, and claimed to be able to prove, that the God of
the Jews was none other than Dionysos Sabazios, and it is
perhaps to this strange identification that Tacitus alludes when
he says (*Hist.*, v, 5) that some maintain the rites of the Jews
to have been founded by Dionysos.   On the other hand, Valerius
Maximus relates (i, 3, 2) that the prætor C. Cornelius Hispallus,
in the consulate of M. Popilius Lena and Cn. Calpurnius, about
139 B.C., sent back home, hence expelled from Rome, certain Jews
who, under pretext of worshipping Sabazios-Jupiter, strove to
corrupt the morals of the Romans (*Judaeos qui Sabazi-Jovis
cultu simulato mores Romanos inficere conati sunt, domos suas
repetere coegit*).   Since the passage treats of the Jews, the
words *Sabazi-Jovis* must be an error and should be *Sabazios-
Jahweh*.   Furthermore, there exists in the cemetery of Prætex-
tatus, in a crypt which perhaps did not belong to it at first
and has been added by an unskilled excavation, a celebrated
tomb, called the tomb of Vincentius, decorated with interesting
paintings.[1]   Here there is depicted a deceased woman named
Vibia being introduced into the Fields of the Blessed by a good
angel (*angelus bonus*) of Jewish origin, as the accompanying
description shows.   On the other hand, Vincentius describes
himself as the " *servant of Sabazios*."   Here, then, we have
the statement of Valerius Maximus confirmed, and evidence
that a community of Sabazios, probably of syncretistic type,
existed in Rome.[2]

   Jewish influence, which is certain in the cult of Sabazios,
seems probable in that of Attis and Cybele.[3]   We might even
go farther and infer, for instance, from the affinity of that
cult with the worship of Mithra, that the latter was subjected
to the same influence.[4]   Such a conclusion must, however, be
supported by documentary evidence.   Those sources to which
I have referred, and which come from the Bosphorus, seem
indeed to attest the existence in that region of a cult the basis
of which was pagan, but which had been influenced by Judaism.
No doubt, there were others syncretistic in type and diverse
in nature, but which, at least in outward appearance, seemed
to acknowledge the deity as Hypsistos, so much so that the
devotees of such cults actually took, or received, the name of
Hypsistarians, or, *Hypsistanians*.   Traces of them were sufficiently discernible in the fourth and even the fifth century to
attract the attention of Gregory of Nazianzus, Gregory of
Nyssa, Cyril of Alexandria and even of Augustine.   The latter
calls them *Caelicolae*, and it is, at least, curious that the famous

[1] CCCXXVI, i, 249.   [2] CCCXXXIX, 12.
[3] CCCXII, 98 *ff*.   [4] CCCXXXIX, 13.

Codex Bezae renders the term σεβόμενοι in Acts xiii. 50 and
xvii. 4 by the word *caelicolae*.[1] This term naturally recalls
the line of Juvenal, xiv. 97 : " *Nil praeter nubes et coeli numen
adorant* " (" they worship nought save clouds and heaven's
power "), which might more fittingly refer to the people under
discussion than to genuine Jews.

Hence we have sufficient evidence to support the statement
that in more than one respect pagan cults were subjected to
Jewish influence, manifesting itself in the production of more
or less interesting syncretistic forms.

It is, however, the reverse influence which, from our present
point of view, it is important to detect and apprehend, because
it is more likely that nascent Christianity was affected by a
syncretism whose basis was Jewish than by one whose basis
was pagan. Unfortunately, nowhere do we suffer more from
the absence of explicit and dated texts than on this point.

Nevertheless, we possess one text which, though far from
teaching us all that we seek to know, yet claims our attention,
and whose very gaps are instructive. It is Colossians ii. 8–10
and runs as follows : " *Take heed lest there shall be anyone
that maketh spoil of you through his philosophy and vain deceit,
after the tradition of men, after the rudiments of the world,
and not after Christ* " (κατὰ τὰ στοιχεῖα τοῦ κόσμου καὶ οὐ κατὰ
χριστόν).

These words, at first sight so puzzling, must be compared
with the passage in Galatians iv. 8–11, where the " *rudiments* "
recur again with the meaning " gods " : " *Howbeit at that time,
not knowing God, ye were in bondage to them which by nature
are no gods : but now that ye have come to know God, or rather to
be known of God, how turn ye back again to the weak and beggarly
rudiments, whereunto ye desire to be in bondage over again* ? "
It is quickly apparent that this passage is dealing with speculations concerning the cosmic spirits who govern the stars and
who are, in a sense, identical with them. ‹ We are plunged
into the depths of *astrological gnosis*, and everything leads
to the belief that it was in this direction that the Jews of
the Diaspora turned when they surrendered to syncretistic
tendencies.

[1] CCLXVII, v, 95.

III
THE SYNCRETISTIC GNOSIS

We know that *gnosis*, which is the *revealed* knowledge of
the world, of life, and hence of salvation,[1] is something entirely
different from *human* knowledge, that is, knowledge gained by
study and by sense-experience. It remains on an infinitely
higher plane, since its objects are superior to those attained by
common information. Philosophic speculation and mystic
views may render it complex and give it an appearance of
unfathomable metaphysical depth, but in principle it represents
essentially the communication, by direct instruction, reserved
for the chosen and initiated devotees, of a mystery which reason
alone could not discover.

In fact, it is usually the outcome of a combination, often
complex and obscure, of astrological ideas [2] and religious desires
expressed as positive conclusions, in short, a system divorced
from reality. This takes the form of a dialectic which, based
on statements incapable of proof, passes nevertheless for
demonstration. Syncretism and gnosticism are entirely compatible ; the one nourishes the other.

We know that there was a specifically Jewish gnosis, which
drew its sustenance from the astrological and metaphysical
speculations of the Gentile gnosis. In the writings of Paul
occur a number of technical terms belonging to the vocabulary
of gnosticism,[3] such as *Mystery, Gnosis, Epignosis, Pleroma,
Archons, Initiation, Perfection, Firstborn of the Cosmos,* etc.
The profusion of these proves the thorough familiarity of the
Apostle with at least certain gnostic turns of speech, foreign
to pure Judaism.

The very teaching of the Apostle, that is to say, Paulinism
considered as a whole, affords further proof of the existence
of this gnosis. Clearly, Paul starts from the idea that the
Cosmos has fallen into chaos, since according to him it is not
only man, but the whole of nature which needs to be reconciled

---

[1] On the origins of Gnosticism, see **CCLXXVI,** i, 90–120 ; W. Köhler,
Die Gnosis, Tübingen, 1911, 4 *ff.* ; H. Holtzmann, *Lehrb. d. neutestament-
lischen Theologie,* 2nd edit., Tübingen, 1911, vol. i, pp. 553–61 ; S. Angus,
The Religious Quests in the Græco-Roman World, London, 1929, chap. xx ;
W. Bousset, *Hauptprobleme der Gnosis,* Göttingen, 1907.

[2] On the underlying influence of Babylonian astrology, *cf.* W. Anz,
Zur Frage nach dem Ursprung des Gnostizismus, Leipzig, 1897 ; S.
Minocchi, *I miti babilonesi e le origini della gnosi,* in *Bilychnis,* December,
1914, and April, 1915.

[3] **CCCXXXIX,** 15 *ff.*

to God : " *For we know that the whole creation groaneth and travaileth in pain together until now* " (Rom. viii. 22). According to the Testament of Solomon,[1] it is the " *rudiments* " (στοιχεῖα), or astral powers which govern the world (τὰ λεγόμενα στοιχεῖα, οἱ κοσμοκράτορες τοῦ κόσμου τούτου), and it is these " *rudiments* " which Paul calls " the *archontes* of this world." Hence it is clear, first, that these " *rudiments* " were considered by certain Jews as gods, or, at least, as spirits worthy of worship, and Saul of Tarsus himself might well have shared this belief before his conversion : " *I beseech you, brethren, be as I am, for I was as ye are* " (Gal. iv. 12) ; secondly, that the worship of these " *rudiments* " was connected with astrological calculations of which one aspect is related to the Jewish preoccupation with the succession of the ages. Indeed, the two were often and for a long time confused with one another (" *Ye observe days and months and seasons and years*," Gal. iv. 10). In the passage of the Testament of Solomon referred to above, seven spirits are represented as appearing to Solomon, which are the " *rudiments* " or cosmic powers [2] ; their names are given as Apathé, Eris, etc.

Paul is thus seen to be surrounded by a star-worshipping gnosis ; and in certain Jewish centres of the Diaspora, among the Galatians and Colossians, where he had lived, this gnosis was Jewish, that is to say, it had become blended with the religion of Israel. Paul seeks to oppose it, and especially to prove that the " *archontes of this world* " had been vanquished by Christ, the cosmic powers subjected to the Lord (Col. i. 18– 20 ; 1 Cor. xv. 24–5). His method of refutation was somewhat confused,[3] a point which we shall examine later ; but its dominant purpose, at least, admits of no doubt ; it attests not only the existence, but also the success and power of this astrological and syncretistic gnosis in certain Jewish or Judaizing centres of the Diaspora. Considered from this point of view Paulinism is an anti-gnosis ; nevertheless, it is itself permeated by gnosticism.

The question now arises whether the speculations of this Jewish and syncretistic gnosis were confined to the birth, organization, government and life of the Cosmos, or whether they did not also concern themselves with the question of its salvation. Judging from Paul, I am inclined to think that the

---

[1] This apocryphal book is of Jewish origin, but is written in Greek, and is therefore a product of the Diaspora. *Cf.* **EB**, i, col. 254, 14.

[2] **CCCXXXI,** 52 : καὶ τὰ ἄστρα ἡμῶν ἐν οὐρανῷ εἰσιν . . . καὶ ὡς θεὰς καλούμεθα.

[3] **CCCXVIII,** 115 *ff.*

latter was the case.   For, if we analyse the Pauline Christology [1] and remove from it everything peculiar to Christianity, there remains, it would seem, a coherent soteriology, clearly related to Jewish Messianism, yet something more, and constituting a kind of pre-Christian Christology.   Hence we may ask whether in these Jewish gnostic circles of the Diaspora there had not already been a certain amount of speculation concerning the Messiah in which the narrow nationalistic conception of him current in Palestine had been transformed, and in which his traditional function had been spiritualized by seeing it, so to speak, in gnostic terms, and regarding it as his rôle to draw men away from the death of sin, and to guide them into the Kingdom of the Spirit.

This is highly probable [2] and it bears not only, as we shall see, on the conversion of Paul, but also on the preparation for and introduction of Christianity to the Græco-Roman world. Moreover, various other indications confirm the supposition that speculations concerning a Saviour who had come, or rather who was to come, formed the central religious interest of the syncretistic sects in Judaism and in Judaizing gnostic centres.[3]   It matters little that the Saviour was still represented on occasions as the great Conqueror who would usher in the Kingdom of God after having triumphed over his enemies.   This was merely a relic of Jewish Messianism and does not invalidate the anti--Palestinian character of everything else.

IV
The Jewish Sects

We have just spoken of *sects*.   This demands a few words of explanation.   In the syncretistic combinations at which we have glanced it was still only a question of interpretations, additions and arrangements, grouped more or less arbitrarily round a body of Jewish teaching which claimed to be orthodox because, in all likelihood, its daily life was still governed by the precepts of the *Torah*.   The methods by which these peculiar medleys attained success are not so far removed from those of Philo as to be incomprehensible to us.   But we have glimpses of certain groups of Judaizers who by their manner of life, as well as by the nature of their beliefs, seem, indeed, to set them-

---

[1] Brückner, *Die Enstehung d. paulin. Christologie*, Strasburg, 1903, 93 *ff.*

[2] CCCXVIII, 158 and 169.

[3] CCLVIII, 100–17 ; CCCVIII, 173 *ff.*

selves apart from the true religion of Israel. To these we may give the name of sects.

We may first of all mention the Essenes whose synagogue has been said to be the true offspring of the Diaspora.[1] By this is meant that the Hellenism of the latter had penetrated the life of the former. There can, in fact, be no doubt that Essenism was a form of syncretism. Side by side with its attachment to the Law, the sincerity of which is beyond suspicion, it rested upon secret doctrines which occupied a large place in its interests.[2] We cannot say for certain whence these teachings came, nor even describe them exactly, but it is not too rash to suspect that they were influenced, at least to some extent, by those pseudo-Pythagorean speculations in which the pagan world was steeped towards the time of the birth of Jesus. The question has been raised whether the Essenes were conversant with the ideas of astrological metaphysics. It may be so, since Josephus speaks of them as awaiting the sunrise in an attitude of meditation and invocation, and as addressing prayers to it in order to hasten its appearance [3]; hence they may have regarded the sun as a conscious cosmic power, which is one of the basic ideas of the religion of the " *rudiments.*" In short, the Essenes have been regarded as pre-Christian gnostics.[4] Their monastic life was the life of salvationists, that is to say, of men preoccupied with the problem of salvation; their repugnance to sacrifices suggests the Pythagorean doctrine of metempsychosis, or at least the idea that the fallen *essence* is condemned to journey through all the living forms of matter. All this, of course, is far from anything which usually passes under the name of *Mosaism*.

Nevertheless, these Essenes were Jews whose outward conformity to the Law was still sufficiently strict to disguise the peculiarities which marked the rest of their religious life. Moreover, their home was Palestine, and their settlements did not extend far beyond its borders.

With the Therapeutae we go a step farther.[5] They too passed for Jews, and doubtless believed themselves so to be, but there was no longer anything distinctively Jewish in their mode of life. It was confined within the walls of monasteries of a kind built not far from Alexandria on the shores of Lake Mareotis. The men lived there apart from the women, but

---

[1] CCLVIII, 60 ; CCCXVII, 114–68.—On the Essenes, see *supra*, pp. 172–90.

[2] Jos., *Ant.*, xxi, 10, 6.   [3] *B.J.*, ii, 8, 5.

[4] CCLXXVI, i, 149 *ff.*

[5] CCCXXI, 135 and 183, n. 19 (bibliography).

both alike spent their days in spiritual meditation and philosophic reflection. They plumbed the depths of Holy Scripture in order to discover its hidden and mysterious meaning. In other words, they gave to the *Torah* a symbolical and allegorical sense, as did Philo, and we are not surprised to find that the philosopher was interested in them. It is probable that their thought was also devoted to the popular subject of soteriological metaphysics, and to gnostic ideas more or less tinged with Pythagorean speculations. They gathered every seventh day to celebrate the Sabbath, but it was a Sabbath of the learned, a metaphysical and mystical Sabbath wherein each enriched the rest with the fruits of his own solitary meditation during the past week.[1]

Were not the Therapeutae, then, on the borderline of Judaism ? Were they not really an heretical sect, a kind of perfected Essenism ? They may have been, but it is impossible to prove it, since the description of them given in the treatise of Philo whence our information is derived, namely, the *De Vita Contemplativa*, is a purely ideal picture. It has been said above that, in a sense, Philo was a witness to this Judæo-pagan syncretism and that he was a typical representative of it, rather then an exceptional individual or a strikingly original personality. His was a syncretism of the *philosophic* type, that is to say, a form of speculation which takes as its point of departure the study of Greek philosophy. This, however, was only one stream of thought, and there were others less rationalistic in their inspiration and far more coloured by Oriental mysticism.

Philo himself gives us a glimpse [2] of certain effects, certain forms of expression, resulting from these complex and obscure influences. He speaks of *Cainites*, *Ammonites*, and *Moabites*, whom he regards as heretics ; hence it is a question of Jewish syncretists. Some of these appear to have been *pneumatics* who directed their speculations towards the spirit, whereas others were *materialists* who reduced them to the level of matter, as in the case of the Christian gnostics. These sects challenged the *Torah*, setting up Cain in opposition to Moses, and holding that the world and the Law were the work of a Demiurge who had attempted to usurp the place of the true God in the minds of men. Viewed from another angle, they fell into line with the great stirring of interest in soteriology which seems to have been the religious malady of the age. They take their place among the enthusiasts who were awaiting the fulness of the times. We shall find all this again among the pagans ; there

[1] Philo, *De vita contemplativa*, 2.
[2] **CCCLVIII,** 75.

is no watertight division between the Jewish and pagan currents of thought.

This Judaizing pre-Christian gnosticism [1] should not be regarded as a *system*, but rather as a *tendency* which varied in depth and development with different individuals and environments.   To some it was no more than the complement of their orthodox Judaism, orientating their thought in a direction foreign to the *Torah*, while to others it offered the main value, and Judaism did not interest them except as one element in a more or less complex whole.   The logical result of the movement was the formation of sects, those closed circles the members of which believed that they were the possessors of absolute Truth and of Salvation.   It is unfortunate that no precise information has come down to us concerning the chronology, geographical distribution and numbers of these sects, so that any study of them pursued and sustained on the basis of reliable documents is at present impossible.

The question has been asked why the early Christian writers of the second century, such as Justin, Irenæus or Tertullian, whose works have been partially preserved, do not enlighten us concerning these sectaries, and why they did not study them at close quarters, as the origin and probable source of the Christian gnosis.   The answer usually given [2] is that they were hypnotized by the gnostics of their time who claimed to be Christians and who, indeed, gave themselves out as the only true Christians, thus constituting a danger to the ordinary believer.   The Christian teachers, so it is asserted, were far too prone to consider gnosticism as a Christian heresy, or collection of heresies, and it was only the later historians of heresy, *e.g.* those of the third century, such as the author of the *Philosophumena*, or of the fourth and fifth centuries, such as Epiphanius, Philastrius and Augustine, who looked beyond the second century and paid attention to our Judæo-gnostics. These writers, however, were unfavourably situated for the study and understanding of the earlier gnostics, and their information is full of confusions, obscurities and gaps which they could not avoid, but which are a great hindrance at the present time.   The question, therefore, remains open and it is to be feared that it will long continue to remain so, if not for ever.

The historians of heresy appeared to have been specially intrigued by certain sectaries whom they call Ophites, Cainites, and Sethites, among whom the influences of Greek thought

[1] M. Friedländer, *Der vorchristliche jüdische Gnostizismus*, Berlin, 1898.
[2] **CCLVIII**, 79.

seemed to have been combined with Jewish speculations, and with Oriental elements of a more obviously gnostic type. These heretics, who were probably confused with those known to Philo, were only interested in the Jewish Scriptures in so far as they could interpret them in such a way as to destroy their authority. According to their beliefs, the true God was not the Creator, Jahweh, of the Book of Genesis, who was reduced to the rôle of sovereign over matter. Everything in the Scriptures which was opposed to their view-point they attributed to the "Spirit of the world" (Epiph., *Haer.*, xxvi, 6 : ἀπὸ τοῦ πνέυματος τοῦ κόσμου) and the remainder to the "Spirit of truth" (ἀπὸ τοῦ πνεύματος τῆς ἀληθείας).

The *Ophites*,[1] for instance, who seemed to have been of Phrygian origin, considered Jahweh as a mere divine *dynamis*, one of the creator angels who had usurped the place of God. It was the serpent who had exposed this fraud, and it was therefore the serpent whom the Ophites worshipped and from whom they derived their name. They regarded him also as a divine *dynamis*, the incarnation of Wisdom (Σοφία), the Christ himself.[2]

The *Cainites*, so Augustine assures us (*Haeres.*, viii), "blaspheme against the world and against God, the Author of the Law, and deny the resurrection of the flesh." The *Sethites* awaited a Christ who would be of the race of Seth, the son of Adam, or else believed that Christ was Seth himself.[3]

This is merely a superficial account of these vagaries, and it is not necessary to dwell on them here ; but in truth, we have not yet any clear idea of their source ; above all we cannot date with any measure of accuracy those ideas which the historians of heresy most often present to us as a unity, but which must have undergone a process of evolution. Nevertheless, all the probabilities are in favour of the view that we are really concerned with Judaizing and gnostic sects, anterior, at least in their origins, to the establishment of Christianity.

In this depressing confusion one name arrests our attention, that of Simon the Samaritan,[4] the famous Simon Magus who passes across the stage of primitive Christianity and occupies a place in the Petrine legend. In making of him " the father

---

[1] *Philosophumena*, 5 ; *cf.* CCLXXVI, ii, 25–82.

[2] Irenæus, *Haer.*, i, 30 : " *Quidam enim ipsam sophiam serpentem factam dicunt.*"—Epiphanius, *Haer.*, xxxvii, 2 *ff.* ; Philastr., *Haer.*, i ; *Praedestinatus*, 17 : " *Quem colubrum suum Christum appelant.*" On this *Praedestinatus*, largely a plagiarism from Augustine, *cf.* CCCXXV, 106.

[3] Epiph., xxxix, 3 ; Philastr., iii.

[4] CCLXXVI, i, 172 *ff.* ; CCLXVII, v, 151 *ff.* (by Casey), where references are given to texts and literature.

of all the heresies " the Christians have rendered an ill service
both to him and to us. This notoriety has its origin in Acts
viii. 10, where it is said that he was the great sorcerer of
his country whose magic arts had dazzled and seduced his
fellow-citizens. He, himself, claimed to be " *some great one* "
(λέγων εἶναι τινα ἑαυτὸν μέγαν) and " *all gave heed to him
from the least to the greatest, saying, This man is the* dynamis
of God, which is called Great " (οὗτός ἐστιν ἡ δύναμις τοῦ θεοῦ
ἡ καλουμένη μεγάλη). At first, according to the redactor, an
adherent of the infant Church (viii. 13), Simon ends up by
appearing in his eyes as the first anti-Christian, after he had
sought to buy from the Apostles the secret of their miracles.
Nevertheless, it is possible that, behind the tendentious arrangement of Acts, there is a nucleus of truth. Simon claimed that
he was the *great power of God*, and various items of evidence
which we possess about him agree as to this claim. It probably
means that he presented himself as a kind of Messiah—so much
the phrase " *gave himself out to be some great one* " suggests
—an envoy of God, filled with his Spirit for the execution of
designs of which we know nothing. In relation to Christianity
Simon is not, therefore, to be regarded as a heretic, but rather
as a precursor and a rival. He was certainly a gnostic and
a syncretist, who appears to have borrowed largely from Stoic
cosmology and ontology, whilst his composite theology was
inspired by the methods of which Philo affords us the most
perfect example.[1] Moreover, it is scarcely probable that his
was an isolated case, for we know that there existed in Samaria
a centre of gnostic thought, heretical in relation to pure Judaism.
At a later date Dositheus represented variously as a disciple
and a rival of Simon, emerged from the same strange environment
and presented himself likewise as a kind of Messiah.[2] Similarly,
Menander, the pupil of Simon, met with some success at Antioch,
possibly at the same time as Christianity was being established
there.[3] There is today a tendency to believe that from this
Samaritan environment and from Simon himself there proceeded various influences which seriously affected the form and
early development of Christian thought.[4] Unfortunately, this
is easier to suspect than to prove. The statement that Simon
was the incarnation of the " *great power of God* " in itself
claims our attention, because it proves that the Pauline idea

---

[1] **CCLXVII**, v, 160.
[2] Origen, *C. Celsum*, i, 57 ; vi, 15 ; *In Ioannum*, xiii, 27.
[3] Justin, 1 *Apol.*, 26 ; Irenæus, *Haer.*, i, 23.
[4] **CCCXVIII**, 74 ; Alfaric, *Christianisme et Gnosticisme*, in **RH**, cxlv,
1924, 45.

of Incarnation was not so great a novelty in the Jewish world as has been believed. It is difficult not to compare this quality of the Samaritan with that which Paul attributes to Jesus Christ : " Power of God and Wisdom of God " (Χριστὸν Θεοῦ δύναμιν καὶ Θεοῦ σοφίαν).

It is not altogether impossible for us to read between the lines of the early Christian criticisms [1] the chief features of Simon's teaching. They suggest a gnostic system, probably perfected and completed by several generations of disciples, since we know that the Samaritan founded a school, but whose essential character is not in doubt.

If we have diverted our attention for a moment to Palestine, it is because the three Samaritans whom we have found there seem to offer striking and instructive examples of those gnostic syncretists whose speculation took its point of departure from Judaism, or ran parallel with it, and was then nourished by Greek and Oriental sources.[2] It is altogether improbable that such men appeared only in Samaria, and we know that they themselves did not always remain there, since it was at Tyre that Simon, " the Father," discovered his consort Helena, named by him Ennoia, or the Thought ; Menander, too, settled near Antioch. Indeed, according to Justin Martyr,[3] Christian legend placed the figure and fame of Simon in the capital of the Empire.

It would seem likely that wherever Judaism came into contact with Hellenistic or Græco-Oriental influences it allowed itself to be more or less penetrated by them and in turn reacted upon them. The more advanced forms, and the most coherent, gave rise to definite sects, some still very Jewish or Judaizing, others, on the contrary, definitely hostile to Jahweh, his Torah and the Jewish spirit.

The circles in which such religious forms arose were disturbed, confused, diverse, the meeting-place of tumultuous streams of divergent thought. Here there sprang up a fertile but chaotic mingling of beliefs, hopes, speculations, and revelations, which afforded an inexhaustible store of nourishment for the new religion which was about to emerge in this seething world, offering certain clear and simple principles, sufficiently elastic to allow of indefinite expansion.

[1] Irenæus, Haer., i, 28 ; Philosophumena, vi, 19–20.

[2] CCLXXVI, i, 180 ff., where an attempt is made to differentiate the several elements which went to make up Simonism.

[3] Justin, 1 Apol., xxvi, 2 and 3. On this complicated legend, cf. Ch. Guignebert, La primauté de Pierre et la venue de Pierre à Rome, Paris, 1909, pp. 203 ff.

CONCLUSION

PALESTINE had long since lost her independence. Successive conquerors of Syria had annexed her. As a rule, she had accepted her fate without much resistance, rebelling only when some foreign overlord, like Antiochus Epiphanes, had shown contempt towards Jahweh and his Law, and had attempted to sever the Chosen People from its God, and to subject them to the accursed idols of the Gentiles.

If, amid all these tribulations, Israel still preserved its racial identity, and was not scattered into isolated units, this was due entirely to its religion—a religion which grew more rigid and jealous as the political fortunes of the people darkened. And while that people, sorely tempest-tossed, was exalting its God to the supreme dignity of Creator and Ruler of the Universe, it clung with all the greater tenacity to the hope, nay, certainty, that a shattering vengeance would overwhelm its oppressors. For it was impossible that Jahweh should belie his promises and allow the Gentiles to mock his sovereign power for ever.

This comfortable hope was nurtured upon two illusions. The first was based on an exaggerated idea of the glories of Israel at the time of King David. This energetic " unifier " of the Jewish territory around Jerusalem, who had begun life as a simple Judæan adventurer, and thence developed into a soldier of fortune and large-scale bandit, ultimately to become the prince of his people, seemed to constitute the ideal type of conqueror, after Jahweh's own heart. The restoration of his reign was thus tantamount, in popular thought, to the realization of the most glowing dreams of the future.

The second illusion was connected with the Maccabæan revolt against the Seleucid monarchs. It was agreeably portrayed as a brilliant triumph, and a complete restoration of Israel, accomplished by the special favour of Jahweh.

In both cases, the reality was far more modest than they imagined. Nevertheless, it is not difficult to understand that these illusions afforded a source of permanent and effective encouragement for all those enthusiasts who believed that they had felt the stirring of the breath of Jahweh, and that they acted as a ferment of revolt among the people. The conviction grew that Jahweh was waiting His hour, but that when it struck He would reveal Himself in an irresistible burst of glory. It was believed also that this event might be hastened by a stringent observance of the *Torah*, and in this way political interests came to be mingled with those of religion.

Yet even from this point of view, it would be an exaggeration to regard the outlook of the Palestinians as homogeneous. Not all of them were equally disposed to surrender themselves to the dreams of nationalism. The upper classes were, in general, prepared to accept the foreign domination with which they made their peace for the sake of greater personal profit. Thereby they retained their influence and consolidated those material advantages which they had acquired by birth. Their fathers before them had become Grecized, and they themselves now became Romanized. Indeed, down to the time of the insurrections in the first and second centuries A.D., and especially during the reigns of Caligula and Claudius, the imperial court was frequented by Jewish princes. When it came to repressing the Great Rebellion, Vespasian and Titus found support in a strong Roman party which saw no profit in headstrong action, and was therefore inclined to display a disapproving and non-committal attitude. These "*politicians*" were particularly numerous among the ranks of the priesthood. Adventure did not attract them, and they set their faces from the start against those fiery spirits who were all too ready to both invoke the anger and the favour of Jahweh, to the danger of all, and especially of those in high places.

Diametrically opposed to this attitude was that of the Zealots, who welcomed every attempt at revolution : they exploited the smallest opportunity and the flimsiest pretext to stir up the people. They magnified petty incidents and resorted to violence at the first excuse. In a word, they lived in a constant state of excitement of which their foreign masters were aware and which, with good reason, they dreaded.

The mass of the people certainly did not share this chronic excitement of the Zealots, but in moments of crisis they were none the less capable of being roused by it. It may be said, indeed, that their chief characteristic was a propensity towards headstrong action. Having yielded to this impulse, they lost their heads and shrank from no kind of excess, so that even in cases where their risings had at first a good ground and a valid excuse, they soon committed inexcusable crimes which, in the eyes of their foreign masters, justified the sternest measures of repression.

So far as we can judge, the leaven of all Palestinian uprisings at the time of Jesus lay in the Messianic hope. Apart from the numerous enthusiasts who claimed " *to be someone,*" *i.e.* attempted, whether in good faith or not, to pass themselves off as " *The Coming One,*" every petty incident between Zealots and Roman police seemed in the eyes of its leaders to be indeed the Great Beginning and an enterprise sure of Jahweh's aid. For this reason, the most crushing failures never damped their ardour. Last time, they said, God's hour had not struck, but every day brought it nearer, and who could tell whether this time it had not arrived ? Such was the thought, or at least the feeling, of all those enthusiasts who were eager for adventure.

It was rare indeed even for the most paltry pretender to be unable to enlist in his cause some hundred credulous souls, and it only needed a glimmer of success to swell the hundreds into thousands. The people were not, perhaps, living at such a high tension as has been supposed, but the livelier elements among them certainly were, and their activity, ever ready to burst restraint, quickly spread the infection of frenzy and fanaticism around them, producing the rashest adventures. Romantic memories of the Davidic or Hasmonæan past, the recollection of Jahweh's promises, prophecies drawn from contemporary events, miracles and *signs* of divers kinds, all would serve to obliterate reason and foster hopeless enterprises. The Romans had good reason for adopting towards these Palestinians an attitude of distrust and suspicion, easily regarded by these chronic malcontents as in itself a provocation. It was all a fatal vicious circle, whose evil effects went on increasing from the period with which this book closes until the middle of the second century A.D.

From the purely religious point of view, it is necessary to abandon, once for all, the time-honoured picture of the *closed fence*, cutting Israel off from its geographical neighbours and from the whole life of the East. We have seen that there were large breaches in the fence through which influences of the most varied origin and nature penetrated to the heart of Jahwism. In order best to describe the real state of affairs, we have been obliged to speak of variety, mixture, and syncretism. Undoubtedly, our first impression is one of rigorous legalism, meticulous observance, excessive religious scruples, and pedantic interpretation of the Law. The Scribe and Pharisee seem to dominate Jewish piety and religion. This, however, is a false impression, explicable by the fact that most of the documents preserved to us come from the hands of priests or doctors of the Law, and direct our attention only to the outer surface of the religious life. How could a people, placed by the countless demands of its daily life in constant and prolonged contact with its neighbours to the south, the east and the north, have escaped their influence only in the pattern of its religious life, when that very life was for them the all-important thing ?

In seeking to analyse and reduce that life to its basic elements, it is the diversity and contrasts of those elements which strike us most. Over against the belief and practice of priest and Rabbi, with their rigid observance, which had for them, nevertheless, its emotional value, we find the warm and living religion of the simple folk, born of a robust faith in the power and righteousness of Jahweh, together with an astonishing receptive credulity and a surprising mass of superstitions. From this it is only too clear that even men reputed to be learned were not always proof against contamination. All the natives of Palestine, in greater or lesser degree, took dreams seriously ; unexpected noises alarmed them ; everywhere around them they felt the presence and activity of good and evil spirits, and believed that they could defend themselves by means of amulets, magical formulæ, exorcisms and incantations. Indeed, all this childish and cumbrous sorcery seems to be as foreign to the religion of the heart as the mechanical dryness of legalism ; and it is a cause for wonder that it should have met with such success in Palestine. Even the schools were not always immune from it.

But this is the very state of mind which was characteristic of the whole of the Hellenized East [1] at that time, and for long after. We catch a glimpse of it in the environment of Apollonius of Tyana at the end of the first century A.D., and in the circle of Alexander of Abonoteichos, under Marcus Aurelius. Moreover, in the light of this simple fact, we are at once able to understand why Judaism never succeeded in protecting itself effectively against the disease of syncretism, of combining heterogeneous beliefs ; it was caught up, by the force of circumstances, in the great religious stream which was then flowing through the ancient world. Only its nationalistic character saved it from the danger of complete absorption. Jahwism, however, did at least derive from the religions with which it came into contact elements which enriched it and profoundly transformed it.

The point which must always be stressed is the cardinal fact that in all these Palestinian regions, alongside of the precepts of the priest, the dogmas of the scholar, and the formulæ of the quack, we find a true, solid, deep piety, closely

[1] CCLXXVIII, i, 413, n. 3.

bound up with the related ideas of the power, righteousness, and *faithfulness* of Jahweh. It vitalizes both the faith of a member of the ʿam ha-areṣ in his village synagogue, and that of the Pharisee in the school of his Rabbi, that of the Sadducee in the Temple, or of the Essene in his monastic seclusion. It is susceptible of a variety of forms and takes on a different colour in different places ; everywhere it is supreme. Israel, as a whole, remains the one people which has both lived by its religion and has lived its religion.

When we turn our attention especially to the upheavals which shook the nation and finally brought about its downfall, we recognize that it was the Messianic hope, conceived of either as the immediate assumption by Jahweh of the government of the world, or as the beneficent and blessed rule of a representative of the divine Majesty, which stirred up and sustained them all. In actual fact this line of thought was translated into action by two different forces, the one represented by the Pharisees and the other by the Zealots. Neither of these, doubtless, numbered many adherents, but both of them, the former by means of legalistic observance and the latter by means of open revolt, claimed the attention of the common folk and guided them, each in its own direction, according to circumstances, with varied success. Thus the mass of the population sometimes listened in quiet admiration to the Pharisees, and sometimes sprang to arms at the bidding of the Zealots, and were always ready to lend an ear to a *nabi* foretelling wonders.

The analysis which we have attempted of the overflowing activity of religious thought in Palestine has deceived us on more than one important point, above all because we have not always been able to distinguish and to separate from one another the various religious currents which crossed and mingled on this soil, where men and ideas from every direction met. Nevertheless it has at least allowed us to recognize in the spiritual life of Judaism a greater variety, complexity and elasticity—in short, a greater degree of freedom—than was hitherto suspected.[1] It would appear that the varied expressions of this culture nevertheless flowed finally into two main channels clearly indicated in the vast but chaotic literature [2] in which we now seek them : they led, that is to say, on the one hand to the *Talmud* and on the other to the Gospel.

But it must be understood that neither the *Talmud* nor the Gospel are the immediate products of this Palestinian environment. Those New Testament writings, such as the Book of

[1] **XXXIII,** 78 *ff.*   [2] **LXXXVIII,** 297.

Revelation and the so-called Epistle of James which seem most Jewish in appearance, did not proceed directly from it. Similarly, the *Talmud* is rather to be regarded as a monument witnessing to the religious vitality of Israel after the catastrophe which shattered and dispersed the Jewish nation in A.D. 70. Indeed, it is not impossible that it would never have come into being had not that very catastrophe rendered it necessary, in order to serve as a repository of all the traditions and hopes of Jahwism and of all the interpretations and thoughts of its learned men which might survive that bitter experience with its hateful memories. In the anguish of the terrible disillusionment of the first and second centuries, the vital elements of Judaism which are contained therein were revised and determined. They were brought together into an organized system for the sustenance, consolation and instruction of the scattered people.

As for the *Gospel*, it was in origin the book in which a sect, originally issuing out of Israel, had laid down the first principles of its hope and faith, but it was born outside of Israel, and the writers who have given us the three oldest versions of it, *viz.* the Gospel according to *Mark*, *Matthew* and *Luke*, and still more to the author and redactor of *John*, were already completely outside Judaism. Nevertheless, just as the elements which make up the oldest parts of the *Talmud* derived their origin from the Schools of the Scribes and the inspiration of the Pharisees, so the Jewish basis of the *Gospel* proceeds at one and the same time from the religion of the *'anavim* and from the piety, principles and hopes of Pharisaism. Moreover, these two sources alone do not exhaust the whole content of the complex soul and heterogeneous spirit of Israel, as it has been revealed to us.

Perhaps in course of time the discordant elements which we have met in Palestinian Jewry might have been reconciled, and all the divergent tendencies co-ordinated in a single movement, but we cannot imagine what could have become the principle and actuating force of this happy harmonization. In the present confusion it is the Messianic hope alone which appears to have been sufficiently widespread and deeply rooted in the masses of the people to constitute such a force. It had within it the power, even if imperfectly realized, *i.e.* only on the human level and in the unstable form of the political emancipation of the people of God, to rally round it all the Jews of Palestine.

The final goal of the Messianic movement was, undoubtedly, the establishment of the Kingdom of God upon a regenerated earth. Nevertheless, from the ways and means by which its foundation was visualized, the forms under which its realization was envisaged, and from the dreams which its expectation aroused and the pictures it evoked in the hope of the Jews, it is clear that this vision of regeneration assumed an entirely nationalistic expression. In one sense, it presented itself as the final and overwhelming victory of those who had always been the conquered, and it was taken for granted that its natural prelude would be a revolt. " *God helps those who help themselves* " might well have served as the war-cry of the Zealots. It is precisely for this reason that the message brought by Jesus (if, indeed, it was such as the Synoptic Gospels represent it to have been), calling for the moral transformation of the individual and for a spirit of resignation whose only reward was the promise of supernatural bliss in " *the Coming Kingdom*," had no chance of acceptance, and was not in fact accepted, by the prophet's fellow-countrymen.[1]

The small band of the Nazarene's disciples continued in Jerusalem for some years after his death, in a state of arrested development, and only succeeded in making a very small number of converts. Statements to the contrary in the Acts of the Apostles [2] will not bear the most superficial criticism.

On the other hand, the testimony of those whom we call the Apostles found more willing ears among certain Jews of the Dispersion whose religious duties brought them on pilgrimages to the Holy City. Such men, living outside Palestine, in a Gentile environment, no longer clung so firmly as did their brethren to the expectation of a warrior Messiah or the hope of a nationalistic revival of the Davidic Kingdom.

There came a day, probably not long after the death of Jesus, when certain of the Hellenistic Jews who had been converted to the Galilean hope began to vex the pure Jews of Jerusalem by entering the synagogues and advocating their faith with undue zeal. In consequence of this, they were all expelled from the city and scattered abroad, the greater part of them, no doubt, returning to their homelands. This was an event of cardinal importance, since the message which these men carried with them found on the soil of the Diaspora more favourable conditions of survival and of development than in Palestine, even among the genuine Jews whom constant intercourse with the Gentiles had broadened. Their nationalism had become blunted and their Messianism, gradually contaminated by the mixed environment of Greek thought and Oriental mysticism, evolved in time into a kind of universalist

[1] *Cf. Jesus*, 231 *ff*.   [2] Acts ii. 41, 47 ; iv. 4 ; vi. 1 and 7.

salvationism. Above all, their synagogues were surrounded by proselytes whose religious needs, interests and aspirations remained at root intensely personal, nay, individual, and who therefore evinced but little sympathy for the religious " totalitarianism " of orthodox Jewry and for its painful and uncomfortable demands. It was among these men that true Christianity, regarded as a religion, came to birth.

It was probably at Antioch that " *the brethren who called on the name of the Lord Jesus* " first became a conscious entity, and it was in that city that they received from the pagans the name by which they were to be noted through the ages, *viz. Christians,* or *believers in Christ.*

Behind the converts to Judaism there was the mass of pagans many of whom found themselves stirred by the same unrest as had led the Judaizers to the synagogue, and who were ready to be attracted to the Church. To them—and it may be said, through them also—the Jewish Messiah assumed the complexion and rôle of a *Soter* and rose inevitably to the status of absolute divinity.

We can well understand that Jesus of Nazareth should have been born in Galilee, and that the impulse behind his career should have been the expectation of the Messianic Kingdom; we can also understand that he should have drawn from the religion of the ʿanavim and the piety of the Pharisees the fundamental elements of his spiritual development, the inspiration of his mission, and the substance of his teaching, welding together these various influences and stamping them with his own forceful personality. Indeed, as he appears behind the veil wherewith early Christian imagination has shrouded him, he is plainly inexplicable except as the product of this environment. It is, moreover, by no means impossible that there were other prophets of the same order, at present unknown to us, who arose in Palestine at the same time. If so, and if they really existed alongside of or in competition with the more warlike agitators, their obscure fate has been shrouded in oblivion, for lack of that apotheosis which martyrdom alone can earn. In any case, men of this type, to which Jesus himself belonged, could not possibly hope for success in Palestine. The prophet of Nazareth never gave voice to the sentiments necessary, if not to interest, then at least to attract and move the mass of his countrymen. It is, therefore, readily comprehensible that they did not follow him.

On the other hand, it is equally easy to understand how his personality and his utterances, when transplanted and adapted to the environment of the Diaspora, were found acceptable there, and, by the help of certain accommodations whose number and consequences were limited by no insurmountable obstacle, they there became the centre of a powerful and fruitful religion.

Developed to its logical extreme, Palestinian Judaism led perforce to the Great Rebellion, and hence to the downfall of the Jewish nation. Similarly, the spiritual evolution of the Judaism of the Diaspora would produce a religion, based on Israelitic monotheism and the ethic of the Mosaic Law, but based on the form and spirit of a universalist Salvationism, ready at all times to assimilate anything of religious vitality which came within its range.

Such a religion indeed saw the light of day, and it goes under the name of Christianity. To the historian, it might possibly appear as no more than the natural consequence of the appearance on Palestinian soil of a Messianic prophet of distinctively Jewish character. In reality, however, its true antecedents lie on Hellenistic soil, for it was in Hellenistic Judaism that it found its *raison d'être*, there it was born, nurtured and reared, and there it fulfilled its destiny.

BIBLIOGRAPHY

PERIODICALS, DICTIONARIES AND REPORTS

Abhandlungen der Berliner Akad. der Wiss., phil.-hist. Klasse	**ABA**
Académie des Inscriptions et Belles-Lettres, comptes rendus des séances	**AI**
The American Journal of Semitic Languages and Literatures	**AJSL**
Archiv für Religionswissenschaft	**AR**
Beihefte zur Zeitschrift für die alttestamentliche Wissenschaft, Giessen, Töpelmann	**BZAW**
Bulletin de correspondance hellénique	**BCH**
The Cambridge Ancient History, Cambridge Univ. Press, vol. ii, 1924	**CAH**
Corpus inscriptionum semiticarum	**CIS**
Dict. d'Archéologie chrétienne et de Liturgie (Dom F. Cabrol and Dom H. Leclercq, Paris, 1903 *ff.*, (the work has reached the CXXXIst part, and the syllable *Nat*) .	**DACL**
Dict. of the Bible (J. Hastings, 5 vols., Edin., 1897–1904)	**DB**
Encyclopedia Biblica (Cheyne and Black, 4 vols., Lond., 1899–1903)	**EB**
Encyclopaedia judaica, Das Judentum in Geschichte und Gegenwart (Klatzkin and J. Elbogen, Berlin, 9 vols. appeared (1934) of 15 announced) . . .	**EJ**
Expository Times	**ET**
Handkommentar zum A. T. (Nowack), Göttingen, Vandenhoeck and Ruprecht	**HK**
The Harvard Theological Review	**HTR**
The Jewish Encyclopedia, New York, 1901 *ff.*, 12 vols..	**JE**
Journal of Biblical Literature	**JBL**
The Journal of Egyptian Archaeology, London . .	**JEA**
Journal of Theological Studies	**JTS**
Keilschriftliche Bibliothek	**KB**
Kommentar zum A. T. (Sellin), Leipzig, Deichert .	**KAT**
Kurzer Hand-Commentar zum A. T. (Marti), Tübingen, Mohr.	**KHC**
Kurzgefasstes exegetisches Handbuch zum A. T., Leipzig, Hirzel	**KEH**
Mémoires présentés par divers savants à l'Académie des Inscriptions et Belles-Lettres	**MAI**
Mitt. der Vorderasiatischen Gesellschaft . . .	**MVAG**
Museon	**MUS**
Orientalistische Literaturzeitung	**OLZ**
Palaestinajahrbuch	**PJ**

Palestine Exploration Fund . . . . .   **PEF**
Real-Encyklopaedie für prot. Theologie und Kirche, 3rd
   edit. (Alb. Hauck, 22 vols., Leipzig, 1896–1909) .   **HRE**
Recherches de science religieuse . . . . .   **RSR**
Recueil de travaux relatifs à la philologie et à l'archéologie
   égyptienne et assyrienne . . . . . .   **RTEA**
Die Religion in Geschichte und Gegenwart, Tübingen, Mohr.   **RGG**
Revue d'Assyriologie . . . .   **RA**
Revue Biblique, Paris, Gabalda . . . . .   **RB**
Revue des Études anciennes . . . . .   **REA**
Revue des Études grecques . . . . . .   **REG**
Revue des Études juives . . . . . .   **REJ**
Revue des Études sémitiques . . . . .   **RES**
Revue d'histoire et de philosophie religieuses, Strasburg-
   Paris, Alcan . . . .   **RHP**
Revue de l'histoire des Religions . . . . .   **RHR**
Revue de théologie et de philosophie, Lausanne . .   **RTP**
*Sitzungsberichte der Preussischen Akademie der Wissen-
   schaften*, phil.-hist. Klasse . . . . .   **SBA**
Syria, Revue d'art oriental et d'archéologie, Paris, Geuthner   **SY**
Theologische Blätter, Leipzig, Hinrichs . . . .   **TB**
Theologische Literaturzeitung, Leipzig, Hinrichs . .   **TLZ**
Theologische Quartalschrift . . . . . .   **TQS**
Theologische Rundschau . . . . . .   **TR**
Theologische Studien und Kritiken, Gotha, Perthes .   **TSK**
Theologisch Tijdschrift . . . . . .   **TT**
Transactions of the Society for Biblical Archaeology .   **TSBA**
Zeitschrift der Deutschen Morgenlaendischen Gesellschaft,
   Leipzig, Brockhaus. . . . .   **ZDMG**
Zeitschrift des Deutschen Palästinavereins, Leipzig,
   Baedeker . . . .   **ZDPV**
Zeitschrift für Assyriologie . . . . . .   **ZA**
Zeitschrift für die alttestamentliche Wissenschaft, Giessen,
   Töpelmann . . . .   **ZATW**
Zeitschrift für wissenschaftliche Theologie (Hilgenfeld) .   **ZWT**

GENERAL WORKS

I. BENZINGER, *Hebraeische Archaeologie*, 3rd edit., Leipzig,
   Pfeiffer, 1927 . . . .   **I**
PHILIPPE BERGER, *Histoire de l'écriture dans l'Antiquité*,
   Paris, Imprimerie nationale, 1891 . . . .   **II**
ALFRED BERTHOLET, *Histoire de la civilisation d'Israël*,
   trans. by JACQUES MARTY, Paris, Payot, 1929 .   **III**
R. BEVAN and CH. SINGER, *The Legacy of Israel*, Oxford,
   1928 . . . .   **IV**
La sainte Bible, traduction nouvelle d'après les meilleurs
   textes, avec introductions et notes (Bible du Centenaire),
   Paris, Société biblique protestante de Paris, 1916 *ff.*   **V**
KARL BUDDE, *Geschichte der althebraeischen Literatur*,
   Leipzig, Amelang, 1906 . . . . . .   **VI**
D. BUZY, *Les symboles de l'Ancien Testament*, Paris,
   Gabalda, 1923 . . . .   **VII**

ANTONIN CAUSSE, *Les dispersés d'Israël*, Paris, Alcan, 1929   VIII

A. CAUSSE, *Les " Pauvres " d'Israël (prophètes, psalmistes, messianistes)*, Strasburg-Paris, Istra, 1922.   IX

CARL HEINRICH CORNILL, *Einleitung in die kanonischen Bücher des Alten Testaments*, Tübingen, Mohr, 5th edit., 1905   X

SAMUEL IVES CURTISS, German trans. by H. STOKES, *Ursemitische Religion im Volksleben des heutigen Orients*, Leipzig, Hinrichs, 1903   XI

LOUIS DELAPORTE, *La Mésopotamie. Les civilisations babylonienne et assyrienne*, Paris, Renaissance du livre, 1923   XII

JOSEPH DERENBOURG, *Essai sur l'histoire et la géographie de la Palestine, d'après les Talmuds et les autres sources rabbiniques*, Paris, 1867   XIII

PAUL DHORME, *Choix de textes religieux assyro-babyloniens*, Paris, Lecoffre, 1907   XIV

BERNHARD DUHM, *Das Buch Jesaia*, Handkommentar zum Alten Testament, iii, 1, Göttingen, Vandenhoeck and Ruprecht, 1892   XV

B. DUHM, *Die Theologie der Propheten*, Bonn, 1875   XVI

HANS DUHM, *Die bösen Geister im Alten Testament*, Tübingen, Leipzig, Mohr, 1904   XVII

RENÉ DUSSAUD, *Les origines cananéennes du sacrifice israélite*, Paris, Leroux, 1921   XVIII

R. DUSSAUD, *Topographie historique de la Syrie antique et médiévale*, Paris, Geuthner, 1927   XIX

OTTO EISSFELDT, *Einleitung in das Alte Testament*, Tübingen, Mohr, 1934   XX

JAMES FRAZER, *The Golden Bough*   XXI

GAUDEFROY-DEMOMBYNES, *Contribution à l'étude du pèlerinage de la Mekke*, Paris, Geuthner, 1923   XXII

LUCIEN GAUTIER, *Introduction à l'Ancien Testament*, 2 vols., Lausanne, Bridel, 1st edit., 1906 ; 2nd, 1914   XXIII

GEIGER, *Urschrift und Uebersetzungen der Bibel*, Breslau, 1857   XXIV

GRAETZ, *Histoire des Juifs*, trans. by WOGUE, vol. ii, Paris, 1884   XXV

GEORGE BUCHANAN GRAY, *Sacrifice in the Old Testament. Its Theory and Practice*, Oxford, Clarendon Press, 1925   XXVI

HUGO GRESSMANN, *Altorientalische Texte und Bilder zum Alten Testament*, 2 vols. (I Texte, II Bilder), 2nd edit., Berlin-Leipzig, de Gruyter, 1926   XXVII

HUGO GRESSMANN, HERMANN GUNKEL, MAX HALLER, HANS SCHMIDT, WILLY STAERK, PAUL VOLZ, *Die Schriften des Alten Testaments in Auswahl übersetzt*, Göttingen, Vandenhoeck and Ruprecht, 1st edit., 1910 ff. ; 2nd, 1921 ff.   XXVIII

HERMANN GUNKEL, *Genesis*, Handkommentar zum A. T., 3rd edit., Göttingen, Vandenhoeck and Ruprecht, 1910   XXIX

HERMANN GUTHE, *Geschichte des Volkes Israel*, Tübingen, Mohr, 2nd edit., 1904 ; 3rd, 1914   XXX

H. GUTHE, *Kurzes Bibelwörterbuch*, 1905   XXXI

JOSEPH HALÉVY, *Mélanges de critique et d'histoire*, Paris, Maisonneuve, 1883   XXXII

R. T. HERFORD, *Judaism in the New Testament Period*,
London, 1928. . . . . **XXXIII**

GUSTAV HÖLSCHER, *Die Bücher Esra und Nehemia*, in
EMIL KAUTZSCH, *Die Heilige Schrift des Alten Testaments*, 4th edit., Tübingen, Mohr, 1923, ii, pp. 491–562 **XXXIV**

G. HÖLSCHER, *Geschichte der israelitischen und jüdischen
Religion*, Giessen, Töpelmann, 1922 . . . . **XXXV**

G. HÖLSCHER, *Die Profeten, Untersuchung zur Religionsgeschichte Israels*, Leipzig, Hinrichs, 1914. . . **XXXVI**

A. VAN HOONACKER, *Les douze petits Prophètes traduits et
commentes*, Études bibliques, Paris, Gabalda, 1908 . **XXXVII**

HENRI HUBERT and MARCEL MAUSS, *Essai sur la nature et
la fonction du sacrifice*, Paris, Alcan, 1899 . . **XXXVIII**

PAUL HUMBERT, *Recherches sur les sources égyptiennes de la
littérature sapientiale des Hébreux*, Neuchâtel, Secrétariat
de l'Université, 1929 . . . . **XXXIX**

MORRIS JASTROW jr., *Aspects of Religious Belief and Prac-
tice in Babylonia and Assyria* (American Lectures on the
History of Religions, 9th series, 1910), New York-
London, Putnam, 1911 . . . . **XL**

MORRIS JASTROW jr., *Die Religion Babyloniens und Assyriens*, 2 vols., Giessen, Töpelmann, 1912 . . **XLI**

J. A. JAUSSEN, *Coutumes des Arabes au pays de Moab*,
Paris, Gabalda, 1908 . . . . **XLII**

CHARLES F. JEAN, *La littérature des Babyloniens et des
Assyriens*, Paris, Geuthner, 1924 . . . . **XLIII**

CHARLES F. JEAN, *Le milieu biblique avant Jésus-Christ*,
Paris, Geuthner, 1st vol., 1922 ; 2nd, 1923 . . **XLIV**

ALFRED JEREMIAS, *Das Alte Testament im Lichte des Alten
Orients*, Leipzig, Hinrichs, 1904 ; 2nd edit., 1906 ; 3rd,
1916 ; 4th, 1930 . . . . **XLV**

JOSEPHUS, *Œuvres complètes de Flavius Josèphe*, traduites
en français sous la direction de THÉODORE REINACH,
Paris, Leroux, 1900 *ff*. . . . . . . **XLVI**

JEAN JUSTER, *Les Juifs dans l'Empire romain, leur condition juridique, économique et sociale*, 2 vols., Paris,
Geuthner, 1914 . . . . **XLVII**

EMIL KAUTZSCH, *Die Heilige Schrift des Alten Testaments*,
2 vols., Tübingen, Mohr, 3rd edit., 1908 ; 4th, 1922–3 **XLVIII**

RUDOLF KITTEL, *Geschichte des Volkes Israel*, 6th edit.,
vol. ii, 1925, Gotha ; vol. iii, 1929, Stuttgart, Kohl-
hammer . . . . **XLIX**

J. A. KNUDTZON, *Die El-Amarna Tafeln mit Einleitung
und Erlaeuterungen*, 2 vols., Leipzig, Hinrichs, 1915. **L**

M. J. LAGRANGE, *Le Judaïsme avant Jésus-Christ*, Paris,
1931 . . . . **LI**

C. F. LEHMANN-HAUPT, *Israel, Seine Entwicklung im
Rahmen der Weltgeschichte*, Tübingen, Mohr, 1911 . **LII**

LUCIEN LÉVY-BRUHL, *La mentalité primitive*, Paris, Alcan,
1922 . . . . **LIII**

MARK LIDZBARSKI, *Handbuch der nordsemitischen Epi-
graphik*, Weimar, Felber, 1898 . . . . **LIV**

ADOLPHE LODS, *L'ange de Yahwé et " l'âme extérieure "*
(Wellhausen-Festschrift, pp. 263–78), Giessen, Töpelmann, 1914 . . . . **LV**

AD. LODS, *La croyance à la vie future et le culte des morts dans l'antiquité israélite*, 2 vols., Paris, Fischbascher, 1906 LVI

AD. LODS, *Israel, from its Beginnings to the Middle of the Eighth Century.* Eng. trans. by S. H. HOOKE. Kegan Paul, London, 1932 LVII

ALFRED LOISY, *Essai historique sur le sacrifice*, Paris, Nourry, 1920 LVIII

A. LOISY, *La religion d'Israël*, 2nd edit., Ceffonds, 1908 ; 3rd, Paris, Nourry, 1933 LIX

KARL MARTI, *Das Buch Jesaja*, Kurzer Hand-Commentar zum Alten Testament, x, Tübingen, Friburg-Leipzig, Mohr, 1900 LX

K. MARTI, *Das Dodekapropheton*, Kurzer Hand-Commentar zum Alten Testament, xiii, Tübingen, Mohr, 1904 LXI

K. MARTI, *Geschichte der israelitischen Religion*, 5th edit., Strasburg, F. Bull, 1907 LXII

S. MATHEWS, *The History of the New Testament Times in Palestine*, New York, 1910 LXIII

JOHANNES MEINHOLD, *Einführung in das Alte Testament*, Giessen, Töpelmann, 1919 LXIV

MOMMSEN, *Histoire romaine*, trans. by CAGNET and TOUTAIN, vol. xi, Paris, 1889 LXV

SIGMUND MOWINCKEL, *Psalmenstudien*, 6 vols., Kristiania, Dybwad, 1921–4 LXVI

W. O. E. OESTERLEY and THEODORE H. ROBINSON, *Hebrew Religion. Its origin and development*, London, S.P.C.K., 1930 LXVII

W. O. E. OESTERLEY and T. H. ROBINSON, *A History of Israel*, 2 vols., Oxford, Clarendon Press, 1932 . . LXVIII

JOHS. PEDERSEN, *Israel, its Life and Culture*, i–ii, London, Milford, 1926 LXIX

C. PIEPENBRING, *Histoire du Peuple d'Israël*, Paris, 1898 LXX

ERNEST RENAN, *Histoire du Peuple d'Israël*, Paris, Lévy, 1887 *ff.* LXXI

GIUSEPPE RICCIOTTI, *Storia d'Israele*, 2 vols., Turin, Soc. editrice internaz., 1932 LXXII

C. W. ROGERS, *Cuneiform Parallels to the Old Testament*, Oxford, University Press, 1912 LXXIII

A. SCHLATTER, *Geschichte Israels von Alexander dem Grossen bis Hadrian*, 1906 LXXIV

EMIL SCHÜRER, *Geschichte des jüdischen Volkes im Zeitalter Jesu Christi*, Leipzig, Hinrichs, 2nd edit., 1886–1890 ; 3rd and 4th, 1909 LXXV

R. P. SCHWALM, *La vie privée du peuple juif à l'époque de Jésus-Christ*, Paris, Gabalda, 1910 LXXVI

ERNST SELLIN, *Einleitung in das Alte Testament*, Leipzig, Quelle and Meyer, 1st edit., 1910 ; 2nd, 1914 . . LXXVII

E. SELLIN, *Geschichte des israelitisch-jüdischen Volkes*, 1932 LXXVIII

E. SELLIN, *Das Zwölfprophetenbuch* (Kommentar zum A. T., xii), 2nd and 3rd edns., Leipzig, Deichert, 1929–1930 LXXIX

S. SPINNER, *Herkunft, Entstehung and antike Umwelt des hebraeischen Volkes*, Vienna, Vernay, 1933 . . LXXX

WILLY STAERK, *Das assyrische Weltreich im Urteil der
Propheten*, 1908 . . . .   **LXXXI**
BERNHARD STADE, *Geschichte des Volkes Israel*, 2 vols.,
Berlin, Grote, 2nd edit., 1889 . . . . .   **LXXXII**
B. STADE, *Biblische Theologie des Alten Testaments*, 2 vols.,
Tübingen, Mohr, 1905 . . . . . .   **LXXXIII**
EDMOND STAPFER, *La Palestine au temps de Jésus-Christ*,
Paris, 1897 . . . .   **LXXXIV**
TIELE, *Kompendium der Religionsgeschichte*, trans. by
F. W. T. WEBER, 3rd edit. revised by NATHAN SÖDER-
BLOM, Breslau, Biller, 1903 . . . . .   **LXXXV**
PAUL VOLZ, *Der Geist Gottes und die verwandten Erschei-
nungen im Alten Testament und im anschliessenden
Judentum*, Tübingen, Mohr, 1910 . . . .   **LXXXVI**
JULIUS WELLHAUSEN, BLEEK'S *Einleitung in die Heilige
Schrift, I*er *Theil, Einl. in das A. T.*, 4th edit., Berlin,
Reimer, 1878 . . . .   **LXXXVII**
J. WELLHAUSEN, *Israelitsche und jüdische Geschichte*,
Berlin, Reimer, 2nd edit., 1895 ; 6th, 1907 ; 7th, 1914   **LXXXVIII**
J. WELLHAUSEN, *Die Composition des Hexateuchs und der
histor. Bücher des A. T.*, 2nd edit., Berlin, Reimer, 1889   **LXXXIX**
J. WELLHAUSEN, *Reste arabischen Heidentums gesammelt
und erlaeurtert*, 2nd edit., Berlin, Reimer, 1897 .   **XC**
ALEXANDRE WESTPHAL, *Les sources du Pentateuque*,
2 vols., Paris, Fischbacher, 1888–1892 . . .   **XCI**
A. WESTPHAL, *Les prophètes*, 2 vols., Paris-Lausanne, 1924   **XCII**
HUGO WINCKLER, *Alttestamentliche Untersuchungen* .   **XCIII**
H. WINCKLER, *Untersuchungen zur altorientalischen
Geschichte*, Leipzig, 1889 . . . . . .   **XCIV**
HEINRICH ZIMMER and HUGO WINCKLER, *Die Keilin-
schriften und das Alte Testament*, 3rd edit., Berlin,
Reuther and Reichard, 1902 . . . . .   **XCV**

SPECIAL WORKS

1. THE PRE-EXILIC PROPHETS AND THEIR TIMES

G. CH. AALDERS, *De Profeten de Ouden Verbonds*, Kampen,
Kok, 1918 . . . .   **XCVI**
A. ALLWOHN, *Die Ehe des Propheten Hosea in psychoanaly-
tischer Beleuchtung*, Giessen, Töpelmann, 1926 . .   **XCVII**
ALBRECHT ALT, *Israel und Aegypten*, 1908 . . .   **XCVIII**
HEDWIG ANNELER, *Zur Geschichte der Juden in Elephan-
tine*, Berne, 1912 . . . .   **XCIX**
WILLIAM FREDERIC BADÈ, *Der Monojahwismus des Deu-
teronomiums*, **ZATW**, 25 (1910), pp. 81–90 . .   **C**
WALTER BAUMGARTNER, *Ein Kapitel vom hebraeischen
Erzaehlungsstil, Eucharisterion*, Gunkel-Festschrift .   **CI**
A. BENTZEN, *Die josianische Reform*, Copenhagen, 1926   **CII**
L. E. BINNS, *The Book of the Prophet Jeremiah* (Westmin-
ster Commentary), London, 1919 . . . .   **CIII**
BUDDE-FESTSCHRIFT, **BZAW**, 34 (1920), Giessen, Töpel-
mann . . . .   **CIV**.

BIBLIOGRAPHY

KARL BUDDE, *Auf dem Wege zum Monotheismus*, Rektoratsrede, Marburger akademische Reden, Marburg, Elwert, 1916 CV

WALLIS BUDGE, *Egyptian Hieratic Papyri*, British Museum, 2nd series, 1923 CVI

ANTONIN CAUSSE, *Les prophètes contre la civilisation* (Christian social), Alençon-Cahors, Coueslant, 1913 . CVII

A. CAUSSE, *Les plus vieux chants de la Bible*, Paris, Alcan, 1926 CVIII

CHAINE, *Introduction à la lecture des prophètes*, Paris, Gabalda, 1932 CIX

STANLEY ARTHUR COOK, *The Religion of Ancient Palestine in the second millennium B.C. in the Light of Archœology and the Inscriptions*, London, Constable, 1908 . . CX

J. CULLEN, *The Book of the Covenant in Moab*, Glasgow, 1903 CXI

RENÉ DUSSAUD, *Observations en faveur de l'authenticité de la lettre adressée par Sennachérib à Ézéchias et rapportée dans II Rois xix, 10–13 (Isaïe xxxvii. 10–13).* Actes du Congrès international d'Histoire des Religions tenu à Paris en octobre 1923, Paris, Champion, 1925, vol. ii, pp. 5–6 CXII

OTTO EISSFELDT, *Die Bücher der Könige*, in EMIL KAUTZSCH, *Die Heilige Schrift des A. T.*, 4th edit., Tübingen, Mohr, 1923, i, 492–585 CXIII

ADOLF ERMAN, *Eine ägyptische Quelle der Sprüche Salom.*, Sitzungsberichte der Preussischen Akademie der Wissenschaften, P. H. Kl., 1924, xv–xvi, 86 *ff.* . . . CXIV

C. J. GADD, *The Fall of Nineveh, the newly discovered Babylonian Chronicle*, no. 21901 in the British Museum, London, Brit. Mus., 1923 CXV

ALAN GARDINER, *Admonitions of an Egyptian Sage*, Leipzig, 1909 CXVI

GÖTZEL, *Hizkia und Sanherib*, B. Z., 1908, pp. 133 *ff.*. CXVII

GRENFELL and HUNT, *The Hibeh Papyri*, i, 1906 . CXVIII

HUGO GRESSMANN, *Die neugefundene Lehre des Amenemope und die vorexilische Spruchdichtung Israels*, **ZATW**, 42 (N. F. 1), 1924, pp. 272–296 . . . CXIX

F. L. GRIFFITH, *Catalogue of the Demotic Papyri in the John Rylands Library*, Manchester, 1909 . . . CXX

JOHANNES HEMPEL, *Die Schichten des Deuteronomiums*, Leipzig, 1914 CXXI

H. W. HERZBERG, *Prophet und Gott*, Gütersloh, Bertelsmann, 1928 CXXII

H. V. HILPRECHT, *Explorations in Bible Lands* . . CXXIII

GUSTAV HÖLSCHER, *Das Buch der Könige, seine Quelle und seine Redaktion*, Eucharisterion, pp. 158–213, Göttingen, 1923 CXXIV

G. HÖLSCHER, *Komposition und Ursprung des Deuteronomiums*, **ZATW**, 40 (1922), pp. 161–255 . . . CXXV

F. HORST, *Die Anfänge des Propheten Jeremias*, **ZATW**, 41 (1923), 94 *ff.* CXXVI

F. HORST, *Die Kultusreform des Königs Josias*, **ZDMG**, 77 (1923), 220–38 CXXVII

L. P. HORST, *L'extase chez les Prophètes d'Israël d'après les travaux de Hölscher et Gunkel*, **RHP**, 1922, pp. 337–48 CXXVIII

FRÉDÉRIC HROZNY, *Code hittite provenant de l'Asie Mineure* (*vers 1350 avant J. C.*), Paris, Geuthner, 1922   .   **CXXIX**

PAUL HUMBERT, *Essai d'analyse de Nahoum, 1, 2-2, 3* (extrait de **ZATW**, 1926), Giessen, Töpelmann   .   **CXXX**

P. HUMBERT, *Un héraut de la justice : Amos* (inaugural lecture), Lausanne, La Concorde, 1917   .   **CXXXI**

P. HUMBERT, *La logique de la perspective nomade chez Osée et l'unité d'Osée 2, 4-22* (Vom Alten Testament, Karl Marti . . . gewidmet, Giessen, Töpelmann, 1925, pp. 158–66)   .   .   .   .   .   **CXXXII**

P. HUMBERT, *Le problème du livre de Nahoum*, **RHP**, 12 (1932), pp. 1–15   .   .   .   .   .   **CXXXIII**

P. HUMBERT, *Quelques aspects de la religion d'Amos* (**RTP**, lxxiii, 1929), 1930   .   .   .   .   .   **CXXXIV**

P. HUMBERT, *La vision de Nahoum 2, 4-11* (extrait de *Archiv für Orientforschung*, Bd v, Heft i, 1928)   .   **CXXXV**

W. JACOBI, *Die Extase der alttestamentlichen Propheten* (Grenzfragen des Nerven- und Seelenlebens), Munich, Bergmann, 1923   .   .   .   .   **CXXXVI**

JOHNS, *Assyrian Deeds*   .   .   .   .   .   **CXXXVII**

H. JUNKER, *Prophet und Seher in Israel*, Trêves, Paulinus, 1927   .   .   .   .   .   **CXXXVIII**

R. H. KENNETT, *The Date of Deuteronomy*, **JTS**, 1906, 481–500   .   .   .   .   .   **CXXXIX**

R. H. KENNETT, *Deuteronomy and the Decalogue*, Cambridge, 1920   .   .   .   .   .   **CXL**

RUDOLF KITTEL, *Die Bücher der Könige*, Handkommentar zum A. T., i, 5, Göttingen, Vandenhoeck and Ruprecht, 1900   .   .   .   .   .   **CXLI**

AUGUST KLOSTERMANN, *Der Pentateuch, neue Folge*, Leipzig, Deichert, 1907.   .   .   .   **CXLII**

ABRAHAM KUENEN, *De Propheten en de prophetie ouder Israel*, 2 vols., 1875   .   .   .   .   **CXLIII**

STEPHEN LANGDON, *Die neubabylonischen Königsinschriften*, 1912   .   .   .   .   **CXLIV**

JULIUS LEWY, *Forschungen zur Geschichte Vorderasiens* (**MVAG**, 1924, 2), Leipzig, Hinrichs, 1925   .   **CXLV**

JOH. LINDBLOM, *Hosea literarisch untersucht*, Helsingfors, 1927   .   .   .   .   .   **CXLVI**

J. LINDBLOM, *Die literarische Gattung der prophetischen Literatur*, Upsala, 1924   .   .   .   **CXLVII**

J. LINDBLOM, *Micha literarische untersucht*, Åbo, 1929 .   **CXLVIII**

ADOLPHE LODS, *La divinisation du roi dans l'Orient méditerranéen et ses répercussions dans l'ancien Israël*, 2e congrès national des sciences historiques, Alger, 1932, pp. 261–75   .   .   .   .   **CXLIX**

AD. LODS, " *L'étang supérieur* " *et l'approvisionnement en eau de la Jérusalem antique.* 5e Congrès int. d'Archéologie (Alger, 1930), Alger, 1933, pp. 183–204   .   **CL**

MAX LÖHR, *Das Deuteronomium*, Berlin, 1925   .   **CLI**

LUCKENBILL, *Ancient Records of Assyria and Babylonia*.   **CLII**

LUCKENBILL, *Annals of Sen.*, 1924   .   .   .   **CLIII**

JOHANNES MEINHOLD, *Die Jesaiaerzählungen*, 1898   .   **CLIV**

ADALBERT MERX, *Die Bücher Moses und Josua*, Rel.-gesch. Volksbücher, Tübingen, Mohr, 1907   .   **CLV**

SIGMUND MOWINCKEL, *Die Chronologie der israelitischen und jüdischen Könige*, Leyden, Brill, 1932 . . **CLVI**

S. MOWINCKEL, *Le Décalogue*, Paris, Alcan, 1927. . **CLVII**

NAGEL, *Der Zug des Sanherib*, 1902 . . **CLVIII**

ÉDOUARD NAVILLE, *La découverte de la loi. Une interprétation égyptienne d'un livre biblique* (extrait des Mémoires de l'Acad. des Inscriptions et Belles-Lettres, vol. xxxviii, 2), Paris, Imp. Nat., 1910 . . . **CLIX**

É. NAVILLE, *Le Deutéronome, un livre mosaïque*, Fontenay-sous-Bois, 1924 . . . . . **CLX**

T. OESTREICHER, *Das deuteronomische Grundgesetz*, Gütersloh, Bertelsmann, 1923 . . . . **CLXI**

ORR, *Le problème de l'Ancien Testament*, Geneva, 1908. **CLXII**

OTTO PROCKSCH, *Jesaia I übersezt und erklärt* (Kommentar zum A. T. von Ernst Sellin, ix), Leipzig, Deichert, 1930 . . . . . **CLXIII**

A. F. PUUKKO, *Das Deuteronomium*, Beiträge zur Wiss. vom A. T. (Kittel), 5, Leipzig-Stuttgart, 1910 . . **CLXIV**

GEORGE A. REISNER, *Recent Discoveries in Ethiopia*, The Harvard Theological Review, xiii (1920), 23–44 . . **CLXV**

G. L. ROBINSON, art. *Deuteronomy* in *International Standdard Bible Encyclopedia*, 1915 . . . . **CLXVI**

THEODORE H. ROBINSON, *Baal in Hellas*, Classical Quarterly, 1917 . . . . . . **CLXVII**

T. H. ROBINSON, *The Ecstatic Elements in Hebrew Prophecy*, Expositor, 1921, pp. 217 *ff.* . . . **CLXVIII**

T. H. ROBINSON, *Prophecy and the Prophets in Ancient Israel*, London, Duckworth, 1923 . . . **CLXIX**

H. WHEELER ROBINSON, *Prophetic Symbolism* (*Old Testament Essays*), London, Griffin, 1927, pp. 1–17 . . **CLXX**

R. W. ROGERS, *Sennacherib and Judah* (Studien zur Semitischen Philologie und Religionsgeschichte, pp. 319–28) **CLXXI**

HANS SCHMIDT, *Das deuteronomische Problem*, Theologische Blätter, 37 (1927), pp. 40–8 . . . **CLXXII**

H. SCHMIDT, *Geschichte Judas unter König Josia*, Schriften des A. T. in Auswahl, 2nd edit., ii, 2, pp. 177–202, Göttingen, 1923 . . . . . **CLXXIII**

H. SCHMIDT, *Die Herkunft des Propheten Amos*, **BZAW**, 34 (1920), pp. 158–71 . . . . **CLXXIV**

KURT SETHE, *Die Aechtung feindlicher Fürsten Völker und Dinge auf altägyptischen Tongefässscherben des mittleren Reiches* (Abhandlungen der preuss. Akad der Wiss., 1926, ph.-hist. Klasse, no. 5), Berlin, 1926 . . **CLXXV**

ARTHUR ROBERT SIEBENS, *L'origine du code deutéronomique*, Paris, Leroux, 1929 . . . **CLXXVI**

J. SKINNER, *Prophecy and Religion*, 2nd edit., Cambridge University Press, 1926 . . . . . **CLXXVII**

SIDNEY SMITH, *Bab. Hist. Texts*, 1924 . . **CLXXVIII**

W. SPIEGELBERG, *Zur Datierung des Deuteronomiums*, **OLZ**, 26 (1923), 481–2 . . . . **CLXXIX**

C. STEUERNAGEL, *Das Deuteronomium und Josua*, Handkommentar zum A. T., Göttingen, Vandenhoeck and Ruprecht, 1898, 2nd edit., 1923 . . . **CLXXX**

C. STEUERNAGEL, *Die Entstehung des deut. Gesetzes*, Halle, 2nd edit., 1901 . . . . . **CLXXXI**

VATER, *Commentar über d. Pentateuch*, 1805 . . **CLXXXII**

VATKE, *Die biblische Theologie*, 1835 . . . . **CLXXXIII**

PAUL VOLZ, *Der Prophet Jeremia* (**KAT**), Leipzig, Deichert, 2nd edit., 1928 . . . . **CLXXXIV**

A. C. WELCH, *The Code of Deuteronomy*, London, 1924. **CLXXXV**

A. C. WELCH, *Jeremiah* . . . . . . **CLXXXVI**

W. M. L. DE WETTE, *Dissertatio critico-exegetica*, Jena, 1805 . . . . **CLXXXVII**

HAROLD WIENER, *Das Hauptproblem des Deuteronomiums*, Gütersloh, Bertelsmann, 1924 . . . . . **CLXXXVIII**

H. WIENER, *The Altars of the Old Testament*, Leipzig, Hinrichs, 1927 . . . . **CLXXXIX**

WILKE, *Das Skythenproblem im Jeremiabuch* (Alttestamentliche Studien für Rudolf Kittel, pp. 222–54) . **CXC**

WILKE, *Jesaia und Assur*, 1905 . . . . . **CXCI**

HUGO WINCKLER, *Die Keilschrifttexte Sargons*, 1889 . **CXCII**

2. EARLY JUDAISM

H. I. BELL, *Jews and Christians in Egypt*, Brit. Mus., 1924 . . . . **CXCIII**

ALFRED BERTHOLET, *Das Buch Hesekiel*, Kurzer Hand-Commantar zum A. T., xii, Friburg-Leipzig-Tübingen, Mohr, 1897 . . . . **CXCIV**

A. BERTHOLET, *Die Bücher Esra und Nehemia*, Kurzer Hand-Commentar zum A. T., xix, Tübingen, Leipzig, Mohr, 1902 . . . . **CXCV**

ANTONIN CAUSSE, *Israël et la vision de l'Humanité*, Strasburg-Paris, Istra, 1924 . . . . . . **CXCVI**

PAUL DHORME, *Le livre de Job* (Études bibliques), Paris, Gabalda, 1926 . . . . **CXCVII**

AUGUST DILLMANN, *Die Bücher Exodus und Leviticus*, Kurzgefasstes exegetisches Handbuch, xii, Leipzig, Hirzel, 3rd edit., 1897 . . . . . . **CXCVIII**

BERNHARD DUHM, *Die Psalmen*, Kurzer Hand-Commentar zum A. T., xiv, Friburg-Leipzig-Tübingen, Mohr, 1899 . . . . **CXCIX**

GADD and LYRAIN, *Ur Excavations, Royal Inscriptions*, 1928 . . . . **CC**

LUCIEN GAUTIER, *La mission du prophète Ézéchiel*, 1891 **CCI**

HERMANN GUNKEL, *Ausgewählte Psalmen*, 4th edit., 1917 **CCII**

H. GUNKEL, *Die Psalmen*, Handkommentar zum A. T., Göttingen, Vandenhoeck and Ruprecht, 4th edit., 1926, ii, 2 . . . . **CCIII**

O. E. HAGEN, *Keilschrifturkunden zur Geschichte des Königs Kyrus*, 1891 . . . . **CCIV**

J. HERMANN, *Ezechielstudien*, Beiträge zur Wissenschaft vom Alten Testament (Kittel), 2, Leipzig-Stuttgart, 1908 **CCV**

J. HERMANN, *Ezechiel*, Kommentar zum A. T. (Sellin), Leipzig, Deichert, 1924 . . . . . . **CCVI**

HILPRECHT and CLAY, *Bab. Exped.*, vols. ix, x, 1898, 1904, 1912 . . . . **CCVII**

GUSTAV HÖLSCHER, *Hesekiel, der Dichter und das Buch*, 1924 . . . . **CCVIII**

* CLÉMENT HUART, *La Perse antique et la civilisation iranienne*, Renaissance du livre, 1925 . . **CCIX**

MORRIS JASTROW jr., *The Book of Job. Its Origin, Growth and Interpretation*, Philadelphia and London, Lippincott, 1920 CCX

PIERRE JOUGUET, *L'impérialisme macédonien et l'hellénisation de l'Orient*, Paris, Renaissance du livre, 1926 . CCXI

KARL KAUTZSCH, *Das sogenannte Volksbuch von Hiob*, 1906 CCXII

KING and THOMPSON, *The Sculptures and Inscription of Darius the Great on the Rock of Behistûn in Persia*, London, British Museum, 1907, pp. xxxvi–xxxviii . CCXIII

KLOSTERMANN, *Ezechiel. Ein Beitrag zur besseren Würdigung seiner Person und Schrift*, TSK, 1 (1877), 391–439 CCXIV

RICHARD KRAETZSCHMAR, *Das Buch Ezechiel*, Handkommentar zum A. T., iii, 3, 1, Göttingen, Vandenhoeck and Ruprecht, 1900 CCXV

LACHMANN, *Das Buch Habakkuk. Eine textkritische Studie*, Aussig, 1932 CCXVI

ADOLPHE LODS, *Recherches récentes sur le livre de Job*, RHP, 1934, pp. 501–33 CCXVII

AD. LODS, *Éléments anciens et éléments modernes dans le rituel du sacrifice israélite* (RHP, 1928, pp. 399–411), Paris-Strasburg CCXVIII

AD. LODS, *L'Ecclésiaste et la philosophie grecque*, Paris, Jouve, 1890 CCXIX

AD. LODS, *Les découvertes d'Éléphantine et l'Ancien Testament*, Revue Chrétienne, Montbéliard, 1910 . . CCXX

AD. LODS, *Le monothéisme israélite a-t-il eu des precurseurs parmi les " sages " de l'ancien Orient ?* RHP, 1934, pp. 198–205 CCXXI

WILLIAM LODS, *Les Juifs en Égypte à l'époque ptolémaïque et romaine d'après les textes papyrologiques et épigraphiques* (thèse inédite de la Fac. de Théol. prot. de Paris), 1925 CCXXII

ALFRED LOISY, *La consolation d'Israël*, 1927 . . CCXXIII

A. LOISY, *Les mythes babyloniens et les premiers chapitres de la Genèse*, Paris, Picard, 1901 CCXXIV

JACQUES MARTY, *Les chapitres 56-66 du livre d'Ésaïe*, Nancy, Berger-Levrault, 1924 CCXXV

JOHN A. MAYNARD, *The Birth of Judaism, a Study of Hebrew Religion during the Exile*, London, Luzac, 1928 CCXXVI

EDUARD MEYER, *Die Entstehung des Judentums, eine historische Untersuchung*, Halle, Niemeyer, 1896 . . CCXXVII

E. MEYER, *Der Papyrusfund von Elephantine*, Leipzig, Hinrichs, 1912 CCXXVIII

ALDO NEPPI MODONA, *La vita pubblica e privata degli Ebrei in Egitto nell' età ellenistica e romana*, Aegyptus, ii (1921), pp. 253–75 ; iii. (1922), pp. 19–43 CCXXIX

SIGMUND MOWINCKEL, *Statholderen Nehemia*, 1916. *Ezra den Skriftlærde*, 1916 CCXXX

FIRMIN NICOLARDOT, *La composition du livre d'Habacuc* (thèse de la Fac. des Lettres de Paris), Paris, Fischbacher, 1908 CCXXXI

G. PINCHES, *Journal of the Victoria Inst.*, 1896, pp. 8 *ff.* CCXXXII

E. H. PLUMPTRE, *Ecclesiastes*, Cambridge, 1881 . . CCXXXIII

E. PODECHARD, *L'Ecclésiaste*, Études Bibliques, Paris, Gabalda, 1912 CCXXXIV

Rost, *Altorientalische Studien*, f. B. Meissner . . CCXXXV

J. W. Rothstein, *Die Nachtgesichte des Sacharja*, Beiträge zur Wissenschaft vom A. T. (R. Kittel), 8, Leipzig, Hinrichs CCXXXVI

Eduard Sachau, **ABA** *vom Jahre 1907*, Berlin, 1908 . CCXXXVII

E. Sachau, *Ein altaramäischer Papyrus aus der Zeit des ägyptischen Königs Amyrtaeus*, Florilegium Melchior de Vogüé, 1909 CCXXXVIII

E. Sachau, *Aramäische Papyrus und Ostraka aus einer jüdischen Militärkolonie zu Elephantine*, Leipzig, 1911 . CCXXXIX

Sayce and Cowley, *Aramaic Papyri discovered at Assouan*, London, Morning, 1906 CCXL

H. H. Schaeder, *Ezra der Schreiber*, Beiträge zur hist. Theol., 1930 CCXLI

Hans Schmidt, *Das Gebet der Angeklagten im Alten Testament*. Old Testament Essays, London, Griffin, 1927, pp. 143–55 CCXLII

H. Schmidt, *Das Gebet der Angeklagten im A. T.*, **BZAW**, 49 (1928), Giessen, Töpelmann CCXLIII

Rudolf Smend, *Der Prophet Ezechiel*, Kurzgefasstes exegetisches Handbuch, viii, 2nd edit., Leipzig, Hirzel, 1880 CCXLIV

Sidney Smith, *Babylonian Historical Texts relating to the Capture and Downfall of Babylon*, London, 1924 . CCXLV

W. Staerk, *Die jüdisch-aramäischen Papyri von Assuan, sprachlich und sachlich erklärt*, Bonn, Marcus Weber, 1907 CCXLVI

Charles C. Torrey, *The Composition and Historical Value of Ezra-Neh.*, 1896 CCXLVII

Th. Tyler, *Ecclesiastes*, London, 1874 . . . CCXLVIII

Paul Volz, *Jesaia II* (**KAT**), Leipzig, Deichert, 1932 . CCXLIX

WORKS RELATING TO THE SECOND VOLUME
Late Judaism
A. *PALESTINIAN JUDAISM*
I. General Works

Abrahams (I.), *Studies in Pharisaism and the Gospels*, Cambridge, 1917 and 1924, 2 vols. . . . CCL

Bertholet (A.), *Apokryphen und Pseudepigraphen, in Geschichte der Althebräischen Literatur* of K. Budde, Leipzig, 1906 CCLI

Bertholet (A.), *Die Jüdische Religion von der Zeit Ezras bis zum Zeitalter Christi* (vol. ii of *Biblische Theologie des Alten Testaments* by Stade), Tübingen, 1911 . CCLII

Bousset (W.), *Die Religion des Judentums in neutestamentlichen Zeitalter*, 3rd edit. revised and edited by Gressmann, Tübingen, 1926 CCLIII

Charles (R. H.), *The Apocrypha and Pseudepigrapha of the Old Testament*, Oxford, 1913, 2 vols. . . CCLIV

Dewick (E. C.), *Primitive Christian Eschatology*, Cambridge, 1913 CCLV

Dussaud (R.), *Introduction à l'histoire des religions*, Paris, 1914 CCLVI

FEINE (P.), *Theologie des N. T.*, Leipzig, 4th edit., 1912   CCLVII
FRIEDLAENDER, *Synagoge und Kirche in ihren Anfängen*,
  Berlin, 1908   CCLVIII
GRESSMANN (H.), *Der Messias*, Göttingen, 1929 . .   CCLIX
GRESSMANN (H.), *Der Ursprung der israelitisch-jüdischen
  Eschatologie*, Göttingen, 1906   CCLX
GUNKEL (H.), *Zum religionsgeschichtlichen Versi'ändnis des
  N. T.²*, Göttingen, 1910   CCLXI
HERFORD (R. T.), *Pharisaism, its Aim and Method*, Lon-
  don, 1912   CCLXII
HERFORD (R. T.), *Les Pharisiens*, Paris, 1928 . .   CCLXIII
HERFORD (R. T.), *Pirké Aboth. Introduction, Translation
  and Commentary*, New York, 1925   CCLXIV
HOENNICKE (G.), *Das Judenchristentum im ersten und
  zweiten Jahrhundert*, Berlin, 1908   CCLXV
HOLTZMANN (H.), *Lehrbuch der neutestamentl. Theologie²*,
  edited by A. JÜLICHER and W. BAUER, Tübingen, 1911,
  2 vols.   CCLXVI
JACKSON (F.) and LAKE (K.), *The Beginnings of Chris-
  tianity*, vol. i, London, 1920   CCLXVII
JACKSON (F.), *Josephus and the Jews. The Religion and
  History of the Jews as explained by Flavius Josephus*,
  London, 1930.   CCLXVIII
KAUTZSCH (E.), *Die Apokryphen und Pseudepigraphen des
  A. T.*, Tübingen, 1900, 2 vols.   CCLXIX
KENNETT (R. H.), *Old Testament Essays*, Cambridge, 1928   CCLXX
KITTEL (G.), *Die hellenistische Mysterienreligion und das
  A. T.*, Stuttgart, 1924   CCLXXI
KLAUSNER (J.), *Jésus de Nazareth*, Paris, 1933 . .   CCLXXII
KOHLER, *The Origins of the Synagogue and the Church*, New
  York, 1929   CCLXXIII
KREGLINGER (R.), *La Religion d'Israël²*, Brussels, 1926   CCLXXIV
LAGRANGE (M. J.), *Le Messianisme chez les Juifs*, Paris, 1909   CCLXXV
LEGGE (F.), *Forerunners and Rivals of Christianity*, Cam-
  bridge, 1915, 2 vols.   CCLXXVI
LÉVY (Is.), *La Légende de Pythagore, de Grèce en Palestine*,
  Paris, 1927   CCLXXVII
MEYER (Ed.), *Ursprung und Anfänge des Christentums*,
  vol. ii, Stuttgart and Berlin, 1921   CCLXXVIII
MOORE (G. F.), *Judaism in the first centuries of the Christian
  Era*, Cambridge (U.S.A.), 1925 and 1927, 3 vols. .   CCLXXIX
NICOLAS (M.), *Des doctrines religieuses des Juifs pendant
  les deux siècles antérieurs à l'ère chrétienne*, Paris, 1860   CCLXXX
OESTERLEY (W. O. E.), *The Sayings of the Jewish Fathers*
  (Pirké Aboth), London, 1919   CCLXXXI
PIEPENBRING (C.), *Théologie de l'A. T.*, Paris, 1886 .   CCLXXXII
SILVER (H.), *A History of Messianic Speculation in Israel,
  from the First to the Seventeenth Century*, New York, 1927   CCLXXXIII
VOLZ (P.), *Jüdische Eschatologie von Daniel bis Akiba*,
  Tübingen, 1903   CCLXXXIV
WEINEL (H.), *Biblische Theologie des N. T. Die Religion
  Jesu und des Urchristentums*, Tübingen, 1911, 2nd edit.,
  1928   CCLXXXV
WELLHAUSEN (J.), *Die Pharisäer und die Sadducäer*, Han-
  over, 1874, 2nd edit., 1924   CCLXXXVI

II. WORKS DEALING WITH SPECIAL POINTS

BERNOUILLI (C. A.), *Johannes der Täufer und die Urgemeinde*, Basle, 1917 . . . .   **CCLXXXVII**

BRÜCKNER (M.), *Der sterbende und aufstehende Gottheiland in den orientalischen Religionen und im Christentum*, Tübingen, 1908, 2nd edit., 1920 . . . .   **CCLXXXVIII**

EISLER (R.), *IHΣOYΣ BAΣIΛEYΣ OY BAΣIΛEYΣAΣ* Heidelberg, 2 vols., 1930 . . . . .   **CCLXXXIX**

GOGUEL (M.), *Au seuil de l'Évangile : Jean-Baptiste*, Paris, 1928 . . . .   **CCXC**

KITTEL (G.), *Die Probleme des palästinischen Spätjudentums und das Christentum*, Stuttgart, 1926 .   **CCXCI**

LAKE (K.), *Landmarks in the History of Early Christianity*, London, 1920. . . . .   **CCXCII**

LEITPOLDT (J.), *Sterbende und aufstehende Götter*, Leipzig, 1923 . . . .   **CCXCIII**

LOISY (A.), *Les Évangiles synoptiques*, Ceffonds, 1907 and 1908, 2 vols. . . . .   **CCXCIV**

LOISY (A.), *Les Actes des Apôtres*, Paris, 1920 . .   **CCXCV**

LOOFS (F.), *Leitfaden zum Studium der Dogmengeschichte*[4], Halle, 1906 . . . .   **CCXCVI**

MONTEFIORE (C. G.), *Judaism and St. Paul*, London, 1914   **CCXCVII**

NIELSEN (D.), *Der dreieinige Gott*, vol. i, Copenhagen, Berlin, London, 1922 . . . . . .   **CCXCVIII**

OESTERLEY (W. O. E.) and Box (G. H.), *A short Survey of the Literature of Rabbinical and Mediaeval Judaism*, London, 1920. . . . .   **CCXCIX**

PRESSENSÉ (DE), *Le siècle apostolique*[2], Paris, 1887 .   **CCC**

RENAN (E.), *Vie de Jésus*[6], Paris, 1863 . . .   **CCCI**

RÉVILLE (A.), *Jésus de Nazareth*, Paris, 1906, 2 vols. .   **CCCII**

SANDAY (W.), *The Life of Christ in Recent Research*, Oxford, 1908 . . . .   **CCCIII**

SCHIEWIETZ, *Das morgenländische Mönchtum*, Mayence, 1904 . . . .   **CCCIV**

STRACK (H.) and BILLERBECK (P.), *Kommentar zum Neuen Testament aus Talmud und Midrasch*, vols. i and ii, Munich, 1922 and 1924 . . . . . .   **CCCV**

TOUSSAINT (C.), *L'Épitre de St. Paul aux Colossiens*, Paris, 1921 . . . .   **CCCVI**

TOUSSAINT (C.), *L'hellénisme de l'Apôtre Paul*, Paris, 1921   **CCCVII**

WENDLAND (P.), *Die hellenistich-römische Kultur*[2], Tübingen, 1912 . . . .   **CCCVIII**

B. *THE DIASPORA*

BERNAYS (J.), *Ueber das Phokylideische Gedicht*, 1856 .   **CCCIX**

BERTHOLET (A.), *Biblische Theologie des Alten Testaments. Die jüdische Relig. von der Zeit Esras bis zum Zeitalter Christi*, Tübingen, 1911 . . . . . .   **CCCX**

BRÉHIER (E.), *Les idées philosophiques et religieuses de Philon d'Alexandrie*, Paris, 1907 . . . .   **CCCXI**

CUMONT (F.), *Les religions orientales dans le paganisme romain*[4], Paris, 1929 . . . . . .   **CCCXII**

DECHARME (P.), *La critique des traditions religieuses chez les Grecs, des origines au temps de Plutarque*, Paris, 1904   **CCCXIII**

DEISSMANN (A.), *Paulus*, Tübingen, 1911. Since re-edited .   **CCCXIV**

DIETERICH (A.), *Eine Mithrasliturgie*, 1903, 3rd edit., 1925   **CCCXV**

DUCHESNE (L.), *Histoire ancienne de l'Église*, vol. i, Paris, 1906 .   .   .   .   **CCCXVI**

FRIEDLAENDER (M.), *Die religiösen Bewegungen innerhalb des Judentums im Zeitalter Jesu*, Berlin, 1905 .   **CCCXVII**

GOGUEL (M.), *Jésus de Nazareth, Mythe ou histoire ?* Paris, 1925 .   .   .   .   **CCCXVIII**

GOMPERZ (Th.), *Les penseurs de la Grèce* (trans. A. REYMOND), 3 vols., Paris, 1903–10 .   .   **CCCXIX**

GRESSMANN (H.), *Jewish Life in ancient Rome*, in *Studies in Memory of Israel Abrahams*, pp. 170 *ff.*, New York, 1927   **CCCXX**

GUIGNEBERT (Ch.), *Le Problème de Jésus*, Paris, 1914 .   **CCCXXI**

HARNACK (A.), *Mission und Ausbreitung des Christentums in die drei ersten Jahrhunderten*[2], Leipzig, 2 vols., 1906. Since re-edited .   .   .   .   **CCCXXII**

HARNACK (A.), *Gesch. des altchristlichen Literatur.* pt. ii : *Ueberlieferung und Bestand*, 2 vols., Leipzig, 1893 .   **CCCXXIII**

HERRIOT (E.), *Philon le Juif ; essai sur l'école juive d'Alexandrie*, Paris, 1898 .   .   .   .   .   **CCCXXIV**

JORDAN (H.), *Gesch. der altchristlichen Literatur*, Leipzig, 1911 .   .   .   .   .   .   **CCCXXV**

LECLERCQ (H.), *Manuel d'Archéologie chrétienne, depuis les origines jusqu'au VIII*[e] *siècle*, 2 vols., Paris, 1907.   **CCCXXVI**

LOHMEYER (E.), *Soziale Fragen im Urchristentum*, Leipzig, 1921 (Coll. *Wissenschaft und Bildung*) .   **CCCXXVII**

OMODEO (A.), *Paolo di Tarso, apostolo delle Genti*, Messina, 1922 .   .   .   .   **CCCXXVIII**

REINACH (S.), *Judaei* (in *Dict. des Antiquités grecques et romaines* of DAREMBERG and SAGLIO) .   .   **CCCXXIX**

REITZENSTEIN (R.), *Die hellenistichen Mysterienreligionen*, Leipzig and Berlin, 1910, 2nd edit., 1920 .   **CCCXXX**

REITZENSTEIN (R.), *Poimandres, Studien zur griechisch-ägyptischen und frühchristlichen Literatur*, Leipzig, 1904   **CCCXXXI**

RENAN, *Les Apôtres*, Paris, 1866 .   .   .   **CCCXXXII**

RENAN, *L'Église chrétienne*[4], Paris, 1879 .   .   **CCCXXXIII**

RENAN, *Les Évangiles*, Paris, 1877 .   .   .   **CCCXXXIV**

RÉVILLE (J.), *Le Logos d'après Philon d'Alexandrie*, Geneva, 1877 .   .   .   .   .   .   **CCCXXXV**

RÉVILLE (J.), *Les origines de l'Épiscopat*, Paris, 1894..   **CCCXXXVI**

RÉVILLE (J.), *Le Quatrième Évangile*, Paris, 1901 .   **CCCXXXVII**

SABATIER (P.), *La Didaché ou l'Enseignement des Douze Apôtres*, Paris, 1885 .   .   .   .   **CCCXXXVIII**

TOUSSAINT (C.), *L'Epitre de St. Paul aux Colossiens* (trans. and comm.), Paris, 1921. .   .   .   .   **CCCXXXIX**

ZELLER (E.), *Die Philosophie der Griechen*, part iii[4] (1903 and 1909) .   .   .   .   .   **CCCXL**

I regret that I was not able to make use of the important work by P. J. Bonsirven, S.J., *Palestinian Judaism in the Time of Jesus Christ*, Paris, 1935, 2 vols., which appeared after the present book had been set up in type (1935).

INDEX

Library of the Mystic Arts

A LIBRARY OF ANCIENT AND MODERN CLASSICS

BARTON, R. F. Autobiographies of Three Pagans in the Philippines. intro. by Dr. Nancy Oestreich Lurie. ill. index bibliog. 320 pp. 5½" x 8¼" 62-19195. $7.50   ANTHROP
"It is difficult to realize that the people in these autobiographies, two men and a woman live on the same planet that we do. Head-hunting and spearing your enemy are everyday occurrences. Anyone who knows your kin is an enemy, unless he is your kin. It is the savage eye for an eye and tooth for a tooth of Biblical times, even though coming of the Americans has discouraged some of the practices. R. F. Barton was among the Ifugaos long enough to select three representatives of the tribe. In the autobiographies he gives their life history before marriage, including many of their ceremonies and customs. It is an interesting and informative anthropological study." — WICHITA EAGLE & BEACON

BERNHEIM, H. Hypnosis and Suggestion in Psychotherapy: The Nature and Uses of Hypnotism. intro. by Ernest R. Hilgard. index. 428 pp. 6⅛" x 9¼" 63-22664. $10.00   PSYCH
Hypnosis has had a checkered career over a period of centuries, going through cycle after cycle of general approval and total eclipse. The fate of this book indicates how fragile the reputation of hypnosis has been; written almost eighty years ago, and translated into English a few years later, it has always been acknowledged as a great classic. Yet it has been out of print for some seventy years. It was not obsolete; nor was it suppressed. It has simply been neglected — as has hypnotism itself. It was the Second World War that reintroduced hypnosis in psychotherapy, and the widespread contemporary interest dates from that time. Today its potential is recognized by practically all medical societies over the world, and courses in hypnotism are appearing in medical school curricula and in training programs for psychiatric residents. Numerous psychologists are also turning to hypnosis as a fertile field for research and therapy.

BULLOUGH, Vern L. The History of Prostitution. index. 320 pp. 6⅛" x 9¼" 64-16619. $7.50   HIST
Prostitution, like the weather, has often been talked about, but very rarely has any scholar bothered to do any research on the topic. Few serious studies on prostitution have been undertaken by social scientists over the past fifty years. Although an occasional sociologist, psychologist, psychiatrist, or anthropologist has concerned himself, the historian has totally neglected the subject. As a result this book is the first attempt at a serious history of prostitution in English in this century.
The author, Dr. Vern L. Bullough, is a historian who has specialized in the history of medicine and science. He has published numerous articles, primarily on medical history, in various learned journals. He was assisted in his researches by his wife, Bonnie L. Bullough.

COOMARASWAMY, Ananda Kentish. Buddha and the Gospel of Buddhism. intro. by John C. Wilson. ill. index. bibliog. glossary. 370 pp. 6⅛" x 9¼" 64-16160. $10.00   REL
A classic introduction to Buddhism, Coomaraswamy's book was originally published in England in 1916. It was reprinted without change in 1927, and it is now finally available in its original form in an American edition. The author was revered both in the East and the West for his unique contributions to art

and philosophy as well as religion. An ardent Indian nationalist, his life work became the preservation of India's heritage and the monumental task of teaching the West to respect and revere the great civilization of India.

When Coomaraswamy died, Aldous Huxley spoke of his "unique importance as a mediator between East and West."

The author was fond of calling himself a traditionalist and often emphasized the virtues of orthodoxy. He was always suspicious of the Western fashionable interest in Buddhism and frequently spoke with considerable irony of the contemporary offbeat Zen enthusiasts. "The suspicious popularity of 'Buddhism' in Europe," he wrote in 1938, "has rested upon a very thorough misunderstanding of what Buddhism really means. The essential doctrines of Buddhism, like those of all orthodox relgions, are in radical opposition to our modern individualism."

The book continues to be a solid exposition of Buddhistic thought and its reissue should be timely in view of current rapprochment between the West and Eastern religious systems. Some twenty plates add interest and value.—VIRGINIA KIRKUS SERVICE.

FEILDING, Everard. Sittings with Eusapia Palladino and other Studies. intro. by E. J. Dingwall. 324 pp. 6⅛" x 9¼" 63-18682. $10.00
PARAPSYCH
"The author, well known as an objective observer of psychical phenomena, presents primarily a detailed report of 13 seances with the noted Italian medium of the 20th Century. There are included accounts of other mediums and of the stigmata of a French abbe. Facts are given; conclusions are left for the reader." — JOURNAL OF THE AMERICAN MEDICAL ASSOCIATION

"William James deplored the cheating and the vulgarity connected with the mediumship of Eusapia Palladino, but he believed that there was a residuum of phenomena in her performances which could not be explained. So did Everard Feilding of the Society for Psychic Research. He put her through the most rigid tests possible early in this century and concluded that she possessed some inexplicable power which caused tables to levitate, bells to ring, and lights to flash. In this most interesting collection of Feilding's writings we find that although he was a serious researcher, he always retained a sense of humor and a healthy skepticism. Eric Dingwall, who was his friend, has contributed a witty and appreciative introduction which reinforces the impression one gets from these papers that Feilding was a "most acute and well-balanced investigator" of ESP. Recommended for all libraries interested in this field of research." — LIBRARY JOURNAL

GUIGNEBERT, Charles. Jesus fwd. by Joel Carmichael. index. bibliog. xv + 560 pp. 6⅛" x 9¼" 56-7837. $10.00
REL
This historical study of the life of Jesus and the origins of Christianity has received the highest possible praise from biblical scholars of the status of Niebuhr, Barth and Pfeiffer. Its author, Charles Guignebert, is generally considered one of the finest examples of European scholarship. He spent a lifetime of research into the genesis of all forms of religious belief; toward the end of his life he held the chair of the History of Christianity at the Sorbonne.

REINHOLD NIEBUHR: "The virtue of Professor Guignebert's venture lies in his comprehensive analysis of the scholarship of the past decades in this field. The specialists are acquainted with all the evidence which he analyzes. But there is no book of recent years which will give the interested layman a more comprehensive account of what has been written and said about the life of Jesus and a fairer estimate of conflicting evidence. Naturally the author has a position of his own to maintain, but the reader is permitted to see how he arrived at it, and with what cogency and plausibility he defends it against contrasting views."

ROBERT H. PFEIFFER: "Aside from Guignebert's JESUS, only Goguel's LIFE may be regarded as a serious attempt to write a critical and objective historical work.